# Who's Who in
# Late Hanoverian Britain

# Who's Who in Late Hanoverian Britain

## (1789-1837)

*being the seventh volume in the*
*Who's Who in British History series*

## GEOFFREY TREASURE

### Series Editor:
### GEOFFREY TREASURE

### SHEPHEARD-WALWYN

First published as *Who's Who in History* Vol. V
by Basil Blackwell, 1974

This revised and enlarged edition published in 1997 by
Shepheard-Walwyn (Publishers) Ltd
Suite 34, 26 Charing Cross Road, London WC2H 0DH

*British Library Cataloguing in Publication Data*

A catalogue record of this book
is available from the British Library

ISBN 0 85683 094 1 cased
ISBN 0 85683 137 9 limp

Typesetting by Alacrity, Banwell Castle, Weston-super-Mare
Printed in Great Britain by BPC Wheatons Ltd, Exeter

# CONTENTS

*To my sisters, Pamela and Anne*

# GENERAL INTRODUCTION

With the simultaneous publication of this volume and the Victorian one, the series which was re-launched in 1988, is complete. Published as *Who's Who in History* by Basil Blackwell between 1962 and 1974, the original five volumes offered a biographical companion to British history. In this enlarged series, with four new, and four extensively revised volumes, we trust that we have remained faithful to the ideal of the original general editor, the late C. R. N. Routh, who wanted the short 'life' to be a fruitful meeting ground for the historian-author, the student, and the 'general reader'. Each author has sought in his own way to convey more than the bare facts of his subject's life, to place him or her in the context of the age and to evoke what was distinctive in character and achievement. By using a broadly chronological rather than alphabetical sequence, and by grouping together similar classes of people, each volume provides a portrait of the age. So, we dare hope, the reader will be drawn to browse, for example in this volume, from Turner to Constable, from Telford to Rennie and Trevithick.

At a time when academic historians seem primarily to be writing exclusively for fellow-historians, when textbooks, too often, have little room for story, character and the individuals who are the life and soul of the past, there is a place for a history of our country which is composed of the lives of those who helped make it what it was — and is. Contributing to this high endeavour, our authors can be said to have taken heed of the warning of Trevor Roper's inaugural lecture at Oxford in 1957 against 'the removal of humane studies into a specialisation so remote that they cease to have that lay interest which is their sole ultimate justification'.

Hard-pressed examinees often need essays which put significant lives into context. From brief accounts they may learn valuable lessons in proportion, conciseness, relevance and style. We hope that they will be tempted to find out more, and so have added, wherever possible, the titles of books for further reading. Mindful of academic demands, we have not, however, confined our attention to those who have left an obvious mark on church and state. The man who invented the umbrella, the archbishop who shot a gamekeeper, an early cricketer and the neglected inventor who pioneered the digital computer, a successful highwayman and an unsuccessful admiral, find a place among the great and the good. Nor have we eschewed anecdote or turned a blind eye to follies and foibles. It is not the authors' view that history which is instructive cannot also be entertaining.

With the development of a secure and civilised society, the range of characters becomes richer, their achievements more diverse. Besides the soldiers, politicians and churchmen who dominate the mediaeval scene there are more scholars, lawyers, writers and artists; merchants, inventors, industrialists; explorers and empire builders. More is known about more people and the task of selection becomes harder. Every reader will find some omission. Behind it there is likely to have been doubt and pain, a decision reached after much heart-searching. Throughout, though mindful of the need to present a balanced picture and a representative cast, the authors have been guided by the criterion of excellence. To record the achievements of those few who have had the chance to excel and who have left a name behind them, be it honoured or execrated, is not to denigrate the unremarkable or unremarked for whom there was no chance to shine, nor chronicler at hand to describe what they made or did. It is not to deny that a Neville or a Pelham might have died obscure if he had not been born to high estate. It is to offer, for the instruction and inspiration of a generation which has been led too often to believe that individuals count for little in the face of the forces which shape economy and society, the conviction that a country is as remarkable as the individuals of which it is composed. In these pages there will be found, in plenty, examples of heroism, genius and altruism; some of self-seeking, treachery and depravity. There will be little that is ordinary. It is therefore the hope of the authors that there will be little that is dull.

GEOFFREY TREASURE
Kington, Herefordshire

# PREFACE

This collection of biographical essays forms the companion volume to *Who's Who in Early Hanoverian Britain* in the revised series, *Who's Who in British History*. Its themes include the wars against revolutionary France, liberal and radical campaigns for the reform of society and institutions, a new and turbulent phase in the 'Irish question', the evolution of a mature imperial power, and the transforming effect of industrialism on a fast-growing population. In the world of the arts the conventional terms 'romantic' and 'neo-classical' scarcely hint at the many-sided genius of the age of Jane Austen and Scott, Wordsworth and Keats, Blake, Constable and Turner. The dates that mark the frontiers of this volume are 1789 and 1837: the French Revolution and Queen Victoria's accession. It is not a long period. The place of Lord Melbourne, as the queen's first prime minister, is in the Victorian volume. Yet as a young man he had sat to Sir Joshua Reynolds who figures in the Early Hanoverian volume.

Contemporaries certainly believed that they were living in a time of unprecedented upheaval. It lacked the moderation of Georgian years; also that confidence in progress, allied to a sense of security, that characterised the central years of Queen Victoria's reign. It is hard to select one date for the end of the 'eighteenth century'; in some aspects it is alive until the Great Reform Bill. It was undoubtedly, however, the French Revolution that did most to destroy the equilibrium, even if not the institutions, of the British *ancien régime*. It helped determine the character of the next fifty years.

The cult of the hero has a central place. The great engineers who tackled the obstacles of nature in the conviction that nothing was impossible, evangelical Christians who felt called to take the Gospel to the furthest parts of the world, artists and writers who responded to the visionary spirit, politicians and students who were intoxicated by the fall of the Bastille, fashionable devotees of the cults of Napoleon and Byron, and the sailors who wept at the death of Nelson: all are unmistakeably children of this uninhibited age.

It is also an age of extremes: wealth turning to excess, poverty grimmer and more widespread than ever. Lord Mornington declared 'you cannot live like a gentleman on less than £50,000 a year' — when agricultural wages in southern England were as low as nine shillings a week. The wealth of the plutocracy — landowners benefiting from the coal or iron that was found on their estates, Cobbett's detested 'stock jobbers' and bankers who could take advantage of the exigencies of war finance, or manufacturers who made fortunes out of new machinery and mass production — mounted in disturbing contrast to the pauperism of field labourers and the child labour of the mills.

Revolution did not occur but violence was endemic. Cobbett's young labourer excused himself from poaching on the grounds that 'it was better to be hanged than to starve to death'. Two prime ministers fought duels; a third was shot by a bankrupt merchant. The Cato Street conspirators planned to blow up the entire cabinet. Surtees, creator of the immortal Jorrocks, lost his way on Epsom Downs: he was relieved to stumble upon an encampment of gypsies because 'these honest people would only rob me at most'. Jack Mytton, brandy-sodden Shropshire squire and pathological practical joker, was one of the folk heroes of the age. It was the heyday of the stage coach and horses were flogged to death in the interests of speed.

Humanitarians, such as Wilberforce, Romilly and Elizabeth Fry, worked for their causes with a zeal that glows in the darkness. In cooler spirit, 'utilitarians' followed the light of reason. This was indeed 'the age of improvement'. But kindness was not at a premium: women, chained in threes, passed through London streets on their way to transportation; the navy recruited ruthlessly through the press gang; the discipline of Wellington's army was based on flogging. In famous schools, boys mutinied against inhuman treatment; at Winchester the military were called in. Husbands and wives were separated in the new workhouses: Mr Bumble awaited the pen of Dickens.

Conflicts became sharper as men sought to preserve the past or shape the future. 'High and dry' churchmen defended the citadels of preferment against evangelical (soon to be 'Puseyite') encroachment. The defenders of classical values fought a rearguard action against 'romantic' advocates of a new freedom in the arts. Conservatives mustered to defend king and constitution against even the most modest proposals of reform. The Plantations interest found unlikely allies in its war against the anti-slavery movement. With *Slavers throwing overboard dead and dying — Typhoon coming on*, and *Coalbrookdale by Night*, Turner and de Louthenberg suggest pictorially the elemental drama of the times.

A composite picture might include the boundless optimism of a Bentham, legislating for mankind; an Owen designing utopia for mill-workers; a Shelley, ever in search of the absolute and universal — but read by a handful; a Raffles founding Singapore; or a Wellesley re-drawing the map of India. Yet there are more modest charms. This is the age of trousers, the waltz and seaside holidays. Mr Pickford's express canal service enjoys a brief splendour. It is not only the men of Hambledon who are playing cricket. The Waverley novels offer a polite substitute for the cruder realities of Highland warfare, for the drawing rooms and parlours whose life Jane Austen depicts with such exact and tender skill.

She deliberately excluded public affairs from her canvas. The historian must dwell more upon politics and war. Half the period under review was spent in war. The army and navy reached heights of performance never before achieved. The war effort, drawing strength from an expanding economy, was on a scale that the elder Pitt could not have envisaged. His son was the very embodiment of resolute and responsible government. Moore, Wellington, Nelson and Collingwood are models for all time in contrasting styles of heroic leadership. They had superb material to work on. Nothing could be finer than the endurance and seamanship of the sailors who manned the blockades which won the war at sea — unless it be the infantrymen of the Peninsular who showed that they could beat the best of the world, when they were well led.

Nor, finally, should the work of the British in India be overlooked. The problems of government presented by the decaying cultures of Moslem and Hindu were tackled by men who enjoyed arbitrary power over vast regions and exercised it, in the main, with a moderation and sense of responsibility for the well-being of the natives that is one of the glories of our history.

After many years of wandering enjoyably in the footsteps of the men and women who appear in these pages, I am left only with regret for those characters who, for reasons of space, have had to be omitted. That they include 'Nimrod' (Charles Apperley), Leigh Hunt and Mary Russell Mitford, will give some idea of the reader's loss in the literary field alone. Given the chance to re-write this volume, twenty-five years after its original publication by Blackwell, I have taken advantage of some recent biographies (for example the completion of Ehrman's magnificent life of Pitt) and changing trends in historiography, to add detail, revise judgements and introduce some new names to the list.

The reader is urged to consult the short bibliography where, besides specific recommendations at the end of each essay, I have listed books which may be of further interest and provide background to the whole period. In the spheres of painting, sculpture and architecture, where my limitations would otherwise have been exposed, I am again specially grateful to Francis Pearson for his fine contributions, robust advice and stimulating friendship over the years. We first met at Harrow. How much, I reflect, I owe to the privilege of teaching there, in the panelled formroom in the Old Schools where Byron's name was carved, where generations of sixth-formers taught me to strive for accuracy in detail and modesty in judgement.

With the simultaneous appearance of *Who's Who in Victorian Britain*, by Roger Ellis, the series is complete. As author of two volumes and as general editor of the series, I wish to thank my fellow authors for what they have contributed to the enterprise, and Anthony Werner, of Shepheard-Walwyn, for his faith in its central idea: biographical essays which provide a comprehensive history and portrait of our country. He has given me steady support and warm encouragement. To my wife Melisa I owe a special debt. For thirty years she has been counsellor, critic, eagle-eyed reader of manuscript and proofs; in successive enterprises, the most imaginative and generous of partners. (She declines to make any corrections to the preceding sentence.)

# LIST OF ILLUSTRATIONS

The author and publisher wish to express their grateful thanks to the National Portrait Gallery in London for permission to reproduce the portraits listed below.

# WHO'S WHO IN
# LATE HANOVERIAN BRITAIN

**WILLIAM PITT** (1759-1806), statesman, was born on 28 May at Hayes in Kent, the second son of William Pitt and Hester Grenville. By the end of that year his father had been immortalized by a succession of splendid victories; despite the vicissitudes of his later career, nothing could detract from the prestige of his name. Resolute, efficient, devoted to her husband, Hester Grenville embodied the better qualities of her proud family and provided her son with a more stable inheritance than that of the Pitts — erratic, violent, sometimes brilliant but sometimes mad. William was notably sane. He announced, when his father was made Earl of Chatham and he was but seven, that he was glad that he was the second son, for he wanted to follow his father's course in the House of Commons. Shy and uneasy in his relations with people, he seemed always to possess the conviction that he must do great things.

Chatham recognized the quality in his son and sought to train his mind. He taught him to think on his feet, by making him read aloud in English from foreign texts; when he came to a difficult passage he would pause until the right words came. He was taught by a tutor, Edmund Wilson, at a pace which invited reaction. At the age of fourteen he went to Pembroke College, Cambridge, in Wilson's words 'to be admired as a prodigy; not to hear lectures, but to spread light'. There his tutor, Tomline, could hardly contain himself: 'his parts are astonishing and universal' — but Pitt fell ill and had to convalesce for six months. The doctor prescribed early rising, daily riding, and port. Thereafter his health remained sound though he came to rely increasingly on his port. In 1776 he took his degree by privilege, but stayed at Cambridge. By now he was an accomplished mathematician and linguist, steeped in Newton, Locke and Hume. Later he was to be an admirer of Paley whose reasoned statement of the *Principles of Moral and Political Philosophy* accorded with Pitt's temperament and views.

He chose law for his profession, went to Lincoln's Inn and was

1

*William Pitt*
(Artist: John Hoppner)

called in 1780. To this period belongs the encounter with Gibbon whom he so worsted in argument that the historian left in a pique and would not return. Since his father's death Pitt was poor and

had to be assisted by Earl Temple, his uncle. His early debts were
to grow steadily all his life. He practised on the Western Circuit
but he was set on politics. In 1780 he came bottom of the poll at
Cambridge, but was promptly provided with a seat for the
amenable borough of Appleby by Sir James Lowther. His training
for politics had been almost entirely academic. With his strict upbringing and his own deliberate preparation, he was markedly
different from the man who was to be his greatest rival: Charles
James Fox had already acquired a host of friends and debts
and was in the course of softening mind and will by reckless
dissipation.

Pitt attached himself to that section of the Whigs who adhered,
under Shelburne, to Chatham's conception of colonial policy and
had therefore opposed the government of Lord North. In February 1782 North fell at last and was succeeded by Rockingham,
who did not offer Pitt a post, despite the latter's interest in parliamentary reform. He had already announced that he would not
accept 'a subordinate situation', but after Rockingham's death in
July, Shelburne made him Chancellor of the Exchequer. 'He is not
a chip off the old block; it is the old block itself,' said Burke after
listening to him speaking. Pitt's mature reasoning impressed the
House; as compared to the dazzling style of Fox it was especially
the architecture of Pitt's speeches that compelled attention. Shelburne valued his talents, his independent views and the patriotic
appeal of his name. Fox, who seems to have hoped that Pitt would
incline towards his group, was affronted by his decision to serve
under Shelburne: his subsequent alliance with North destroyed
Shelburne's government. From March 1783 until the end of the
year, Pitt was therefore free to take his own line again, knowing
that he stood well with the king who had pressed him to succeed
Shelburne. Unpopular in the country, detested by the king, the
Fox-North coalition was too strong in Parliament to be defied at
once. Pitt stood back and waited for power on his own terms. He
took up one of his father's interests when, in May 1783, he introduced proposals for parliamentary reform in alliance with Wyvill
and the Yorkshire Associations. They were rejected, though
Fox spoke for them; so was his bill for reform of the abuses of
administration. In the autumn Pitt travelled to France and met
Talleyrand and Necker, whose wife tried to arrange a marriage
with her daughter. Pitt seems to have been unaware of what was

intended and the future Mme. de Stael was left to find her match elsewhere. He never went abroad again.

On 17 December Fox's India Bill was defeated in the Lords and on the following day George III commanded his ministers to give up their seals. Temple became Secretary of State and Pitt moved into the centre of the storm with the office of First Lord of the Treasury. The risk was great, for the cry of royal tyranny still carried weight in the House. The kingdom 'was trusted to a schoolboy's care'; he was the head of a 'mincepie administration' and the wits had a field day. But he was heartened by Robinson's estimate of voting prospects and gambled on the effect of royal patronage and a turn of opinion in the constituencies. His ministers were weak in talents even before the resignation of Temple, who should have led the Lords. But Pitt stood firm against the opposition's gibes. They weakened their case by their vehemence; division after division their majorities fell. Pitt refused the sinecure of the Clerkship of the Pells. It was vital for him to appear to be independent of the court since in reality he relied so heavily upon it. He presented his own India Bill which provided for the public control which Fox's bill had proposed, through a Board of Control, without giving that body the patronage which made Fox's bill so vulnerable.

The bill was only defeated by eight votes; by March the difference had narrowed to one vote. Fox was discredited by the hooligans who attacked Pitt's coach outside Brooks's Club; Robinson, meanwhile, prepared the ground by discreet use of the king's known favour. On 24 March, Parliament was dissolved and, in the election that followed, Pitt won a triumph which reflected both careful political management and a surge of popular feeling; 160 supporters of Fox and North lost their seats. Returned head of the poll at his beloved Cambridge, Pitt remained its member for the rest of his life.

The next five years, the most satisfying of Pitt's life, saw a series of measures designed to restore England's reputation and finances. The last four years of war alone had cost £80,000,000; the debt stood at £231,000,000. Discontent in Ireland, administrative disorder in India, threatened further expense, if not actual war. Abroad England had no friends. To set against the problems, one hidden advantage must be recorded. The industrial revolution was entering upon its most dynamic phase. The wealth was being created which, tapped by loans and taxes, was to enable England to survive the unparalleled burdens of the Napoleonic Wars. Nonetheless, Pitt's talent for financial administration was a factor in the recovery of the economy in the five years before the French Revolution. 'So perfect a knowledge of the Commerce, Funds and Government of the country', wrote Lady Gower, 'that one must imagine that he had the experience of fifty years.' Largely unoriginal in his measures, he went a long way to implement the free trade advocated by Adam Smith. Like his mentor Shelburne, he paid heed to the views of the intellectuals. At a dinner party in 1787 he complimented Adam Smith thus: 'Nay, we will stand until you are seated, for we are all your scholars.' He showed also a Walpolean grasp of political realities and eschewed the grand projects of the more doctrinaire sort of reformer. He hit smuggling by reducing the duty on tea and other essential imports and simplified the method of collection. The yield on such dutiable goods as wine, spirits and tobacco rose sharply. By an extension of the Hovering Act (1780) he empowered officials to search ships up to four leagues out to sea. Further duties were added, to make up for the deficit arising from the reductions, upon a wide assortment of goods — hats, ribbons and hair powder, linens, calicoes and candles, paper, bricks and tiles, horses and even servants. In general this represents a trend which students of modern governmental finance will recognize: the government seeking to profit from the growth of consumption in an expanding economy.

The fashionable process of 'economical reform' was carried further by an inquiry into 'fees, gratuities, perquisites and emoluments'. The system of government borrowing was altered when loans were raised by tender, and he initiated a modest reform of archaic revenue procedures by creating the statutory Commission for Auditing the Public Accounts. By such measures an annual deficit was turned to a surplus and the means made available for the reduction of the National Debt. For this, Pitt instituted a Sinking Fund, similar to that outlined by Price. He did not, however, as Price proposed, borrow money at simple interest in order to invest at compound interest. He set aside a surplus £1,000,000 a year from the annual revenue. It did pay off several millions of debt, but its greatest service was to restore confidence in the government's solvency. (Pitt was later criticized for clinging to the system in wartime when he had to borrow at high rates in order to maintain the fund.) His triumph of financial understanding and parliamentary stamina was the Consolidation Bill of 1787, containing 2,537 separate resolutions. By the consolidation of customs duties, national book-keeping was vastly simplified. The Treasury account books were reduced from sixty folios to about a dozen. On the eve of war with France, Pitt was able to forecast a continuance of surpluses. It had been an astonishing achievement.

Pitt acquired at once an authority in the House which enabled him to persist in measures which he believed to be justified. Fox and his friends drew upon a fund of anti-French prejudice when they attacked the Free Trade treaty of September 1786. But Pitt had the manufacturing interest behind him and he carried it through with lofty contempt for the arguments of the opposition: 'to suppose that any nation could be unalterably the enemy of another is weak and childish'. Of course the English gained by a treaty which reduced duties on French wines, vinegar and oil and linens, and, correspondingly, duties upon English cottons, woollens, muslins, saddlery, porcelain and pottery. The French came to see the treaty as being the cause of their complex economic misfortunes and Robespierre even claimed that Pitt had deliberately precipitated the Revolution.

Pitt was less resolute in pressing schemes which promised no material advantage. He was not at heart a radical. Reforms, however desirable, had to be placed in the balance with all the needs of government. Few prime ministers have been ready, like Gladstone over Home Rule, to jeopardize a government for a single principle. Advocates of abolition of the slave trade and of the reform of Parliament had to make their way as best they could. Although he consciously tried to lead and direct his ministers, Pitt was forced, perhaps even content, to accept the system of his time, and there was no unanimity in his cabinet about reforms. Furthermore there was no party discipline which could enable Pitt to impose his point of view. He had only some fifty personal adherents as against more than twice that number who could be called Foxites. In 1785 he presented a scheme for the reform of Parliament by the disenfranchisement of thirty-six boroughs, the distribution of seventy-two seats between the larger counties and the cities of Westminster and London and the admission of copyholders in the counties to the franchise. Boroughmongers were to be compensated handsomely; Fox opposed it, but most men accepted the idea of a borough as a piece of property. Pitt was defeated by 74 votes and introduced no further scheme for reform. Since Wilberforce, author of the movement to end the slave trade, was ill, Pitt himself introduced the motion for an inquiry in May 1788. Later the movement ran into entrenched opposition from commercial interests. In 1792 Pitt spoke eloquently for total abolition but the House preferred the compromise of Dundas — regulation of the trade. There the matter was left until 1806.

When Pitt took office, the state of Ireland was alarming. The antagonism of Grattan and Flood and the quarrel about the emancipation of Catholics divided the legislature, while the people suffered from poor trade and welcomed the actions of extremist groups. Pitt saw free trade as one solution, the precursor of that union which he thought must come. His proposals were opposed by the Whigs on the ground that they would ruin British industry. Fox was fêted in Manchester and Pitt modified his proposals: the Navigation Laws were to be binding in both kingdoms and duties were not to be reduced below 10 per cent. It was then the turn of the Irish to protest against what seemed to be a betrayal, and of Fox to declare that he would not 'barter English commerce for Irish slavery'. The problem was therefore allowed to lapse and the distresses of Ireland continued to fester for want of intelligent and enforceable legislation. In Canada, however, in 1791, far-sighted action was taken to avoid racial dispute by the division into Upper or British and Lower or French provinces, each with its elected assembly. The French community remained, however, obstinately separate; and the problems outlined in the Durham Report of 1839 remained to be solved by the Act of 1840.

In 1784 Pitt secured the passage of his India Act. Whigs felt cheated — and made Warren Hastings the target of their revenge, hoping that Pitt would be drawn into the struggle. He, however, voted for indictment on the Benares charge. Justice could therefore take its course without reflection upon the government. As Pitt hoped, Hastings was eventually acquitted upon all charges. Pitt had acted as a politician and sympathy was subdued by calculation. We may recall his action in the first months of his administration when he upheld the election scrutiny against Fox: technically he was right, but it was a time for generosity. Pitt's stature could not be denied; but even his friends wished sometimes that he would glance towards the ground.

Pitt's style of leadership was unusually detached. In Cabinet he was uncommunicative. He entertained little. In the Commons he seemed scarcely to acknowledge the existence of his back-benchers. He detested the business of patronage which had been meat and drink to Walpole and North. But success justified his cautious handling of affairs. His integrity and commanding air earned loyalty, if not love. He could be counted upon not to be extreme. His lavish promotion of peers (119 in his time as Prime Minister) did indeed cause alarm. Pitt was uneasy about it himself, but he was also largely indifferent to the idea of nobility as a caste. He had to balance the Whigs and to compensate for the abolition, in the course of reform, of other forms of patronage. As in other matters he judged every case on its merits.

Under his armour there was a good-natured man, gentler and more uncertain when confronted by a contrary opinion than many supposed. Dundas once warned him of 'the unyielding nature of your temper when you are anxious upon a subject'. His instinct for perfection was constantly challenged by his insight into problems and understanding of what was possible. He did not spare himself the trouble of mastering subjects which he held to be important. Dealing with the Hastings case, he shut himself up with Dundas for ten days to study the intricacies of the Bengal revenues.

In foreign affairs Pitt devoted himself to altering Britain's condition of isolation. In 1783 the Emperor had voiced a common opinion when he said that the country had descended forever to 'the rank of a second-rate power like Sweden or Denmark'. A crisis arose in 1787-8 from the quarrel in Holland between the Republican party and the Stadholder. When collision point had been reached the Cabinet backed the Stadholder with a subsidy and held the fleet in readiness, while Prussian troops marched to defend him. The French accepted the defeat of the republicans whom they had formerly upheld.

Spain, too, yielded to British power. After arresting British ships in Nootka Sound (1790), they subsequently admitted the British right to navigate the Pacific. The Eastern Question cast a larger shadow. After Suvaroff's victories over the Turks in 1791 Pitt became alert to the danger of Poland and the Turkish Empire being dismembered between Russia, Austria and Prussia. He demanded that Russia should restore her conquests, notably

Okzakoff, but the Whigs protested and the Cabinet was divided. Pitt had to retreat: the price paid was the secret partition of Poland in 1793. Nonetheless Pitt was reducing armaments up to the outbreak of war with France in that year.

One of Pitt's recurring problems was caused by the precarious mental balance of the king. Between October 1788 and February 1789, when George III regained his sanity, his future seemed to hang upon the Regency Bill. Essentially Pitt was conducting a delaying action in his search for precedents and his desire for a formula which should give the Regent powers adequate for an emergency. Fox stood for the Regent's inherent right but spoiled his case by careless preparation. When the king recovered, the Regency Bill had not become law, the Whigs were 'un-Whigged' and Pitt could justly claim that he had stood both for the rights of the king and for the privileges of Parliament against a prince whose personal conduct did not commend him to sober citizens. As a gesture of independence he had returned the offer of £100,000 from the merchants of London — though he was short of money as always. His personal reputation was by now secure. Indeed, a note of awe creeps into contemporary accounts of 'the good minister'. His slender figure, the long, haughty nose above a disdainful mouth, his proud and absorbed public manner; his seeming indifference to women and simplicity of life were all so different from the lavish style of Fox. Pitt's friends knew a more spontaneous person — witty, a man who loved children and read the poems of Burns, went dutifully to church but liked to argue points of doctrine; a delightful companion at the dinner table. Richard Wellesley, about this time, described his manners as 'perfectly plain' and thought him endowed 'beyond any man of his time ... with a gay heart and a social spirit'.

In his appraisal of the French Revolution Pitt stood halfway between Fox, who welcomed it effusively, and Burke, who warned of the tyranny that would ensue. He was pragmatic as ever, sympathizing first with the creation of a limited monarchy, then shrinking from the extremes of violence. He judged what was happening in France by its effect upon England. He welcomed Burke's defection from the Whigs but remained unimpressed by his flights of rhetoric and prophecy. The effect of the Revolution was to create a new Toryism, thus seemingly to make Pitt's position impregnable. As the war developed after 1793, Fox's attitude became increasingly unpopular: for some years the opposition virtually withdrew from Parliament. As a war leader Pitt enjoyed the support that men give when faced by a common danger and he could count on patriotic sentiment and generous loans. The price was heavier, however, than even the mounting figures of the National Debt could show. Schemes of reform wilted in the prevailing mood of anti-Jacobinism. Pitt gave expression to this spirit and seldom gave way to its excesses. He was little suited, though, to the needs of 'this war of armed opinions'. It was Pitt's tragedy no less than Fox's; it consumed his spirit.

Pitt upheld the Scottish judiciary in 1793 after treason trials of notorious severity with biased judges. He seems for once to have capitulated before popular opinion. But he panicked less than his associates in the face of the symptoms of social revolution and his 'reign of terror' was relatively mild. There was widespread acquiescence in the anti-Jacobin agitation of 1792-99 — the Aliens Act, the Seditious Meetings Act, the Treasonable Correspondence Act, the suspension of Habeas Corpus and the anti-combination laws. His position was not easy for he was associated with the establishment of wealth and privilege by those who protested against the high price of food. 'No war! No famine! No Pitt!' was the cry of the London mob in 1795.

He always kept negotiated peace in mind but unfortunately the British did not achieve enough success to give them a strong position. Pitt was not a gifted strategist; he seemed to be unable to devise an over-all strategy. He can be criticized for failing to appreciate the impoverished mentality of revolutionary governments who were unconcerned by the loss of sugar islands and trading posts. Their acquisition was moreover of doubtful benefit to England. In the West Indies 40,000 British troops died of disease. Nor did economic warfare bring the success expected; only slowly did Pitt accept that France would not be destroyed by inflation.

Pitt was ill-served by his Continental allies, who accepted his subsidies but could not match the spirit of the French armies, the administration of Carnot or the genius of Napoleon. Successive coalitions were bedevilled by the failure of the powers to act together. English military intervention was also inglorious: the Duke of York's expedition of 1793 to France had to be withdrawn, the Quiberon Bay expedition of 1795 was a fiasco. In 1795

Prussia and Spain left the coalition; in 1796 Spain joined France. The campaigns of Bonaparte smashed the Austrians in Italy and in the autumn of 1797 Britain stood alone and Consols fell to 48. Could 'the efforts of a free, brave, loyal and happy people', in Pitt's words, check France? France came to mean Bonaparte, First Consul in 1799, Emperor in 1801. To his credit Pitt had exempted the navy from his peacetime economies. In Sir Charles Middleton, at the Admiralty, he had a great administrator. England's strength was at sea but, as the naval mutinies of 1797 showed, even there lay danger. The victories of St. Vincent and Duncan restored confidence, however; the brilliant success of Nelson at the Nile in 1800 gave Napoleon a salutary lesson in the importance of sea power, and his victory at Copenhagen in 1801 showed neutral powers what to expect if they took sides in the Great War. These were dour years for Pitt. Long, wearing hours were spent poring over maps, consulting with ministers and commanders, writing and reading correspondence, wrestling with the problems of war finance. He had the moral stature to promote such unpopular taxes as, in 1798, an income tax rising to 2s. in the pound for all above £200 a year. He was hissed by the mob, but the burden was placed fairly on the shoulders of the rich when he raised the land tax; his appeal for an extra voluntary subscription was received with enthusiasm and large loans were floated.

Pitt bore the burden alone. It was expected that he would marry Eleanor Eden, but for some reason, although he seems to have been in love with her, he decided against marriage. His own affairs were utterly confused, debtors pressed. It is odd that he who devoted so much care to the nation's finance could not order his own. Did he foresee that his life would be one of unrelieved cares leading to an early death? Was he unusually considerate — or unfeelingly cold, as his enemies said? He remained a bachelor, living at Downing Street and Walmer Castle (as Warden of the Cinque Ports), with his niece Lady Hester Stanhope as housekeeper. His health deteriorated, he drank deeply but without the gaiety of earlier years. Dundas claimed that he divided his time 'between cellar and garret'. Never methodical, and a neglectful correspondent, he now became increasingly casual about political and personal business. In 1806 there were still odd documents of the 1780s lying about his room. He was usually calm but one incident showed that he could crack: in May 1798 he fought a duel with Tierney on Putney Common after a violent exchange in the Commons.

Negotiations for peace brought their own strains. Fox urged the ministers on with brilliant speeches but others condemned the very idea of parleying with unstable revolutionaries: predictions were hazardous, treaties unreliable. Between the iron obstinacy of Grenville and the wishful thinking of Fox, Pitt had to steer a middle course. As it turned out, Pitt was not the man who made peace.

The problems of Ireland did not wait upon the events of war. By the impetuosity of Earl Fitzwilliam in 1795, who introduced a bill in the Irish parliament for full civil equality for Catholics and Protestants, he was embroiled in a struggle whose outcome, he believed, must be political union. In an hysterical atmosphere calm measures were spurned. Pitt offered a charter for Maynooth College — but Catholic feeling could not be assuaged. The United Irishmen planned a republic, but fortunately for England their title was a misnomer. The Catholic rising in Leinster and Wexford was less a republican movement than an agrarian *jacquerie* fortified by religious fanaticism and, belatedly, by French troops. Hideous atrocities embittered both peasants and troops before the rising was put down by Lake and Cornwallis. Pitt was impressed by the military danger and the cost of 40,000 troops, as well as by the distresses of Ireland. In January 1800 he presented the case for Union in a speech which was masterly, humane, comprehensive. To persuade the Irish borough-mongers to give up their interest, £10,000 was given for each borough; sinecures, titles, further sweetened the pill. The total bill for disenfranchisement was £1,260,000, 46 promotions to the peerage and 20 ecclesiastical appointments. The resolution passed the Dublin parliament in the spring of 1800. Then Pitt ran upon the rocks.

Loughborough, his Lord Chancellor, aroused the king's anxieties about Catholic Emancipation. When Pitt put this before the king the latter talked of conspiracy and insisted upon his oath: he saw the issue, as always, in personal terms and spoke of loyalty. Pitt felt that he was committed to the Catholic cause by the previous transactions, though no formal promise had been given. In February 1801 he resigned. George III lapsed into insanity. Pitt promised that he would not raise the question of Catholic

Emancipation again in George III's lifetime. Addington was left to negotiate the peace of Lunéville. Pitt continued to give support as a private member. Just as he had never seen himself as being, in a modern sense, head of a party, so now he would neither lead any systematic opposition nor listen to suggestions of a compromise ministry. He was reticent in these months to a point that exasperated his friends. They longed, in Canning's words, for the return of 'the pilot who weathered the storm'. He seems to have waited for a spontaneous rush of public opinion and he suffered in health from sudden release from the tensions of high office. Visits to Bath were needed to relieve his gout and biliousness. Only a private subscription among friends saved him from his creditors, but he had still to sell Holwood, his country house.

In May 1803 war was resumed after deadlock had been reached upon the question of Malta. As Colonel of the Kentish Association and Warden of the Cinque Ports, Pitt drilled volunteers. 'He absolutely goes through the fatigue of a drill sergeant' reported Hester. At first he seems to have supported the government. He seems to have hoped for a coalition, but the government's naval policy alarmed him. Then Fox joined him in voting against the Militia Bill and Addington's majority sank. At the end of April 1804 he resigned. George III resisted Pitt's request to have Fox in — and Grenville stayed out in sympathy with Fox. Pitt shouldered his burden with only Dundas close enough to him to be of much use. The impeachment and disgrace of Dundas was a shattering blow. But Pitt planned for a decision: the navy's part, planned by Barham at the Admiralty, was to annihilate the French and Spanish fleets, while on the Continent Austria and Russia were to bring the French to action in Italy. The Mediterranean was the strategic centre. In the event, Napoleon's invasion plans were thwarted, but Trafalgar brought grief as well as the exhilaration of complete victory. Pitt, who admired Nelson intensely, could not sleep the night he heard the news. Napoleon's sea power was destroyed but on land the triumphs of Ulm and Austerlitz were to spell the destruction of Pitt's laborious and expensive design.

In November 1805 he went to the banquet at the Mansion House; the mob untied the horses and dragged his carriage themselves. To the Lord Mayor's toast to the 'saviour of Europe' he simply replied: 'I return you many thanks for the honour you have done me; but Europe is not to be saved by any single man. England has saved herself by her exertions and will, as I trust, save Europe by her example.' The frail figure seemed to embody the collective will of the nation. In December, however, came the news of Austerlitz. He may not have said 'Roll up the map of Europe, it will not be needed these ten years', but he seems to have believed it. Wilberforce spoke of his 'Austerlitz look'. His last weeks were passed in physical agony and the heartbreak of a disappointed patriot. In his last delirium listeners caught the cry 'Hear! Hear!' and later, 'Oh! my country! How I leave my country!' He died in the early morning of 23 January 1806. His last thoughts seem to have been of the Commons, and of the country which he had so nobly served.

Many wept. Lord Malmesbury vowed that in his whole future life he would always act as he believed William Pitt would have wished. For a political following, more generally for a political class, Pitt became, more than a memory, an idea. Because his mind had been so open, his policies so pragmatic, his appeal was broad. It was that which had frustrated Charles James Fox; and it was he who said, after his rival's death, that 'it seemed as if there were something missing in the world'.

J. Holland Rose, *William Pitt and the National Revival, William Pitt and the Great War*, both 1911.
J. Ehrman, *The Younger Pitt*, vol. I, 1969; vol. II, 1983; vol. III, 1996.

**HENRY DUNDAS, LORD MELVILLE** (1742-1811) was a formidable politician, ambitious and adroit in the management of political machinery, a true professional — the sort of man whose outlook and stamina might have carried him today, *mutatis mutandis*, to the Presidency of the United States. His career is important in the conditions created by the Napoleonic Wars, and because of his long association with the younger Pitt. He came from a line of Scottish judges. When he was born his father was Lord President of the Court of Session; when he was called to the bar, a half-brother had succeeded his father as president. Dundas had a fertile practice in the General Assembly and 'twas in the Kirk courts he learn'd his airs'. In 1766 he was appointed Solicitor-General; in 1776 Dean of the Faculty of Advocates in

Edinburgh. This was his anchor even after he was launched in political life and he retained the office of Dean until 1785. In 1774 he became M.P. for Midlothian and at once attached himself to the administration of Lord North. For loyalty and ability he was quickly rewarded: in 1775 he became Lord Advocate, in 1779 Keeper of the Signet for Scotland — in George III's words, in order that 'Lord North might be certain of an able debater at all times in the House of Commons'. He was a steady defender of the war in America and believed that 'to bring America to reason we must make her feel our power', but he found himself able to sit in office under Rockingham in 1782. With the formation of the Fox-North coalition he passed over, however, to Pitt. His friendship was of immense value to the austere young man who became Prime Minister in 1784, for he had negotiated himself a position at the heart of the complex bargains and understandings which bound together the Scottish interest. He had been Treasurer of the Navy under Rockingham and Shelburne; in 1784 he became President of the Board of Control. In the latter capacity he worked harmoniously with Pitt in the promotion of the useful measures of these years. His principal rôle was the organization of places and jobs. The East India Company was the natural objective for ambitious and impecunious Scots and Dundas saw to it that they arrived there, to the benefit of both the government and the Company. Pitt could rely upon the Scottish members for steady support since the representation of her docile counties and decayed burghs, only 4,000 voters in all, was firmly in his friend's hands.

Dundas was wary, pragmatic and entirely devoted to the concept of efficient government. No one worked harder. He remained Treasurer of the Navy until 1800 and President of the Board of Control until 1801. For three years, 1791-4, he was Home Secretary. From 1794 he was Secretary of State for War, but did not have control of the militia, the main home force, until 1798. With Grenville he was the third member of the governing triumvirate. He was not a man to break under the nervous strain imposed by revolution and war. Indeed he supplied an admirable foil to Pitt's finer temperament. Over many bottles of port they discussed the affairs of state in the realistic terms which both understood.

What use did Dundas make of his power and patronage? He

was more interested in facts and results than in ideas and the excitements of the French Revolution washed about him without effect. But he was not lacking in human sympathy and as an administrator he was adventurous. At different times he interested himself in the abolition of serfdom in Scotland, the regeneration of the Highlands and Free Trade with Ireland. Politically he was indeed illiberal. He opposed Sheridan in 1789 on the matter of reform of the Scottish boroughs. Though prepared to consider the gradual abolition of the slave trade he was opposed to drastic action. Over Hastings he preserved a judicial open-mindedness. He showed sympathy with Catholic Emancipation and resigned with Pitt on this issue in 1801, but in general the impression that he leaves is one of archetypal conservatism. He was not a man to attach himself to a hopeless cause simply because he thought it right. If all men did this, how would the king's government be carried on?

Created Viscount Melville by Addington, he returned to office with Pitt in 1804 as First Lord of the Admiralty. Before Trafalgar he was out of office since in the spring of 1805 he was impeached after an inquiry which reported malversations of funds by the former Treasurer of the Navy. He had in fact, in a way more negligent than corrupt, mingled public and private accounts. When the motion of Whitbread for an impeachment on the grounds of malversation was voted on, there were 216 votes cast for and against. Speaker Abbot gave his casting vote for the impeachment — and Pitt was overwhelmed: his pride was hurt, the image of probity tarnished, his friend and supporter disgraced. Friends crowded round him so that the Opposition should not see the tears rolling down his face. Melville of course resigned but the impeachment which followed failed and he was acquitted on all charges involving his honour: 'light delinquency' was Fox's phrase. He retired to live quietly in Scotland at his seat near Comrie.

There is irony in the manner of his disgrace for he had done much for the navy and for his country. It is arguable that he was a sounder strategist than Pitt. He was an energetic naval administrator trusted by the sailors. Exponent of 'a war for colonial resources', he was a staunch and intelligent imperialist: the territories and trade won in 1815 owe much to him. He was a man of courage. In the days when he supported North, Wilberforce had described him as the first man on the ministerial side and referred to 'a manliness in his character which prevented his running away from the question'. In his own words he had been 'a cement of political strength'.

H. Furber, *Henry Dundas, First Viscount Melville 1742-1811*, 1931.
J. Ehrman, *The Younger Pitt*, 3 vols., 1969, 1983, 1996.

**WILLIAM WINDHAM** (1750-1810) was war minister under Pitt and Dundas from 1794 to 1801, and later briefly in the 'ministry of all the talents'. He was one of the best parliamentary speakers of his day and an imaginative minister. In his ardent pursuit of new ideas and hasty, sometimes injudicious, efforts to execute them he recalls the youthful Churchill. He lacked the patient application of Castlereagh, who succeeded him in 1807, and he cannot be counted among great war ministers. As a politician he exposed himself to the charge of inconsistency. But the young man who became one of Dr. Johnson's dearest friends, the middle-aged patriot who befriended Cobbett and sought to make that awkward individualist a good government man, the civilized Norfolk squire who was one of the earliest patrons of Humphrey Repton, cannot be judged as a politician alone. 'Weathercock Windham' was one of the most agreeable as well as one of the most capable men in public life.

The son of William Windham, a cavalry officer, and member of parliament, the author of a military manual and supporter of Chatham's militia scheme, he grew up at the family seat, Felbrigg, and went to Eton, Glasgow University, where he studied under the philosopher John Anderson, and University College, Oxford. His was a keen, ingenious mind. He was always fascinated by novelties: for a time he was much concerned with balloons. His friendship with Dr. Johnson was a formative, inspiring experience. The old sage warmed to his enthusiasm and lively scholarship. 'Such conversation I shall not have again till I come back to the regions of literature; and there', said Johnson, 'Windham is *inter stellas luna minores*'. Windham tended his last illness and acted as a pallbearer at his funeral. For a time he carried on a hopeless, possibly platonic, affair with the wife of a Norfolk friend, John Byng. He was liable to bouts of melancholy and was happiest among his pictures and books at Felbrigg, or when he had important work to do. Reynolds' portrait of him in later life shows fine, sensitive features, the face of a man of feeling — but one accustomed to thought.

He first tasted politics when he became secretary to the Lord Lieutenant of Ireland in 1783. 'Don't be afraid, sir,' said Johnson, when Windham consulted him upon a question of ethics, 'You will soon make a very pretty rascal.' But Windham was ever the most scrupulous of men, always threatening resignation on some point of principle when in office, happier when he was free to criticize. In 1784 he became member of parliament for Norwich. Like his Norfolk colleague, Coke of Holkham, he was a keen Whig. He assisted in the impeachment of Hastings. Later he followed Burke in opposition to the Revolution. Pitt recognized the value of this convert who was convinced of the necessity of war against France. In 1794 he made him Secretary at War with a seat in the cabinet, but under Dundas, who had over-all powers of direction. Unfortunately Windham was, like Dundas, an amateur in strategy. His approach was coloured by his chivalrous sympathy for the *émigrés*, for whom he was made specially responsible. Lord Guilford once said that he could never see Windham without picturing Don Quixote with a barber's basin on his head. He never overcame his regret for the Bourbons. Veneration for Burke was his dominant political idea. The Breton fiasco of 1795 was a disillusioning reminder of the hazards of supporting a local rising in anything but overwhelming strength. British support was inadequate and the Vendéan rising was suppressed. If anything the British patronage of exiled nobles and Breton peasants strengthened the revolutionary government; it certainly contributed to the rise of Napoleon. Windham ought not to be blamed too severely for this or other failures of strategy. Pitt and Dundas allowed themselves the luxury of dispersal of effort when the army was too small and too badly trained for one successful expedition, let alone for a global war. Their policy was almost a caricature of the successful straegy pursued by the elder Pitt. Windham at least contributed a passionate will to win. He actually visited the campaign area during the Duke of York's operations in Flanders. And he perceived more plainly than others the need to improve conditions of pay and service. He understood the importance of propaganda and patronized Cobbett's *Porcupine*, then helped him found the *Political Register*. It is typical of the way in which Windham's schemes went awry that this paper, which began life as friend of church and state, became the most effective of radical journals, the scourge of governments.

He resigned with Pitt over the king's refusal to add Catholic Emancipation to Irish Union. He derided Addington and savaged the peace of Amiens; he was impatient with Pitt for not doing the same. His militant views lost him his seat at Norwich and, temporarily, his friendship with Coke. He could hardly be described now as a Whig. 'Who would repair their house during a hurricane?' was his rejoinder when men talked of reform. He returned to parliament as member for a Grenville borough. In 1804, however, he showed that he had his share of the spirit of party when he declined to enter Pitt's second administration. He was also convinced about the necessity for a settlement of the Irish question. In 1806 he became Secretary for War and Colonies in the 'ministry of all the talents' and put forward the scheme that embodied his thinking and experience, the General Training Act. The whole population was to be trained in batches of 200,000 at a time. Men were to be allowed to enlist for a short period and they were offered higher rates of pay if they chose to re-engage. The volunteer system was ended. The conception was sound, the execution poor. Windham should have given the business his whole time. Unfortunately he preferred to plan operations.

After the disastrous failure of Pitt's last coalition it seemed pointless to contest Napoleon's grip on the Continent. The new world offered more scope; great trading interests were at stake. So ambitious operations were mounted. Popham captured Buenos Aires but it was subsequently lost. Whitelocke was sent to retrieve the situation and establish a permanent base. The idea was that the colonists would welcome the British as liberators. But Whitelocke failed to capture Buenos Aires after bloody assaults and sailed for home and court martial. Castlereagh inherited a bleak situation indeed. His first measures included a drastic reassessment of the rôle of the militia; he took thirty thousand to be trained along with regulars. Windham naturally preferred his own scheme and attacked Castlereagh's. He opposed the assault on Copenhagen (1807) and the expedition to Walcheren (1809). He supported the Peninsular war, however, and it is sad that he did not live to see Wellington's final victories.

R. W. Ketton-Cremer, *The Early Life and Diaries of William Windham*, 1930.

**HENRY ADDINGTON, 1st VISCOUNT SIDMOUTH** (1757-1844), is one of the least regarded of our Prime Ministers. 'Pitt is to Addington, as London is to Paddington' — Canning's epigram summarizes what is usually felt about the man who succeeded Pitt as Prime Minister in 1801, negotiated peace with Bonaparte, saw this peace dissolve within eighteen months and had to give way again to the man who epitomized the spirit of national resistance. This bathetic interlude, the venomous wit of Canning, who took it upon himself to represent the interests of Pitt, and the lack of distinction of his subsequent spells of power help to explain why Addington is dimly known. No reappraisal can make a great man of him, but his solid achievement deserves a fairer perspective.

The son of a court doctor, he was educated at Winchester and Brasenose College, Oxford, read law and followed the younger Pitt into political life. He was elected in 1783 for the seat of Devizes. In 1789 he was made Speaker, in which capacity he pleased the Tories by his mild conservatism and impressed the house by his tact. When in 1801 Pitt was forced to resign upon the issue of Catholic Emancipation, Addington, whom George III had used as his emissary to Pitt in the last stages of the dispute, was asked to form a ministry. He was well liked. Although his own following was small, some dozen friends who looked to him for advancement, there were many others who wanted him to make peace. There are analogies to this situation. Henry Pelham in the eighteenth century, Baldwin in the twentieth, men of sense and integrity, answered to a similar mood of war-weariness, a desire for economies and for good order — for 'safety first'. It was widely felt that the war against the revolution had become meaningless; furthermore that the war could not be won, nor allies obtained. Addington himself is recorded as saying that 'there was not the least prospect of obtaining such alliances' for the present. Gold payments to continental allies had already exhausted much of the Bank of England's reserves; the pound depreciated, trade was disturbed, bread was expensive.

Addington, with a somewhat weak ministry, palpably stuffed at the lower levels with friends and relations, negotiated the Treaty of Amiens upon the premise that peace was needed at once. Except for Trinidad and Ceylon — taken from Spain and Holland respectively, conquests were to be handed back. France agreed to help to obtain compensation for the House of Orange and to evacuate Italy. Wyndham, Canning and, more surprisingly, Grey criticized the Peace of Amiens and 'Britain's guardian gander' who made it. But Pitt continued to back 'The Doctor' in the most generous fashion. The peace, however, crumbled as France went from one provocative act to another. Napoleon accepted the 'presidency' of the Cis-Alpine republic, annexed Piedmont, enforced France's control of Switzerland by military intervention. The English, concerned about the spirit in which Napoleon interpreted the peace, held on to their Indian posts and to Malta (to be returned to the Knights of St. John), as bargaining counters. They declared war in May 1803 and Addington had to contend with the threat of invasion. The navy had been reduced from 130,000 to 70,000; the regular army establishment was reduced to 95,000. In all this Addington had not been merely destructive. Alongside a saving of £25 million in one year went a new method of annual budgeting, based upon a complete survey of the accounts, and a reform of the civil list by which Parliament took care of the payments for the salaries of departments, instead of the king. He also abolished the income tax.

'He was not well fitted for the warfare of St. Stephen's.' (Wilberforce.) He was insecure, as if on a temporary lease, and hesitant in debate. War further exposed Addington's limitations. He wanted a defensive war: granting that Napoleon would master the continent, he relied upon the navy to hold the Channel. He increased the Militia but created confusion by appealing for Volunteer companies, setting in motion a patriotic movement with only the haziest idea of how to control it. Priority was not given, as it should have been, to training a regular army to defeat the French on the Continent, for Addington lacked vision. Many still trusted him: Southey, Hastings, even Nelson. He was calm in crisis and he wisely made no fuss about the affair of Colonel Despard, a crazy officer who planned to murder the government and was executed for it in 1803. He was also willing to come to terms with Pitt, but on terms which looked condescending. When Pitt formed his new government in May 1804, several of Addington's followers, such as Hawkesbury and Eldon, were included. Addington himself returned in January 1805 as Lord President, with the title of Viscount Sidmouth. Too much bitterness had been caused, however, by the machinations of the last part of his ministry to allow for an easy assimilation of Addington men. The impeachment of Pitt's friend and First Lord, Melville, increased the strains, since Addington's following voted with the opposition, against Melville, in a division which went, by the casting vote of the Speaker, against the First Lord. Melville resigned in May 1805, Sidmouth in June.

He reappeared in the 'ministry of all the talents' (1806) as Lord Privy Seal and later Lord President of the Council. In 1812 he became Home Secretary in Liverpool's government and remained there until 1821. In the face of the hardships which followed the war, the social evils of industrialization and widespread agitation, Sidmouth's policy was bleakly repressive. The Suspension of the Habeas Corpus Act in 1817, the Six Acts of 1819, were the policy of the government, not his alone. But his shortcomings during this period are exposed by the reforming activity of his successor, Robert Peel. Strong nerve, patience and staying power Sidmouth and his colleagues undoubtedly possessed. But the will and imagination to look at the causes of the evils of society were wanting.

P. Ziegler, *Addington*, 1962.

**HENRY GRATTAN** (1746-1820), Irish statesman, played a principal rôle in the attainment of legislative independence for Ireland in 1782 and fought, less effectively, against the Act of Union which brought that independence to an end eighteen years afterwards. Sidney Smith said of him that 'He thought only of Ireland, lived for no other object; dedicated to her his beautiful fancy, his elegant wit, his manly courage and all the splendours of his astonishing eloquence'. We may observe that the crises in Anglo-Irish relations have tended to coincide with times of danger for the mother-country. But the 'Irish Demosthenes', demagogue though he was at times, was no common agitator; reckless in rhetoric, he was capable still of larger views. He was at heart a Whig: a man of the establishment, committed to the preservation of property and the Protestant ascendancy, who nonetheless hoped for salvation for his country from Catholic Emancipation.

Grattan, the son of a recorder of Dublin, was called to the Irish bar after he went down from Trinity College, Dublin. But he was drawn to politics by the rising force of Irish nationalism. The Irish saw 'the Castle' in the same light as the American colonists saw the redcoats and revenue officers of King George — aliens, instruments of exploitation. Grattan excelled in epigram, in aphorism; he was a fastidious but passionate debater, another Burke but without the hysteria. 'The Irish Protestant can never be free until the Irish Catholic has ceased to be a slave'; again, 'Let the kingly power that forms one estate in our constitution, continue for ever: but let it be, as by the principles and laws of these countries it should be, one estate only — and not a power constituting one estate, corrupting another, and influencing a third': there we have a summary of his views upon the two issues that concerned him most.

He was brought into the Irish House of Commons by his friend Lord Charlemont in 1775. He proposed motions for free trade and the repeal of the acts which kept Ireland subject to the English Privy Council and Parliament. Concessions were secured: in 1778 Roman Catholics were allowed to inherit property and to hold long leases; in 1779 Irish ships were allowed to sail as British. In 1782 the Irish parliament got its independence. The only link that remained was the king, head of the executive of both countries. 'Spirit of Swift, spirit of Molyneux, your genius has prevailed! Ireland is now a nation!' Could the system work, when the Viceroy and chief secretary in Dublin were in the last resort responsible to an English government dependent on an English parliament? Ireland knew some prosperity during the two decades of independence. But in Ireland Grattan's party were convinced that their parliament must be reformed, the Catholics given civil rights. In England after 1793 it seemed that he was irresponsible, rousing the Catholic poor who would welcome French invaders. Pitt's Catholic Relief Act of 1793, admirable in intention, made matters worse, and Fitzwilliam's rashness, in 1795, speaking precipitately about the Emancipation for which Pitt was more subtly working, put Grattan in a difficult position. To avoid losing control over the popular movement, he had to attack Pitt. When, in 1797, with French invasion threatened, (the force was rounded up at Fishguard), the government, in the shape of Lord Camden, set about the disarmament of Ulster, Grattan and his friends seceded from the Irish Parliament. In truth they were irrelevant.

After the Civil War of 1798 Pitt moved towards Union. Despite Grattan's impassioned protests the Union was forced through, with titles, compensation and a strong understanding that emancipation would follow. Grattan fought a duel with Isaac Corry, who had attacked his speech against the Bill. He had remained 'faithful to her freedom, faithful to her fall' — but the real disaster for Ireland was the refusal of George III to grant Catholic Emancipation. The good of the Union was undone, its bitterness remained. Pitt resigned, while Grattan resolved to fight for the measure in the English parliament.

He sat for Malton in 1805, thereafter for Dublin. He had long been a friend and admirer of Fox, who offered him a post in his ministry of 1806. Grattan refused it. By instinct he was an opposer, a tribune rather than an administrator. He continued to delight the House by his style and to press for Emancipation. He carried the motion for an inquiry in 1811; the nearest he could get to satisfaction. Neither Jacobin nor democrat, he supported the war effort. It is fitting that he was buried in Westminster Abbey between Pitt, who had worked so hard to find a solution to the problems of the two countries, and Fox whom, in his love of liberty he so much resembled.

Stephen Gwynn, *Henry Grattan and his Times*, 1939.
R. B. McDowell, *Ireland in the Age of Imperialism and Reform, 1760-1801*, 1979.

**THEOBALD WOLFE TONE** (1763-98), Irish revolutionary leader, was the son of Peter Tone, a Protestant coachmaker of Dublin. A clever but lazy boy who would have preferred to go into the army, Tone became a pensioner of Trinity College, Dublin, in 1781. He was nearly expelled for acting as second in a duel in which a man was killed, and he eloped with a girl of sixteen, Matilda Witherington. They were happy but penniless. After the birth of a daughter Tone went to London and enrolled as a student in the Middle Temple. He scarcely opened a law book, but with his younger brother, home from service in the East India Company, he devised a scheme for a military colony in a South Sea island: Pitt was not interested. Tone returned to Ireland after nearly two years (Christmas 1788) and was called to the Irish bar. Thomas Russell, the main founder of the United Irish Society, was an important influence on Tone at this time. Tone became a republican and avowed his aims: 'To break the connexion with England, the never-failing source of all our political evils' and 'to substitute the common name of Irishman in place of the denominations ...'.

With Henry Flood he was elected an honorary member of the first company of Belfast Volunteers. He assisted Russell in the formation of the United Irishmen and devoted himself to bringing together the various interests in the patriotic movement. He played a major part in the great Catholic convention of December 1792 but he was disappointed by the failure of his leader, John Keogh, in negotiation with Lord Buckinghamshire. He decided to try more extreme tactics.

Revolutionary France seemed to be Ireland's natural ally. A memorandum for the agent William Jackson, urging that the time was ripe for a French invasion, was betrayed to the government. By agreement with the government Tone took himself off to America in June 1795, a month after the United Irishmen had reorganized themselves on a rebellious basis. In Philadelphia he met the French ambassador, who approved his plan, worked out with Emmet and Russell, for securing French aid. In February 1796 Tone, alias James Smith, was in Paris, discussing invasion with Carnot and de la Croix.

He was given the commission of *chef de brigade*, but there were delays. Bad seamanship then spoiled the first attempt in December 1796. The French could have landed 12,000 men on an undefended shore; they delayed, a storm blew up, they cut their cables and ran. The death of Hoche, Tone's main ally, was a further set-back (September 1797). Bonaparte was more interested in Egypt than in Ireland; later he was to regret it. When news came of the rising in Ireland (June 1798), he was on his way east and the Directory would only sanction small expeditions to different points along the coast. Humbert sailed in August with a thousand men. In September Napper Tandy landed on Rutland Island with a band of Irish refugees. Tone himself sailed from Brest with General Hardy, the battleship *Hoche* and three thousand men. Contrary winds delayed them and they did not arrive off Lough Swilly until October 10th. Before they could land they were attacked by an English squadron. The *Hoche* surrendered and Tone was taken prisoner. He was court-martialled: against the charge of treason he pleaded his duty as a French officer. He was only allowed to read portions of a prepared statement declaring his aims. He was found guilty; his request to be shot as a soldier was refused. To save himself from the gallows he cut his throat with a pen-knife. Meanwhile efforts had been made to transfer his case to the civil courts. The chief justice ordered the suspension of execution but a week later, 19 November, Tone died of his self-inflicted wound.

Tone's *Journals* present an entertaining picture of the man, but they were written mainly to amuse his wife and his friend Thomas Russell and should not be treated too seriously. His reputation in English history is that of a reckless rebel. 'I hated her [England] before my exile and I will hate her always.' By Irishmen, however, he can justly be seen as a patriot: optimistic, brave, an Irish Danton. His son William Tone served actively in the French and later in the American army, and subsequently wrote a life of his father. Today Irish exponents of violent revolution revere his name.

T. Pakenham, *The Year of Liberty*, 1969.
Marianne Elliot, *Wolfe Tone*, 1989.

**WILLIAM HENRY BENTINCK, DUKE OF PORTLAND** (1738-1809) was twice First Lord of the Treasury. A cartoon of 1807 shows an irascible John Bull surveying a figure, upright and rigid in a chair of blocks of Portland stone; on his chest is hung a placard, 'Repaired and whitewashed in the year 1807'. In this year Portland became First Lord of the Treasury for the second time. He was the nominal leader of a ministry of various and discrepant talents at a dispiriting juncture of the Napoleonic war. He had played a leading part in politics for thirty-five years but few men who have had such eminence are less known. He is indeed a fair example of the type of English magnate who has enjoyed high office as much by virtue of honesty as by the influence of broad acres, who was essentially the safe, dull man who could be relied upon to lead brilliant ministers less steady or more factious than himself.

After Eton and Christ Church Portland joined the following of Rockingham, whose career in some respects resembled his own. In 1782 he was Lord Lieutenant of Ireland in Rockingham's second ministry, when legislative independence was given to the Irish parliament. After Shelburne's short, unpopular administration he became the nominal head of the Fox-North coalition. He might have become the head of a greater partnership, between Fox and Pitt, if his terms had been less binding or Pitt's independence less proud. As it was he saw Pitt go from strength to strength in the years after 1784. In July 1794, after the outbreak of war with Revolutionary France and the resounding conversion of Burke to Tory principles, he followed some of his friends among the right wing of the Whigs to Pitt and to a new alignment along a broad front of anti-Jacobin and anti-reform principles which was to survive until the Great Reform Bill. As Home Secretary, from 1794 to 1801, Portland provided stability and soundness of administration. He was a realistic patriot but no zealot; the relatively mild action of the government against subversive elements reflects his calm approach. He opposed Catholic Emancipation and stayed in Addington's Cabinet after Pitt's fall in 1801. From January 1805 he served Pitt again, though without office.

On the fall of the 'ministry of all the talents', again upon the Catholic issue, he emerged to head a government — 'all Pitt's friends, without Mr Pitt' (Sir John Moore) — which was torn apart by the mutual hostility of Canning and Castlereagh, its ablest members. His grasp was by then faltering; he was much weakened by the gout. In the months before his death he could read nothing and transact no business. He spent much time asleep. Hansard does not record a single speech in two and a half years. Perceval gained authority; Canning intrigued against Castlereagh. Military misfortunes culminated in the failure of the Walcheren expedition and Castlereagh called Canning out to a duel. Shortly afterwards Portland had a fit and died. 'It is not', said Perceval, 'because the Duke of Portland is at our head that the Government is a Government of departments, but it is because the Government is and must essentially be a Government of departments that the Duke of Portland is our head.'

**WILLIAM WYNDHAM, BARON GRENVILLE** (1759-1834) was Pitt's foreign minister for ten years and later, after Pitt's death, the head of the 'Ministry of all the talents'. He was a cleverer man than his father, George Grenville, George III's Prime

Minister (1763-5), and a more constructive politician than Grey, with whom he led the opposition after 1807. Yet he sacrificed the chance of office at critical periods of the war, when his experience would have been invaluable, for adherence to a principle. What he saw as principle others saw as pride. He was an upright man, but above all he was a Grenville. The Grenvilles stand out like an island in the choppy sea of Georgian politics. Frowning cliffs and rocky shoals defended their privileged base. Distinctive, clannish and exclusive, they were willing to exert themselves in the public interest and to receive the rewards of public life. They were unwilling to join any association except on their own terms, which were invariably pitched very high. Earl Temple, his uncle, damaged the Pitt administration at the outset by a resignation which has never been satisfactorily explained. His elder brother, Buckingham, made demands on him which became, inevitably, demands on the state. In 1806 Fox had to introduce a special bill to enable Grenville to continue to hold the office of Auditor and Comptroller-General concurrently with the Lord Treasurership: in the one capacity Grenville was to control and audit what in his other capacity he was to spend!

William Grenville was the younger son of George Grenville and Elizabeth Wyndham. He was the first cousin of William Pitt, whose mother, Hester Grenville, was his mother's sister. After Eton and Christ Church he entered Parliament for the family borough of Buckingham at the age of twenty-three. He was liberal in his economic views, a student of Adam Smith and a natural ally of Pitt, whose administration he joined in 1784 as joint Paymaster-General. He became later Home Secretary and, in 1791, after the resignation of Carmarthen over the Okzakoff question, Foreign Secretary. His capacity for detailed study and patient handling of complex issues can be seen to advantage in his handling of the Canada problem. He did much spade-work for the Canada Act of 1791 though Pitt managed its passage through the Commons. Its authors had learned the lessons of the revolt of the American colonies: the governor was given extensive patronage and a church establishment was provided. The laws and religion of French Lower Canada were preserved. Both parts of the country were given a legislative assembly on British lines while council, executive and governor broadly represented the British institutions of upper house, ministers and king. Grenville believed that 'the constitution of Great Britain is sufficient to pervade the whole world'. Such magnificent whiggishness made him an unbending opponent of Jacobin and Bonapartist extremes. Grenville was foreign minister until 1801 and the resignation of Pitt. From 1793 England was at war with France. Grenville never wavered. Financial matters were, of course, of less concern to him than they were to Pitt, and where Pitt was willing to compromise and negotiate, Grenville was for fighting on. This intelligent, steady man epitomized the stubborn will of his countrymen. Defeats, mutinies, deficits were brushed aside as of no consequence; peace on any other terms than those of Great Britain was unthinkable. He stood on traditional grounds of national security when the French renounced the Scheldt treaties, saying that his government could not watch with indifference any nation make herself 'sovereign of the Low Countries or general arbitress of the rights and liberties of Europe'. He distrusted the German statesmen who regarded England as an inexhaustible milch cow. He was relieved when French intransigence wrecked peace negotiations in 1797. He wrote then: 'it would be ten thousand times safer to face the storm than to shrink from it'. He rejected Bonaparte's overtures of 1799 and opposed the terms of the Peace of Amiens in 1801: 'England has given up everything everywhere'. He was consistent throughout. Since Chauvelin could not claim to represent his king he had no official status. He was therefore shown to the smallest chair in the room (he promptly sat down on the largest). When Bonaparte, newly made First Consul, sent an ingratiating letter to George III, as one ruler to another, Grenville replied with a memorandum stating coldly that the British government saw no reason for departing from established methods and manners in diplomacy: 'the best way for the French people to achieve peace would be to restore their proper rulers'.

After 1801 Grenville moved towards Fox and Grey. Family loyalty, common interest and a similar style in politics and personal life had helped to bind him to Pitt. The cousins looked physically alike. Now in opposition, however, differences emerged. Grenville, like Spencer and Windham, was impatient with Pitt's tolerant attitude towards Addington. When Pitt tried to form a national government of all parties, Grenville refused to join it. George III had refused to accept Fox as foreign minister, and Grenville would not abandon Fox or the cause of Catholic

Emancipation. 'I will teach that proud man', said Pitt, 'that I can do without him, though I think it will cost me my life.'

Pitt's death seemed to make possible the 'ministry of all the talents' that he had failed to achieve in life. Grenville was its head. In reality its composition was narrower than the name suggests. The old Portland group was represented strongly: Spencer and Windham were fellow secretaries of state with Fox. But the Pittites were excluded and these began to act as a coherent opposition. The administration was not fruitless. Windham instituted universal military training, in place of the volunteer system. The power of government was put behind the anti-slavery movement and a generous measure was promoted. Grenville defeated diehard resistance in the Lords by his own advocacy. The slave trade was abolished by Britain as the ministry came to an end. Fox's tragic death had robbed Grenville of his ablest minister. But the end came over an issue which need never have been raised. To secure a token victory for his ministers' principles Grenville had sought to gain royal assent for further concessions to Roman Catholics. It could be argued in the interest of military efficiency that Roman Catholic officers should hold ranks up to colonel. Was it wise to raise this question at a critical juncture of the war — or to require from the king, when ministers offered to drop the bill, that they should be allowed nevertheless to put their case to their followers? So, in Sheridan's phrase, 'they built a wall against which to run their own heads'. The king acted with doubtful propriety when he demanded a pledge from ministers that they would never again raise the question. But the Whigs had shown more confidence than their parliamentary position warranted. The king was ready with an alternative ministry. The Whigs were not to have power again for twenty-three years.

Grenville and Grey had chances of office in 1809, 1811 and 1812. Principle and prejudice combined to prevent them from leaving their tents. Grenville was almost hysterically pessimistic about the outcome of the war. Like Grey he was devoted to his country house. 'Lord Grenville's attachment to Boconnoc surpasses anything I have yet seen', wrote Auckland: 'Politics are no more alluded to in conversation than astrology'. In 1811 the prince toyed with the idea of having Wellesley as head of a Grenvillite ministry. Grenville attacked Wellesley's view of the war. After Perceval's assassination there were further negotiations.

Grenville demanded Catholic relief and a cut in public expend-
iture. From all the parleys came a mixture much as before: the
Pittites now under Liverpool. As the largest cohesive group in
Parliament the Whigs feared to lose their identity in a coalition.
The history of liberalism in the twentieth century suggests that
they may have been right.

In 1815 Grenville and Grey fell out over the future of
Napoleon. Grenville was for destroying him, Grey for coming to
terms. In the post-war years Grenville voiced strong views about
sedition and public order. Liverpool was sufficiently impressed by
his energy to offer him a post; he declined, but let some of his
followers join. In 1823 he retired from public life, to spend time
where he had always been happiest — in the country; no longer in
his beloved Cornwall but at Dropmore where a magnificent
library solaced his declining years.

P. Jupp, *Lord Grenville, 1754-1834*, 1985.

**CHARLES JAMES FOX** (1749-1806), statesman, received an
education which made the most of his splendid talents. Both at
Eton and at Hertford College, Oxford, he showed that he could
work diligently at the classics that he loved. His father, Henry
Fox, besides being a very capable politician, was a pleasant, easy
man; his mother was descended from Charles II. He himself was
not good looking but he was made to be admired, swarthy, somewhat heavy in features but with magnificent eyes; his voice and
smile went to the heart. When inherited wealth and natural ability combined to make the prospect sweet, only a sensible discipline was needed to train him for a purposeful life; but he was
outrageously spoiled by his father. At fourteen they went together
to the gambling haunts of the Continent and Charles returned to
Eton devoted to cards and dice. 'Too witty to live there — and a
little too wicked' is the comment in the Eton College Register. His
too indulgent father later took him away from Oxford. That was
his undoing. 'An egoist through and through', Ehrman calls him:
'his causes were always splendid, his failures never his fault.'
Charles learned the languages of several countries. After two
years he returned to take a seat in Parliament for Midhurst. At
nineteen he was still ineligible, but all rules gave way before his
prodigious self-assurance. He made an immediate impact. His

*Charles James Fox*
(Artist: Karl Anton Hickel)

ready command of words and an ability to think on his feet which allowed him to appear almost negligent in manner, seemed to promise a great career. This promise was never wholly fulfilled.

The legend of Charles James Fox is made up of charm, ability, wit and waste. He 'banked his treasure in the hearts of his friends', as Churchill said of Birkenhead, but he also drew endlessly upon their money and their patience. His political achievement is small and most of his life was spent in opposition; even there the story is largely one of futile tactics and improvident attitudes, relieved only occasionally by fine words and gestures. Yet his name stands along with that of Pitt, whose personal and political virtues emphasize his rival's faults. 'Two young men', Jenkinson called them, 'both of great parts and great Ambition, and from their different Tempers and Characters, I am afraid, irreconcilable.' It is of course a Whig legend, but it has survived much reappraisal of the Whig tradition. Fox's career is paradoxical and poignant. The spell that contemporaries felt is not without power today. Earthy and even gross he may have been, corrupt he certainly was, yet he seems to have been oddly naïve. For all his precocious maturity, he never acquired the wary, responsible sense that the highest levels of political management demand. Did constant indulgence sap his willpower? Was he more interested in the ornaments of power than in its uses? Or was it circumstances that thwarted him — the dominance of Pitt, the enmity of George III and the conservative, patriotic spirit engendered by the Revolution which Fox so passionately admired?

'His judgements are never wrong; his decision is formed quicker than any man's I have ever conversed with; and he never seems to mistake but in his own affairs'. This was the estimate of his friend Lord Carlisle in 1771. He had an exceptional ability to master arguments and to develop them in his oratory; he was especially fine when called upon to attack the whole body of the opposition's case. He could work up a brief to an imposing strength, but all too rarely would he pore over his material; so often he would come flushed and unprepared from the dinner table. His gift of spontaneity encouraged him to rely on the inspiration of the moment. He was indeed a gambler all through and his vein of recklessness only grew with age. It was not so much that he was lazy, for he could work intensively and rapidly, but he preferred to improvise. There is no more telling example than Fox of the casual amateurism so often held to be a cause of weakness in English political leadership. He was made a member of the Board of Admiralty when barely twenty-one, but he attended seldom, or not at all. In 1792 he moved for leave to introduce a bill for the repeal of Lord Hardwicke's Marriage Act without having taken any steps to prepare the bill. When the second reading was due he was so late back from Newmarket that the bill was thrown out in his absence. Even where the nation's interests were at stake he could be culpably careless. An omission in the preparation of diplomatic instructions led to the Spanish gaining a point at the negotiations before the peace of Versailles in 1783; it made it no better that Fox openly admitted his omission.

Fox's political career is hard to follow unless it be realized that, besides being a Whig, he was also a complete individualist, who sat loosely towards any grouping. Never fully a North man, though he had a seat on the Treasury Board for a year (1773-4), he was also never properly a Rockinghamite, as he showed in 1783 when he made his ill-starred alliance with North. He had taken into politics the fatal legacy of his father's enmities. Personal friendships and enmities guided his erratic course. He lost his place on the Treasury Board because, being disappointed in his efforts to secure a concession for Richard Burke (in return for a share in the profits), he set out to embarrass North in every way. When, in 1792, Burke broke with him publicly over the Revolution, it was 'the loss of friends' that seemed to upset him more than the clash of principle. Fox often, however, spoke the language of 'party' in the sense of a coherent body of opposition to the king's government, an essential check which served to prevent the 'euthanasia of absolute monarchy'.

In some ways Fox was perfectly suited to lead young men. He had an eye for talent, encouraged young Grey and Erskine. The latter so enjoyed the experience of a weekend spent with Fox at St. Anne's Hill that he coined a new expression, 'to Charley it'. But he had, however, neither the temperament nor the equipment to be a good party man. He formulated the watch-words of a liberal policy that was as deeply felt as it was superficially planned: 'Peace, Economy and Reform'. But he never came to terms with the implications of this policy, except in the case of the abolition of the slave trade, where the hard work was done by others and altruism did not conflict unduly with political interests.

In his advocacy of parliamentary reform Fox was complacent to the point of absurdity. He epitomized the extravagant privilege of a tiny aristocratic group; in everything his method was that of the eighteenth century: favouritism, jobbery and regard for the vested interests. He was a frank agnostic who believed that, for Irish bishops, classical scholarship was more important than residence in the diocese. He had little conception of the new forces in electoral society that gave urgent force to the reform movement. For all his forays into the streets of radical Westminster, he was content to browse upon the lush meadows of the landed aristocracy. He did not wish to see the smoking chimneys of the other England. He held court at Brooks's: its card tables, the drawing-rooms of his friends, the admiration of Whig hostesses, the attentions of his mistress, Mrs Armistead, to whom he was steadily faithful and whom he eventually married, and the crowded benches of the House of Commons, were enough, it seemed, for him.

During the American War Fox was a loud critic of the government's policy; wildly and openly he supported the colonists and denounced the military actions of the ministry abroad and the apparent growth of royal influence at home. After the fall of North in March 1782 he took office as Secretary of State in Rockingham's administration with the avowed object of ending the war and reducing crown patronage by 'economical reform'. Within months, however, he was ready to retire after disagreement with the other Secretary of State, Shelburne, about principles and methods of negotiating with the Americans. Fox wanted to begin by recognizing independence of the Americans; Shelburne preferred to stress mutual trading interests and to work from there towards political understanding. In the event Rockingham died on 1 July, Fox resigned and Shelburne was left to complete the peace. Fox and North then joined forces in a surprising alliance to destroy Shelburne, and took office together in February 1783. Fox seems to have believed that it was a marriage of convenience between those who wanted constructive reform and those who had the experience and support on the back benches, to secure the passage of such reform. The ministry lasted only for ten months; it was destroyed on the initiative of the king himself, who had detested it from the start and secured the defeat of the India Bill in the Lords.

For Fox this ministry, and the four months of febrile opposition which ensued before a General Election confirmed the authority of Pitt, were a débâcle from which his reputation and prospects never recovered. He forgot perhaps the effect of his own oratory. He had swayed Parliament upon questions of principle, and many were now shocked at what seemed like a cynical preference for power. He under-estimated the tenacity and wiliness of the king; for dealing with this now-experienced royal politician geniality was not enough. In Pitt he had an opponent who could learn from his rivals' mistakes, a man of superb ability, a name to conjure with — and an image of probity. Fox's India Bill, admirable in conception, ingenious in detail, was fatally compromised by the appointments to the new Board of Commissions, all North and Fox men. Fox, who had denounced the evils of patronage, was especially vulnerable to the charges now laid against him; he became Carlo Khan, the fat and greasy mogul of pamphlet and cartoon. In the new warfare of satirical prints, even his appearance told against him. That Pitt's subsequent India Bill reproduced many of the best features of Fox's was no compensation for the fact that, on the day of reckoning, in the General Election of April 1784, 160 of Fox's friends were defeated at the polls, 'martyrs' to his misjudgements. Fox was reduced to the status of the head of a clique.

In 1788 the king's madness seemed to afford an opportunity to secure power again through his friend the Prince of Wales, Regent-designate. In the arguments over the constitution of the Regency, Fox went to the length of insisting upon the automatic right of the heir to full royal power once the incapacity of the king was recognized; when the king recovered he was therefore in a weaker position than ever. George III's detestation of his heir embraced his reckless political adherents as well. Fox's rhetoric in the Hastings trial (1788) did not mend his position since Pitt was studiously non-committal, and Hastings was ultimately acquitted.

Fox welcomed the French Revolution with ecstasy, both as a romantic and as a Whig. His mood was expressed in terms which are as endearing as they are absurd — but no more so than Burke's later effusions from the opposite side. The fall of the Bastille was the greatest and happiest event in the history of the world! With firm consistency he held to this view, despite the evolution of democratic licence into military dictatorship, and he continued to admire Bonaparte at a time when he was tyranny and Jacobinism personified to the average Englishman. On many occasions between 1793 and 1797 he defended the essential liberties of speech and thought against government restrictions: when the power of speaking is taken away, what is left but ...

implicit submission? He seemed to provide his own despairing answer when he led his friends in 1797 into voluntary retirement from the House. The 'secession' meant that for two years, political opposition ceased to matter.

The removal of Pitt in 1801 upon the issue of Catholic Emancipation brought no dividend to Fox. His personal following of about ninety remained loyal, but Fox could no more influence affairs than he could order his own debauched life. Ambitious and able men, like Canning, gravitated towards Pitt and power. Only such radicals as Romilly and Whitbread, to whom Fox's refusal to swim with the tide appealed, party faithfuls and friends, and the remoter aristocrats, like Grey, who was disinclined to office anyway, held to Fox. At last, however, upon the death of Pitt in January 1806, Fox returned to office, under the nominal leadership of Grenville, in the 'ministry of all the talents'. As Secretary of State, Fox negotiated to end the war, only to find that Napoleon was more interested in conquests. Perhaps now, in a new-found mood of seriousness, he might have become the tough war-minister that this coalition needed. In Scott's noble words he 'stood to his country, glory fast, And nailed her colours to the mast'.

Unfortunately he was physically spent. In July his health gave way, on 13 September he died. He was on the point of introducing the bill to abolish the slave trade which was subsequently passed.

Generous and altruistic, gloriously irrelevant to the critical problems of the war, that bill provides a fitting epitaph to the career of a statesman whose faults and virtues were open for the world to see, who was often unwise but seldom mean.

Loren Reid, *Charles James Fox*, 1969.
L. G. Mitchell, *Charles James Fox and the Disintegration of the Whig Party*, 1971.

**RICHARD BRINSLEY SHERIDAN** (1751-1816), dramatist and politician, was the grandson of an Irish clergyman, a Jacobite and a friend of Swift, who lost his living with a sermon, on the anniversary of George I's succession, on the text 'Sufficient unto the day is the evil thereof'. His father earned some fame as actor, dramatist and manager of plays, and as author of a pronouncing dictionary. His mother, Frances, was no mean actress. Sheridan inherited his parents' talents and interest in the world of theatre.

He went to Harrow School (1762-8). He subsequently lived on the hill in a house which is, today, one of the school's boarding houses. Meanwhile the family lived in Bath, where he met Elizabeth Linley. He eloped with her to France, fought two duels with the Welsh beau whom she had thus escaped, and came home, not to the intended career at the bar, but to marriage and the precarious life of writing for the theatre.

Beaux and Bath, courtships, elopements and duels — these were good ingredients for a comedy. Throw in a bumpkin or two, an irascible father, a disreputable Irishman, Sir Lucius O'Trigger, and a lot of the verbal rapier work of the sort that audiences delight in — and there is *The Rivals*. Produced at the beginning of 1775, it was not at first well received; revised and re-cast, it won acclaim. He had given familiar situations and characters new freshness. Its brittle elegance and exuberant spirits have won playgoers ever since. Mrs Malaprop's verbal misfortunes still amuse but his Faulkland, an introspective sentimentalist, is a subtler study.

Looking for someone to succeed him as manager and proprietor of Drury Lane Theatre, Garrick saw in the young Sheridan a man with a rare sense of theatre. He became a partner, with two wealthier backers. One of them, Thomas Linley, provided the music for *The Duenna* (1776), whose charming lyrics and intriguing plot earned great popularity. Its 75 performances exceeded the 62 credited to *The Beggar's Opera*, the previous record. *St. Patrick's Day* and *A Trip to Scarborough* are pleasant pieces, but better known today are *The School for Scandal* and *The Critic*. The former earned him the title of 'The modern Congreve'. Combining innocence and sophistication, Lady Teazle, country girl amazed and pleased by the sexual licence of high society, gives the actress glorious opportunities. Insincere specimen of 'the man of feeling', Joseph Surface stands out among other parts, each cleverly matched to the skills of his cast. With its lively ridicule of affectation and pretentiousness, it may be considered the greatest comedy of manners in the language. *The Critic*, first performed in 1779, again showed how Sheridan could improve on an earlier model: in this case Villiers' *The Rehearsal*. Puff is a type, Sir Fretful Plagiary has more individuality: unkindly modelled on the dramatist Richard Cumberledge he epitomises the vanity of authors.

Unfortunately for the theatre, Sheridan's career as playwright virtually ended when he entered politics in 1780. *Pizarro* (1799) would be found derivative and mediocre. He was already a luminary of society, upon Dr Johnson's instance a member of 'the Club'. Now as a Foxite Whig he displayed wonderful powers of oratory. In 1782 he became an Under-Secretary; then in the coalition of Fox and North Secretary to the Treasury. His unfailing good nature and ready wit made him many friends, notably the Prince of Wales, now aspiring to a political role; but this association did Sheridan little good. With Fox and the Prince he gambled and drank of nights, was encouraged to think of political questions in personal terms, and became implicated in the unfortunate Regency issue. In 1788 he championed the Prince's claim to be regent during the insanity of George III. It was Fox rather than Sheridan who put the Regent's claims in such an uncompromising way that they seemed to flout the constitutional right of Parliament, but Sheridan's prospects were blighted by the débâcle which ensued when George III recovered his wits. The impeachment of Warren Hastings in Westminster Hall did not improve the position of the Whigs, even though the subject of Sheridan's first speech, the Begums of Oudh, gave him the material for a masterpiece of rhetoric, for Pitt's neutrality deprived the trial of political significance. Before Sheridan had finished his peroration and collapsed melodramatically into the arms of Burke, experienced politicians were overcome by emotion and fashionable ladies fainted in the galleries. Sheridan soon tired of the trial, however, and began, with the other friends of Fox, to experience the frustration of opposition. He made his mark from time to time, in defence of the Revolution and in attacks on Pitt, notably upon his policy of coercion and the infamous Scottish trials.

Sheridan was ever a friend of liberty but he was also a patriot. As a good Irishman he strove to prevent the Act of Union but when invasion of England threatened he raised his own regiment of volunteers. Later he supported the Peninsular War. He had little talent for administration and it may be that his political achievement would have been superficial, even if he had been luckier, or less steadfast, in his political connexions. In his last years he drank heavily and became a figure of derision in the House of Commons which he had once adorned. Yet he could argue well on occasion. The speech he made when moving that there be an inquiry into Irish affairs, in August 1807, showed him at his best. To the end of his life he could rise above party considerations to humane and patriotic statesmanship. He held office once again, as Treasurer for the Navy, in the coalition of 1806, but soon thereafter resigned. After Fox's death he was treated coolly by the Whig leaders, as if he were a cast-off entertainer. He lost credit further during the complicated negotiations of May-June 1812 over the formation of an administration to follow Perceval's because he was thought to have deliberately withheld information that he had received from Lord Yarmouth, the Regent's friend, and so materially damaged Whig changes of office. He embarrassed the House by his faltering explanation of his conduct. At worst he was guilty of misjudgement. But clear thinking was now beyond him. He looked as debauched as he was. His once expressively handsome face was swollen, his nose scarlet; only the brilliant eyes recalled his youthful charm.

Recklessly generous when he had any money, Sheridan was unlucky in business ventures. In 1791 old Drury Lane was burned down and had to be re-built at great expense; it was burned down again in 1809. He died deeply in debt. We may regret that the man whose plays gave such delight, whose speeches had improved so many parliamentary hours, should have found so little fulfilment in his political career. When the Whigs had no man that was 'at all a match for little Perceval', the eclipse of Sheridan was sad. He does not seem, however, to have become bitter or depressed. Of all the great Whigs he is in some ways the most likeable personality.

W. S. Sichel, *Sheridan*, 2 vols., 1909.
J. H. W. Morwood, *Sheridan*, 1985.

**THOMAS ERSKINE, 1st BARON ERSKINE** (1750-1823) was a brilliant barrister and an ambitious politician He lived at a time when the established lawyer was held in great respect and he earned briefs in political trials especially suited to his style of advocacy. At a crucial time, he made a lasting contribution to the liberties of the subject.

The son of the tenth Earl of Buchan and of Agnes Stewart, Erskine was born at Edinburgh and educated at St. Andrews. At the age of fifteen he went to sea as a midshipman. Three years later he exchanged naval life for a commission in the 1st Royals. He spent two garrison years in intensive reading. He left the army, entered Lincoln's Inn in 1775, Trinity College, Cambridge in 1776. In 1778 he was called to the bar and enjoyed an immediate success in the case of *Rex v Baillie*. Baillie was a naval captain and governor of Greenwich Hospital: he was tried for libel after criticizing Lord Sandwich's administration and was acquitted after Erskine had gone over to the offensive and attacked the Admiralty more vigorously than had his client. In 1779 he defended Lord Keppel with equal success: the charge was declared 'malicious and ill-founded'. A more difficult client (1781) was Lord George Gordon, the notorious rabble-rouser, but he secured his acquittal from the charge of treason. In 1783 Erskine entered Parliament, but he made an unsuccessful start. His style was too extreme and dramatic for the Commons. He was not the most sensitive of men; maybe success came too early and easily and he was not prepared to modify or adjust. He became Attorney-General to the Prince of Wales (an office which he subsequently lost by appearing for Tom Paine!), spoke on behalf of Fox's India Bill and vehemently opposed Pitt's India Bill. Between 1786 and 1790 he was out of Parliament. He was busy at the bar, developing English commercial law.

He was employed as defence counsel in many of the political cases of the early war years. As a founder member of the Friends of the People he was a natural choice. His greatest effort was, perhaps, the defence of Hardy, Horne Tooke and Thelwall in 1794. He was helped by the government's insistence upon pressing charges of treason. English juries had also been strengthened by the timely passage (1792) of Fox's Libel Act. Erskine was himself an expert on the subject and contributed to Fox's success. Juries proved themselves to be bulwarks of free speech. When one compares the acquittal of Hardy and his fellow 'Jacobins' with the brutal sentences passed on Muir and Palmer in Scotland in 1793, the importance of the jury system is emphasized — and with it the achievement of the man who stood up to the government's law officers and relentlessly cross-examined their witnesses until their case was seen to be absurd. Is it fair to suggest that Erskine was inspired by other motives besides chivalry and love of battle? The defence of persecuted individuals against a background of popular sympathy undoubtedly appealed to his vanity.

When his friends came into power in 1806 he became Lord Chancellor and Baron Erskine of Restormel. His decisions earned the name 'The Apocrypha'. It was his misfortune to be compared with Eldon, a legal heavyweight indeed: Erskine had but a slight acquaintance with the principles of Equity; nor was he generally held to be a sound common lawyer. After his resignation in 1807 he had little political influence. To the end he adopted liberal causes. He opposed the Bill of Pains and Penalties against Queen Caroline in 1820 and the Six Acts; and he wrote a pamphlet on behalf of the Greek independence movement. In later life he became an advocate of negro emancipation, wrote *Armata*, a political romance, took up farming and married a second wife at Gretna Green.

Lovat Fraser, *Life of Lord Erskine*, 1932.

**SAMUEL WHITBREAD** (1758-1815) was a wealthy brewer, a liberal-minded Whig member of Parliament and a strong advocate of political and social reforms. His career is coloured by some of the virtues and values which we associate with the Victorians. But he is also a typical figure of the earnest, optimistic, industrious manufacturing class of the late eighteenth century. 'He felt himself an honest tradesman in an assembly of politicians' (Roberts). He was one of the early patrons of Watt, whose steam engine, which he installed in 1785 to drive the barley mills in place of twenty-four horses, was one of the sights of London. So was his curricle, built on the model of a modern bus: 'the body of it is near seven feet long; it will accommodate fourteen persons. It is in the form of a car, and made of wicker, painted yellow' (*Morning Chronicle*, August 1811). He was equally radical in his approach to politics.

He became member for Bedford in 1790. As the Eton friend and brother-in-law of Lord Grey he soon made his way into the charmed circle of Whig leadership. He was an effective orator in a somewhat bludgeoning manner and he showed a fine Foxite regard for principle. He moved the impeachment of Dundas in 1804. His speech upon the case of Mrs Clarke and the Duke of York filled eighty columns of *Hansard*. Ultimately, however, he failed to find fulfilment in politics. The limitations and prejudices of the Whig grandees, his own faults of personality, and political circumstances combined to thwart this man, whom Thomas Barnes, the radical editor of *The Times*, called 'England's greatest and most useful citizen'.

After the deaths of Fox and Pitt, on both sides of the house there ensued a chaos of personal groups. Grey and Grenville had sufficient experience in government of the ambition and duplicity of Napoleon to understand that England had to fight: their opposition was confined to methods of conducting the war. Whitbread and his friends of 'the Mountain' opposed the war from pacifist principles which appeared to their critics to be unpatriotic. He also went further than the official leadership in his support of reform. He wanted to draw the party into co-operation with the Burdett group and the extra-parliamentary movement. So the opposition became 'confoundedly embarrassed how to act with Whitbread and the *enragés*', as Lord Bulkeley observed. Whitbread's apparent irresponsibility was not due solely to his radical views. He was relentless in harrying ministers and uncovering scandals. He might justly claim to be more faithful to the tradition of Fox than Tierney, Petty or Ponsonby. Yet it was Ponsonby, a dull politician, who was chosen to lead the Whigs in the Commons. Whitbread was also passed over for ministerial office in the 'ministry of all talents'. From the fall of that administration until the assassination of Perceval (1807-12) he was the government's most persistent critic. When Castlereagh was the government's main representative in the Commons, the debate often resolved itself into a forensic duel between Whitbread and the foreign minister. And yet his liberalism and ambition made him as awkward to his own party as to the ministry. He was considered to be ill-mannered and he had a disconcerting temper. Whitbread lacked the tact and flexibility of the born politician. His dogmatic and outspoken manner was the opposite of Grey's reticence and patrician detachment. As the prospect of office receded, Whitbread's behaviour and pronouncements became more violent; the way in which he embraced the cause of the Princess of Wales disgusted many supporters. He could not recover the rôle which Brougham was later to assume — that of the educator of his party.

In 1806 Whitbread had brought forward, though without success, a bill for a rate-aided system of education. That the 'march of intellect' meant something more than a political slogan to him can be seen from the contents of his fine library, which contained a great range of pamphlets and books, the work of authors such as Bentham, Burke, Clarkson, Malthus, Paine, Priestley and Young, upon a variety of subjects, but especially the slave trade, Poor Law reform and the education of the working class. He put money and care into the management of the Drury Lane Theatre. He had his old house at Southill in Bedfordshire rebuilt by Henry Holland. Furniture and gardens were designed to fit the whole conception. The result was a complete and beautiful work of late Georgian art. But neither politics nor art brought serenity of mind to Whitbread. He suffered from periods of depression. In the end he cut his throat with a razor.

Roger Fulford, *Samuel Whitbread, 1764-1815*, 1967.

**SIR SAMUEL ROMILLY** (1757-1818), law reformer, was born in Frith Street, Soho, the son of Huguenot parents. His father, a jeweller, had emigrated from Montpellier; his mother brought some wealth into the family. With the help of his autobiography we can trace the melancholy of his later life to a lonely childhood. Left largely to a nurse who read to him from Fox's *Book of Martyrs* and the *Newgate Calendar*, taught the strictest tenets and traditions of Calvinism, Romilly might well, when he came to lose his faith, have lapsed into a nervous prostration. From this state and from the drab life of his father's shop he was saved by a legacy from a relative of his mother, which enabled him to read at the Bar. He made there a great reputation and an income, at his prime, of £15,000 a year. He also acquired an unequalled knowledge of the criminal law both of England and the Continent. He studied the work of Beccaria, the Italian jurist, and Bentham, another reformer who preached the principle of 'equal punishment for the same crime'. The importance of Romilly in the history of legal reform is that he was a passionate idealist, but a profound lawyer and a working politician as well. He became Solicitor-General in the 'ministry of all the talents' in 1806, though he was not then a member of Parliament. That year saw his Bankruptcy Law, a valuable civil law reform. He remained in the House of Commons after the fall of the Ministry in 1807 and began, in the following year, his campaign to bring some reason and humanity into the penal code.

To his work he brought a reputation for high-mindedness and a manner that was severe, but sincere enough to impress his most obdurate opponents. We may be shocked at the arguments of those who defended a situation in which children of twelve could be executed for stealing 25p. (like Lord Ellenborough who opposed an amendment to raise the amount to 50p.) but we should recall that they were prisoners themselves of conventional thinking, the love of liberty and the desire to protect property, at a time when there was no adequate police force, no proper prisons, no deterrent except the awesome ceremony of the Black Cap and the public horror of execution. That Romilly achieved anything at all at a time when all change was suspect as tending to Jacobinism and when he was known to have been an admirer of Napoleon, was because he was practical in his objectives, argued as a lawyer before lawyers, and never let himself be branded as a mere doctrinaire. At the height of the excitement of 1789 he, who had travelled in France and knew the country so well, had sent to Mirabeau an abstract of the Rules of Procedure of the British House of Commons for the use of the States-General! How unfortunate, we may think, that they were never adopted — but how typical of Romilly that he should have seen in the constitution of England the salvation of France. He was indeed no democrat. He sat for a succession of boroughs, but resolutely refused to commit himself to his electors upon anything 'calculated to court political favour'. He was appalled by the business of electioneering, even by celebrations of victory, and would have preferred, as he admitted, to have purchased a seat with cash. He may thus be seen as a Whig of the Whigs, an extreme case of the gulf between enlightened opinion in Parliament and people in the constituencies.

Successive bills presented by Romilly were rejected by the Commons or the Lords. The fourth time he moved his Bill to repeal the Shop-Lifting Act, in 1816, he was able to tell the House that, even as he spoke, a boy convicted of shop-stealing was awaiting execution in Newgate gaol. He managed to secure the abolition of the death penalty for the crime of stealing from bleaching grounds, in England and Ireland, on petition of the manufacturers themselves who said that the severity of the sentence made the Act ineffective, prosecutions being rare and convictions rarer still. He also secured the repeal of an old statute making it a capital offence for a soldier or sailor to beg without a pass. In 1818, however, the

Lords threw out yet again his Bill to repeal the Shop-Lifting Act; shortly afterwards his wife died, and Romilly killed himself in a sudden fit of despair. Lord Eldon came into court the next morning and saw the empty place in court where Romilly had been accustomed to sit. 'His eyes filled with tears: "I cannot stay here," he exclaimed; and rising in great agitation, he broke up his court'. Peers, bishops, judges might vote against him, his achievement might seem barren, but his career saw the tide turn. The month after Romilly's death, petitions began to flow in, demanding a revision of the Criminal Code. In 1819 a Committee of Enquiry was set up. Subsequently Peel, the practical, conservative statesman, put Romilly's hopes and ideas into effect and hacked through the jungle of penal laws.

Fastidious, fair-minded, humane, patient in the face of disappointment, Romilly was one of the men who kept alive the conscience of the nation at a time of peril. It is easy to forget that his decade as a reformer coincided with a crisis of the Napoleonic Wars and unnerving disorders at home. In these years he managed to persuade moderate politicians that his cause was right.

C. G. Oakes, *Sir Samuel Romilly*, 1935.

**GEORGE TIERNEY** (1761-1830) was leader of the Whigs in the House of Commons from 1818 until his retirement from politics in 1828. The leaders of the several Whig factions that made up an opposition to Lord Liverpool's government sat in the House of Lords. It is surprising nonetheless to learn that the spokesman of these aristocratic politicians in the Commons was the son of a Spanish merchant. His early success in politics testifies to the impact of his personality. He began as the people's idol, another Burdett. His later career was a long anticlimax. It was generally held in the time of his leadership that he was lazy. He seems however to have had a clearer idea of the rôle of the opposition than his chief, Lord Grey. For failures of opposition Grey must take equal blame. Until they were presented with the Reform movement in 1830 the opposition simply lacked a policy upon which they could unite.

Tierney was born in Gibraltar, but he had some Irish forbears and his firm dealt with English trade; he was educated at Eton and Peterhouse College, Cambridge. Although intended for the law, he enjoyed sufficient means after the deaths of his brothers to enter politics. In 1788 he boldly put himself forward as a candidate for Colchester, although that town was notorious for the length and expense of its elections: three recent candidates there had each become bankrupt. Tierney opposed the government candidate, George Jackson, but each candidate scored exactly the same number of votes and he was admitted to Parliament only after a committee had investigated the election. He was nevertheless unseated in the following year. Some gentlemen in Southwark offered to put him forward as a candidate and pay his expenses. His opponent was George Thellerson, a director of the East India Company, a body that had been the subject of much pamphlet-attacking by Tierney. Thellerson was victorious, but Tierney, acting as his own counsel, petitioned against him and accused him of breaking a law of William III's day which forbade 'treating' — or offering free entertainment and drink to voters. The election was repeated, so was the 'treating' and so was Tierney's petition. Thellerson was finally unseated and Tierney elected in his place. Southwark later rejected him when he accepted an office under Addington in 1803.

He was an active opponent of William Pitt and in 1798 the two quarrelled violently in the Commons: Pitt asserted that Tierney's opposition to a bill 'for suspending seamen's protections' proceeded from 'a desire to obstruct the defence of the country', and Tierney demanded an apology, which Pitt refused, or a duel. It was no light matter, at a dark moment in the continental war, for the Prime Minister to risk his life in a duel on Putney Heath. As Pitt was thin and Tierney exceptionally corpulent, wits declared that Pitt's silhouette should be traced out on Tierney as the proper target area. Both parties missed with their first shots and Pitt fired into the air with his second. Honour satisfied, the duel was called off.

As England faced the danger of invasion Tierney was one of many who joined the Volunteer Movement. He was Lieutenant-Colonel Commandant of the Somerset House volunteers, composed of clerks and government servants. He was Treasurer of the Navy, 1803-4, and President of the Board of Control for India for a few months in 1806. At the end of his career he was made Master of the Mint, 1827-8, by Canning, as part of the alliance between the new Prime Minister and the Whigs. Between these two short episodes in office he was a prominent Parliamentary opponent of the government and was considered leader of the opposition from 1818, after the death of Ponsonby. By then he was ineffective, though the repressive policy of the government gave opposition plenty to work on. During this period the Whigs, about 150, were a reasonably solid phalanx. But ministers like Peel and Huskisson took social and economic initiatives which disheartened Tierney and he did not live to see electoral reform become the issue which returned the Whigs to power. When Lord Goderich's Ministry came to an end, in 1828, he retired from politics. He remained a cheerful man until the day of his death, despite the frustration of his dreams of office and asthmatic and dropsical complaints.

At his best Tierney had been a dreaded speaker in the House, noted for his sarcasm; Castlereagh suffered especially from his barbed wit. He was known to some of the younger members of the party as *Mother Cole*, after his habit of referring to himself as a plain, honest man, like the lady in Foote's farce who ran a brothel in Covent Garden, but protested stoutly that she was an honest woman.

H. K. Olphin, *G. Tierney*, 1934.
Austin Mitchell, *The Whigs in Opposition*, 1967.

**GRANVILLE SHARP** (1735-1813), philanthropist, was a leading personality in the anti-slavery movement. He was a scholar who acquired most of his extensive knowledge in his scanty spare time, a man of strong principles who fought for what he believed right with extraordinary tenacity. His enthusiasms sometimes led him into eccentric paths. He was unwise to try to persuade Charles Fox that Napoleon was the 'Little Horn' of Daniel's prophecy or to suggest at a public meeting that soldiers of the Peninsula should be provided with bales of wool to make a rampart against enemy attack. He had done so many good and generous things that he might be forgiven for tilting at a few unlikely windmills in his old age. In the words of James Stephen, 'As long as Granville Sharp survived it was too soon to proclaim that the age of chivalry was gone.'

He was born at Durham, the ninth son of Thomas Sharp, prebendary of Durham and a theological writer of some note, and the grandson of John Sharp, Archbishop of York. His father's family being larger than his means, Granville was sent to London at the age of fifteen to be apprenticed to a linen draper. Since successive masters were Quaker, Presbyterian, Irish Roman Catholic, and atheist, it is not surprising that he followed his father's inclination to theology and taught himself Greek and Hebrew. In 1758 he obtained a post in the Ordnance Department. He wrote two Old Testament studies and *A Short Treatise on the English Tongue* (1767). He never became a Quaker, though his work brought him into contact with them. He was never ordained — but showed where his sympathies lay when, after the American war, he started a successful movement for the consecration of bishops in New York and Pennsylvania.

In 1765 Sharp befriended a negro, Jonathan Strong, whom he found wandering destitute, having been deserted by his master, James Lisle. Later Lisle had Strong imprisoned as a runaway slave, but Sharp secured his release and prosecuted Lisle for assault. A counter-action was brought against Sharp for detaining another man's property. Sharp found that he had no legal case: masters had property in their slaves even when in England. He wrote about and researched into the law of personal liberty and interested himself in similar cases. Eventually, in the case of James Sommersett (1772), the judges laid down the great principle that 'as soon as a slave sets foot upon English territory he becomes free'. A first step had been taken towards the suppression of the trade and it was the work of Sharp who, 'though poor and dependent and immersed in the duties of a toilsome calling, supplied the money, the leisure, the perseverance and the learning required for this great controversy'.

Beyond doubt Sharp enjoyed litigation. He defended, with success, the claim of the Duke of Portland to the forest of Inglewood and the castle of Carlisle (against the rival claim of the Lowthers). He agitated on behalf of the Caribees, the original West Indians, when it was reported that the government planned to eliminate them. He supported the American colonists and resigned his ordnance post when war began (1776). He joined Oglethorpe in his crusade against the press-gang. But slavery remained his main interest. Tracts flowed from his pen, five in 1776 alone. In 1787 he was appointed chairman of the largely Quaker committee set up to gather 'such information as may tend to the abolition of the

Slave Trade'. One difficulty was the number of liberated slaves in England. From 1783 he was planning for the settlement of a colony at Sierra Leone. The first ship-load sailed in 1787; the freed slaves were accompanied by a number of 'whites, chiefly women of the lowest sort'. Four years later the Sierra Leone Company was set up to run the enterprise. There were immense problems; eventually the crown took over the colony (1808). The affair provides a good example of the way in which the state was saddled with territorial concerns after private enterprises, commercial and philanthropic, had failed to solve problems of their own making.

Sharp had the happiness of seeing the slave trade abolished (1807). His approach to this evil was always that of an evangelical Christian. In 1804 he was chosen first chairman of the British and Foreign Bible Society, which he had helped to found. He helped to start the African Institution in 1807 and the Society for the Conversion of the Jews in 1808. There was a narrow, prejudiced side to his zeal. In 1813 he was first chairman of the Protestant Union, founded to fight against Catholic Emancipation. Perhaps the greatest work of his later years was the enunciation of 'Granville Sharp's canon' — a vital linguistic contribution to the orthodox trinitarian case against the Unitarians. Sharp never married and lived usually in rooms in the Temple. His good and useful life is well summarized by James Stephen: he had 'the most inflexible of human wills united to the gentlest of human hearts'.

Roger Ansley, *The Atlantic Slave Trade and British Abolition, 1760-1810*, 1975.

**THOMAS CLARKSON** (1760-1846), anti-slavery agitator, was the son of the Rev. John Clarkson, headmaster of the grammar school at Wisbech. He went to St. Paul's, and St. John's, Cambridge, as a sizar. At Cambridge he won university prizes for Latin essays two years running: the subject of the second (1785) was the moral question '*Anne liceat invitos in servitutem dare*'. Study for the essay absorbed him. He read it in the Senate House and was acclaimed. His material disturbed him deeply. Could slavery be justified? He secured publication of his essay in translation by the good offices of a Quaker friend, Joseph Hancock. His acquaintance with the publisher, James Phillips, led to introductions to

other men already committed anti-slavers. In May 1787 a committee including Granville Sharp and Samuel Hoare was formed
for the suppression of the slave trade: apart from Clarkson, Sharp
and Philip Sansom, all were Quakers.

Clarkson had been ordained a deacon but made no attempt to
pursue a religious calling. He was single-minded about slavery to
the point of obsession. With his fellow-workers, he collected
information at first hand, organized meetings and distributed
tracts. In February 1788 a committee of the privy council was
instructed to inquire into 'the present state of the African trade'.
In May Pitt, deputizing for Wilberforce who was ill, opened a
debate about the trade. Sir William Dolben moved a bill, which
was only passed after fierce opposition, limiting the number of
slaves that could be carried in one ship: mortality on the voyage
across the Atlantic was frequently over fifty per cent. In April
1791 the government's committee completed its work of hearing
evidence. Clarkson, meanwhile, had been travelling and working
indefatigably to further the cause. In August 1789 he went to
France and stayed for six months, trying to persuade the French,
who were changing so much, to abolish the slave trade. To
Mirabeau he wrote a long letter every other day for months.
To track down a key witness Clarkson boarded naval ships in five
dockyards — and found him on the fifty-seventh vessel he had
tried! His intense labours ruined his health and finances. He was
sustained in the early years more by hope than by success. Wilberforce's motion for stopping the African traffic was defeated,
despite the firm lead of Pitt, Fox and Burke, by seventy-five votes.
In 1794 Clarkson's health gave way. A subscription among his
friends provided for his modest needs. After nine years he
returned to work on the committee. A national tour, in the later
part of 1805, was a great success. In March 1807 Lord Grenville's
bill for the abolition of the trade received the royal assent.

In 1818 Clarkson had an interview with the Emperor of
Russia at Aix-la-Chapelle to secure his influence with the other
sovereigns at the forthcoming congress in favour of abolition
throughout their territories. In August 1833 the final emancipation Bill was passed and 800,000 slaves became free men. Clarkson was then almost blind with cataract, but in 1836 a successful
operation restored his sight. In June 1840 he made his last public
appearance and spoke at the Anti-Slavery Convention. Haydon's

picture of the scene can be seen at the National Portrait Gallery. 'He had a head like a patriarch' wrote the painter. Frail as he was, Clarkson lived to a great age, latterly at Playford Hall, near Ipswich. More than any man he had been responsible for the success of the movement's propaganda. Men who had accepted slavery as a natural feature of the economy now condemned it as a monstrosity. In the words of Wordsworth's sonnet of 1807 in honour of Clarkson, it had indeed been 'an obstinate hill to climb'.

R. Coupland, *The British Anti-Slavery Movement*, 1933.

**WILLIAM WILBERFORCE** (1759-1833), evangelical Christian, politician and social reformer, is best known for his part in the abolition of the slave trade, an act of unselfish policy which is among the best things done by an English Parliament. His work and influence extended also to many causes less famous. No Englishman of his time did more for his fellow-men.

His father, a wealthy Hull merchant, died when he was nine. From St. John's College, Cambridge, he went into Parliament; his first election at Hull in 1780 cost him £8,000. After 1784 he was one of the county members for Yorkshire. He had a good voice and was a fluent speaker, 'the nightingale of the House'. Pitt was devoted to him, but his friendships included also Fox and Sheridan. A delightfully open and humorous character made him popular in the House, but his unique position of moral authority came from his personal commitment to good causes. He was fearlessly independent: inclining always to pacifism he risked Pitt's anger in 1795 by speaking in favour of peace. Later he hurt Pitt deeply (and swayed the issue) by voting for the impeachment of Dundas. He seemed to be interested in political life only in so far as it gave him the opportunity to promote reform. In 1787 he wrote in his journal: 'God Almighty has placed before me two great objects, the suppression of the slave trade and the reformation of manners.'

Under the influence of Milner, fellow and later President of Queen's College, Cambridge, and Newton, London vicar and former slaver, Wilberforce experienced 'a conversion' to evangelical Christianity. His conviction was fortified by the friendship of his aunt, Mrs Wilberforce of Wimbledon, her brother, John Thornton of Clapham, and his son Henry Thornton. With the latter he

*William Wilberforce*
(Artist: George Richmond)

lived for two years; at about the same time John Venn became vicar of Clapham. With Lord Teignmouth, Zachary Macaulay and James Stephen these men formed a circle of devout, practical

Christians who, because of their tendency to think and act together upon social and political questions, came to be called 'the Clapham Sect' or 'the Saints'. Single-minded, experts on their own chosen subjects and untied to any party or programme, they had an authority in Parliament far larger than their voting strength might suggest. Wilberforce, regular in committee work and in attendance in the House, a competent and sometimes moving speaker, was their acknowledged leader. His life was grounded upon prayer and Bible-reading, and he conducted a steady offensive for the reform of the Church of England in the interests of 'vital religion'. But he was able to work with radicals, utilitarian or agnostic in their views, such as Bentham, Brougham, Romilly and Mackintosh. 'If to be an anti-slavist is to be a Saint' wrote Bentham, 'Saintship for me'. A few, notably Cobbett and Hazlitt, thought his religion pious cant because of his political conservatism. They marked his loyalty to traditional notions of class, his friendship with astute bankers. He was indeed orthodox in his view of society, but sensitive also to the conditions of the English poor.

He was one of the three founders of 'The Society for Bettering the Conditions and Increasing the Comforts of the Poor' which cared for the casualties of a raw industrial society. He supported Peel's Factory Bill of 1802 and asked that its benefits be extended to other industries. In 1812 he moved the promotion of 'An Association for the relief of the Manufacturing and Labouring Poor'. As member for Yorkshire he worked for the interests of the small farmer and manufacturer; in 1826 he directed a movement of private charity to relieve the suffering of the people. Two of the pioneers in the Factory Reform projects, Oastler and Wood, had been agents in the anti-slavery movement; a third, Sadleir, was Wilberforce's political agent in Yorkshire and a close friend. As Halévy wrote: 'The historian of the movement which produced the Factory Acts must not forget the many tributaries that swelled the main stream. But the source of the river was the piety and Christian sentiment of the Evangelicals'.

In an age when the State played a negative rôle, their initiatives were crucial. Wilberforce supported legislation to abolish the lottery, and duelling in the services. In tract and speech he attacked bull and bear baiting. He lent his weight to the campaign of Romilly for reform of 'our murderous laws'. He visited Newgate with Elizabeth Fry and he secured the passage of a bill (rejected by the Lords) to end the practice of employing 'climbing boys' as chimney sweeps. A strong believer in elementary education for all, he became a vice-president of the British and Foreign School Society. He encouraged Hannah More in her work for Sunday Schools and wrote a book whose heavy title, *A practical view of the Prevailing Religious System of Professed Christians in the Higher and Middle Classes in this Country contrasted with Real Christianity*, did not prevent its running into five editions in six months. Its message is essentially that Christianity was the only remedy for the selfishness engendered by wealth, and the moral decline of England's expanding population in a time of revolution. Wilberforce contributed much to the growth of the spirit of moral earnestness which characterized the Victorians.

The committee for the abolition of the Slave Trade was formed in 1787. Its leaders wanted a spokesman in Parliament. Neither Fox nor Pitt would take an initiative which might fatally divide their followings; Pitt did support Wilberforce and when, in 1788, the latter fell seriously ill, took charge of the first motion for an investigation, but the Revolution and ensuing war damaged the cause of Abolition. Pitt concentrated upon the war; public opinion was alarmed by the rebellion of black slaves in St. Domingo; reform receded before the spectre of Jacobinism. Yet the movement grew, with Clarkson organizing corresponding committees, agents, public meetings, pamphlets, all rousing people to awareness. The methods adopted were important. According to G. M. Trevelyan, 'Public discussion and public agitation of every kind of question became the habit of the English people, very largely in imitation of Wilberforce's successful campaign'. The going was hard, and in 1800 he even dropped his annual motion for comprehensive abolition. In May 1804, however, his bill passed the Commons for the first time. After Pitt's death, Grenville, Grey and Fox put the weight of government behind the Bill. In February 1807 both Houses passed it, and Wilberforce received a memorable ovation.

He laboured on, for the enforcement of the Act and towards its logical successor. At the end of the war Castlereagh insisted upon an anti-slave trade clause in the Treaty of Vienna: 'The nation is bent on this object. I believe there is hardly a village that has not met and petitioned upon it. Ministers must make it the basis of their policy.' Now the campaign for the abolition of slavery in the colonies passed to younger men. Wilberforce resigned from Parliament in 1824 and died a few months before the Act was passed in 1833.

Coupland summarizes his achievement, after pointing out that the abolition came just in time, before the development of Africa could turn the Continent into a vast slave plantation: 'More than any other man he had founded in the conscience of the British people a tradition of humanity and responsibility toward backward black people whose fate is in their hands.' Mackintosh 'never saw any one who touched life at so many points ... When he was in the House of Commons he seemed to have the freshest mind of any man there'. Wilberforce had his critics; he had no enemies.

John Pollock, *Wilberforce*, 1977.

SIR THOMAS FOWELL BUXTON, Baronet (1786-1845) was born at Earl's Colne in Essex. The influence of his mother, an earnest and intelligent Quaker, was most important in his early life. He later entered the close Quaker circle of Earlham when he married Hannah Gurney, daughter of John Gurney, the Norwich banker, and sister of Elizabeth Fry. He seems to have been ill-treated at school at Kingston and he was placed for a time under a tutor, Dr. Burney of Greenwich, brother of the diarist Fanny Burney. He went to Trinity College, Dublin, and there won the university's gold medal. Indeed, his academic successes were so great that he was pressed to stand for parliament as member for Trinity College. Instead he began a business career with Truman, Hanbury and Buxton, the brewers. His practical approach to social reforms was to owe much to this experience, as well as to the first-hand knowledge he gained of the conditions of the urban poor in Spitalfields and neighbouring parts of expanding London. In 1816 his impassioned speech at a Mansion House meeting helped to raise more than £40,000, with which he embarked upon systematic relief work.

Together with Mrs Fry he began to look into prison conditions and published his critical findings in a forceful pamphlet. In the same year he entered parliament for Weymouth. He was a natural ally of Sir James Mackintosh, the leading parliamentary advocate of penal reform. 223 offences were punishable by death when Peel became Home Secretary. Peel's critics said that he listened too much to judges. But he listened attentively too to the reformers' arguments and acted upon some of them, while at the same time taking measures to make police more effective. Buxton's interest in this and other humanitarian causes, such as the abolition of *suttee* in India, attracted the notice of Wilberforce, who handed over to him the leadership of the anti-slavery movement.

In 1823 the Commons passed Buxton's resolution that slavery, 'being repugnant to the Christian religion and the British Constitution, ought to be abolished at the earliest period compatible with the safety of all concerned'. For the next eight years he and his helpers mobilized public opinion against slavery. In the autumn of 1830 there were 2,600 petitions. They gradually wore down the resistance of planters, colonial assemblies and those politicians who saw the plantations as an outpost of the citadel of property. After 1832 the abolition of slavery became official government policy; in the autumn Lord Howick, Under-Secretary for the Colonies, proposed immediate emancipation. The plantation interests were obstructive. The next year Buxton raised the matter in parliament and Stanley, the Colonial Secretary, carried through a revised scheme. All slaves were to receive their freedom within twelve months; slaves engaged in agricultural work would be apprenticed to their former masters until 1840, domestic slaves until 1838. Compensation of £20,000,000 was allowed to the slave owners, equivalent to £37.10s. a slave, roughly the market price. 700,000 slaves were freed as a result.

Buxton turned his attention to the slave trade abroad and exposed the dreadful conditions in which Africans were being stolen, shipped and sold. In *The Slave Trade and its Remedy* (1839) he proposed the deliberate civilization of Africa by a joint missionary, political and economic team. It was the dream of 'the Saints' in new form: practical rescue work in the spirit of the gospel, personal conversion and the transformation of a culture. His own attempt to show how this could be done, in the form of a huge expedition up the Niger in 1841, was a failure. Buxton was practical and effective as an organizer and a lobbyist, but he was wholly unrealistic in his African schemes. There was no shortage of Mrs Jellybys to support his 'Borrioboola-Gha' nor, wrote Miss Martineau, 'of public meetings, with Prince Albert in the chair, so crowded that persons were carried out fainting ... of grand subscriptions and yet grander hopes'. An expedition of three iron steamers, two of which were called, appropriately, the *Albert* and the *Wilberforce*, sailed for the Niger, to open up trade and to establish a model farm. Numbers died of fever and the attempt was given up. 'The King of Borrioboola-Gha' wrote Dickens in *Bleak House*, ten years later, 'wanted to sell everybody — who survived the climate — for rum.'

It is easy to criticize Buxton and his fellow evangelicals. They paraded their principles with more confidence than discretion. 'Cant', said Cobbett, who could not forgive the anti-slavery lobby for being, seemingly, more interested in negroes than in hungry English labourers. But Buxton was a good man, of wide interests. He maintained his interest in prisoners to the end. In 1839 he toured Italy, investigating the crimes of bandits and the condition of Roman gaols. He was generous as well as devout in support of Bible and missionary societies. His honesty was unassailable. He lost his seat at Weymouth in 1837 because he would not give 'loans'. He was a great lover of children and animals. Domestic tragedy did not sour him, though it may have contributed to the compulsions of his public life. In 1820 his eldest son and three other children died. He lived latterly at Cromer Hall. Around about were his model farms and plantations at Runton and Trimingham. For an essay on the management of estates he won the Royal Agricultural Society gold medal in 1845. He was buried in the ruined chancel of Overstrand church, a peaceful spot above the encroaching North Sea.

Ed. Charles Buxton, *Memorials of Sir T. F. Buxton, Bart.*, 1872.

**JEREMY BENTHAM** (1748-1832), philosopher and jurist, was an original critic of institutions and a constructive advocate of radical reforms. His father was a well-to-do London attorney, who took, perhaps, excessive pains over the details of his schooling and upbringing, and nourished dreams that the precocious boy would become Lord Chancellor. His intensive education left little time for the usual concerns of boyhood. Westminster received him at seven; Queen's College, Oxford, at twelve, and already a ripe classical scholar. Predictably he was a somewhat lonely undergraduate, shy, sober and deferential in manner. He showed, however, that he had a mind of his own. It was with

*Jeremy Bentham*
(Artist: Henry William Pickersgill)

reluctance that he subscribed to the statutory Thirty-Nine Articles, since he found them both unscriptural and unreasonable. When he began to practise law he was repelled by the self-satisfaction, ethos and rules of the Bar, the needless complexity of laws and the chicanery of legal practice. He was unimpressed by the *mystique*: of what use were such phrases as 'the rule of law' or 'the balance of the constitution' if the courts were inefficient, justice partial, and the constitution nothing but a conspiracy of vested interests? He could not accept the view popularized by Blackstone that the Common Law, built upon precedents and tested by time, had the validity of revealed truth. Bentham saw, rather, some sound laws and some bad ones, wrapped in a tissue of absurdities. In the *Fragment on Government* (1776) he accepted that law was the tie which bound society together, but he insisted, too, that it was only a set of rules to achieve certain ends; when it became, with changing circumstances, inefficient, it should be altered.

Since this had never been done, he proposed an entirely new code which should be scientific, objective and humane: its criterion should be the good of people as they are — not the abstract creations of the philosophers. The publication dates of Bentham's works are not those of their composition: his *Introduction to the Principles of Morals and Legislation* was privately printed in 1780 and not published until 1789. It is therefore hard to chart the progress of his thought, but it matters little: it was based on certain fixed principles and evolved by logical methods which took little account of local conditions and institutions. In a time of turbulence he preferred to trust to time and the essential soundness of his ideas. He eschewed the London Corresponding Society and even those Whigs who still called for reform. His ideas were formulated in lonely meditation. In his capacity for generalization, in his persistent appeal to reason, in detachment and scientific bent, he stands apart from other English philosophers and reformers.

Bentham was not gifted with a strong sense of humour, but he was not unsociable. He never lacked friends, even if, like Lord Shelburne, they were valued most when they appreciated his ideas. There is a quality of eagerness in Bentham, something between naïvety and assurance, that lends itself to satire. He was prepared to make a new constitution to order, to draw up plans of reform in any subject that attracted him and to go into minute detail. He would have made an admirable minister in an enlightened despotism. He never went into Parliament, though he would undoubtedly have appreciated a pocket borough; instead he tackled legal and social questions in a stream of pamphlets.

Bentham even planned a new sort of prison. His *Pantopticon or Prison Discipline* was a proposal for a circular prison building, 'a glass lantern about the size of Ranelagh, the prisoners in the cells occupying the circumference; the officers in the centre'. In this prison, where the inmates were to be taught 'to love labour' by being made to do useful work and to share in their produce, they could also be kept under constant surveillance by officials 'concealed by blinds and other contrivances'. Bentham sank much of his own money in his project, which met with little response from ministers preoccupied with the French war. Nor did the penitentiary at Millbank (constructed at a cost of half a million pounds) do as much by itself to relieve the squalor and cruelty of prisons as the steady pressure of Elizabeth Fry, Hoare and Buxton of the Society for the Reformation of Prison Discipline. Bentham did, however, influence his generation by his *Principles of Penal Law*. In no country were so many offences punishable by death and the number grew continually: 160 in 1760, a further sixty-three were added in the next sixty years. Many sentences were remitted, but in London and Middlesex alone there had been ninety-seven executions in 1785, including but one murderer. That a start to reform was made in Bentham's lifetime must be ascribed primarily to Romilly and Mackintosh, but Bentham himself played a great part. Becoming more extreme with age, he denounced as 'weak and feeble' the work of Peel who, in the 1820s, reduced over three hundred statutes into four intelligible acts and made it possible for courts to withhold the death sentence for all but murders. He had by then come to demand the abolition of the death sentence, even for murder. More important than specific proposals, he had 'found the philosophy of law a chaos, and left it a science' (J. S. Mill).

'The age we live in is a busy age; in which knowledge is rapidly advancing towards perfection. In the natural world, in particular, everything teems with discovery and improvement.' This trend must, in Bentham's view, lead to the examination of institutions, so that the greatest happiness of the greatest number — 'the measure of right and wrong' — could be realized in society. From his critical analysis of law it was but a short step to the British constitution. When Bentham came to study the electoral structure he found many obstacles to the free operation of his utilitarian principle. He tended towards democracy because he held that governments normally created — or allowed to grow — systems of law and administrations which defied the laws of human behaviour. Because conflict was inherent in human society, the only way of reconciling people to the decisions of government was to make the government depend upon the will of the majority. How was this to be ascertained? Not by a franchise in which constituencies were unequal and in which excessive influence attached to landed property. In the old electoral system, where others saw picturesque differences, liberties, checks and balances — even the fostering of responsibility in the wealthy classes — Bentham saw corruption, hypocrisy and inefficiency. His reiterated questions — 'What is its use? How does it work?' — exposed more effectively than any demand for rights the arguments that rested upon tradition.

Bentham was not surprised that the French Revolution gave rise to the despotisms of Robespierre and Napoleon. In Britain too he saw new fictions foisted upon a public whose eyes were so riveted upon the excesses of Jacobin France that they could not see what was wrong at home. In 1809 he wrote his *Plan for Parliamentary Reform in the Form of a Catechism*: it was not published until 1817. Then, with the confidence of middle age and his widening acquaintance with such reformers as Burdett, Place and Cochrane, he threw off caution and clarified his position. He played a significant part in the reform movement of the post-war years, providing it with a statement of radical principle that was neither irrelevantly antiquarian nor tainted by Jacobinism. Indeed, it was an important part of his argument that the greatest danger to institutions came from the unreasoning defence of anomalies and relics of the past; from taking honest criticism for treason. In *Radicalism Not Dangerous*, written in 1819-20, Bentham advocated secret ballot, virtually universal suffrage, and annual Parliaments.

Bentham played an active part in the establishment of University College, in 1827 where there were to be no credal tests and the emphasis in teaching was to be on modern subjects. Ignorance must be combated in every way. When he died, he bequeathed his body for anatomical dissection; when the doctors had finished with it, the mummified body was to rest in the college he had helped to found. There it can be seen.

His followers tended to interpret his belief in individuals and distrust of the state as meaning that there must be, for example, no factory legislation; they elevated efficiency above humanity. But Bentham had meant by enlightenment something different. Where there was exploitation by privileged classes or individuals, he believed that the legislator should intervene: utility could justify state action as well as state inaction. In Bentham's writing, utility was the servant of humanitarianism. But in the hands of the Mills, or Edwin Chadwick, the principle underwrote a new authoritarianism. 'The letter of Benthamism prevailed; the spirit of Benthamism died' (Derry).

In assessing the significance of Bentham we must distinguish the original from the imitators. We must also beware of the tendency to label all reforming legislation as being Benthamite. A more practical approach to legislation, interest in poor law and sanitary reforms, a root and branch attack upon abuses in politics and society, were not the monopoly of Bentham and his followers. Yet his was indeed, as John Stuart Mill wrote, one of the great 'seminal minds' of the nineteenth century. Without Benthamism, Victorian radicalism would have been quite different. He helped to make the idea of reform respectable by persuading men to accept utility as a valid test. He died on the evening before the Reform Bill received royal assent. The bill was 'the greatest of the silent revolutions', a landmark in the age of improvement, a tribute to 'the great questioner of things established'.

Jeremy Bentham's determination to expose fictions led him to take an advanced view of sexual relations. The most powerful of human drives should be accepted for what it is: pleasurable, natural, useful, legitimate in all forms except where public decency was offended. Surely, Bentham was a townsman to the marrow, yet he bought himself an old, romantic house, Ford Abbey in Dorset. He had always combined frugality with a certain elegance. He was temperate and complacently self-sufficient, but his greatest admirers became also his trusted friends. Few important thinkers have been so unassuming in their ways. He did not play the prophet or indulge in controversy for its own sake. Mild and magnanimous, he was a good advertisement for his principles.

Mary P. Mack, *Jeremy Bentham: An Odyssey of Ideas*, 1962.
J. W. Derry, *The Radical Tradition*, 1967.

**JOHN HORNE TOOKE** (1736-1812) was a radical clergyman with scholarly interests and a flair for publicity, who first made his name during the Wilkes affair and was still politically active in a somewhat anachronistic way at the turn of the century. He was the son of a well-to-do poulterer called Horne. (He later adopted the name of a friend, Tooke.) He seems to have been a clever, rather opinionated and argumentative boy. On one occasion he ran away from his tutor on the ground that the tutor was 'bad at grammar'. He lost the sight of an eye in a fight with a schoolfellow. He distinguished himself at St. John's College, Cambridge, and took orders, but without enthusiasm.

In 1760 he became the incumbent of a chapel of ease at Brentford. He preached good, practical sermons and studied medicine in order to set up a dispensary for parishioners. He grew increasingly casual, however, about their spiritual needs. In dress and conduct he was decidedly unclerical. He spent some time travelling abroad and fathered at least two illegitimate children. In 1766 he wrote a notorious letter in which he apologized for 'having the infectious hand of a bishop waved over me'. He made the acquaintance among others of Voltaire and Sterne and his ideas and style during this period show their influence. Rationalist and individualist, he was also a man who liked to make startling statements. 'I will have my black coat dyed red', he announced to the startled freemen of Middlesex. He seemed to enjoy a contest. He accused George Onslow of selling an office and was fined £400 after a celebrated libel case. He had the last word, however, since he appealed and secured a verdict against the great Mansfield in the Court of Common Pleas.

Along with some prominent and wealthy men Tooke founded the Society of the Supporters of the Bill of Rights, in February 1769, to support 'Mr Wilkes and his cause'. He soon fell out with the people's champion, whom he suspected of marshalling support largely for his own benefit. In 1771 he formed the

Constitutional Society. He was naturally regarded as a renegade by Wilkesites and he was burned in effigy by the mob during the election of sheriffs for the city in that year. He was indeed better suited to guerilla operations than to the more organized forms of political warfare. In 1774 he was summoned before the House of Commons to account for a violent attack on the Speaker, Norton. He escaped punishment on that occasion, but he was fined and imprisoned for a few months in 1778 for publishing a resolution to raise a subscription for the American colonists.

He was refused admission to the Bar by the Benchers of the Inner Temple. It was a cruel blow, as he had proven legal abilities and had already been offered some briefs. For a short time he set up as an agriculturalist with a farm at Witton in Huntingdonshire. It was hardly his *métier* and he soon gave up with an ague. Fortunately he inherited some money from his father and was enabled to live comfortably in Dean Street with his two daughters. He subsequently went to live at Purley. It was there that he wrote Ερεα πτερόεντα or *Diversions of Purley* (two volumes, 1786 and 1798) which established his reputation as a philologist. Philology, in his view, subserves philosophy: every word means a thing and reasoning is the art of putting words together. In his philosophical approach he influenced James Mill, amongst others, while in his emphasis upon the importance of studying Anglo-Saxon he has a significant place among early grammarians.

Dislike of Fox led him to contest Westminster against Fox in the election of 1790; he came bottom of the poll. Pitt allowed him to be tried for high treason in 1794, after a sham confession to being a spy. It may have been a foolish joke; it can hardly have deceived the ministers. He had Erskine to defend him; he enjoyed himself, mocking at the Attorney-General and clowning in the dock. He was very properly acquitted. He was no Jacobin and, if he occupied a position to the left of the parliamentary Whigs, it was only the position of an old-fashioned city tribune, who resented aristocratic privilege. His appearance suited the part. He was sturdy, keen-eyed and dressed like a prosperous tradesman. In 1796 he was again unsuccessful in a Westminster election, but in 1801 Lord Camelford brought the persistent old man in for Old Sarum. An act was subsequently passed declaring clergymen ineligible for parliament.

After 1792 he lived in a house on Wimbledon Common where he gardened and kept cows. He was greatly attached to his tomcat. He was also celebrated for his Sunday dinners. He was formerly a great drinker of wine and is said to have left Porson and Boswell, two noted topers, under the table. In later life, however, he was abstemious. He claimed to have acquired his painful gout from drinking bad claret in prison. His friendships did not rely solely on his generous table. Men like Bentham, Paine, Thurlow and Erskine appreciated his mind and conversation. 'Your political principles', Burdett once remarked, 'are as much out of fashion as your clothes!' 'I know it', said Tooke, 'but the fashion must one day return or the nation be undone.'

A. Stephens, *Memoirs of John Horne Tooke*, 2 vols., 1813.

**JOHN CARTWRIGHT** (1740-1824), 'the Father of Reform', was the third son of William Cartwright of Marnham and Anne Cartwright of Ossington: he was descended on both sides from the old Northamptonshire family of that name. An early memory was of an uncle, Viscount Tyrconnel. stirring the fire violently during family prayers when the prayer for Parliament was being read, and muttering to himself 'Nothing but a miracle can mend them.' He went to the grammar school at Newark and entered the navy. A zealous officer, he devised improvements in gunnery and bombarded the government with plans for perpetual timber supplies for the navy. He believed so strongly in the cause of American independence that he refused to join Lord Howe when he was ordered to America. He settled instead to farming and the cause of parliamentary reform. His first reform pamphlet, *Take Your Choice*, appeared in 1776. For the rest of his life, in innumerable letters, pamphlets, through clubs and journals, he worked to spread the gospel.

From the start he called for annual parliaments, universal suffrage and the ballot: if this programme was unrealistic in the Chartist 1840s it can be imagined how bold it sounded in the age of Rockingham, Burke and 'economical' reform. He was too extreme for the Whigs, though they respected him as a gentleman and patronized him as a man of principle. After a county meeting at Nottingham in 1780 the Whig leaders met Cartwright and passed resolutions upon the inadequate representation of the people. In that year Cartwright promoted the Society for Constitutional Information. At its dinner in 1782 toasts were drunk to Magna Carta, 'the Majesty of the People' and 'America in arms, despotism at our feet'. The French Revolution brought new stimulus. Cartwright attended a public meeting to celebrate the taking of the Bastille and forfeited his commission in the Nottinghamshire militia.

Cartwright's design for a temple of naval celebration, the 'Hieronauticon', was the most ambitious to be submitted for that romantic project. *England's Aegis; or the Military Energies of the Constitution* was a patriotic plea to the authorities to repair the country's defences. He worked indefatigably for the various reforming causes; in turn the patriots of Spain and Greece claimed his pen and purse. He was in demand as a speaker at such gatherings as that of the meeting of 1,200 at the Crown and Anchor on May Day, 1809, when he moved resolutions inviting every town to petition Parliament. His personal tour of the midland counties in 1811 did more than anything to promote the cause in the country at large.

In 1812 he joined with Burdett in forming the Hampden Club in London. In 1813 he made another excursion into the manufacturing districts of the midlands and north; the Hampden Clubs that sprang up in his wake were the prime movers in the great petitioning movement of 1816-17. He was over seventy, but apparently, he thought nothing of travelling nine hundred miles in winter weather. When his friends urged him to rest, he replied: 'English gentlemen are perpetually travelling. ... Some go to see lakes and mountains. Were it not allowable to travel for seeing the actual conditions of a starving people?'

The London Hampden Club was a gathering of 'men of wealth and influence'. As Cartwright realized, this prevented it from becoming the nucleus of a national union. Indeed, he felt that he had to resign his own membership for one year because it was hinted that persons of rank were deterred by his presence. The club did not, as has been suggested, provide the focus of reform politics and it was never the hotbed of sedition that ministers seem to have feared. It was, however, Cartwright's inspiration, the model which he offered to working men to copy in their own small associations. 'His experience of the lower orders', wrote his niece and biographer, 'led him to remark that they preferred confiding their interests to persons of more consideration than themselves.' Cartwright travelled about like a methodist preacher on circuit, spreading the gospel of reform. 'One step more', he wrote to his wife, 'and your prophecy will be completed, that I shall become a field preacher.'

How effective was his mission? He claimed that the Hampden Club, though it was 'lamentably defective, cold and inefficient', had 'been instrumental in generating the petitions for reform of more than a million of men'. Cobbett advised his readers 'to have nothing to do with any political clubs, any secret *Cabals*, any *Correspondencies*'. Bamford was sympathetic but unimpressed: 'the worthy old Major remained at his post, brave as a lion, serene as an unconscious child; and also, in the rush and tumult of that time, as little noticed'. The reverent attitude of some provincial leaders towards London and anyone who came thence, claiming to represent the Hampden Club, had its dangers, as is illustrated by the successful tactics of Oliver the government spy. Undoubt-edly Cartwright claimed more than he achieved. He was naïve, a fundamentalist among reformers. One can search his prosy, stereotyped writings in vain for signs of development of thought; he reproduces the clichés of the age of reason for the earnest artisans of Regency England. He sets out to teach the people the 'First Principles of the Law of Nature' and he looks forward to a return to the virtuous democracy of the Saxons (overlaid and distorted by alien Normans).

Major Cartwright may in fact have been something of a bore. Did he not urge his nephew to hang up the Declaration of Rights in his room at Oxford? He objected to giving presents to children because it was 'a species of immorality to employ bribery and corruption even to a child'. And yet there was something grand about the man. He brings courage to a bleak scene. Tall, thin, with long, wrinkled face and wide, thin mouth, dressed as he usually was in a loose jacket and breeches, his grey hair flowing lank under a battered cocked hat, he inspired more love than ridicule among 'the people'. They were certainly no abstraction to him. He was no stranger among them. He accepted all discom-forts and snubs, everything except the possibility of defeat. 'Of course', he once said, 'I get heartily cursed for disturbing the quiet of the country'. Horne Tooke wrote to him in 1797: 'I think the cause of reform is dead and buried.' The Major endorsed the letter, 'But J. C. is a believer in the Resurrection.' He did as much as any man to see that it came about.

F. D. Cartwright, *Life & Correspondence of Major John Cartwright*, 2 vols., 1826.
A. Goodwin, *The Friends of Liberty, the English Democratic Movement in the Age of the French Revolution*, 1979.

**CHARLES STANHOPE, 3rd EARL STANHOPE** (1753-1816), politician and scientist, was a man of diverse talents and interests who could be relied upon to be original in any situation. Egocentric, sometimes ridiculous, callous in his private life, in public affairs ranging from the perceptive to the perverse, his inventive talents amounted to genius, even if they were often misapplied. Educated largely at Geneva, where his parents moved when he was ten, Lord Mahon, as he was styled until he inherited the earldom in 1786, early displayed radical inclinations. In 1780 he harangued the Gordon rioters and advocated the end of hostilities in America. Although he sat for the rotten borough of Chipping Wycombe, by the patronage of Shelburne, he persistently advocated parliamentary reform. He attacked Pitt's Sinking Fund with sound reasoning. He was married to Pitt's aunt, but became permanently estranged from the family after the French Revolution. 'Citizen Stanhope' had an excessive zeal for the principles of the revolution and imposed them upon his unhappy family. Lady Hester, his daughter, like the others was disinherited: she became housekeeper to Pitt until his death; later she displayed all her father's pride and eccentricity, settling eventually to the life of an Arab sovereign among the Druses of Mount Lebanon.

It is easy to conclude that Stanhope was a little mad. He lent himself to caricature and was a favourite subject of Gillray. He undoubtedly enjoyed the notoriety he acquired through his advocacy of friendship with the French republic and the speeches that he made in the House of Commons upon this theme. His London house was fired by rioters in 1794. But his inventions were remarkable. Around 1777 he had constructed two calculating machines. He patented steam vessels, in 1790 and 1807, which were adopted by the Admiralty. He invented a microscope lens and his process of stereotyping was acquired by the Clarendon Press in 1805. In 1811, after some years in which he had retired from Parliament in dudgeon, he had a success with his Gold Coin and Banknote Bill. He was interested in canals and projected one from Holsworthy to the Bristol Channel. He wrote upon many subjects from electricity to musical tones. In the year of his death he was pressing for a committee of Parliament to reform weights and measures. Political life would have been duller without him, society the poorer.

A. Newman, *The Stanhopes of Chevening*, 1969.

**SIR FRANCIS BURDETT** (1770-1844), the fifth baronet of his line, was a sturdy Tory radical whose impetuous attacks upon the government during the Napoleonic Wars earned him a well-deserved popularity with the mob. He came of a line of Warwickshire squires and he inherited a traditional Jacobite Toryism in the Bolingbroke style. Like Cobbett's, his was a countryman's view of government: regretful about declining squires and yeomen, and suspicious of the new plutocracy of city and government — 'nabobs', bankers and brokers. He wanted reform of Parliament because he detested the power of borough-mongers — especially the new ones. He incited the mob in order to bring pressure upon Westminster, not to school them in principles of democracy. He was an effective politician because of his splendid presence and rhetoric — but also because of an independent income which came largely from his marriage to Sophia, the daughter of the banker Thomas Coutts. He was a rebel by temperament. At Westminster he had taken part in a revolt against the headmaster, Dr. Smith, who had knocked him down with a cudgel and then expelled him.

After leaving Christ Church Burdett went to France. In Paris he sampled the vivid oratory of the National Assembly. In 1791 he wrote some verses on the Revolution in uncomfortable French. Despite his marriage (1793) he seemed to lack stability of purpose and was somewhat moody. His father-in-law prompted him to a political career and in 1796 he was returned for Boroughbridge, a seat in the Newcastle interest. The Commons took notice of a natural orator, with a fine voice and manner, pretty hot when he was roused and capable of stinging sarcasms. Disraeli was later to idealize his 'Norman' looks and his Tory radicalism: the view is coloured by his own political philosophy. Burdett was a figure of romance to Disraeli. But he is surely right in placing Burdett in the line of such stalwart 'country party' Tories as William Wyndham and John Hinde Cotton: they, like he, had advocated annual parliaments and wider suffrage as a means of breaking the grip of the borough-mongers upon government. Burdett can also be classed as an extreme Whig, in his passionate assaults upon tyranny in any guise, whether Catherine the Great annexing helpless Poles or the British Home Secretary detaining prisoners without trial. In 1799 he was one of the few Whigs to raise a serious opposition to the Combination Acts.

In 1802 he was elected for Middlesex after a rowdy contest. Burdett had taken up the case of the 'Habeas Corpus prisoners', notably Colonel Despard, held by Governor Aris in Coldbath Fields prison, after receiving an appeal from a prisoner written, according to Cobbett, 'upon the fly-leaf of a book with a splinter of wood dipped in blood'. Burdett's quixotic act of rescue made him a second Wilkes in the popular estimation and he defeated the ministerial candidate Mainwaring to cries of 'Burdett and no Bastille'. Afterwards there were illuminations to rival those of the peace celebrations. A petition was presented against his return but in 1804 it was declared void. He stood again and was elected by one vote, amid tumultuous excitement, before the sheriff reversed the decision on a technicality. In 1806 he plumped for an austere campaign to meet allegations of bribery and to test what he called 'the unassisted public principle': he eschewed canvassing, treating and transport for elderly voters. His vote was halved!

Burdett was sufficiently disillusioned to decline to stand for Westminster when first asked. He then fought a duel with 'the game-cock' James Paull, who was to be his fellow-candidate. Eventually he came out top of the poll with the radical sailor Cochrane second and Sheridan, the Whig, far behind: Westminster was safe for radicalism until the Reform Bill. Burdett was still popular, but his electoral triumph owed much to Francis Place and his organizing skills. Soon Cobbett was to dismiss him as 'Old Glory' and Hunt was to become the darling of the crowds. The future of radicalism lay primarily with such men. Burdett's concern was with political rights rather than with social change. By exposing individual cases of oppression and defending general principles he sustained the cause of reform more effectively than the official Whigs could do.

In 1810 an alleged violation of the privileges of the House when he was defending the freedom of the press (in the person of John Gale Jones) led to an order for his arrest by Speaker Abbot. He issued a defiance from his Piccadilly home. 'Power and Privilege', he declared, 'are not the same things, and ought not to be confounded together. Privilege ... was by law secured to the third branch of the Legislature in order to protect them, that they might safely protect the people; not to give them power to destroy the people.' While his Westminster *sansculottes* guarded his house, the authorities dallied. Eventually troops had to be brought up to assist them in forcing an entrance and carrying him off to the Tower. There he lived comfortably to the end of the session, received deputations and brought, but lost, an action against the Speaker. He was re-elected for the City in 1812 and concerted a programme of reform with Cartwright. Together they founded the Hampden Club to provide a radical cadre. Burdett and Place tried to concentrate upon securing household suffrage. Playing the demagogue, Burdett never became a democrat. But he remained vigilant as ever against oppression. In 1820 he suffered imprisonment and a fine of £2,000 for denouncing the Peterloo magistrates.

The passage of Catholic Emancipation and the Reform Bill made it possible for Burdett to return to Toryism. The Whig Poor Law aroused his wrath. He was a Benthamite in his desire for law reform (and Hobhouse called him the best constitutional lawyer in England) but was out of sympathy with the stricter utilitarians. In 1835 he resigned his Westminster seat and was elected at once for North Wiltshire. The Radical press denounced him as a renegade, 'in his second childhood' and 'a faded fox-hunter'. He was certainly a keen follower of the Quorn. He could be taken as the model of a squire of the old school. Disraeli was among those who were captivated by the man. 'He was extremely vain but not offensively so; his high breeding prevented that; and under all circumstances, he was distinguished by simplicity. I think he was the greatest gentleman I ever knew.'

M. W. Patterson, *Sir Francis Burdett and his Times*, 2 vols., 1931.

**WILLIAM COBBETT** (1762-1835) was the founder and editor of *The Weekly Register*. This journal reached people who had

*William Cobbett*
(Artist: George Cooke)

never before been informed about political and social questions. *The Register* has some claim to be the first modern newspaper. It embodied its editor's spirit of opposition and independence.

Though exasperatingly dogmatic in the way of a self-educated man, he wrote with great sympathy for people.

Cobbett's father was a yeoman of Farnham in Surrey who kept an inn, farmed a few acres and enjoyed a local reputation as a settler of disputes. The third of four children, William was bred to the plough and learned little more than to read, write and do arithmetic, and to fend for himself. 'I do not remember the time', he later wrote, 'when I did not earn my living.' His first occupation was bird-scaring: 'When I first trudged afield, with my wooden bottle and my satchel swung over my shoulders, I was hardly able to climb the gates and stiles.' At the age of eleven he walked to Kew to work on the royal estate. On the way there he had purchased *The Tale of a Tub* in Richmond, with the three pennies he had saved for his supper. The awkward lad in blue smock coat and red gaiters was given work at Kew. But he was already restless and Swift's strange satire had fired his imagination to be more than a gardener. After more years at home he tried unsuccessfully to enlist in the navy. He went to London and spent unhappy months in an attorney's office. When he left to soldier in a line regiment he spent his time as a recruit 'not in the dissipation common to such a way of life, but in reading and study'. He trained himself in the rules of grammar by learning Dr. Lowth's *English Grammar* off by heart. Cobbett was a soldier in the 54th for nine years, most of this time in New Brunswick. He was soon promoted to sergeant-major over the heads of senior men. He practised his prose style in the drafting of official reports. By his account he virtually ran the regiment. Inevitably he encountered corruption. To trap a fraudulent quartermaster he copied out parts of the regimental accounts, secured evidence of other peculations and, after obtaining a discharge, pressed for a court martial. Suspecting that official obstruction made a successful outcome improbable, he absented himself from the trial. The case went by default and he came in for scornful censure. Matters were little improved by the appearance of a pamphlet, *The Soldier's Friend*, which attacked corruption and stated the case for the private soldier. This was the only way in which Cobbett felt that he could tackle the great wall of the army establishment. He had received a salutary lesson. His own trumpet could not bring down that wall. He must enlist a greater force — public opinion.

In 1792 Cobbett married Ann Reid, a New Brunswick girl, who had proved herself worthy of her unusual swain. He had given her 150 guineas from his savings: she had kept the sum intact and worked as a servant until he was ready to marry her. He was a devoted but demanding husband, she a staunch wife, in a life which took him twice to America, once to Newgate and exposed them to the hazards of a tribune of the people. He went to Revolutionary France, and then to America, where he lived for seven years. Democratic Philadelphians found that they had in their midst a British patriot with a genius for pamphleteering. He began by attacking the ideas of Joseph Priestley, who had recently come from England, having had his home burned by a mob in the name of Church and King. Cobbett went better than his king who had gloried 'in the name of Briton'. The British lion has never roared louder than in his pamphlets, culminating in *The Life and Adventures of Peter Porcupine.* 'Who will say', he asked, 'that an Englishman ought not to despise all nations in the world?' To publicize his works he set up his own bookshop and defied the mob that came to protest. He inspired change of heart. George III was toasted at public dinners. Many Americans admired Cobbett's courage and some even subscribed to his views. Eventually his blundering found the wrong target. He attacked Judge McKean, a notorious anglophobe. McKean ordered his property in Philadelphia to be seized. This was the end of his daily *Porcupine Gazette.*

In 1800 Cobbett took his leave for England where, in the words of his parting address, 'neither the moth of *Democracy* nor the rust of *Federalism* doth corrupt ...'. The war minister, William Windham, invited him to a dinner at which he, the prime minister and Canning discussed the uses of propaganda. Cobbett was offered sole running of the government-controlled *New Briton*. 'The pen of a slave seldom produces effect', he informed Pitt. The clumsy directness of the words is as typical as the prickly instinct for independence. Cobbett edited instead an English *Porcupine*, patriotic and Pittite. George III referred delightedly to 'my friend Cobbett's paper'. He opposed the peace of Amiens and had his windows smashed by the mob. The *Porcupine* lost money but Windham found capital for a new paper, the *Weekly Political Register*. He was ill-rewarded. Cobbett's enthusiasm for war cooled when he came to study its financial implications. He saw the country flooded with a depreciated paper currency, 'Jews and jobbers' everywhere, building their houses in Surrey and Hampshire, turning out the old squires. Cobbett was obsessed by the idea that government and high financial interests conspired together to rob honest men. Emigration, craftsmen, enclosures, pretty country 'boxes', new barracks, martello towers — all these offences were traced to 'The Thing', the 'Great Wen', 'Our big gentlemen at Whitehall', 'tax-eaters' or some other name for the unnatural growths that had sprouted out of the French wars. So patriotism took a radical hue. The puritan in Cobbett despised a system which enabled men to make money out of money. He found poignant contrasts between the vast sinecures of a favoured few and the sullen labourers of factory and field. He seized upon particular cases of injustice. He denounced the flogging of some young militiamen of Ely by a Hanoverian regiment. His generous temper still burns through his article: 'Five hundred each! Aye, that is right! Flog them! Flog! Flog! Flog! They deserve a flogging at every mealtime. Lash them daily!' The government tried him for sedition. In July 1810 he was found guilty after an inept defence.

Cobbett had bought an estate at Botley and enjoyed there the strenuous, well-ordered life of an old-fashioned yeoman. There Mary Mitford saw him presiding over his family. 'There was not the slightest attempt at finery, or display or gentility. They called it a farm, and everything was in accordance with the largest ideas of a great English yeoman of the old times.' She admired his Indian corn, Carolina beans and water-melons. 'There was something of Dandie Dinmont about him', she wrote. 'He was a tall, stout man; fair and sunburnt, with a bright smile, and an air compounded of the soldier and the farmer, to which his habit of wearing an eternal red waistcoat contributed not a little.'

Now Cobbett had to leave Botley. He was imprisoned for two years and fined £1,000; he afterwards maintained that the sentence had been meant to kill him. He seldom failed in self-dramatization. In fact he lived comfortably in the sheriff's lodgings, received visitors and wrote as much as he wanted. It did not harm Cobbett in the eyes of the people that he had become a martyr for popular liberties; the experience affected him adversely, however. Resilience, humour, sense of proportion were all damaged: the Cobbett of the post-war years was vindictive, a man of grievances amounting in some respects to paranoia. His political philosophy was spelt out grossly in a catalogue of hatreds and caricatures. What did not square with the idealized version of a self-sufficient rural England was liable to be rejected. And yet his view remained a broadly humane one. Feeling won its battles over reason — but reason, we may decide, had exponents enough in the years of Bentham, Ricardo, Brougham and Mill. It was, for example, on humane grounds that he wrote, in 1816, his *Letter to the Luddites*, in which he defended machines as 'the produce of the mind of man' whose existence 'distinguishes the civilized man from the savage'. Machines were not necessarily an evil; a degree of urbanization was inevitable. What Cobbett maintained was that government should be conducted so as to minimize the ill-effects of this process; instead it was in the hands of speculators and 'Scotch feelosophers'.

In November 1816 he brought out a special, cheap edition of the *Register*, subtitled an *Address to the Journeyman and Labourers of England, Scotland and Wales* and sold two hundred thousand copies. In 1817, after the suspension of the Habeas Corpus Act, he set off for America and stayed there until November 1819. Radicals at home were unconvinced by Cobbett's talk of 'a long arm' against corruption and accused him of cowardice. Leadership was always for Cobbett a matter of self-expression and if he could not speak freely he could not lead. Did even Cobbett realize what power he had won by his 'Twopenny Trash'? Hazlitt called him 'a kind of fourth estate in the politics of the country'. Bamford testified to the way in which Cobbett diverted working men from rioting to planning for political reform. After he returned from America, bearing with him the bones of Tom Paine, he stood for parliament at Coventry and was defeated. The Six Acts, by one of their provisions, compelled him to raise the price of the *Register* to sixpence.

Cobbett started business as a seed-merchant and set out on the first of his *Rural Rides*. He issued the *Grammar of the English Language* which he had composed in the tranquillity of Long Island: examples present Cobbett's political views in a droll but effective way. Thus the subjunctive: 'If he *write*, the guilty tyrants will be ready with their dungeons and axes.' To refute the idea that he was an atheist, he published *Twelve Sermons*, simple

homilies, the more effective because of his unwonted restraint.
The *Cottage Economy* was a manual of practical instruction in
self-sufficient living. It is an attractive work. His own favourite
was the *Poor Man's Friend* (1826), the theme of which was that no
man can be happy unless he has a full belly — government's chief
function being to fill it. The book was Cobbett's reaction to an
election, at Preston, in which he had come bottom of the poll. In
1824 he had written his *History of the Protestant Reformation*: it
was the genesis of 'the Thing', 'engendered in lust and brought
forth in hypocrisy and fraud'. The maligned Catholic Church had
preserved 'old English hospitality', built the great cathedrals and
devoted a third of its wealth to the care of the sick and destitute.
His whole argument was designed to serve the cause of Catholic
Emancipation. It fits with his nostalgic picture of a Merry
England, now in the last stages of spoliation.

Cobbett loved to teach and any subject was grist to his mill.
Luckily he chose to ride out into the land for his greatest essay in
national education. *Rural Rides* is one of the delights of our literature, because Cobbett the scolding pedagogue and Cobbett the
politician share the saddle with Cobbett the observant countryman. At past sixty years of age he would ride more than forty
miles in all weathers, eating nothing but a rasher of bacon and
a handful of nuts or an apple or two. Mainly in the south and
midlands he noted everything he saw, from a well-drilled field of
mangel-wurzels to the tithe-gathering parson or a new barracks.
Every sight yielded its moral. 'At leaving Whitchurch we soon
passed the mill where the Mother-Bank paper is made! Thank
God, this mill is likely soon to want employment! Hard by is a
pretty park and house, belonging to "*Squire*" Portal, the *paper-
maker*. The country people, who seldom want for sarcastic
shrewdness, call it "Rag Hall"! (23 November 1821).' He looked
with disapproval on two miles of 'new stock-jobbers" houses
on the road to Croydon, with pity on a bunch of pretty girls reap-
ing in a field, 'as ragged as colts and as pale as ashes, whose blue
arms and lips would make any heart ache but that of a loan-
jobber'.

In 1829 Cobbett wrote a didactic fragment of autobiography:
in *Advice to Young Men* he offered them some of the lessons of
his own life. The philosophy that emerges is a puritan one; it is
centred upon the dignity of work. An important place is given to

the upbringing of children: preferably their education should be undertaken by their parents. He was not destined to spend his last years in domestic peace. 1830 was the year of Captain Swing, when the agricultural labourers rose in their misery, burned corn ricks and smashed threshing machines. Cobbett now spoke for the labourers. 'I thank God', he said, 'that they will not live on damned potatoes while the barns are full of corn, the Downs covered with sheep and the yards full of hogs, created by their own labour.' Cobbett was unfairly accused by the government of being an instigator of revolt. He confounded the attorney-general by an alert defence and the case was dismissed. He was at large to preach his gospel of comprehensive reform: annual parliaments, universal male suffrage, cancellation of pensions and sinecures, discharge of most of the army, abolition of tithes, confiscation of church property and crown lands and their sale to pay off the national debt. He was elected M.P. for Oldham in 1832, receiving four times as many votes as the next man. Cobbett's opening remark was a collector's piece. 'It seems to me that since I have been sitting here I have heard a great deal of unprofitable discussion.' At first he spoke excessively, then with more tact. He mellowed. But life in the Commons exhausted him. Stuffy evening sessions were too much for this early riser. He went to Ireland to recuperate and saw scenes of poverty which surpassed the worst of England. He made great efforts in 1835 to oppose the Malt Tax. In May he spoke at length on the question of agricultural distress. Then he went down to Normandy Farm in Surrey, the farm he had recently bought. It was near his birthplace; and there he died.

In his heyday Cobbett was perhaps the most popular writer the country has known. This is because he was a great attacker. He expressed men's bafflement in the face of changes inexplicable in origin but hurtful in results. He offered neat solutions: get rid of Jews and paper-money and all will be well. His range of targets is absurdly large: Wilberforce and Quakers (cant), railways (urbanization) understandably — but why tea? Why was Owen, struggling to bring co-operation into industry, accused of being 'monkish'? His more grotesque sallies were all part of his art as a journalist. He wrote for the moment, rapidly, and let himself be carried away. His art was the literary equivalent of the cartoon as executed by a Hogarth or a Gillray: distortion was of the essence.

G. D. H. Cole, *Life of William Cobbett*, 1924.
W. B. Pemberton, *William Cobbett*, 1949.

JOHN THELWALL (1764-1834), political reformer and pioneer in speech therapy, was the son of Joseph Thelwall, a silk
mercer of London who died when his son was eight. He was sent
to school at Highgate, but he was removed at thirteen and put
into business. Independent opinions and an addiction to books
prevented him from progressing as a tailor. He studied law for a
time, but he preferred philosophy to copying 'the trash of an
office'. He also had a strong objection to the taking of oaths. He
became entirely dependent on the pen for his living. 1789 found
him a natural subject for revolutionary propaganda.

He joined in turn the Society of Friends of the People and
Hardy's Corresponding Society. Despite a hesitation of speech
and a slight lisp he became an effective speaker. His radical
diatribes at the Coachmakers' Hall attracted the attention of
ministers. In 1793 his pamphlet *Politics for the People, or
Hogswash* led to the prosecution of the printer, Eaton — an
unwise and unsuccessful move, which did not deter ministers from
charging Thelwall and eleven others with treason in the following
year. When Thelwall's turn came, in December 1794, Hardy and
Tooke had already been acquitted and the government's case torn
to shreds. Thelwall might have proved an easier victim, or the jury
might have been less sympathetic to a man who made his living by
lectures largely devoted to passionate attacks upon the constitution. It was possible to conceive of Thelwall, this stocky,
muscular, figure with the tastes and talents of a demagogue, as an
English Danton. He was brave, original and uncompromising; he
was also a poet and philosopher, with a lot of his friend Coleridge
in him. 'The minds that really govern the machine of society are
at all times few', said Coleridge. Thelwall, an *exalté* among the
radicals of his time, would not make a promise lest he should be
unable to keep it. He dealt in absolutes. He believed that he had
a mission.

He can appear in a somewhat ridiculous light, as in this
description retailed by Walsh, the spy, of his appearance at a
dinner in Somerset: 'The little stout man with dark, cropt hair ...
wore a white hat and glasses ... talked in a great passion.' Yet
at the height of the terror in France and in the first year of an

ideological war, Thelwall's activities alarmed the government; their mistake was to pitch the charge too high. 'Seditious conspiracy' might have secured a conviction, but even Thelwall's record could hardly sustain a charge of treason. He was defended by Erskine. Thelwall had wanted to defend himself. 'If you do, you will be hanged', wrote Erskine. 'Then I'll be hanged if I do', replied Thelwall. He was acquitted.

Fortunately for Thelwall he had another life besides political agitation. In 1791 he married Susan Vallum of Rutland, his 'good angel'. She bore him four children. He had begun to study medicine and wrote, in 1793, an essay, *Animal Vitality*. *Poems written in close confinement in the Tower and Newgate* provided an outlet for his romantic yearnings. From 1796 to 1798 he travelled about the country denouncing the government through the medium of 'Lectures upon Roman History'. Sometimes his meetings were broken up by hired mobs. When he stayed with the Coleridges he was being watched by a government spy — but this may have been because of the odd conduct of Coleridge and Wordsworth. In 1798 he went for a rest to a small farm near Brecon and when he returned to London two years later he discarded politics for elocution. His cure for stammering was original, effective and popular. He saw speech impediments as a part of the whole personality of the sufferer. Crabb Robinson describes how he went to hear *Comus* recited by a group of Thelwall's 'stammerers'; he went to be amused, but he stayed to praise.

In 1818 his wife died and three years later he married Cecil Boyle, much younger than he, a woman of social charm and literary ability. He lived to see the reform of parliament. He had then long ceased to be a fire-eater and his friends testified to his integrity and good nature. He had been, however, one of the most effective of the 'English jacobins'. He had helped to keep alive the spirit of radical protest in unpropitious times.

Charles Cestre, *John Thelwall*, 1906.
C. B. Crone, *The English Jacobins: Reformers in the Late Eighteenth Century*, 1968.

**ELIZABETH FRY** (1780-1845) was a brave, devout and warmhearted Quaker who devoted her life to the cause of female prisoners. She grew up in the exquisite house near Norwich that will be familiar to readers of Percy Lubbock's *Earlham*, the third of seven daughters of John Gurney, a wealthy Quaker banker. Her mother was the grand-daughter of Robert Barclay, author of the *Apology for the People called Quakers*. But the Quakerism to which Elizabeth was brought up was not of the severest kind. She studied music and dancing and she did not have to wear distinctive clothes. But she was lovingly trained in the spirit of practical service. A peaceful piety ruled the Gurney household: 'the fear of the Lord was constantly set before the children as the supreme principle of life and action'. Mrs Gurney taught her daughters — as we learn from her diary — to be 'virtuous and good on the broad, firm basis of Christianity', and gentle in manner, to which they 'may be led without vanity and affectation by amiable and judicious instruction'. Her mother (who died when Elizabeth was twelve) called Elizabeth 'the dove-like Betsey', but there was more to her character than gentle diffidence. She worked hard, thought for herself and did not hesitate to do what she thought right. She enjoyed the lively, cultivated society life of Norwich. 'Old Crome' was the girls' drawing master for a time.

As a girl of seventeen who enjoyed going out to dances, Elizabeth expressed in her journal 'the greatest fear of religion', because she 'never saw a person religious who was not *enthusiastic*' (my italics: words like 'intense' or even 'obsessed' best convey the meaning of that word). An encounter with William Savery, an American Quaker, seems to have been the beginning of a new attitude. She visited London and tested her vocation against 'the vanity and folly of what are called the pleasures of this life'. As a mark of her new earnestness she adopted the plain Quaker cap and put away her 'scarlet riding-habit'. She started a small school for poor Norwich children and soon had seventy pupils. At twenty she married Joseph Fry in the Friends' Meeting House at Norwich and moved to London. Her husband practised a Quakerism so strict that Elizabeth was now 'the gay instead of the plain and scrupulous one of the family'. Her house became a centre for Friends from all parts of the country. Later, when her husband's father died, the family moved to his country seat, Plashet in Essex.

After her father's death in 1809 she became a 'minister' — or one who was prepared to obey 'the inward voice' by 'bearing testimony at the prompting of the Holy Spirit' in the Quaker manner. The succession of pregnancies and births would have tied most women to a domestic life: like her mother, she had twelve children. But Plashet became a charitable centre. A poor community of Irish people in the neighbourhood and a tribe of gypsies were among those who received her practical aid. She was uncondescending, undogmatic, unprejudiced — and willing to face anything. In 1813 she made her first visit to Newgate and found her life's work in that grim place, where about three hundred women were crammed into two cells and two wards, - with their children, under the care of one old man and his son. They lived, cooked, washed and, when they could beg money, drank spirits from the prison tap; the governor was reluctant to go near them, some of the women were frenzied and dangerous and gaol fever was not the worst of the health hazards. To a gently nurtured woman the sights and smells and language must have been sickening.

Mrs Fry was not the first pioneer or the only protagonist. John Howard had done a great work of publicity and reform. Romilly's supporters kept the issue of prison reform alive in Parliament. But she achieved a breakthrough at Newgate by force of personality, at a time when public opinion was being roused, and official indifferences giving way to concern. From Christmas 1816, with friends like Anna Buxton, she began regular visiting of the prisoners, provided them with clothes and work, and set up a school for the children. Most of the women seem to have accepted her as a woman whom they could respect and love. She treated the most degraded as individuals and seemed to be more interested in their needs than their crimes. Maria Edgeworth, the novelist, recorded these impressions of Elizabeth Fry visiting Newgate after her reforms had taken effect: 'Enter Mrs Fry, in a drab-coloured silk coat, and plain, borderless Quaker cap; a most benevolent countenance; Guido Madonna face, calm, benign … . Her first smile, as she looked upon me, I can never forget. The prisoners came in an orderly manner and ranged themselves on the benches. All quite clean faces, hair, caps and hands. On a very low bench in front little children were seated, and watched by their mothers. Almost all these women, about thirty, were under sentence of transportation. … She opened the Bible and read in the most sweetly solemn sedate voice I have ever heard, slow and distinctly, without anything in the manner that could distract attention from the matter.'

To discover what lay behind this calm scene the reader should turn to the evidence presented to Parliament's inquiry into the metropolitan prisons in 1818: Mrs Fry's evidence was minutely informed and unemotional. Prison reform was to be a slow business despite the work of James Nield and T. F. Buxton, Elizabeth Fry's brother-in-law. Many probably sympathized with Sydney Smith: 'Mrs Fry is an amiable excellent woman and ten thousand times better than the infamous neglect that preceded her, but hers is not the method to stop crimes.' He believed in severity. 'There must be a great deal of solitude; coarse food; a dress of shame; hard, incessant, irksome, eternal labour; a planned and regulated and unrelenting exclusion of happiness and comfort.' There is little in this prescription of the idea of 'there, but for the grace of God, go I' which surely moved Mrs Fry and her friends.

Elizabeth Fry did not enjoy the public acclaim that followed her work — but she never shrank from interviews, meetings and travels that would benefit her causes. She took up the cause of women sentenced to be transported. Convicts who found, when they arrived in Australia, work, shelter and provision, might become the useful citizens that the new country needed. The same practical aims can be seen in the association she founded for improving the condition of female prisoners in Newgate: aims included the separation of the sexes, classification of prisoners according to the nature of their crimes, female supervision for them, useful employment and adequate education. The success of her methods led to their adoption elsewhere. In 1818 she toured the prisons of Scotland and the north of England with her brother, Joseph Gurney. A visit to Ireland in 1827 led to her becoming interested in other places of detention besides prisons. Her report in 1828 led to some improvement in hospitals and in the treatment of the insane. She corresponded a great deal with reformers on the continent and later travelled abroad as well, inspecting prisons and reporting to governments. The Tsarina of Russia followed her advice when she was working on the improvement of lunatic asylums. Queen Victoria, like Queen Charlotte before her, took a personal interest in her work.

To the end of her life Mrs Fry worked for her various causes: libraries for coast-guard stations and a charity for servants in distress were among them. One of her happiest moments was when she was able to present no less than twenty-five grandchildren to the King of Prussia! She had not allowed her husband's business failure in 1828 and their subsequent comparative poverty to deflect or depress her, but family bereavements saddened her last years, notably the death of her son William and two of his daughters from scarlet fever. But her end was tranquil. She died at Ramsgate in October 1845.

Mrs Pitman, *Elizabeth Fry*, 1884.

HANNAH MORE (1745-1833) was a pioneer in writing about religious matters in a popular way; she was also influential in the movement for religious education of the poor. Her activities may suggest a woman of narrow absorption and a presumptuous piety. Brave, devoted, idealistic though she was, the evangelical, *élitiste* tone of her writing, with its pervasive sense of class, is not appealing. Set in her own time against the degradation of many of the poor, and the indifference of many of the rich, her work and personality acquire new significance. The youthful friend of Dr. Johnson and David Garrick, the flirtatious blue-stocking and author of the *Bas Bleu* (a description of the life of the literary ladies of London), she retained much of her liveliness as the serious part of her personality emerged and she sought to 'escape from the world'. A sense of humour becomes, however, more difficult to trace in 'Saint Hannah', who said that she would derive more gratification from being able to lower the price of bread than from having written the Iliad', the sabbatarian who wrote of Pitt's duel on Putney Heath: 'to complete the horror, they chose a Sunday'.

Her father, a Norfolk gentleman who had been reduced by the failure of a law-suit to take the mastership of a school near Bristol, sensibly brought up his daughters so that they could earn their own living. Hannah was precocious, a voracious reader and anxious to write. She improved her French by talking to French prisoners on parôle. In 1757 she joined her elder sister, who had set up a school in Bristol, continued her education and later taught there. In about 1767 she received her first proposal of marriage from a Mr Turner, a Bristol merchant about twenty years her senior; he prevaricated strangely and after six years the engagement was broken off, though he provided her with a small annuity. She would never afterwards listen to talk of marriage. She was excited by her meeting with Dr. Johnson who, with amiable hyperbole, declared that she was 'the most powerful versiatrix in the English language'. Garrick persuaded her to write a play: *Percy*, for which he wrote both prologue and epilogue, ran for twenty-one nights at Covent Garden. She afterwards said that she had liked Garrick despite his profession, that she never saw cards — and but one other actor in his house! She enjoyed her *succès d'estime*, and only gave up writing plays when Garrick died (1779). Her *Sacred Dramas* (1782) were not intended for the stage.

In 1784 Hannah More left London, renounced its dinners and routs and settled in a cottage she had built at Cowslip Green, ten miles from Bristol. There she gardened, wrote, observed the world and considered her spiritual position. In 1788 there appeared anonymously the result of her reflections: *Thoughts on the Importance of the Manners of the Great to General Society*. Meanwhile the state of the Somerset poor had attracted her attention. In Cheddar and Blagdon, Shipham and Rowberrow, the people were almost pagan, wild and depraved in morals.

Following the example of Robert Raikes, Hannah and her sisters founded schools for village children and gave them respectability in the eyes of the prejudiced or cynical by assuring them (as in a letter to a bishop who was perturbed by the possibility of 'enthusiasm') that she taught on weekdays only 'such coarse work as may fit them for servants ... only habits of industry and piety'. Of course she was accused of 'methodism', a useful bogey word for idle clerics — but also a growing movement, a living reproach, if not a threat, to the establishment of what Brougham called a 'quiet and somewhat lazy church'. In the Mendips, thirteen adjacent villages were without resident clergy. She was also attacked by local farmers, who thought that religion would 'ruin agriculture' and by mothers, who wanted to be paid for sending their children to school. She was actually summoned before the Dean's Court to answer the charge that a school she had started at Blagdon was a conventicle and was illegal because unlicensed! By the time of this 'Blagdon controversy' (1800-1802) she had moved on to the national stage — at least to that wing of it occupied by the evangelicals.

After the success of *Village Politics* (1792) she wrote a series of tracts, secured the backing of committees all over the country and the formation (1799) of the Religious Tract Society. To a man like Bishop Porteous of London, who caused a theatre manager to drop the curtain in the middle of a ballet at midnight on Saturday rather than face prosecution for playing on the sabbath, Hannah was a valued spiritual adviser. An aunt was distressed by her niece's 'seriousness' until she was relieved — and converted — by reading Hannah More's *Coelebs in Search of a Wife* (her most popular book, published in 1809). Hannah More wrote in 1817 of the death of Princess Charlotte, for whom she had written *Hints towards Forming the Character of a Young Princess*, that it was a punishment for the national lack of piety. The next year she wrote: 'It appears to me that the two classes of character are more decided than they were; the wicked seem more wicked, and the good better.' If the 'good' were indeed 'better', or if there seemed to be, as a clergyman correspondent of hers wrote, 'a more lively impression of the importance of Christianity among the great', this determined lady had had some part in it.

M. G. Jones, *Hannah More*, 1952.

**RICHARD MARTIN** (1754-1834) was much loved for his compassionate and generous nature and earned the name 'Humanity Martin' for his work for animal welfare. As benevolent Irish landowner and diligent parliamentarian he might be honoured above those less scrupulous about how they used their rental incomes. More especially he should be remembered as the founder, in 1824, of The Royal Society for the Protection of Animals.

From County Galway he went, like other scions of Ascendancy families, to Harrow and Trinity College, Cambridge. He returned to the Irish Bar and Parliament, and management of the 200,000 acres around his family seat, Ballinahinch Castle. He was a keen supporter of the Act of Union and, from 1801 to 1826, represented Galway at Westminster. Like some other Protestant landowners who knew their Catholic tenants and sympathised with their aspirations, he supported Emancipation. George IV was otherwise inclined, but appreciated Martin's wit and remained his friend. 'I hear you are to have an election in County

Galway. Who will win?', he asked. 'The survivor, sire' replied Martin. He was known as a man of quick temper and fought more than one duel.

Unusually at a time of lavish promotion among Irish families, Martin refused the offer of a peerage. But it was his constancy in cherished causes that made the greatest impression. In 1822 he saw through Parliament a law that made Britain the European leader in the field of animal welfare, 'to prevent the cruel and improper treatment of cattle'. He was no less zealous in following up and prosecuting breaches of the Act.

**MARY WOLLSTONECRAFT** (1759-97), or Mrs Godwin as she became, was ahead of her time in her courageous championship of the rights of women. She was the child of an unhappy marriage. Her father was a gentleman-farmer who squandered his inheritance. Besides her mother, one of her two sisters and her close friend Fanny Blood (the first unhappily married, the second apparently kept on a string by a man who professed love but would not commit himself to marriage) exemplified for her the cruel lot of women under the man-made laws and conventions of society. Mary herself had to take work as a governess after trying to run a school at Newington Green with her married sister Eliza (Mrs Bishop, who had eventually run away from her husband). Her experience as governess of Lady Kingsborough's children in County Cork opened her eyes to Irish extremes of wealth and poverty. She visited peasants in their cabins, brooded upon her dependent status, read Rousseau and wrote an autobiographical novel, *Mary*. Joseph Johnson, the progressive publisher, who had already given her £10 for *Thoughts on the Education of Daughters*, accepted the novel and urged her to come to London and a literary life.

Miss Wollstonecraft reviewed books, translated, wrote articles, and sharpened her mind in Johnson's *salon* in St. Paul's Churchyard. With Paine, Godwin and the artist Fuseli for friends, she became an agnostic and a radical. Fuseli she loved in a demanding but Platonic fashion. 'If I thought my passion criminal', she wrote 'I would conquer it or die in the attempt.' Intellectual power and passionate feeling could find no synthesis in her hectic but essentially lonely life. In 1788 she wrote *Original Stories from Real Life*. In 1792, in response to Burke's *Reflections* and as a sequel to

*Mary Godwin née Wollstonecraft*
(Artist: John Opie)

her own *Rights of Man*, came an immediate success, *Vindication of the Rights of Women*. The book is long, its reasoning often cogent, but marred by an incoherent style, as if she were overcome by the strength of her feelings. Democracy was astir and events in America and France excited this sensitive, spirited woman, who craved independence, and male companionship on equal terms.

She wanted a proper education for women, believing that they would no longer 'degrade their characters with littleness, if they were led to respect themselves, if political and moral subjects were opened to them'. She advocated a freedom in morality which shocked people who were ready, nonetheless, to accept fashionable liaisons. She went to Paris, where she saw Louis XVI going to his execution, met revolutionary leaders, the Rolands, Brissot, and 'Citizen' Paine, and lived with an American, Gilbert Imlay, by whom she had a child, Fanny (May 1794). When he was unfaithful, she tried to drown herself. She found a brief happiness, however, with William Godwin, author of *Political Justice*, an admirer and suitable soul-mate. In Godwin's words, 'Friendship melted into love'. She married him in March 1797, but died in September of the same year at the birth of their daughter Mary, who was to be the second wife of the poet Shelley.

Claire Tomalin, *The Life and Death of Mary Wollstonecraft*, 1974.

**WILLIAM GODWIN** (1756-1836), political philosopher, was born in Wisbech, Cambridgeshire, where his father was a dissenting minister. He was nurtured upon an unquestioning faith of the narrowest sort. He read such books as *The Pious Deaths of many Godly Children*, accepted the Calvinist notions of sin and damnation, indeed pressed them upon his fellow school children, and acquired the habit of moral inculcation which never deserted him in his later and atheist life.

From school at Norwich he went to Hoxton Academy, where he stayed for five years, being taught principally by Dr. Kippis, the friend of Dr. Priestley. He was already imbued with the ideas of Sandeman, a Scottish divine who taught that political methods of reform were less effective than the dissemination of the spirit of Christ. Godwin's study of philosophy led him to doubt the existence of a God, but this did not prevent him from entering upon the ministry and for about five years he was pastor of a congregation at Stowmarket. Compromise was not in his nature. Calvinism, based rigidly upon predestination, passed easily into the worship of natural reason in that rationalist age. Priestley had moved in the same direction — only he stopped short at unitarianism. Godwin was humourless, sentimental and vain; literate and logical, but a child in experience of the world outside his books. 'All my amusements were sedentary; I had scarcely any pleasure but in reading.' From a scheme for starting a seminary at Epsom only the prospectus emerged. It was largely composed of excerpts from Rousseau and Holbach. 'The state of society' said Godwin, 'is incontestably artificial.' He told, in his autobiography, a story which is more revealing than if it had been told against him. As a boy he attended the Assizes and, feeling tired, he rested his elbow on the corner of the cushion placed before the judge, who 'laid his hand gently on my elbow and removed it. ... I recollect having silently remarked, if his lordship knew what the lad beside him will perhaps one day become. I am not so sure that he would have removed my elbow.' He was never sensitive to other people's susceptibilities. Crabb Robinson described him thus at a party (1815): 'Godwin was in high spirits, but hardly in good spirits. He laughs long and loud without occasion ... he is vehement and intolerant'.

Godwin's reputation was based on one work: *Political Justice*, written with great deliberation over a period of nearly two years and published in January 1793. In the same month Louis XVI was executed and England prepared to go to war with France. Godwin, who had until then written little of note, chose to meet the tide of reaction full on and his boldness brought him fame. Since the book cost three guineas there was little fear that the government would think it worth prosecuting him. Despite its avid reception by radicals, 'jacobins' and agnostics, it was revolutionary neither in argument nor tone. Indeed, what specially appealed to a man like Wordsworth was that it offered an alternative to revolution. Godwin appealed, with all the confidence of the age of the *philosophes*, to immutable principles of justice and reason, and he addressed himself to 'men of study and reflection'. His central argument is that man can advance to perfection by the gradual improvement of human surroundings and institutions. It rests upon the idea that the 'moral qualities of men are the produce of the impressions made upon them'. As obstacles to the expression of truth were removed, truth would prevail, by means of literature, education, and political justice, whose object was the general good. In Godwin's ideal society, 'private judgement was not a right but a duty': every man was therefore 'inquisitor-general' of the moral conduct of his neighbours. To a rational being in this situation there could be but one rule of conduct — justice; and but one way of ascertaining this rule — the exercise of the understanding. This conception of man as 'a being capable of justice, virtue and benevolence' is the best part of the book. So believing in human perfectibility, Godwin was able to remain an individualist. Even national education he rejected as being likely to produce too much uniformity of thought.

Godwin proclaims that men's characters are the product of circumstances; but as moralist and educator he is anxious to alter circumstances so as to produce the character he thinks proper. Following Holbach, Godwin holds that Nature bids men be sociable, peaceful and beneficent. Yet the institutions which men have fashioned are unnatural: if man wants to improve his lot, he must therefore act. Wordsworth moved on to a deeper conception of nature as 'feeling', the source of joy and man's tutor, if he would but listen. Wordsworthians therefore reject Godwin's ideas as poisonous nonsense. Professor Garrod hints at their first impact however, describing 'the spells by which that impossible Pretender — the *archimagus* of a metaphysic quackish beyond redemption — bound the most exalted spirits of the time'. Wordsworth reacted against Godwin with the violence of the convert. But it should be allowed that Godwin himself altered his ground: in the second edition of *Political Justice* (1795) he modified some extreme views.

Godwin was writing at the end of a tradition: he reflects the prevailing optimism of the Age of Reason in his notion of human perfectibility. He under-rates, perhaps, the complexity, the emotional, acquisitive, illogical character of man. He gave an appearance of logical and scientific precision to a work which was really based on human sentiment. Hazlitt, who made an independent study of Hartley and Helvetius and arrived at different principles from those of Godwin, described how at first he 'blazed as a sun in the firmament of reputation; no one was more talked of, more looked up to, more sought after, and wherever liberty, truth, justice was the theme, his name was not far off'. Twenty-five years afterwards, it was a different story: 'Now he has sunk below the horizon, and enjoys the serene twilight of a doubtful immortality.'

In 1797 he married Mary Wollstonecraft: she died in the same year on the birth of their daughter — the future Mrs Shelley. The difference between his novels, *Caleb Williams* (1794) and *St. Leon*

(1799), hint at the change wrought in him by this experience. The first is an exposition in terms of a personal conflict of the principles of *Political Justice*. In the preface to the second occurs this passage: 'I apprehend domestic and private affections inseparable from the nature of man, and from what may be called the culture of the heart'. Marguerite, the heroine of this novel, was an idealized portrait of Mary Wollstonecraft. In 1801, after several refusals from other ladies, Godwin married Mrs Clairmont, the widowed mother of Claire Clairmont who was to achieve notoriety as Byron's mistress. Neither his growing family, nor his literary pursuits now brought him much satisfaction. He wrote in several *genres*: history, children's stories, moralizing (*Thoughts on Man*, 1831), and essays that were published posthumously. He set up in book-selling and publishing but this did not prosper.

Godwin had been at the centre of a notable circle of writers and radical politicians. He had won acclaim as the defender of Horne Tooke, his friend Holcroft and others in the trials of 1794, when the feeling of triumph amongst the friends of liberty was universal. He had earned the respect at different times of men as different as Coleridge, Mackintosh, Parr and Lamb. Now he had become known as an insensitive, cantankerous hanger-on. He was a man to be avoided, with a habit of borrowing money which he could not repay. To Shelley he was a shamelessly demanding father-in-law. Solemn, short and stout, with a bald dome of a head, a reedy voice and an air of seeming half-asleep when he walked or even when he talked, he could seem a figure of pathos. Harriet Martineau, who met him in 1833, the year when he acquired the sinecure of Yeoman Usher of the Exchequer, looked on him as 'a curious monument of a bygone state of society'. Crabb Robinson recorded in his diary in April 1836: 'There died a few days ago another person who had a mighty influence on my early life — Godwin. I had lost all my personal respect for him. These are melancholy experiences in life. Godwin had no sense of *meum* and *tuum*.'

P. H. Marshall, *William Godwin*, 1984.

**SAMUEL BUTLER** (1774-1839) was headmaster of Shrewsbury from 1798 to 1836. In this time the school, from being a decayed country grammar school with a glorious past and some fine buildings, became in some respects the first of the 'reformed' public schools. When Butler was appointed to succeed Atcherley by the fellows of St. John's, Cambridge, the numbers had declined to about twenty. Butler had to struggle, against burgesses who wanted 'commercial education' for their sons, and boys who fought back against his new discipline. By his victory in the matter of the Albrighton tithe, after a marathon run in the law courts, he relieved the school's finances. By his inspired teaching he attracted pupils from all over the country. He was to be followed by two more exceptional men, his pupil Kennedy, and Moss, so that the school maintained its supremacy in scholarship among those leading public schools which were influential in church and state.

Since Butler personally taught all the boys in the fifth and sixth forms, numbering about a hundred, Shrewsbury's fame was essentially his. He was never quite a national figure, however, such as Arnold became. He was no prophet. Like his namesake, the eighteenth-century bishop, he mistrusted 'enthusiasm' and thought impossible what Arnold was soon to achieve, the instilling of a spirit of spiritual earnestness through chapel services. He discouraged organized games and thought that football was 'only for butcher boys'. Butler did, however, take seriously the claims of moral education. He made lasting friendships with boys who appreciated his selfless and scholarly concern for excellence. He instilled a discipline that did not rest solely upon flogging — though this was the age of Eton's grim Dr. Keate, and of epic turbulence in public schools. Shrewsbury's 'praepostors' anticipated Arnold's 'prefects' in assuming responsibilities for discipline. Shrewsbury, like Eton and Winchester, had its mutiny. But the praepostors who led the walk-out in 1829 over the state of their pickled beef were reinstated.

A modern scholar has seen in Butler's methods a tendency to produce prizemen for whom the classics were no more than a graduated sequence of problems to be solved, rather than a great literature. Butler was accused of cramming — but not by the pupils who experienced his teaching. In his concentration on classical studies he was a man of his time — and of the foundation which he served. Moral lessons, the Greek and Roman virtues, geography and history were to be picked up incidentally from the study of texts. If the curriculum was narrow, Butler's methods and style were inspiring. He was a man of broad culture, a linguist, a fluent writer. He built up a fine library, wrote books on geography and compiled atlases. If his edition of Aeschylus was imperfect it was largely because he could not detach himself sufficiently from his teaching.

He was a conscientious archdeacon of Derby in his latter years at Shrewsbury; when he left the school to become Bishop of Lichfield, failing health did not deter him from working hard at his duties. But his fame depended primarily on his teaching. 'There is nothing in scholastic history which can be fairly compared with your career except that of Busby', wrote the Bishop of Gloucester. 'Everyone exclaims against your monopoly of university scholarships', wrote a pupil who had gained the Ireland. The headmaster of Harrow came down with one of his assistants to hear Butler teaching his form. The headmaster of Eton wrote inquiring about the details of his scheme of competitive examinations — 'the emulative system', as it was called, soon to become universal. Kennedy and Brancker won the Porson and Ireland prizes respectively while still at school. Shrewsbury boys dominated university prize, scholarship and first class lists in a way that cannot be explained by clever teaching alone; those boys carried with them from Shrewsbury what, in the words of Stephen Paget, was 'that inestimable blessing, the pride of scholarship'.

S. Butler, *Life and Letters of Samuel Butler*, 1896.

JOSEPH LANCASTER (1778-1838) was a pioneer in the field of elementary education at a time when the growth of population was not accompanied by any serious attempt by church or state to provide teaching facilities. Private enterprise had to supply the need. Whatever his faults, Lancaster was both enterprising and charitable. His father was a private soldier who served in the American War. Joseph was intended for the nonconformist ministry, but at fourteen he left home with the intention, it seems, of going 'to teach poor blacks the word of God'. Penniless at Bristol, he joined the navy; after one voyage he was released from his engagement by friends. He became a Quaker and began a little teaching at home.

In 1801 he opened a school in London, offering free education to those who could not afford his modest fee. To deal with the large numbers who came, since he could not afford to hire an assistant, he set senior boys to teach the junior ones under his supervision. He managed to instil a strong spirit of community and self-help. The instruction was necessarily simple: reading, writing and arithmetic were learned by drill. The children were given flat desks with layers of sand to write on; large letter sheets and printed passages of the Bible were their only aids. There were elaborate punishments on the principle that it was better to shame than to pain. Boys were suspended in cages and tied to pillars; they were also encouraged by orders of merit and systematic promotion, while promising scholars were prepared for teaching.

The Quaker found himself famous. Visitors were impressed by the discipline of an establishment of almost a thousand, where a child could be taught for an estimated cost of seven shillings a year. At an audience at Weymouth in 1805 George III told Lancaster that it was his wish 'that every poor child in my dominions should be taught to read the Bible'. The religious argument could also be used against Lancaster. To opponents like the formidable Mrs Trimmer it was the main fault of his system that it was not subject to church control.

Andrew Bell, founder of the 'Madras system' of teaching, became his relentless opponent and with the formation of rival societies a feud developed which enlisted support from nonconformists, radicals and whigs on Lancaster's side, Tories and church establishment on Bell's. Brougham saw in Lancaster a leader in the 'march of mind'; Southey admitted that great good had been done, but only in the way that 'the devil has been the cause of Redemption'. Lancaster was copied. In 1810 he claimed to have promoted fifty schools for 14,200 children. The more extravagant his claims, the more unpractical he became about ways and means. In 1808 Fox and Allen, Quaker philanthropists, came to the rescue of his school and the Royal Lancastrian Society was set up with a board of trustees. Lancaster claimed that he was being over-ruled by the trustees and seceded from his own movement: he set up a school at Tooting, which soon failed.

Thereafter his life was spent in travelling, pontificating about his methods and quarrelling with those who disagreed with him. He was imprisoned for debt and his wife went out of her mind. He found listeners and imitators in the United States, Canada and Venezuela. He wrote pamphlets obsessively and self-pityingly, in the way of a frenzied pedagogue, with plentiful use of italics, capitals and irrelevant biblical quotations. 'Be assured that the fire which kindled Elijah's sacrifice has kindled mine', he wrote. Wherever he was, even when he was alone, he would keep his Quaker Sunday morning of silence and 'waiting on the spirit'. In October 1838 he died of injuries received in a street accident in New York. We should look away from the forlorn end to the earlier achievement. His intentions had been unselfish, his method both original and, within its limits, effective. He had done much to reveal the need and had pointed to ways in which it could be met.

D. Salmon, *Joseph Lancaster*, 1904.

RICHMAL MANGNALL (1769-1820) was the author of *Questions*. Hers was a name of power in the nineteenth century schoolroom. Her little book, privately printed in 1800, then taken up by the shrewd firm of Longman, had appeared by 1857 in 84 editions. It was the stand-by of generations of governesses and other teachers, especially in girls' schools like that at Crofton Hall, where Miss Mangnall was for many years headmistress. The confident style of the answers, expressing truths assumed to be beyond questioning, evokes the spirit of the Enlightenment. Judgements are level, plain, humane. Opinions presented as facts are an easy target for a scientific age. Miss Mangnall would not have liked later tendencies to doubt, to qualify, 'to be fair'. Fairness for this high-minded lady was to give to child and teacher the gist of current knowledge and the best of her understanding, patriotic, protestant and humane. She believed in 'the superior excellence' of the British constitution. She was also proud of her country's claim to have 'struck off the chains that galled the African slave'. In praise or censure she sought to improve the occasion. So the duke of Wellington 'rebuked by his conduct restless vanity, and reprimanded the morbid sensibility of irregular egotism.' The works of Rabelais, 'a Frenchman', were 'greatly deficient in that delicacy without which genius may sparkle for a moment, but can never shine with pure, undiminished lustre.'

Pupils may have wished to know more about 'the abominable Sylla'. They may not have cared 'Whence are cocoa-nuts procured?', nor shared Miss Mangnall's liking for classification games: 'Name the four most ambitious men in Rome'. Her name, and her questions, may have been hateful to them. The answers still had to be learned. Looking at the Victorian age we seek cultural influences among the great, a Coleridge, a Carlyle. We should not forget Miss Mangnall.

**RICHARD PORSON** (1759-1808), classical scholar, was born on Christmas Day at the Norfolk village of Ruston and was educated at the village schools of Bacton and Happisburgh. His father, an intelligent man, was parish clerk, but it was a curate, Mr Hewitt, who gave the boy a grounding, and a neighbouring squire, Mr Norris, who got him a place in College at Eton. Some friends of Norris (who died in 1777) provided for him to go to Trinity, Cambridge, where he won the Craven and First Chancellor's medal and became a Fellow of the college. At Cambridge Porson showed that his friends' enlightened trust was justified, for he displayed a powerful mind, prodigious memory and an acuteness of judgement that made him a formidable critic. He contributed to reviews and magazines and acquired a name for caustic truthfulness, wit and penetration. He had scruples about orthodox belief which are sometimes found amongst men who are passionately concerned with the validity of texts, and he would not follow the usual academic path of ordination. He therefore lost his Fellowship in 1792, but was provided by friends with a small annuity and was also made Professor of Greek, at £40 a year. In 1796 he married a widow, but she died within a few months. He then lived in chambers in Essex Court in the Temple.

Porson's accomplished work was less than his reputation for learning would suggest, but everything he did was of the highest quality. Restricted somewhat in imagination, he was unequalled in judgement and his critical emendations were based on solid reading and thought. His favourite tragedian was Euripides. He hoped to be remembered as 'one who had done a good deal for the text of Euripides' and his editions of *Hecuba*, *Orestes*, *Phoenissae* and *Medea* justify his ambition. He also collated the Harleian manuscript of the *Odyssey* for the Oxford Homer. Like A. E. Housman, whose character and work recalls traits of Porson, he did not confine himself to academic studies. His *Letters to Travis* in which he belaboured an unfortunate clergyman who had criticized Gibbon, and a letter in the *Morning Chronicle*, in which he made fun of Ireland's forgeries on Shakespeare, show the delight he took in exposing what he took to be fraud. His mordant wit, and his puns, often in Greek, have a place in scholarly legend. He was often unwashed and unkempt, frequently rude and neglectful of ordinary civilities, and seldom wrote letters, even to foreign scholars who corresponded hopefully with him. He developed a famous thirst, but it may be that he drank to overcome the distress of chronic asthma and insomnia. His uncompromising honesty was perhaps his most attractive feature. 'He had no equal', wrote a fellow scholar, 'in the most pure and inflexible love of truth'. It would have pleased him to know that he would be buried near to Bentley, in the antechapel of Trinity.

J. E. Sandys, *History of Classical Scholarship*, 1903-8.

**WILLIAM BECKFORD** (1759-1844) enjoyed a very long and very odd life. Students of the Gothic revival, however, find in his career more than eccentric passing interest. The son of William Beckford, the London merchant and friend of Pitt, he inherited an enormous fortune: no unmixed blessing, as his neurotic life was to show. After the death of his father, Beckford was educated by a private tutor. Dr. Lettice was attentive, but he could do little to control his precocious and wilful charge. He was taught music by Mozart. Lord Chatham took a benign interest. 'All air and fire' he called him. At seventeen he showed his ability in his *History of Extraordinary Painters*, an elaborate satire upon the biographies in *Vies des Peintres Flamands*. He did not attend a university since his mother disapproved of them. He went instead to Geneva; then travelled extensively in Europe.

In 1781 he wrote *Vathek*, in French, at a single sitting of three days and two nights. An anonymous translation presented the work to English readers (apparently without Beckford's leave) before the original appeared in Geneva in 1787. It is an Arabian tale, of great splendour and imaginative force. In 1783 Beckford married Lady Margaret Gordon, daughter of the Earl of Aboyne; he lived with her in Switzerland until her death in 1786, and they had two daughters. Beckford therefore missed three things that could have helped or restrained him: a public school, a university and a lasting marriage. He was abroad for most of the next few years, managed to be on hand at the destruction of the Bastille, went to Lausanne, where he bought Gibbon's library, and retired into hermit-like seclusion in order to read its contents. In Portugal he wrote his famous accounts of Batalha and Alcobaca and their exuberant Gothic.

Between 1784 and 1794 he had been a member of Parliament. He retired in the latter year, but was re-elected, for Hindon, in 1806 and sat until 1820. There can hardly have been a more scandalously indolent member. In 1796 he settled at his father's house at Fonthill Giffard and embarked upon the architectural extravaganza which brought him more fame than any of his writings. As a boy Beckford had disliked his father's house. He wanted something more in tune with his own romantic temperament. So he commissioned Wyatt to create a ruined monastery — with some habitable rooms! His appetite grew with the feeding and to Wyatt's elegant design was added a great wing and an octagon tower. The tower fell down in 1800 but was rebuilt. In 1807 Beckford decided to live there, sheltered from the common view by eight miles of high estate walls. The building was spectacularly inconvenient: the tower was 276 feet high, the hall 120 feet high. The long projecting wings were more suited to the cells of the imaginary monks than to the apartments of an eighteenth-century gentleman. The building was not so much Gothic as an eighteenth-century body in medieval clothes.

Beckford's cathedral of follies, together with the mysterious character of its owner, created a legend. Here was indeed the romantic quality of the sublime. The house was built fast to meet Beckford's frenzied schedule; communities of workmen camped around the site, five or six hundred; the work went on through winter nights by the light of huge bonfires. The house cost a quarter of a million pounds. Wyatt did not supervise the work properly, the contractors were fraudulent. After Beckford had sold the place to Mr John Farquhar he was called to the death-bed of the man who had been clerk of the works, who confessed that the solid foundations for the tower, though paid for, had not been provided. One night in 1825 the tower subsided; there is now little trace of the giant structure.

Beckford disclaimed any influence in the movement of Gothic revival. 'I have enough sins', he said, 'without having that laid to my charge.' He commissioned innumerable purchases but he was not unusually interested in medieval art. When his collection was sold by Farquhar, the sale lasted thirty-seven days. 'Mr Beckford has undoubtedly shown himself an industrious *bijoutier*, a prodigious virtuoso, an accomplished patron of unproductive labour, an enthusiastic collector of expensive trifles', wrote Hazlitt. But the best of the books and pictures were removed to Lansdowne Terrace, Bath, where Beckford constructed a miniature Fonthill, this time in the classical style. He went on collecting avidly, 'all agog, all ardour, all intrepidity' as he wrote. In 1836 he re-published the letters which he had deliberately suppressed in 1783: they showed him a talented word-painter, a virtuoso of the picturesque. Those who penetrated his seclusion found a kind and courteous old gentleman. He was kind to dependents and animals. He was less misanthropic than egotistic, with a streak of megalomania. That his wealth, especially his West Indian plantations, implied any social responsibility did not, apparently, occur to him.

H. A. N. Brockman, *The Caliph of Fonthill*, 1956.

**HENRY HALLAM** (1777-1859), historian, provided, in the most magisterial of his works, an account of the development of the constitution which was not seriously challenged until the publication of Stubbs' *Constitutional History* in 1873-8. His father was a canon of Windsor and Dean of Bristol. After Eton he went to Christ Church, Oxford; thence to the bar. With sufficient private money he devoted himself to literary pursuits. In 1805 he began to write for the *Edinburgh Review*. His family tradition was Whig; so were his political sympathies and most influential friends. His history was unequivocally Whig, marked by confidence in the possession of the past and in understanding of the present. 'It is a generous pride that entwines the consciousness of hereditary freedom with the memory of our ancestors'.

Hallam's ambition was high, his range wide, his research deep. He was over forty when he published *A View of the State of Europe during the Middle Ages* (1818). He returned to Europe in his last work, *The Introduction to the Literature of Europe in the Fifteenth, Sixteenth and Seventeenth Centuries* (1837-9). Most important, however, was *The Constitutional History of England from Henry VII to George II* (1827). It would one day be regarded as the hallmark of the true historian that, as Lord Acton wrote of

Stubbs, he 'never lets us know what he thinks of anything but the matter before him'. In Hallam's day the duty of the historian was, in the language of Macaulay, the impression of 'general truths' upon his readers as to the art of government and the progress of society. History was the handmaid of politics and lived in current debate. The seventeenth century, wrote Hallam, 'was the period from which the factions of modern times trace their divergence, which still calls forth the warm emotions of party spirit, and affords a test of political principles'. It is that spirit of engagement that makes Macaulay, politician as well as historian, so stirring — and unreliable. Significantly, it was Macaulay, reviewing Hallam, who described the Constitutional History as 'the most impartial work we have read'. For where Macaulay was advocate, Hallam was judge. Examining the tenets of the two great parties he observed: 'It is one thing to prefer the Whig principles, another to justify ... the party which bore that name'. In that spirit he pondered, in a famous passage, 'whether a thoroughly upright and enlightened man would rather have listed under the royal or the parliamentary standard'.

Hallam married, in 1807, a Miss Elton of Clevedon. By 1840, when she died, eleven children had been born. Only four survived early life. On one son, Arthur, were fixed specially high hopes. His sudden death, in 1831, inspired Tennyson's poem *In Memoriam*: to the parents, and to Emily, the poet's sister, whom Arthur hoped to marry, it was a shattering blow. Bereavement was a recurring theme; grief a bitter private counterpoint to the lofty music of his writing.

Accurate and thorough, Hallam's style boasted of few adornments or special effects; indeed it could be called dry, even ponderous; the drama is in the story; the emotion in its message, its robust certainties echoing the *ex cathedra* style of his conversation. J. W. Burrow sees 'an almost liturgical solemnity about his periodic acts of thanksgiving for English history'. Especially Hallam celebrated the gift, under 'gracious providence', of a unique kind of liberty grounded in the common law, 'gradually wrought by the plastic influence of civil rights'. It was 'the destined means' by which his country had come to enjoy its uniquely successful parliamentary regime.

J. W. Burrow, *A Liberal Descent*, 1981.

WILLIAM PALEY (1743-1805), archdeacon of Carlisle, was the author of textbooks upon moral and religious subjects which so successfully defined the thinking of the time that he influenced a generation — the last generation of the age which has been described (by Whitehead) as 'an age of reason based on faith', and the last which was prepared to take seriously books which 'proved Christianity to be true'. His *Principles of Morals and Political Philosophy* (1785) was adopted as a textbook at Cambridge and went through fifteen editions in the author's lifetime; it provoked Bentham, to write his celebrated *Principles of Morals and Legislation*. Frankly utilitarian, lucid in exposition and edifying in tone, Paley served a readership which wanted to be reassured. *Evidences of Christianity* (1794), his best known book, countered the shocks of revolution with the quiet arguments of the eighteenth-century divine for whom God was not mysterious, for whom the consequences of men's actions provided the safest test of virtue. He defined virtue as 'doing good to mankind in obedience to the will of God and for the sake of everlasting happiness'. Some of his adherents, like Jebb, became unitarian. Paley remained orthodox, saying, when urged to support a move for the relaxation of the terms of a clergyman's subscription to the Thirty-Nine Articles, that 'he could not afford to keep a conscience' and on another occasion that the Articles were merely 'articles of peace'; they contained 'about 240 distinct propositions, many of them inconsistent with each other' so that no one could expect any man to believe all.

Paley was the son of the headmaster of Giggleswick: the family had been settled in the neighbourhood for many generations. His father had the highest opinion of his talents: 'He has by far the clearest head I ever met with in my life', and William never lacked confidence, though he was a clumsy fellow and cut an odd figure at Cambridge — absent-minded, liable to fall off his horse or lose his notes. He was laughed at when he recited a prize essay in the Senate House. He never lost his strong Yorkshire accent, but he became a popular lecturer when he became a fellow of his college, Christ's, in 1768. He did much to raise the standard of tuition: indeed, he presents a pleasant picture of the friendly young don, an intellectual all-rounder, interested in his pupils and more conscientious than his somewhat cynical utterances might suggest. He was less at home, perhaps, in the country living that he accepted after his marriage to Jane Hewitt (1775). He divided his time between his parishes (he usually had two), his public interests (he was an early opponent of the slave trade) and his writing. *Reasons for Contentment* was the title of one of his more complacent books (1792). He had good reasons. Preferment came steadily to him as his services as defender of the establishment became recognized. In 1795 he became rector of Bishop Wearmouth, worth £1,200 a year — an immense sum for those days. He had eight children by his first wife. He married again, four years after her death, in 1795. Latterly he grew very stout.

Paley was exceedingly fond of fishing, but most of his time was given to writing and he was always jotting down stray thoughts, until his notebooks became a 'confused, incoherent and blotted mass'. His thinking was plain enough, however, and his style was warmly praised by Pitt, whose judgement we may respect. As to his religious teaching there must be reservations. It was a short step from this Christian utilitarian to James Mill, who excluded orthodox religion from serious thought, and to evangelicals who excluded thought from religion. Perhaps, as Coleridge said: 'belief in God could not be intellectually more evident, without becoming morally less effective'.

**WILLIAM CAREY** (1761-1834), missionary, was born at Moulton in Northamptonshire and was apprenticed shoemaker to Thomas Gotch. When he was not cobbling he studied languages, Greek, Hebrew, French and Dutch, in order to become a Baptist pastor and schoolmaster. His employer learned of his desire to be a missionary and gave him money to complete his studies. He encountered apathy among his fellow-Baptists, but he gradually built up support for a missionary society to work in Asia and Africa. In 1792 the Society began with an income of £13.12. When William insisted upon going to India with his wife and four children, his own father thought him mad. He was treated coldly by the East India Company in Bengal, which was anxious to avoid any cause of friction, but Carey mastered Bengali and made a start.

For a time he had to make his living by working as foreman in an indigo factory. After five years he moved to Serampore, where he was welcomed by the Danish authorities. His college there became the centre of 26 vernacular schools; his printing house-produced the Bible in many tongues, including Chinese. In 1801, recognized now as an authority on Indian languages, he was appointed professor at the newly-founded Fort William College; characteristically he gave his salary to found a mission at Calcutta. He brought out a grammar in native tongues, started India's first newspaper, the *Friends of India*, and campaigned against superstition, widow-burning and infant sacrifice. He died in 1834, after repeated attacks of fever.

A self-effacing man, a Christian of the finest mettle, Carey has few rivals for devoted scholarship under arduous conditions and for personal witness in the face of ignorance and scorn. 'If a tinker is a devout man he is infallibly sent off for the East, benefiting us more by his absence than the Hindus by his advice' was Sidney Smith's scathing comment on the work of the Baptist missionaries in Bengal. From the complacency of the pluralist of St. Paul's we may turn with admiration to the simple, active faith of Carey and those who followed in his steps.

S. Pearce, *William Carey, D.D.,* 1926

**CHARLES SIMEON** (1759-1836), was one of the most influential evangelical churchmen of his day. His territory was a small one. In all his life he was but Fellow of King's, and Vicar of Holy Trinity, Cambridge which became a mission centre for the conversion of Englishmen to the Evangelical idea: intense belief in the saving force of the Gospel, in the necessity of personal conversion. The moral earnestness, the ordered lives of men who lived hourly under 'the great taskmaster's eye', the prayerful, regulated charity of the men who came under Simeon's spell, were to have a bracing effect upon English society.

Simeon's was only one voice among several. But his own standing and personality, the consistency of his preaching over a period of fifty-three years at Holy Trinity, the strategic importance of Cambridge, home of an earlier reformation, all contributed to his unique fame. His sermons are almost unreadable today, his church was sometimes the scene of crude riots, his efforts met with apathy and hostility. His style would seem odd to us and lent itself, in lesser imitators, to caricature. 'Mama, what is the gentleman in a passion about?' said the small girl who was taken to hear him. Not many of his disciples could obtain preferment, for Low

Church and 'High and Dry' alike mistrusted their zeal. Bishop Marsh of Peterborough even invented a 'trap', eighty-seven carefully worded questions, for all who sought a living in his diocese. They could usually hope to impart their message only through proprietary chapels and afternoon lectures. But they won disciples and touched the moral life of the nation at every point.

'The deepest and most fervid religion in England', said Liddon, 'during the first three decades of this century was that of the Evangelicals.' Some of the best of these, like Henry Martyn, 'the pious chaplain', and Daniel Corrie, first bishop of Madras, acknowledged Simeon to be their inspiration and accepted his guidance. Simeon founded a trust to secure benefices for evangelicals and helped to found the Church Missionary Society. Without his preaching and example evangelical religion might not have been the force it was inside the framework of the Church of England.

H. C. G. Moule, *Charles Simeon*, 1948.

**THOMAS CHARLES** (1756-1814) was perhaps the most important of that devoted group of men who sought to bring learning and religion to the inhabitants of 'Wild Wales'. Though John Wesley declared once that the Welsh were as ignorant of the Gospel as Cherokee Indians, he commented too on the religious instincts of the people. In 1721, in his melancholy description of the state of the diocese of St. Davids, Erasmus Sanders had described 'the extraordinary disposition of the Welsh peasants to religion'. Unfortunately the ministrations of the established church fell far short of the needs of the people. The church needed the leadership of 'men of piety and intellect, prepared to spend their energies in the religious and administrative reform of their sees'. Such, with rare exceptions it was denied. 'Throughout the century it suffered from an alien and non-resident episcopate' (M. G. Jones).

Charles, the son of a Carmarthenshire farmer, a student at Llanddowror school and at Jesus College, Oxford, ordained in 1778, could find no scope in this church. As he wrote, he was 'turned out of three churches in this country without prospect of another'. After some wrestling with his conscience he became minister of a congregation of Calvinistic Methodists at Bala

(1784). The year before, he had married the daughter of a wealthy tradesman and settled in that grey Merionethshire town by its famous lake. Nowhere else did Methodism spread so rapidly as in Wales. In this movement education played an essential part. Charles had much to build on. Griffith Jones, also of Llanddowror, had inspired the establishment of local schools and the preparation and distribution of a Welsh bible. Howell Harris, Daniel Rowland and Howell Davies, Methodist leaders in Wales, looked to these schools as the means by which they could bring about the spiritual regeneration of the people.

Charles made long preaching journeys across Wales; his sermons were practical, like all his evangelical work. In 1785 he started training the teachers himself for the work of instructing village children in the Welsh Bible; when enough had been learned in these 'circulating schools' the teachers passed on to the next village. In the next decade great assemblies were held of representatives from local Sunday schools, so large, wrote Charles, that no building could accommodate them. His output of writing was prodigious. A Welsh catechism and a quarterly religious magazine were among his more important efforts. In 1802, in London, he contributed to the genesis of the British and Foreign Bible Society. It has now published the Bible in 283 languages: its first venture was 20,000 Welsh Bibles. In 1803 a press was set up at Bala under his auspices for Welsh religious writing; by his death fifty-five books had been published. In 1805 he began publication of his *Spiritual Dictionary* which was, 'next to the Bible', according to his biographer, 'the best book in the Welsh language'.

Charles maintained close links with the Calvinistic Methodists of England and made regular visits to London to confer with leaders of the 'serious clergy' and to preach in Lady Huntingdon's Spa Fields Chapel. He was a disciple of Whitefield but tolerant towards Wesleyan Methodists. He was repudiated by Anglicans but he tried to preserve essential links: he was careful to use the Anglican liturgy while, for Holy Communion, Calvinistic Methodists still had recourse to their parish churches. 'Our intention is not to create a schism, a sect or a party, no in the name of God', he declared. Heavy fines, under the Conventicle Act forced them, however, to seek the benefits of the Toleration Act by registering their chapels for nonconformist worship. In 1801 the first definite constitution of the Welsh Methodists had been drawn up.

Ten years later Charles at last consented to the ordination of lay preachers. Separation had come at last.

The vast concourse at Charles's funeral at Llanyeil church mourned the man who had given his life to the ideal of a godly and literate people. There was a severe side: he could not bear to be in the same room as a harpist. In general character, however, he was a fine exemplar of the virtues he preached.

M. G. Jones, *The Charity School Movement*, 1938.

**WILLIAM GRANT BROUGHTON** (1782-1853), missionary, was for a time Bishop of the whole of Australasia. From King's School Canterbury he went for a time to be clerk in the Treasury. A vocation for Christian ministry led to his going to Cambridge and to ordination; the interest of the Duke of Wellington sent him to Australia. The duke offered him the archdeaconry of New South Wales. Observing Broughton's hesitation, he was brisk: 'If in my profession, indeed, a man is desired to go tomorrow morning to the other side of the world, it is better he should go tomorrow, or not at all.'

Broughton's area of jurisdiction was vast, in effect all Australia and Tasmania, with New Zealand; his means of transport primitive. He tried to visit each settlement and encouraged settlers to found churches and schools. He came home in 1835, persuaded his superiors that more was needed, and was consecrated Bishop of Australia. That still included New Zealand until the appointment of Selwyn as its bishop. In 1848 he changed his title to that of Bishop of Sydney and was given metropolitan authority over new bishoprics, Adelaide, Melbourne and Newcastle, as well as those of Tasmania and New Zealand.

In 1850 the bishops resolved to work for the conversion of the aborigines and planned missions among the Pacific Islands. To promote this work Broughton returned to England by a little tried route, across the Pacific and over the Isthmus of Panama. His ship, the La Plata, had an outbreak of fever. Broughton administered to the dying and remained till the last invalids could leave the ship. His health suffered and he died before he could return to Australia. His bones lie in Canterbury Cathedral, mother church of the world wide Anglican communion of which he was such a potent pioneer.

THOMAS CHALMERS (1780-1847), Presbyterian minister and philanthropist was the leader of the movement which led to the disruption of the kirk. He was the son of John Chalmers, shopkeeper and provost of Anstruther. He was educated at the burgh school and went on at the age of twelve to wear the scarlet gown of a student at St Andrews. He was a big, rough fellow, lively-minded rather than industrious, attracted at first to the sciences. His parents were both strict Calvinists but he was a liberal; as such he could find a congenial home in the kirk, dominated as it then was by the Moderates. At best the Moderate party in the General Assembly represented the rational, humane spirit of Principal William Robertson of Edinburgh University. Later, however, under Principal Hill of St Andrews, Moderation took the conservative, oligarchical path of all Scottish institutions in the wartime period, 'becoming little more than the Dundas interest at prayer, with nepotism and pluralism the main order of service' (Ferguson).

Chalmers became a licentiate in 1799, visited England and preached his first sermon at Wigan. He combined studies and teaching at St. Andrews with the ministry of Kilmany in Fife for twelve years. He studied political economy, wrote an *Enquiry into the Extent and Stability of National Resources* and an article on 'Christianity' for the *Edinburgh Encyclopaedia*. The effort of re-appraisal and emotional shocks combined to transform the man and his vocation. He made a happy marriage (1812) but his brother and sister died and he was severely ill: he emerged with a burning evangelical conviction. With Chalmers there were no half-measures. In 1815 he left his douce Fifeshire village for the Tron church at Glasgow. He had already shaken the Assembly by his eloquence. He now applied to parish work his new-found inspiration. In this city, crammed with immigrants, prosperous in the war years, afflicted by the post-war depression, he attacked pauperism, organised bands of helpers and raised private funds for relief.

In 1823 Chalmers was appointed to the chair of Moral Philo-sophy at St. Andrews. His interests were pastoral rather than academic and 'he was a lecturer, rather ardent than exact' (Cockburn). His lectures always began with a prayer. While at St. Andrews he completed his book, *The Christian and Civic economy of large towns*. In 1828 he became Professor of

Theology at Edinburgh, a post which he held until the Disruption in 1843. He was unsympathetic towards a university without a religious basis. He was in many ways a traditionalist. He had a 'moral loathing for they Whigs' and stoutly opposed the Reform Bill. He did, however, want to reform the Church of Scotland, especially to secure a system by which zealous ministers would be appointed in preference to 'safe men' and political time-servers. The crucial issue was patronage.

In 1834 the reforming party secured the right of a congregation to exclude by a majority vote a candidate who was thought to be unsuitable. A majority of the judges in the Court of Session held that such exclusion was illegal. Lord Aberdeen was prepared, in 1841, to introduce a bill giving the presbytery the right to decide upon objections made to a nominee. But attitudes hardened as another bitterly fought test case divided Scotland. The Assembly declared that Parliament had no jurisdiction over the kirk. After further efforts at compromise the government rejected the Assembly's final demands. So reformers became seceders. On 24th May, 1843, 474 ministers left the established church of Scotland and formed the Free Church of Scotland. Within four years of the disruption they had raised over a million pounds and built 654 churches.

In controversy, challenge and sacrifice Chalmers had led the way. He had dreamed of a moral union of church and state; instead he had seen the church in civil chains. He gave to secession not the bitter resignation of defeated men but the creative zeal of a missionary movement. In due course the Established Church was to gain the same freedom as his own. No doubt then, had he been alive, he would have voted for reunion. Circumstances alone made him schismatic; there was no doctrinal difference between the churches. He continued to the end preaching the gospel and ministering to the poor. He became Principal and Divinity Professor of the 'New College' at Edinburgh and he took charge at the same time of a Free Church district in West Port, the poorest quarter of the town.

Cockburn said that he had 'an unusual plainness of Scotch accent' but that he fired men by 'his eloquent imagination and terrible energy'. Jeffrey's account gives some idea of his hold even over intelligent men, used to critical analysis. 'He buried his adversaries under the fragments of burning mountains.' In private life he was simple, affectionate and unspoiled. He never succumbed to the megalomania that often affects great prophets and leaders.

W. G. Blaikie, *Life of Thomas Chalmers,* 1897.

REGINALD HEBER (1783-1826), was a talented writer of verse, hymns and sermons, and a devoted parish priest who left his peaceful Shropshire living to become Bishop of Calcutta. He was a great admirer of Jeremy Taylor, the Caroline priest, poet and author of *Holy Living and Holy Dying*, works which, in Heber's view, with *The Worthy Communicant*, offer 'a complete summary of the duties, and specimen of the devotions, of a Christian'. Heber wrote the life of Taylor: in his own thought and life, rational, courteous, imaginatively devout, he was for his age what Taylor was for the seventeenth century. He well represents the continuity and vitality of the Anglican spirit in a period when the church was generally dull in leadership and lax in example.

He was the son of Reginald Heber, squire and rector of Hodnet, and of Mary Allanson. His half-brother (by his father's first marriage) was Richard Heber, the famous collector of books. Reginald was educated at Whitchurch grammar school and at a private school at Neasden. A cultivated background, good tuition and a scholar's mind combined to make an exceptional undergraduate. At Brasenose College, Oxford, he won Latin verse and English essay prizes, while his prize poem, *Palestine*, was a sensation in its year and survived to be a Victorian favourite. In 1805 he set out, with his friend John Thornton, on an unusual tour of those parts of the Continent still open to wartime Englishmen: Scandinavia, Russia (including the Crimea), Austria and Saxony. His journal gives a vivid account of his two-year odyssey.

On return, in 1807, Heber took orders and the family living of Hodnet. About this time he made friends with Wilberforce and other 'saints' of the evangelical party, but he never tied himself to any party in the Church. He seemed to be content with pastoral work in north Shropshire; he was a model priest, increased the number of services, improved the singing, founded schools for the poor, visited and laboured to instruct his simple people. He was uneasy, however, in his dual position, 'half-parson and half-squire'. He suffered somewhat from the incursions of Richard and Rowland Hill, his evangelical neighbours. In 1807 he married Amelia Shipley, daughter of the Dean of St. Asaph; he became prebendary of St. Asaph in 1812, was Bampton Lecturer in 1815 and preacher in Lincoln's Inn in 1822. He contributed fairly regularly to the *Quarterly Review*. He wrote hymns including 'Holy, Holy, Holy', most magnificent of the Trinity hymns, and the equally familiar 'From Greenland's Icy Mountains'.

In 1822 his college friend Williams-Wynn, president of the India Board, persuaded Heber to become Bishop of Calcutta. The diocese was vast, missionary activity had been unsystematic and largely carried out by dissenters. Heber made it the concern of the church; he travelled adventurously, often out of British territory; he preached, confirmed and arbitrated in the inevitable disputes between missionaries of different persuasions. His Indian journal, published in 1828 after his death, is a quarry for historians of British India. He noted with impartial eye how the people lived, and how the British ruled them. 'The bishop is amiable and acutely intelligent, a strange figure in a land still fierce and turbulent, through which he moves with unruffled courage and an invincible determination to keep his engagements. He moved into the wildest country with the observant tolerance he would have shown to "scenes of Cranford in the village hall".' (Philip Woodruff). He died suddenly in early spring 1826, after a heavy programme of visiting and confirming. He had no son, but the Heber link with Hodnet survived through his sister, who married Algernon Percy, son of the Bishop of Carlisle: he added the honoured name of Heber.

**WILLIAM HOWLEY** (1766-1848) was a Wykehamist and scholar of New College, a clergyman's son who became Bishop of London and Archbishop of Canterbury at a time when the church and her bishops incurred widespread unpopularity. Archbishop Howley opposed Catholic Emancipation and the Reform Bill. He guarded the church's privileged place in education and he proposed but modest reforms in church administration when critics, whether earnest evangelicals or radical outsiders alike, were exposing grave abuses and pastoral neglect. He maintained antique state at Lambeth and he wore his episcopal wig to the last, an eighteenth century survival, it might seem, in a new and unfriendly world.

Yet he was a good man and bishop, who earned the respect and admiration of fellow-churchmen for qualities of mind and character which triumphed over a doddery appearance and a feebleness in speech and sermon that verged on the absurd. Before he went to London in 1813 (he was translated to Canterbury in 1828) he had been Regius Professor at Oxford and he groped for words with a theologian's concern for precise truth. Sometimes the opposite effect was achieved. He contrived to convey in the House of Lords, speaking about George IV's plan to divorce his wife, that the king could do no wrong, morally or constitutionally — even if he misbehaved to his wife! He was putting up a proposition only to disavow it — but it was the proposition that men remembered. He was unlucky in his dealings with George IV, an embarrassing head of the church for any primate to handle, let alone the tactless Howley. When the king complained of muddles in the coronation ceremony, Howley at once assured him that he would see that all went smoothly next time! Has any bishop ever addressed a girls' school as Howley, when, on one occasion, stumbling after suitable words of introduction, he began: 'My dear young friends — my dear girls — my dear young catechumens — my dear Christian friends — my dear young female women'?

'A very ordinary man', said Greville of Howley. Short, slight, frail in appearance, he did not look the part of defender of the faith. In some ways, however, he was an extraordinary man. After his long primacy, when the evangelical, Sumner, was archbishop, churchmen of the high and centre persuasions sighed for Howley's mild and sensible leadership. His mind was clear, his will strong. He was tried by sorrow He had five children: of the two boys, one died at six, the other, the elder, in January 1833, at Lambeth just after he had come down from Oxford. He would not be deflected from what he held to be right. He was apparently untouched by the ceremony and grandeur that surrounded him. He lived to a great age, beloved by the queen who had at first disliked his timid manner. In the words of Professor Chadwick, 'The gentlest and wisest archbishop of the century died as he had lived, fading peaceably and unobtrusively to his grave'.

Owen Chadwick, *The Victorian Church*, part 1, 1966.

**SYDNEY SMITH** (1771-1845) was a country clergyman and liberal journalist, 'the Smith of Smiths' in Macaulay's words; 'a diner-out, a wit, and a popular favourite' in his own words. Smith's life and letters offer valuable insights into the Whig spirit of his day. His honourable sense of duty redeems the coolness of a reluctant clergyman; his kindness and common sense improves the complacent doctrines of the Whig.

Smith was born at Woodford, the son of Robert Smith, a handsome, clever but restless man; his mother was of Huguenot extraction, her father having been a wine merchant in Languedoc. Sydney was unhappy at Winchester, though he became Prefect of Hall, but found New College, Oxford, where he was successively scholar and fellow, more congenial. He wished to be called to the Bar, but lacking private means, he entered the church instead and accepted the curacy of Netheravon on the Salisbury Plain (1794). The isolation of the place depressed him but he worked hard for his poor parishioners and earned the friendship of a sympathetic squire, Michael Hicks Beach. As tutor to the squire's son he went to Edinburgh where, 'amidst odious smells, barbarous sounds, bad suppers, excellent hearts, and most enlightened and cultivated understandings' he found what he needed. To the wit, assurance but essential seriousness characteristic of the best minds of their society, the Scottish Whigs added an earnest desire for liberal reform. Their critics saw also intolerance and dogmatism. Indeed the impact of the French Revolution, the Scottish love of debate, and the personal and professional rivalries of the 'Athens of the North' all helped to put an edge on political argument. Out of this ferment was born the *Edinburgh Review* (1802) when Smith, Jeffrey and Brougham decided to give voice and coherence to liberal views. Its explicit objective was reform at a time when, as Smith later wrote, 'the Catholics were not emancipated, the game laws were horribly oppressive, steel traps and spring guns were set all over the country ... Lord Eldon and the Court of Chancery pressed heavily upon mankind ... the enormous wickedness of the slave trade was tolerated'.

Smith wrote for the *Edinburgh* for twenty-eight years. Upon subjects as diverse as the game laws, the abuses of colonial administration, the spirit of 'fanaticism' in the church, and the woes of Ireland, he compelled attention. Criticism was all the more effective when it was rendered with grace and irony.

The first paragraph, for example, of his article upon a report of the necessity for 'climbing boys' offers the reader the heart-warming picture of 'an excellent and well-arranged dinner ... the most pleasing occurrence, and a great triumph of civilised life'. We see 'the descending morsel and the enveloping sauce ... the rank, wealth, wit and beauty which surrounds the meats' and 'the smiling and sedulous host, proffering gusts and relishes — the exotic bottles — the embossed plate — the pleasant remarks — the handsome dresses ...'. The transition is abrupt. 'In the midst of all this who knows that the kitchen chimney caught fire half an hour before dinner — and that a poor little wretch, of six or seven years old, was put up in the midst of the flames to put it out?'

In 1800 Smith married Catherine Pybus; their match was to prove ideally happy. In 1803 they came south to London. Smith preached in fashionable chapels, lectured to appreciative audiences at the Royal Institution, and became a sought-after guest at dinners. Notably he was to be found at Holland House, the brilliant centre of Whig hospitality, where the memory of Charles James Fox was kept alive and his ideals and causes cherished for the day when a younger generation of Whigs could once more find means of expressing them in political reforms. Smith was devoted to Lady Holland, she, in her somewhat demanding fashion, to him. But he was not rich. He could not refuse the living of Foston-le-Clay which Lord Chancellor Erskine contrived to provide for him (1806).

The arrival of the celebrated wit and writer, 'fresh from London, not knowing a turnip from a carrot', at a Yorkshire village where there had been no resident clergyman for a hundred and fifty years, was quaint enough. What makes the story pleasant and touching is the way in which Smith took to the country life and gave himself to the people. He resolved 'not to smite the partridge; for if I fed the poor, and comforted the sick, and instructed the ignorant, yet I should be nothing worth if I smote the partridge'. He made it his practice to visit London for two months a year. He farmed two hundred acres at Foston, but continued to write. In 1807 the letters of 'Peter Plymley' attracted attention. Written ostensibly to his brother, a country parson, Plymley's vividly satirical letters exposed current views of Protestants towards Catholic Emancipation. Friends recognized Smith behind the pseudonym. Meanwhile he was starting allotments for the poor, befriending farmers and labourers and building himself a parsonage 'equal to any inn on the North Road'. His isolation gave him time to think. His contacts with humble folk enriched the humanity which seldom fails to shine through his most caustic writing. He confessed however to feeling lonely in the countryside. 'Flowers, green turf, and birds: they all afford slight gratification, but are not worth an hour of rational conversation; and rational conversation in sufficient quantities is only to be had from the congregation of some million people in one spot.' From Foston, in 1829, Smith moved to Combe Florey; he was already a canon of Bristol. In 1830 the Whigs gained office and Smith a canonry of St. Paul's. There he preached sound sermons and diffused a spirit of benevolence.

Smith's religion of common sense and kindness had its limitations. It is hard to admire his scornful attitude towards missions. One may look in vain for any understanding of the finer motives of the clerical enthusiasts, high and low, whom he professed to despise. But much may be forgiven a man who, when asked his opinion upon a plan for laying a wooden pavement around St. Paul's, observed, 'Let the Dean and Canons lay their heads together and the thing will be done'; or who said of Macaulay that he was like 'a book in breeches'. Greville said of Smith, on his death, 'he had the true religion of benevolence and charity'. Many of his friends must have hoped that he found his reward, 'eating pâtés de foie gras to the sound of trumpets' — for that, it was reported, was Smith's idea of heaven.

Ed. Nowell C. Smith, *The Letters of Sydney Smith*, 2 vols., 1953. Hesketh Pearson, *The Smith of Smiths*, 1934.


**FANNY BURNEY** (1752-1840) was the daughter of Dr. Charles Burney, musician and author of a celebrated history of music, by his first marriage; her mother was of Huguenot descent. Fanny was intelligent like her four sisters and two brothers, but timid, stoop-shouldered and short-sighted. Her family nickname was 'the Old Lady'; she stayed at home when the sisters went abroad to be educated and escaped without formal education. She encountered some of the best minds of the day, however, in her father's house: his parties were famous and he was popular. Dr. Johnson declared, when he went for a sea-voyage, that no vessel ever put forth with a greater load of good wishes than that which carried Burney. Fanny learned 'the pleasure of popping any thoughts down on paper' and acquired the artless style of an unencumbered mind.

Samuel Crisp, an old friend of her father's, encouraged her to write her journal in the most spontaneous way: 'Harken, you little monkey! Dash away whatever comes uppermost; if you stop to consider what you say, or what may be said of you, I will not give one fig for your letters'. Her diary and her letters provide revealing insight into the social life of her day, and they contain some memorable portraits. Her description of Dr. Johnson — to borrow the phrase of Katherine Mansfield, she 'took him in immensely' — complements Boswell by giving the woman's view. Very fine is her account of the opening day of Warren Hastings' trial. Still better known is her account of George III and court life at Windsor. She was offered, in 1786, the post of Lady-in-Waiting to the Queen, and entered upon a life of stultifying routines and menial tasks. She fastened the queen's stays and noted the absurdity and temporary derangement of the king, not without a certain sympathy for his directness and simplicity of manners. Her portrait of the royal family is indeed acute, vivid and loyal. In 1791 she escaped the court and resumed her literary life.

In 1773 she had *Evelina* published, after some misgivings: it brought her £20 and her publisher over £12,000. Burke, Gibbon and Sheridan all praised the book, which was followed by *Cecilia* in 1782. Nothing she wrote afterwards was so good. Her natural touch deserted her. *Edwy and Elgira*, a tragedy, failed despite the acting of Mrs Siddons. In 1793, to the displeasure of her father, she married a French *émigré*, the upright and courteous General d'Arblay, and lived happily with him. When he returned to France in 1801 she followed him and for eleven years remained out of England. Her odyssey during those years reveals a brave and loyal woman. After the war, he retired on half-pay to England and died at Bath in 1818. She outlived her husband by twenty-two years and her son Alexander by three.

Joyce Henlow, *The History of Fanny Burney*, 1958.

JANE AUSTEN (1775-1817) lived a quiet life and her novels reveal few significant facts about the history of her time. Two of her brothers rose to be admirals in the Napoleonic Wars but one can read her without even realizing that these wars were being fought. She says little, too, about landscape, and then in the most general way, for she had the eighteenth-century reluctance to be too particular. Her social scene is confined to the polite world of the upper and middle classes.

Hers was, in a sense, the last voice of the Augustan age; she wrote with a serenity and elegance which was far removed from the already fashionable mood of the romantics. Human beings were all important to Jane Austen, for what they were rather than for what they did. She may be admired for her irony, her refinement of style and honesty of judgement. Gaiety and a lightness of touch relieve the tensions of social relations. She eschews violence and she only hints at unpleasantness, but she is neither trivial nor insipid. Her leading characters grow quietly upon the reader until at the end he knows them in depth. The quiet chronicler of country house and rectory, drawing-room and watering-place, is indeed one of the world's great novelists. Fielding and Richardson, upon whom she drew avidly, Scott who admired her, are somewhat neglected today, but she is read more than ever. For everyone who makes the acquaintance of Joseph Andrews or Guy Mannering, let alone Pamela, there must be a dozen who are intimate with Mrs Bennet, Mr Collins and Fanny Price.

Jane Austen wrote within the compass of her own experience. Her family was of the upper middle class, small squires, officers in the army and navy, or country parsons like her father, George Austen, who was rector of Steventon in Hampshire, where she was born. He was a sensitive man and scholarly in his interests. Mrs Austen was endowed with sufficient energy to sustain an active life in the county: from her Jane may have derived the comic sense, the terseness and the underlying mockery which characterize her writing. Her sister Cassandra was closest to her: 'they were everything to each other', wrote a niece, and 'they seemed to lead a life to themselves'. Her brothers, too, enjoyed her first essays in writing, small burlesque pieces; indeed, the manuscript of what later became *Sense and Sensibility* but was in its first form *Elinor and Marianne*, a tale told in a series of letters, was first read aloud to the family. Good-looking, high-spirited, the

*Jane Austen*
(Artist: Cassandra Austen)

Austens were a close family, happy together and delicate with one another, the girls enjoying perhaps somewhat of a private world, censorious therefore of others. Jane's formal education was scanty, though she learned French and Italian; her creative talent developed naturally, upon a diet of reading: Cowper, Crabbe, Smollett, Fielding — there was no lack of good models.

Tall and graceful, with fine hazel eyes, good features and brown, curly hair, Jane Austen seems also to have been sweet-natured and an especial favourite with children. She had begun to write as a child and she later delighted in long, improvised stories for her nephews and nieces. In 1801 she went with her family to Bath. Her father died in 1805 and she moved to Southampton and later, in 1809, to Chawton near Alton. It was from Chawton, after careful re-writing, and after earlier discouragements at the hands of printers, that she first gave her work to the world. *Sense and Sensibility* was published in 1811; it was modestly successful. *Pride and Prejudice*, which she knew was a better book, appeared in 1813. 'I have got my own darling child from London', wrote the authoress, after receiving her first copy. Henceforward she would write and talk more freely about her work, but it remained anonymous until her death. Her method of writing was characteristically spontaneous. One of her nieces later recalled how her aunt 'would sit quietly working (sewing) beside the fire in the library, saying nothing for a good while, and then would suddenly burst out laughing, jump up and run across the room to a table where pens and paper were lying, write something down, and then come back to the fire and go on quietly working as before'. She would work on several books at once, re-writing former versions and correcting proofs. As she approached middle age, living with her ageing mother, she seems to have developed her faculty for living in, and re-creating, an imaginary world. Her novels owe much to the fact that they took shape amid the distractions of family life. They reflect a wonderfully cool and uncluttered mind and also a diffidence which made her withhold manuscripts from the publisher for revision, long after they were first penned. They were a growing success. *Mansfield Park* (1814) was well-received. *Emma* (1816) was noticed in *The Quarterly* by Scott himself: he made some sharp criticisms but some compliments as well. The Prince Regent informed her that she might dedicate a future work to him; his librarian suggested that she attempt an historical romance about the House of Coburg. Fortunately she chose instead to prepare *Northanger Abbey* for the press and to begin work on *Persuasion*. She remained self-critical, despite failing health, and carefully re-wrote parts of it. She was busy upon a new work, *Sanditon*, when she became seriously ill. It is typical of her bravery and humour that this novel set out to be a comedy about invalidism. She died in July 1817 in Winchester and was buried in the Cathedral.

Scott, the high priest of romanticism, who required a heightening of effect in fiction, appreciated nonetheless her accuracy of delineation, 'strong resemblance and correct drawing'. Charlotte Brontë, though not in sympathy, yet writes about the 'Chinese fidelity' and 'miniature delicacy' in her writing. Lord David Cecil, in his introduction to *Sense and Sensibility*, rebuts the charge that her view of life lacks serious feeling: 'The visible structure of Jane Austen's stories may be flimsy enough; but their foundations drive deep down into the basic principles of human conduct. On her bit of ivory she has engraved a criticism of life as serene and considered as Hardy's.' He sees it as a protest against romanticism and the high value that it set upon 'passion and sensibility and a heart responsive to the beauties of nature', especially as 'guides to conduct'. Rejecting the wild and tragic in favour of the predictable and comic, deliberately limiting her sphere, Jane Austen was able to control her material so as to achieve a concentration upon the human relationships which were her principal study. 'Think away the surface animation', wrote Virginia Woolf of the ballroom scene in the unfinished story, *The Watsons*, 'and there remains, to provide a deeper pleasure, an exquisite discrimination of human values'. The habitual understatement, which Mary Lascelles compares to a February landscape, and her admirable sense of proportion, convey a timeless quality. With all her fidelity to what she had experienced, Jane Austen was a deeply original artist.

M. Lascelles, *Jane Austen and her Art*, 1939.
R. W. Chapman, *Jane Austen*, 1953.

**MARIA EDGEWORTH** (1767-1849) wrote the first regional novel in the English language. It inspired Sir Walter Scott, as he recorded in *Waverley*, to embark on that great and influential novel 'so as in some distant degree to emulate the admirable portraits drawn by Miss Edgeworth'. *Castle Rackrent* is not only an exact and witty account of an Irish way of life that was not wholly of the past; it was also a landmark in the evolution of European fiction.

Her story is also that of her remarkable father. Richard Lovell Edgeworth, 'irrecoverably a mechanic', was for ever inventing machines and devising schemes for human betterment. First and most important was the education of Maria, his eldest daughter by the first of his four wives — eldest of nineteen. She was to exemplify his Rousseauist principles as expounded in *Professional Education* (1808) and in the book written with Maria, *Practical Education* (1798). Theirs was indeed an extraordinary partnership.

In her Oxfordshire childhood she was noted for her storytelling. After 1773, her mother's death and Richard's second marriage, she first visited the family estate, Edgeworthstown, in County Longford. After schooling at Derby (1775-80) and at Wimpole Street, London (1780-2), it became her home, the setting and source of her stories. She kept accounts for her father, studied the ways and tended the needs of his tenants. With successive step-mothers and an ever-growing family she had plenty for her imagination to work on. Throughout, her father imparted his views, advised, and collaborated in her writing. Published between 1795 and 1847 it would fill forty volumes; several novels were sketched, or partly written, well before publication; most were planned with, or revised by her father. He wrote part of *Ormond* during his last illness. After his death, in 1817, Maria's first concern was to complete his autobiography. His part of the story was more interesting than her respectful tailpiece. Conversely, perhaps significantly, *Castle Rackrent* (1800), her freshest, least overtly didactic work, owed nothing to his tutelage.

'I began to write a family history as Thady would tell it, he seemed to stand beside me and dictate; and I write as fast as my pen would go, the characters all imaginary.' 'Honest Thady' is the Rackrent family's steward through generations of muddle and waste. He is both detached and loyal, observant and tolerant; a chronicler of fecklessness and dissipation all the more devastating, in precision and irony, for his charitable view of the idiots and profligates whom he served. It is a highly intelligent exercise in social criticism by a young woman of exceptional gifts and personality. The tale of drunken Sir Patrick, miserly litigious Sir Murtagh, rakish Sir Kit and absurdly impractical Sir Condy, with his weakness for 'whiskey-punch' is also an entrancing picture of Irish ways of life, an invitation to others to imitate and enlarge.

King George III liked the book: 'he rubbed his hands and said

"What what — I know something now of my Irish subjects."' She
enjoyed a certain fame, visited Paris in 1802 and received an offer
of marriage from a Swedish courtier. She turned it down, perhaps
with sighs, for her father's sake and her Irish life. After *Waverley*
had reached Edgeworthstown she began the correspondence with
Scott which led to her stay at Abbotsford in 1823. There were
further Irish novels: the long, heavy *Patronage* (1813), *Ennui*, and
*The Absentee* which appeared in her *Tales of Fashionable Life*.
*Belinda* (1801) had been her first society novel. *Leonora* (1806), a
romantic letter-novel, had perhaps been written for Edelcrantz.
Each displayed in some way her lively mind and sprightly imagination. With less control of story or refinement of style and sensibility than Jane Austen, she had the same keen eye for human
foibles — and her range was wider. The reader who enjoyed *Sense
and Sensibility* might turn to *The Absentee,* which appeared the
year after, and not be disappointed. In distant Russia Turgenev
would acknowledge his debt to this clever, spirited little lady.

Marilyn Butler, *Maria Edgeworth*, 1972.

JOHN CLARE (1792-1864) is one of the great English poets.
For a short while, visitors came in coaches from London 'to gape
at this miraculous son of toil'. Today his unpretentious, direct
and often lyrical poems of country life and people are appreciated
both for their own sake and as an authentic record of a part of
England that was being changed in his lifetime by enclosures, but
which was wholly untouched by industry.

He was born in a small cottage at Helpstone in Northamptonshire, in the north-eastern part of the county bordering on the
fens. Apart from a few visits to London, a brief confinement in an
asylum at High Beech in Epping Forest and longer subsequent
residence at the Northampton General Asylum, this unremarkable countryside was the whole of his life and experience. Those
who called him the 'peasant poet' were right. He was born as a
peasant, lived among peasants and worked in the fields. He was
closer to rural sights and tasks than any of the 'nature poets' of
his youth. When he was six, *Lyrical Ballads* was published.
Wordsworth's incessant search for experience in the sights and
sounds of nature represented a clear break with the eighteenth-
century poets, Collins, Shenstone and Gray, and his language was

avowedly that of ordinary men. It remained also the language of a scholar and gentleman, more philosophical than minutely observant. In Middleton Murray's view Clare has 'a truer ear and a more exquisite instinct for words' than Wordsworth. He was, of course, attempting something entirely different; and he used the language which was natural to him, that of Northamptonshire villagers at a time when every district had its distinctive dialect and words. The reader of Clare will need a small glossary, though his meaning is usually plain enough: words like *brunny*, *chelping*, *cronk*, *glabber*, *knarl* and *soodle* often give life by their onomatopoeic force, to his verse. He used them not for conscious effect but because they were everyday words; the efforts of his publisher to 'purify' his verse might not emasculate it but certainly altered what he was trying to say.

If Clare had written about mountains, about Scotland, or perhaps confined himself to the prettier adornments of the life around him, he might have won more readers. We may be thankful that he wrote about a whole life and landscape. His poems are fragments, cut out of nature, and minutely described; often preserving intense moments of feeling, but set down in reflective calm. In long stretches of *The Shepherd's Calendar* or shorter poems like 'Pewit's Nest' or 'The Badger', one sees at least a great deal of what the poet himself saw. Long hours in the fields and woods, at work, or sauntering — for he was for long periods unemployed — a fine ear and an artist's eye, and an imagination nourished by deep reading, combine to this end. But he wrote about the miniature landscape of the east Midlands, not even the 'dumpling hills' of south Northamptonshire; his landmarks were Langley Bush, Old Cross, Berry Way, Swordy Well, Sheep Green and Puddock's Nook.

Clare was largely self-educated but his reading was more extensive than early critics imagined. His books can still be seen in Northampton Public Library. They show that beside the great classics of literature he was thoroughly acquainted with the poets of the previous century. His favourite authors were apparently Thomson and Cowper. Compare *The Seasons* or *The Task* with Clare's poems and it will be seen how everyday experience has transformed the classical rustic scene into a living landscape. In a sense Clare was an anachronism, since he was firmly grounded in the 'sensible' poets: he liked the slow Augustan pace and cool manner that it had become fashionable to decry. He was the contemporary of Shelley — and Keats, who said of an early poem by Clare that 'the description too much prevailed over the sentiment'. His publisher deplored this. 'Raise and refine' was his advice, and 'speak of the Appearances of Nature each month more philosophically'. How far this well-meaning man was from appreciating the genius of Clare can be seen from his comment on *The Shepherd's Calendar* (1827) — ' a descriptive catalogue in rhyming prose'.

A crucial agent in Clare's poetry is supplied by his love for Mary Joyce, a farmer's daughter whom he idealized but could not marry; she was his social superior but it is uncertain whether it was the father or daughter who pressed this point. Clare's attitude to her varies. Many of the poems are inspired in some way by her: she remained throughout his life a symbol of innocence, co-dweller in a vanished Eden, the first love who was the touchstone for all his later experience. He married Martha Turner ('Patty') in 1826. Her husband's work, *Poems Descriptive of Rural Life and Scenery*, his erratic ways and brooding manner, must have been puzzling to her: Patty was illiterate. Poems did not pay for the keep of their seven children or repair their damp, insanitary cottage. This first collection of poems sold well — and yet Clare was twenty pounds in debt when at last he received a statement from his publisher. The practice of sharing profits and losses between writer and publisher could produce this odd effect; furthermore there was little market for poetry beyond the few, fashionable names. Clare was assisted by an annuity of £45 from the Marquis of Exeter of Burleigh House, where Clare had worked for a short time as under-gardener. He was always, however, in financial difficulties. He found himself suspended, as it were, between two worlds. He did not lack patrons, notably Lord Radstock, who complained once that he discovered in him 'a want of gratitude and proper feeling towards the opulent and higher orders'; but he could not adapt himself to the rôle of literary man; on the other hand he cut an awkward figure in his village, and with the uncomprehending Patty. Enclosures were altering the landscape and the structure of country life. 'The Parish', his long, satiric poem, is concerned with this process, the clearance of woods and heaths, the planting of new hedges (he worked with a gang on this task), the intensive corn-growing of this period — and the changed position of the parson. In his prose writing he enlarges on this theme.

In 1832 Clare had moved to a cottage in Northborough, about four miles from Helpstone, offered to him by Lord Fitzwilliam. He had friends among Lord Fitzwilliam's servants, but his sense of alienation is recorded in two great poems, 'Decay' and 'The Flitting'. In 1837 he submitted himself voluntarily to the care of Dr. Allen, who ran an asylum in Epping Forest. He suffered from the visitation of 'blue devils' and he believed that he was married to Mary Joyce. He escaped in 1841 and walked home, to be met by Patty with a cart a few miles from their cottage. In December he was removed to Northampton, where he was to spend the rest of his days. His warrant included the words 'for years addicted to poetical prosings'! He was given freedom to go into the town and was for years a familiar figure to Northampton people, sitting on the steps of All Saints' Church. He continued to write poems. Some are love songs harking back to happier days, some show a sense of insecurity and of the imminence of judgement. In 'I am' he wrote of himself as 'the self-consumer of my woes' in 'the nothingness of scorn and noise'. He would have been a great poet if he had written nothing more after he had entered an asylum; he would still be an arresting and moving poet if he had written nothing before.

J. W. and A. Tibble, *John Clare: his Life and Poetry*, 1931.
Frederick Martin, *The Life of John Clare*, 2nd edition, 1964.

**WILLIAM WORDSWORTH** (1770-1850), poet, was born at Cockermouth in Cumberland where the Derwent runs out into the sea. His father, John Wordsworth, was an attorney and agent to the Lowther family. His mother, Ann, was the daughter of William Cookson, a linen-draper of Penrith, and of Dorothy Crackanthorpe; the Crackanthorpes were an old county family. William was the second son. His mother died when he was eight and the family was dispersed. The four boys were sent in turn to Hawkshead grammar school, coming home only for the holidays. After the death of his father in 1783, home was that of an uncle, Christopher Cookson, at Penrith, or Richard Wordsworth at Whitehaven. His headmaster from 1781 to 1786 was William Taylor, lover of poetry and a scholar, who lent William his books.

*William Wordsworth*
(Artist: Benjamin Robert Haydon)

William lodged with a 'dame' and escaped the more rigorous discipline of Taylor's school house. Outside school hours the boys roamed freely. William's father had taught him to learn large portions of poetry and he plunged avidly into Fielding, Swift and

Cervantes. He listened intently to the ballads and border-lore of the country 'back of Skiddaw', and he was always fascinated by the lonely travellers who were later re-created in his poems: the Pedlar, the Discharged Soldier and the Leech-gatherer. Certain things moved him overwhelmingly: a drowned man, a rotting gibbet; or the running water of a stream, the music of a wren, a solitary flute; or wind in fir trees. His youth was marked by 'spots of time', incidents or sights transformed by a capacity for intense emotion, memory pictures to which he 'often would repair and thence drink as at a fountain'.

We can follow in his autobiographical poems the stages of his emotional development. The disciplines of mathematics and classics were balanced by solitary walks, fishing, birds-nesting, skating and other country sports. Chasing lapwings, playing ducks-and-drakes or coursing with his friends, Wordsworth was not a lonely boy. But he had a gift for solitude. On a country walk, he might come suddenly into contact with an experience of 'dream-like vividness and splendour'. So he was 'often unable to think of external things as having external existence'. He went on: 'I communed with all I saw as something set apart from but inherent in my own immaterial nature. Many times while going to school have I grasped at a wall or tree to recall myself from this abyss of idealism to the reality'. From his early observations of natural beauty came the imagery of his greatest poetry. He ascribed to his sister his habit of minute observation 'She gave me eyes, she gave me ears' — but it was also born in him, a natural poet's gift. Dorothy's influence was important: theirs were complementary natures. Her delicate insights and tenderness softened William's 'stiff, violent and moody temper' which had so worried his mother. Her companionship, resumed after 1787, was to him 'a joy above all joys'. Together they explored the fells and vales of Eamont and Eden, read the poems of Burns and 'saw into the life of things'. Thus was established a relationship of trust and sympathy which was to be for both the most important of their lives.

In the same year William went to Cambridge, to St. John's College, where he spent four years 'joyous as a lark'. Finding that he knew much of what was required, he eschewed the prescribed courses and read for pleasure. He learned Italian, read widely and shed conventional religious beliefs. He despised the dons, 'some elderly men unscoured, grotesque in character, tricked out like

aged trees', and deplored the 'frantic and dissolute' undergraduate life. Early poems reveal little originality. Crabbe, Beattie,
Cowper and Collins were the strongest influences on his style. In
1790, with his Welsh friend Robert Jones, he went on a walking
tour in the Alps and whetted his appetite for 'mighty forms'.
Other gentlemen sought the picturesque, but not usually on foot
with but £20 in pocket! In the autumn of 1791, still in wayward
mood, he went back to France. He visited the National Assembly,
became imbued with the spirit of liberty, unsullied as it was then
by terror, and met, among others, Beaupuy, a chivalrous revolutionary, and Annette Vallon.

She was 25, the daughter of a surgeon, and lived in Orleans
where Wordsworth had gone to learn French. They lived together;
but two months before she was due to give birth to his child
Wordsworth returned to Paris. There in December 1792 he heard
of the birth of a daughter and hurriedly left for England. These
facts were unknown for a century because Wordsworth suppressed them; the secret remained with the family and a few
discreet friends. Why did he desert a girl whom he seems to have
loved passionately and to have meant to marry? Did he intend to
return? Was he warned of the forthcoming war with England and
of his own danger? Possibly his slender funds had run out.
Wordsworth had responded joyously to the sense of liberation
and to Beaupuy's love of humanity, when 'to be young was very
heaven'. In his months with Annette his ecstasy was concentrated
in a more personal way: he was capable of intense, worshipping
love. When Wordsworth returned to England his life had been
shaken, and his poetic nature roused, not only perhaps by love but
by the abrupt end, and long suppression, of the affair. Herbert
Read, dwelling on this latter aspect, held that the affair 'transformed his being'. It was the 'deepest experience of Wordsworth's
life — the emotional complex from which all his subsequent
career flows in its intricacy and uncertainty'.

Wordsworth secured the publication of 'The Evening Walk'
and 'Descriptive Sketches' by Joseph Johnson, friend of Blake and
Priestley. He was anxious about the violent trend in France.
A hasty visit to France — the evidence for it is uncertain — would
only have confirmed these misgivings. He did not meet William
Godwin until 1795 but he read *Political Justice* soon after his
return from France. Godwin condemned revolutions because

they 'confound the process of nature and reason'. Journalistic efforts, like his *Letter to the Bishop of Llandaff*, an analysis of the causes of poverty, which even Johnson refused to publish, pointed Wordsworth to a new means of livelihood. He had good friends: Raisley Calvert bequeathed him a small legacy before he died in January 1795. Racedown Lodge, in the Dorset hills, was made available to him, and there he settled down with Dorothy.

At a time when he could have remained in mental chaos, brooding over the past, Dorothy's faith 'preserved him still a poet'. Their *ménage* puzzled the country people. From his habit of wandering round with a small telescope and a notebook, Wordsworth was thought to be bewitching the cattle and later was reported as a spy! Here he rewrote 'Salisbury Plain', composed *The Borderers*, a play on a didactic principle, then some works in a calmer mood, notably 'The Ruined Cottage'. In this poem poverty is still a preoccupation, but Margaret, the humble heroine, emerges as an individual. Wordsworth the social reformer, isolated in his sense of personal suffering, is becoming the poet of the heart and of nature.

In 1796 Samuel Taylor Coleridge fell under Wordsworth's spell. As he described it, Wordsworth's poem 'The Female Vagrant' made a sudden effect on his mind: 'It was the union of deep feeling with profound thought ... and above all the original gift of spreading the tone, the atmosphere ... of the ideal world around forms, incidents and situations of which custom had bedimmed all the lustre'. When the Wordsworths went to stay with Coleridge at Nether Stowey in midsummer 1797, an association of mutual admiration was born. The Wordsworths moved to Alfoxden House near Stowey. They made free with one another's houses, talked endlessly, 'wantoned in wild poesy'. 'Kubla Khan', 'The Ancient Mariner' and 'Christabel' were the result. 'Three people, but one soul' was Coleridge's description of the unusual trio. Dorothy helped turn Coleridge's philosophic mind towards outward things; Wordsworth gave Coleridge understanding; Coleridge gave Wordsworth 'praise and the courage to be himself'. They walked together in November 1797 around the Quantocks and along the coast, and planned 'The Ancient Mariner'.

William settled to writing poetry in the purposeful way that characterized his periodic creative spells. Whole passages that later formed part of 'The Excursion' and 'The Prelude', fragments of blank verse, were written at this time, often incorporating Dorothy's observations as recorded in her journal. Two characteristics of Wordsworth's poetry can be seen already: he looks back upon his youth and its discoveries; and he tries to express the mental states which were produced by his communing with nature. Between February and May 1798 he composed most of the poems which he published in September in *Lyrical Ballads* — and 'Peter Bell'; and the beginnings of 'The Recluse', later to be found in 'The Excursion'. The *Lyrical Ballads* contained 'The Ancient Mariner' and three other poems by Coleridge, but the bulk was provided by Wordsworth's ballads and lyrics; characters of rustic life are the subject of poems like 'Simon Lee' and 'Goody Blake', while other pieces such as 'Lines written in Early Spring' express ideas which Coleridge described as 'semi-atheism'.

'Lines Written a few miles above Tintern Abbey' was added to *Lyrical Ballads* while the volume was in the press: in form an autobiographical sketch and a rhapsody upon his experiences. With Dorothy in July 1798 he toured the Wye valley rediscovering the delectable country through which he had wandered in 1793. He began the poem 'upon leaving Tintern ... and concluded it just as I was entering Bristol in the evening, after a ramble of four or five days ... Not a line of it was altered and not any part of it was written down till I reached Bristol.' Wordsworth describes in 'Tintern Abbey' the change in outlook since he first saw the 'steep woods and lofty banks' of the Wye. Then he consumed the sights of nature with sensuous violence: 'the sounding cataract haunted me like a passion', the forms of nature were 'then to me an appetite'. Now he had learned to listen more calmly to 'the still, sad music of humanity' and he had a clearer sense of the existence all around him of 'a motion and a spirit', universal, vague but immeasurably grand. The intuitions of boyhood are confirmed, nature and humanity reconciled.

In June 1798 the young Hazlitt met Wordsworth and found him more 'gaunt and Don Quixote-like' than he expected. 'He was quaintly dressed ... in a brown fustian jacket and striped pantaloons ... There was a severe, worn pressure of thought about his temples, a fire in his eye (as if he saw more in objects than the outward appearance), an intense, high, narrow forehead, a Roman nose, cheeks furrowed by strong purpose and feeling, and a convulsive inclination to laughter about the mouth'. He talked 'very naturally and freely, with a mixture of clear, gushing accents in his voice, a deep, guttural intonation, and a strong tincture of the northern burr, like the crust on wine'. De Quincey noticed especially the poet's eyes: 'An appearance the most solemn and spiritual that it is possible for a human eye to wear'.

In September 1798 the Wordsworths and Coleridge went to Germany. They divided, the Wordsworths going to Goslar. Wordsworth made slow progress with German, but began what was to be 'The Prelude', besides writing 'Lucy Gray' and 'Ruth'. In May they came back to live at Sockburn-on-Tees, with the Hutchinson family. Mary Hutchinson the Wordsworths had known since their Penrith days. Wordsworth had always been fond of her; she had stayed with them at Racedown. He finally married her in October 1802. She would be the domestic, child-bearing partner in the household of poetry. Before the wedding Wordsworth spent a month at Calais with Dorothy, Annette and his daughter Caroline; perhaps it was to see his daughter, perhaps to convince Annette, who had been living resigned as 'the widow Williams', that marriage was no longer feasible. This encounter seems oddly insensitive. Wordsworth's private relationships were made to fit into the pattern of his work. Dorothy Wordsworth may have loved Coleridge: there are hints of this in her journals. She undoubtedly loved William enough to accept her special position in the *ménage à trois* which was established after the marriage. She was sustained by her admiration for William's genius: she served at his altar. Mary made William a good wife; she seems to have lived contentedly in a household that was surprisingly free of jealousy.

In December 1799 the Wordsworths decided to go and live at Grasmere. They took a cottage at Town End (now Dove Cottage) with an orchard above it whence they could see 'the lake, the Church, Helm Crag, and two-thirds of the vale'. The life they lived is recreated in Dorothy's journal, an intimate, evocative account. They felt they had come home after many wanderings. Their life was austere, for they were as poor as the 'statesmen', farmers of that infertile district. The family was steadily enlarged by the birth of children — five in all — and they were seldom without visitors and guests, notable among them Coleridge, who took a nearby house, Greta Hall.

While much of the poetry of the early Grasmere period was of the ,sort that his critics thought worthless, poetry of the 'light of common day', Wordsworth was also anxious to respond to Coleridge's insistence upon a philosophical scheme. Coleridge could never accept Wordsworth's choice of 'simple and unelaborated expressions', his concern with the 'low and rustic life' in which condition 'the passions of men are incorporated with the beautiful and permanent forms of nature'. *Lyrical Ballads*, from whose preface these words are taken, was an odd match between different kinds of poems, though linked by two agreed principles: 'faithful adherence to the truth of nature' and 'the power of giving interests to novelty by the modifying powers of imagination'. Coleridge could not make Wordsworth a philosopher. But Wordsworth did, in his preface to the second edition of *Lyrical Ballads*, develop his distinctive view of poetry. 'Poetry takes its origins from emotion recollected in tranquillity: the tranquillity gradually disappears, and an emotion, kindred to that which was before the subject of contemplation, is gradually produced, and does itself actually exist in the mind.' No one before had so exactly analysed the process of creation. Dorothy described his ardour once by the word 'kindled' — and his habit of composing out of doors, walking fast between two fixed points, chanting his poetry.

Wordsworth himself preferred to group his poems according to their subject, as for example 'Poems of the Imagination', 'Poems of Fancy', rather than chronologically. His output was enormous though irregular. Critics tend to treat him as a spent force after 'The Excursion' (1814). He was capable, however, almost to the end, of rising above the pedestrian: 'The Power of Sound' was written in 1828, 'Yarrow Revisited' in 1831. He had acquired a bank of imagery upon which, when he was stirred, he could draw for verse which could still please. It is not, however, upon the years of hack-work and homilies that one should dwell, when the mystical power had waned and, as Hazlitt put it, 'the power of his mind preys on itself' — or, as another said, he was 'an owl in the daylight'. The best idea of the poet can be gained from an account of the spring of 1802, Wordsworth's second great time of lyrical creation.

Writing almost every day, in a white heat of inspiration, he got into his stride with a series of poems, like 'Alice Fell' in his simplest style; then the first of the three butterfly poems; on

23 March, 'a mild morning, William worked at the Cuckow poem'. The cuckoo's call was heard in imagination, a herald from a spiritual world: what Wordsworth did to the cuckoo, 'a wandering voice', as he said, dispossesses the bird almost of a corporeal existence. So the poem perfectly represents Wordsworth's imagination, gazing at the world of sense until it 'revealed the invisible world'. 'The Rainbow' and the first lines of 'Intimations of Immortality' followed. 'The Tinker' and several poems about wild flowers were written at this time; so was the first of the skylark poems, whose freedom of metre matches the bird's joyous flight. Finally, on 3-4 May, was written 'The Leech-gatherer or Resolution and Independence', a recreation of an earlier encounter and a detailed illustration of the way in which the poet could still be moved to the point of entering a visionary state. He was just thirty-two and at the mature point of his poetic development. 'William worked at the *Leech Gatherer* almost incessantly from morning till tea time ... and was oppressed and sick at heart, for he wearied himself to death. After tea he wrote two stanzas in the manner of Thomson's *Castle of Indolence* and was tired out'. These stanzas reveal what he thought of himself, the alternating elation and depression, and the way he was mastered by his muse. 'I wandered lonely as a cloud' was to come later; he had seen, this April, the daffodils beside Ullswater and stored the memory away to be recalled at a later date. 'The Solitary Reaper', the rest of 'The Ode' and of 'The Prelude' were not yet written. But he was never again to achieve such an outpouring of genius.

In Wordsworth's move towards the conservatism of his later years certain landmarks may be distinguished. In 1803 Sir George Beaumont, the artist, gave him some land. He became a freeholder of Westmorland, a voter and an active force in local politics. The Wordsworth family had been meanly treated by the first Earl Lowther. The second earl made amends and helped the poet: in March 1813 Wordsworth was made Distributor of Stamps for Westmorland. The duties were not nominal, sometimes vexatious, and always a tie. His gains were not unreasonable for he had to support a growing family and he made pitifully little from his poems. When he flung himself into the celebrated election of 1818, defending the Lowther interest against the whig Brougham with two 'addresses to the freeholders of Westmorland', his critics were quick to point the moral. To men like Hazlitt and Shelley he was simply an apostate. Like so many of his generation Wordsworth had sickened of the Jacobinism that had destroyed the generous revolution of his youth. He had not approved the first war. But after 1803 he responded heartily to the patriotic mood. He became a volunteer at Grasmere. When he ceased to be a revolutionary, he continued to be a puritan: 'plain living and high thinking' was his creed to the end. He clung to his hope of being a prophet of nature, that 'what we have loved, others will love'. He was more sensitive than most of his generation to the wretchedness of industrial towns. His conservatism acquired querulous notes in old age but it was never ignoble or merely defensive. He came to see in the church the natural guardian of good order and morality. In education, under the control of the church, he saw the best cure for moral ills: the ninth book of 'The Excursion' pleads for Anglican primary education for all. If he despised 'the rabble' he also appealed for an early reform of the Poor Laws.

As Wordsworth grew older he had recurring eye trouble, though he never went blind. Domestic calamities pressed hard. A terrible blow was the death by shipwreck in 1805 of his brother John, a good-natured sea-captain, whose ambition was to make enough money to settle down (perhaps marry Sara Hutchinson, Mary's sister) and help the penurious Wordsworths. In 1812 two children (Catherine and Thomas) died. Dorothy had a total breakdown in health in 1829; her mind partially gave way and she became a demanding and trying invalid. Wordsworth has seemed sometimes to be too self-absorbed; if this were true, he made amends in the way in which he accepted the burden of his sister's dotage. Age had not diminished his own capacity for feeling. He had always been prone to tears; when his daughter Dora died in 1847 he was terribly stricken. He died in loneliness. As a poet too he had been essentially a lonely figure. Some young Victorians proclaimed themselves 'Wordsworthians'. In his best work he speaks to every generation. The poet of nature was also the poet of mind which he elevates in a way that leaves little room for a greater being, for the mind 'keeps her own inviolate retirement, subject there to conscience only'. This was a height on which no man could stay for long. The descent may seem that of an egotist, wrapped in self-contemplation. But it was a height that few other English poets achieved.

Dorothy Moorman, *Wordsworth*, 2 volumes, 1957, 1965.
Ed. E. de Selincourt, *Letters of William and Dorothy Wordsworth*, 6 volumes, 1935-9.

SAMUEL TAYLOR COLERIDGE (1772-1834), critic, philosopher and poet, is one of the very few men to whom, without hesitation, the title of genius may be given. The contrast between his gifts and his failures, his virtues and his faults, is so striking that ordinary judgements seem to be out of place. Here apparently is a tragedy of waste. Yet he created several great poems like nothing else in the language and wrote critical and philosophical studies of seminal importance. This rare flower of eighteenth-century culture lived to be the inspiration of the religious revival of the Victorians. Tempted to dismiss him as a mind too nebulous to deserve serious study we are recalled by some special insight, some apt description, and catch an echo of the voice that entranced his listeners. He scattered his seed with careless prodigality — but some fell on rich ground. Most of his life he was oppressed by a sense of failure, but he achieved more than he realized.

He was the son of John Coleridge, vicar of Ottery in Devonshire, an eccentric man, a grammarian of some note; and of Anne Bowdon. His father died when he was nine and he was sent to Christ's Hospital. He attracted the attention of Dr. Boyer, the headmaster, by his proficiency in the classics. However, he became so caught up with philosophy, from about the age of fifteen, that in his own words, 'everything else became insipid'. He proclaimed himself an atheist and thereby earned himself a flogging. He also made the acquaintance of Lamb, who remained his devoted friend in all vicissitudes. He entered Jesus College, Cambridge, in February 1791 and remained there for three years. He won the Browne medal for a Greek ode on the slave trade but could not bring himself to regular study. He was happiest when holding forth upon politics, philosophy, religion — and he seldom lacked an audience. On a sudden impulse he enlisted in a dragoon regiment under the name of Silas Comberbach. Trooper Comberbach was preparing to fight the French while Samuel Coleridge praised the Revolution and denounced the war! '*Eheu, quam infortunis miserrimum est fuisse felicem*' — the lines inscribed on a stable wall roused doubts about him. He was rescued by friends who

*Samuel Taylor Coleridge*
(Artist: Peter Vandyke)

purchased his discharge and he returned to Cambridge. He soon left without taking a degree. (So did Southey and Shelley from Oxford: the ancient universities were uncongenial places for radicals and poets.) Together with Southey, whom he met at Balliol in 1794, he set to planning a communal estate of twelve men and twelve women on the banks of the Susquehanna. The romantic name appealed to him; the practical difficulties he left to Southey. 'Pantisocracy' sought to realize the ideals of Godwin's *Political Justice*; it was never put to the test. Southey's saving caution, and lack of money, killed the scheme. Coleridge gave some lectures in Bristol in which he vehemently upheld Jacobin principles. Rebounding from Mary Anne Evans, his first love, he married Sara Fricker, whose sister later married Southey.

For life with Coleridge a miracle of patience and understanding would have been required. Dorothy Wordsworth later said that Sara's 'radical fault was want of sensibility, and what can such a woman be to Coleridge?' She bore him children and struggled to make an orderly home for him, but he was incapable of meeting the demands of married life and they drifted apart. After 1803 she and her children were supported by Southey; by then Coleridge's efforts to settle down, at Nether Stowey and later at Greta Hall, had broken down in a welter of sentiment and broken resolutions. He went on long excursions with his friends, always leaving her at home. He fell in love with Sara Hutchinson, platonically, as he assured his wife; anyway, she resented Sara less than the Wordsworths who seemed to her to be encouraging her husband's bohemian ways.

Coleridge's happiest years were those of his intimate partnership with the Wordsworths, particularly during the first years, 1797-8, when thought, feeling and purpose were harmonized in periods of visionary exaltation. In 1796 he had projected a paper called *The Watchman*: it was to be the herald of truth and to appear every eighth day, to avoid the Stamp Duty: it never appeared. He wrote verse, notably the 'Visions of the Maid of Orleans'. When his publisher, Joseph Cottle — that enterprising Bristolian who produced the first work of Southey, Coleridge and Wordsworth — was asked by the author what he thought of it, he replied that it was 'all very fine but what it was about I could not tell'. Coleridge himself was only too well aware of what he called 'the swell and glitter both of thought and diction'. He needed a strong personality who could direct him, to help him to contain his own exuberance. He 'wandered in wild poesy' with William and sensed that he was understood. He idolized Wordsworth: 'The only man to whom at all times and in all modes of excellence I feel myself inferior.' Dorothy was no less important: she turned his eye to the minute and intricate things of nature. Longing for 'something great, something one and indivisible', he found these homespun northerners stimulating; but they could not collaborate for long. Wordsworth was more the poet, he more the philosopher: *Lyrical Ballads*, the offspring of their association, presents two entirely different sorts of poem. Wordsworth was aiming at a new poetic language and Coleridge was not particularly interested in this. 'The Ancient Mariner' was Coleridge's great contribution. He called it 'A Poet's Reverie' and it has the irrational, hallucinatory character of a waking dream. The Mariner is a passive figure who acts, as when he blesses the watersnakes, 'unaware'. The active agents in the story are naturespirits. Coleridge himself was unsure whether his poem was to be classed as escapism, pure entertainment, or as a first essay in the exploration of the preternatural condition, accepting abnormal states of mind and psychic events by 'that willing suspension of disbelief for the moment, which constitutes poetic faith'.

Imagination was for Coleridge the sovereign creative force, expressing the growth of the personality. He wrote some less ambitious pieces, intimate and tender: 'conversation poems' like 'The Eolian Harp' and 'The Nightingale', and 'Frost at Midnight', and a series of lyrics inspired by his love for Sara Hutchinson. Always he looked for the sublime. In 'Khubla Khan', as in the 'Mariner', he maintained that his rational mind was in abeyance. This poem was composed in a reverie or dream. The famous story of his writing it in a trance after deep sleep, until disturbed by the untimely arrival of the man from Porlock, if not literally true, may be taken as a parable. For this beautiful poem has a flowing force which suggests sustained inspiration. The rational will suspended, the pen moved as if answering to dictation. Coleridge himself dismissed 'Khubla Khan' as a 'psychological curiosity' but 'Christabel', another unfinished poem, is a different matter. This is a melodrama with a climax of horror which is more effective for remaining unexplained. Coleridge could make people faint in his readings of the poem. Did he hope to arrive at a new synthesis of mind and feeling? Did the fact that it remains uncompleted signify his failure? The poem remains a mystery, unsatisfactory, like so much of Coleridge, because it promises so much. In 'Dejection: an Ode' (1802) he expressed his sense of failure: 'The poet in him' was dying, 'My genial spirits fail'.

In March 1802 Dorothy Wordsworth recorded in her journal the sight of Coleridge when he arrived on a visit: 'His eyes were a little swollen with the wind. I was much affected with the sight of him, he seemed half-stupefied.' Coleridge had become fatally dependent on opium. He had rheumatic fever when he was a boy. Recurrences of this and similar ills gave him much pain. Wordsworth recorded how, on walks in Alfoxden days, he would suffer internal pain which 'sometimes caused him, when we walked together in Somersetshire, to throw himself down and writhe like a worm on the ground'. He first took laudanum to relieve such pain and became addicted. Increasingly he showed its effects. He grew fat and full of self-disgust. That he floated at all on the sea of his troubles was owed to the practical sympathy of friends like Thomas Poole, the tanner who helped to finance some of his literary ventures. Their forbearance was not unrewarded. To help Poole in a problem of chemistry in his tannery, Coleridge obtained information from the young chemist Davy. He always wanted to help people and often showed remarkable resource in doing so. The most extraordinary thing about Coleridge is that his mind went on developing.

In 1798 Josiah and Thomas Wedgwood had offered Coleridge £150 a year on condition that he abandoned his Unitarian preaching and devoted himself to literature. Coleridge had completely given up the Godwinism of his youth: his revolutionary philosophy was in ruins, and he was aware of a void. He went to Ratzeburg to study the German language and its philosophers. He returned home excited by the encounter, and equipped to study and develop along his own lines. On his return to England he produced an excellent translation of *Wallenstein* which hardly sold at all. At this time the lack of a sophisticated readership of any size, outside the academic institutions where taste was dominated by classical studies, discouraged the innovator. In the summer of 1800 Coleridge went to live at Greta Hall, Derwentwater, to be near the Wordsworths. The busy lives of his friends only increased his own sense of purposelessness. In August 1803 he outlined a scheme for a great *Bibliotheca Britannica*, with Southey: the less he achieved the grander his schemes became. In 1804 he went to Malta for his health's sake. He became secretary to the governor, but his health remained bad and he went on to travel in Italy. He returned to England precipitately when he heard a rumour that

Bonaparte had sent agents to seize him because of his hostile essays in the *Morning Post*! The next decade outwardly was one of decline. Southey had taken Greta Hall and his family off his hands. He wandered aimlessly. De Quincey, most impressionable of men, met him in 1807 and promptly sent him an anonymous gift of £300. In 1808 he gave some lectures entitled *Poetry and the Fine Arts*. In 1809 he started *The Friend*. It appeared irregularly, lasted only eight months — and yet it contained some of his finest prose!

In 1810 he gave the first of his celebrated lectures on Shakespeare and Milton. In 1813 his drama *Remorse* was put on at Drury Lane, and was a success. By now he was taking two or three quarts of laudanum a week. In 1816, one happy day, he put himself in the care of Dr. and Mrs Gillman of Highgate: they were both practical and devoted. Now 'Christabel' and 'Khubla Khan' were published and he began to know fame. In 1817 he published his *Sermons* and the *Biographia Literaria*. In 1818 he delivered fourteen lectures. He was given the subject of an extra one, 'The Growth of the Individual Mind', at the last moment, and spoke extempore. Gillman said that his discourse was 'brilliant, eloquent and logically consecutive'. Only notes survive to hint at the quality of his lectures but these, and his *Literary Remains*, show him to have been one of the greatest of Shakespearian critics. Perhaps his finest prose work, *Confessions of an Inquiring Spirit*, was published posthumously in 1840. His last years were more orderly than might have been expected, and not apparently unhappy. He died at Highgate in 1834. For all his apparent self-concern we are left with a sense of his generosity of spirit. There are many paradoxes in Coleridge's career. Leslie, a friend of his later years, expressed one of them: 'His want of success in all worldly matters may be attributed to the mastery possessed over him by his wonderful mind.'

The roaming inquiries that suggest more than they answer have always put people off Coleridge. Moreover his ideas have to be pieced together from a number of sources. He made it as hard for posterity as for his friends. Hazlitt, who, on first acquaintance, had been awed by his eloquence (in a Unitarian pulpit), was also struck by the way he walked: 'In passing from subject to subject, he appeared to float in air, to slide on ice ... He continually crossed me on the way by shifting from one side of the footpath to the other.' Only later did Hazlitt connect the habit with 'any instability of purpose or involuntary change of principle'. Like most people he came to think of him as a random dreamer: 'There is no subject on which he has not touched, none on which he has rested.' Yet, there is an underlying wholeness about Coleridge's life which its fragmented episodes and writings concealed.

In his early years he had been an emotional pantheist: Rousseau made a strong appeal. At the same time he accepted the psychology of Locke and Hartley and the view that sense impressions combined by association shaped the contents of the mind. Wordsworth and then Kant were his guides along the path he took to recover 'the self-directing principle' in his life. In his acquaintance with 'the true and new poet' he came to see an excellence which 'I no sooner felt than I sought to understand'. It was above all 'the original gift of spreading the tone, the *atmosphere*, and with it the height and depth of the ideal world around forms, incidents and situations ...'. From this beginning evolved the important distinctions that he made between fancy and imagination, and between the primary and secondary imagination. The special function of this imagination in the secondary or higher state was to see all things as one, and the one in all things. As a poet this meant creating living metaphors displaying discordant properties, such as novelty and familiarity, internal and external, emotion and order, in balance or reconciliation. It meant directing the 'mind's attention' to 'the loveliness and the wonders of the world before us'. As a critic it means uniting opposites. As a moralist it meant the recovery of truth by the overthrow of 'the mechanic philosophy' which produced offshoots in his own time in the work of the Utilitarians and Benthamites.

The truths of religion and morality could not be demonstrated like geometrical propositions. He began with I *am* as opposed to *it is*, the consciousness of being existent individuals: self-understanding coming with the act of existential choice. He deplored the loss of wholeness in his world in words which must move us today: 'We have purchased a few brilliant inventions at the loss of all communion with life and the spirit of nature.' He came during his painful odyssey from necessitarianism, 'a universe of death', to see that truth could be apprehended at different levels and with different degrees of wholeness: mentally as an abstract demonstration, or embraced by 'the whole soul of man'. So Christianity and Platonism came together in the certainty of a divine ground and meaning in the universe. He set out to show that religion was more truly 'philosophical' than mere enthusiasm (warmth without light, excluding thought from religion), or the gospel of the Godwinites who virtually excluded religion from thought. Coleridge's insistence that Christian faith was the perfection of human intelligence pointed the way to a better future, to Thomas Arnold, F. D. Maurice and Cardinal Newman. It made him a source and inspiration of the Oxford revival and of a school of theologians who were liberated from dependence on literal reading of the Bible. He gave to thoughtful men a conception of society, not as a field of unlimited competition but as a representation of the kingdom of God. Christ, said Coleridge, 'is not a theory or a speculation but a Life; not a Philosophy of Life, but a Life and a Living Process'. And its proof lies in the trial: "Try it."' Coleridge went so deep at several points that it is possible to claim for Lamb's 'fallen archangel' that he was the most important prophet of the nineteenth century.

Richard Holmes, *Coleridge — Early Visions*, 1989.
Rosemary Ashton, *A Life of S. T. Coleridge*, 1996.

**ROBERT SOUTHEY** (1774-1843), poet, biographer and historian, was the son of Robert Southey, a Bristol draper unsuccessful in his business. He was brought up by an aunt, Miss Tyler, a haughty but not ungenerous person, who intended to adopt him but gave up the idea when he took an unorthodox path. A solitary child, he was discouraged from playing lest he should make himself dirty. He was four years at Westminster but was expelled in 1792 for an article in the school magazine in which he attributed the invention of flogging to the devil. At Balliol he read voraciously but left without taking a degree. At this stage he was a rebel of a not unfamiliar sort. He protested against the college rule forbidding the wearing of boots: 'To me it is a matter of indifference, but folly so ridiculous puts me out of conceit with the whole.' He wore his hair unpowdered to show what he thought of Pitt's powder tax. In a slightly aquiline way he was unusually handsome. All portraits catch his proud look, but his manner was gentle: 'An eye piercing with a countenance full of genius, kindliness and intelligence' was how his friend Cottle saw him.

At Balliol he was visited by Coleridge; together in 1794 they sketched out plans for a 'pantisocracy' beside the Susquehanna where men should find regeneration in the communal pursuit of farming. In the event Southey did not travel to utopia in America but to Lisbon, where an uncle was chaplain. There he learned 'to thank God he was an Englishman'. There seems to have been an idea that Southey would be ordained, but his inclination was at this time towards Stoic philosophy and republicanism. Since boyhood he had been writing. His aunt had been interested in the theatre and Southey often went to plays. The great epics of literature stimulated his romantic imagination: 'No one', he later wrote, 'had ever a more decided turn for music or for numbers than I had for romance.' Before he went to Westminster he was writing epics of his own, in blank verse. He now wrote in democratic vein. *Wat Tyler* was unpublished for twenty years and a great embarrassment to Southey when it did appear, unsanctioned by the author. *Joan of Arc*, an epic, was published in 1796 by Cottle.

Before going to Portugal he married Edith Fricker, sister of Coleridge's wife Sarah; on return in 1797 he settled to read law in London and to write for a living. His *Letters from Spain and Portugal* encouraged Charles Wynn his Westminster and lifelong friend, to support him with a small annuity. Southey repaid him by assiduous work. Two themes predominate in his literary life: epic and history. The former he hoped would ensure him a place with posterity, but he was rarely more than a commonplace poet, exceptionally fluent in the Augustan manner. 'Joan of Arc' won many admirers, however. Lamb enthused: 'On the whole I expect Southey one day to rival Milton. I already deem him equal to Cowper and superior to all living poets besides'. Poems like 'Thalabar' (1801), 'Madoc' (1805) (whose relative failure much saddened him), 'The Curse of Kehama' (1810), 'Roderick' (1814) and 'A Tale of Paraguay' (1825) have their merits. Coleridge referred to the 'pastoral charms and wild, streaming lights' of 'Thalabar'. A modern critic has said of Southey that if he had only 'written more of England, which he knew and loved devotedly, instead of dealing with remote subjects ... he might have been a major poet' (Simmons).

Southey never lost his writer's soul or stooped to literary drudgery. His own enthusiasm dictated his choice of subject. He began his *History of Portugal* before his second visit to that country in 1800; only the *History of Brazil*, one section of the larger work, was ever published. He had accumulated too much material for even his busy pen. When he chose a manageable subject, however, he revealed himself a gifted writer of prose. Of his *Portugal* he wrote to Wynn in 1801: 'My heart and soul are in the work. I hope you will like the plain, compressed, unornamented style, in which I endeavour to write strength and perspicuity.' One may regret that he could not have chiselled from his vast quarry some monolith — a life of Henry the Navigator, for example. For when he did match style and subject successfully he was very fine. His *History of the Peninsular War* might have been a classic had it not been trumped by Napier's. His lives of Nelson and Wesley were among the best biographies of their day: brisk, well-proportioned and fair.

After a brief period as secretary to a chancellor of the Irish Exchequer (1801-2) he went to live at Greta Hall, Keswick, where the Coleridges were already established. Here he supported Coleridge's family as well as his own. It was to find a way of describing Southey's steadfast presence that Coleridge conceived the word 'reliability'. Others had harsher things to say about him as the tame government bard, Peacock's 'Mr Feathernest'. He received from 1806 a small government pension and in 1813 he became Poet Laureate. In that capacity he made himself ridiculous by writing 'A Vision of Judgement' (1821) which described the reception of George III into celestial bliss and had the ill-luck to attract the sardonic wit of Byron. Byron said to Moore: 'To have that poet's head and shoulders, I would almost have written his Sapphics.' But in his journal he wrote more sympathetically: 'His appearance is *Epic*; and he is the only existing entire man of letters ... His manners are mild but not those of a man of the world, and his talents of the first order. His prose is perfect.'

Southey's conservatism was more rational and sympathetic than that of Eldon or Sidmouth. This high Tory, who was so upset by the 'madness' of the Reform Bill that he believed an outbreak of cholera to be a divine visitation on a wicked people, was also a strong and practical advocate of the rights of the poor. 'I incline to think there will come a time when public opinion will no more tolerate the extreme of poverty in a large class of the community than it now tolerates slavery in Europe.' He attacked passionately the 'new sort of slave-trade' by which workhouse children were sent off in wagon-loads to supply the new manufactories with cheap labour. His political jeremiads invited ridicule, but his social policies were imaginative and fruitful. They influenced profoundly both 'young England' and the Christian socialists. Newman was one of his most ardent admirers. Shelley, the opposite to him in personality and ideas, found him a sympathetic friend.

He was devoted to his family but he could always find time for friends and visitors. This was real generosity, for time is the wealth of such a writer. He was a sympathetic reviewer and took care to help new authors; not for him the ruthlessness of a Jeffrey or a Macaulay. Even in controversy, as with Byron, he was more self-righteous than vicious. He accumulated a wonderful library and he liked to play with his numerous cats (his correspondence is much concerned with them). There are some delightful things in his occasional writings: *The Cattery of Cat's Eden* and his children's story, *The Three Bears*. He was only a spectator amongst the wild scenes of the Lakes, not essentially a Laker. 'You have been reading the great book of Nature', he said to John Wilson as he stood by the window admiring the view. 'Here' — he pointed to his library — 'are the volumes of men.' He described himself as 'one, at the foot of Skiddaw, who is never more contentedly employed than when learning from the living minds of other ages'. His knowledge was indeed vast: witness the contributions, from 1808 to his death, to the *Quarterly Review*. His letter describing the ancient and beautiful Portuguese university town of Coimbra is as evocative as anything of its sort. His *Letters from England* (1807), purporting to be the translation of a Spaniard's account of travel in England, is a witty, observant, sometimes startlingly sharp documentary on English life and manners. It reveals a sensitive person with a gift for irony.

He had need of stoicism before he died. Three children died; his wife went mad in 1834, died in 1837. His own faculties were clouded thereafter. He married the poetess Caroline Bowles in 1839 for companionship and he toiled on to the end at his books, greeting his friends without knowing them. He died among shadows and there his reputation has remained. And yet where light has been shed there is revealed a good man and a fine writer of English prose.

J. Simmons, *Southey*, 1945.
G. Carnall, *Robert Southey and His Age*, 1960.

CHARLES LAMB (1775-1834), essayist, may have, on the score of his published work, a modest place among English authors, but his life and writing evoke a special affection. No one ever spoke of him without his Christian name. He was a small, clumsy man, who stammered; his eyes were of different colours. De Quincey wrote of his appearance in sleep when his face 'assumed an expression almost seraphic, from its intellectual beauty of outline, its childlike simplicity, and its benignity'. The eyes, however, 'disturbed the unity of effect in Lamb's waking face' and imparted a feeling of restlessness, 'shifting, like Northern lights, through every mode of combination with fantastic playfulness', Lamb's personality intrudes excitably into everything that he writes.

The essays, by which Lamb is best known, elaborate upon his letters and conversation. Part of their appeal is that their author appears to talk to us as intimates, standing upon the common ground of shared experiences. Together his essays amount to an autobiography. Lamb was a Londoner and seldom happy for long away from the crowded and smoky streets of Fleet and Strand, Covent Garden, the narrow lanes of the City and the quiet law courts. With Doctor Johnson and Charles Dickens he is one of the three great Londoners of our literature. As he wrote, in a letter to Wordsworth, comparing his love of London with the poet's 'rural emotions': 'The crowds, the very dirt and mud, the sun shining upon houses and pavements, the print shops, the old bookstalls, parsons cheap'ning books, coffee houses, steams of soups from kitchens, the pantomimes, London itself a pantomime and a masquerade — all these things work themselves into my mind and feed me without a power of satisfying me.'

He was born 'under the shadow of St. Dunstan's steeple' and lived for seventeen years at the Temple, where his father was clerk and servant to Mr Salt, Bencher of the Temple. John Lamb had literary tastes and wrote light verse. His wife, Elizabeth Field, was the daughter of the housekeeper of a fine house in Hertfordshire;

we may read of it, as a child recalled it in 'Blakesmoor in H-shire'. Charles had the run of Mr Salt's library, as valuable, perhaps, as the education he got at Christ's Hospital, where he went at the age of seven. In two of his pleasantest essays he describes the rigours of his boyhood at this school. He became a good Latinist and he acquired an exceptional friend in Samuel Taylor Coleridge. Yet he was unable to reach a university, perhaps because of his stammer. What this deprivation meant to him may be gauged from his essay 'Oxford in the Vacation'. There is pathos in his make-believe: 'When the peacock vein rises, I strut a Gentleman Commoner. In graver moments, I proceed a Master of Arts.'

He went into the East India Company's offices. His brother, twelve years older than he, was already a clerk in the South Sea Company's office where Charles had started. Lamb's essay upon that establishment recalls the best of Dickens and that writer's keen eye for the odd and the archaic. The work in Charles' office was hard. He was there for thirty-three years, six days a week, often working long hours. But in the evenings he lived more agreeably the convivial life of literary conversation. At places like the Salutation tavern in Newgate Street he talked with Coleridge. 'You first kindled in me, if not the power, yet the love of poetry and beauty and kindliness', Lamb wrote when he dedicated his collected works to the poet. There might also be found there William and Dorothy Wordsworth, Keats, de Quincey, Leigh Hunt, Southey, Hood and Godwin. There Hazlitt found Lamb and recalled him for us: 'No one ever stammered out such fine, piquant, deep, eloquent things in half a dozen half-sentences as he does ... What a keen, laughing, hare-brained vein of home-felt truth!'

The background of his life was tragic, the protracted sequel to one awful act. In his later years John Lamb's mind became soft: he was no longer the man whom his son sketches, as Lovel, in 'The Old Benchers of the Inner Temple'. On Mary, ten years older than Charles, fell the brunt of looking after her ageing parents. Charles himself spent a few weeks in an asylum when he was twenty and there was a streak of mental instability in the family. One day in 1796 Mary went out of her mind and killed her mother with a knife. Charles was allowed to take responsibility for her and he looked after her for the rest of his life. Whenever she felt that her reason was giving way she went willingly to hospital. When she was sane she was an intelligent and devoted companion who could, as in their joint *Tales from Shakespeare,* share in his work. It may have been for her sake that he never married. At nineteen he fell in love with a Hertfordshire girl who married someone else. Later he wooed, unsuccessfully, the actress, Fanny Kelly. Some of the restlessness of his nature was surely the result of his anxiety about Mary; he played the buffoon, and drank a lot at parties. Working as hard as he did, reading deeply and caring for his sis- · ter, it is extraordinary that he found so much time for his letters. 'Everybody allows that the art of writing agreeable letters is peculiarly female', says Jane Austen's Henry Tilney to Catherine Morland. 'Letter-writing is a private art: and private life is woman's native and triumphant achievement' writes Lord David Cecil. Lamb's letters are then a *tour de force*: feminine in delicacy and perceptiveness but robust, amusing and above all generous. They must have been delightful to receive.

His first published work consisted of four sonnets in Coleridge's volume of poems (1796). In 1798, with his friend Charles Lloyd, he put out a slender volume of verse which contained 'Old Familiar Faces'. But when he turned to prose he found a richer ore. In 1797 he published his prose romance, *The Tale of Rosamund Gray and Old Blind Margaret.* In 1801 came *John Woodvil,* the product of his intensive study of Elizabethan dramatic poetry, which he helped to restore to fashion. In 1807 he caught public attention with the *Tales from Shakespeare* for Godwin's Junior Library. In the next year *Specimens of the English Dramatic Poets* showed his ripening ability. His taste was for the elaborate and fanciful, the older and quainter the better. Amongst writers he put Shakespeare first; he also had a vast knowledge of the Elizabethan and Jacobean dramatists. He had favourites among prose writers. 'Elia' (Lamb) describes himself as 'hanging over (for the thousandth time) some passage in old Burton, or one of his strange contemporaries.'

His library of books, many tattered bookstall bargains, was an extension of his personality. Another form of escape was the theatre, which he dearly loved: 'A mob of happy faces crowding up at the pit door of Drury Lane Theatre gives me ten thousand sincerer pleasures than I could ever receive from all the flocks of silly sheep that ever whitened the plains of Arcadia or Epsom

Downs'. All the sadder was the fate of the one of his four plays to reach the stage, *Mr H-* (1806). The first-night audience killed it — and Lamb joined in the hissing.

When his essays first appeared in 1820, under the name of Elia, they were a great success. Since the first essay was 'The South-Sea House' it is not surprising that its authorship did not long remain a secret! The lack of constructive power which was fatal to his efforts as playwright, the somewhat artificial style which would have detracted from a novel, do not matter in an essay when the author is talking freely of himself. Lamb is especially an essayist of the feelings. Lynd says of him that 'He seems to steep his very words in some dye of memory and affection that no other writer has discovered' and, again: 'He is at once Hamlet and Yorick in his melancholy and his mirth.' Through his essays he has become with Dr. Johnson and James Boswell the most intimately known character in our literature: how much gentler than Johnson, how much more admirable than Boswell!

Lamb made enough money to avoid debt and provide for his sister. In their later years, Mary and he adopted a girl, Emma Isola. In 1825, in failing health, he retired from his company and was given a generous pension. He settled in Edmonton, in his beloved Hertfordshire, but separation from his friends made him lonely for the first time in his life. In deepening darkness of mind, Mary was to survive him by nearly thirteen years. In January 1834 Taylor the publisher wrote: 'Poor Charles Lamb is dead — perhaps you had not heard of it before. He fell down and cut his face against the Gravel on the Turnpike Road, which brought on the Erisypelas, and in a few days carried him off.'

E. V. Lucas, *Life of Charles Lamb*, 2 vols., Revised edition, 1921.
Edmund Blunden, *Charles Lamb and his Contemporaries*. 1933.

**WILLIAM HAZLITT** (1778-1830) was an awkward individualist of many talents. He was metaphysician, social reformer, painter and student of painting, connoisseur of the theatre, Shakespearian; it was in literary criticism and in the writing of essays that he excelled.

He was born at Maidstone, the son of an Irish Unitarian minister. His mother, Grace Loftus, was the daughter of a dissenting ironmaster. When Hazlitt was five his father went to America for three years: the war of independence was just finished and the political climate appealed to this sturdy dissenter, the friend of Priestley and Price. He once told his son: 'You must fixedly resolve never, through any possible motives, to do anything which you believe to be wrong.' It was to be William's life text. A miniature by John Hazlitt, his brother, shows him as a boy: the face is enchanting, but there is a wayward look and a determined set of jaw.

In 1787 the family settled at Wem and William grew up in the quiet north Shropshire countryside. Though we are told that he was 'moved habitually by the spirit of contradiction', he loved his father. He studied for two years at the New College at Hackney until he decided, in 1795, that he had no desire to enter the ministry. Plays appealed to him more than sermons; he liked philosophy but it did not help him to arrive at any settled convictions. He was always a person of deep feelings, sudden, overmastering revelations. He never forgot the vision of natural beauty aroused by a Walworth garden which he saw in wide-eyed boyhood. 'I set out in life with the French Revolution', he later wrote: it was a shaking and transforming experience. He was ten when the Bastille fell; all his life he adored Napoleon, and he wrote a life in four volumes (1828-30). Luckily he did not live to see the failure of what he meant to be his greatest work. Never disillusioned, obstinately generous, content to run across the grain of contemporary opinion and to be in this, as in so much else, the brilliant outsider, Hazlitt described at the end of his life how 'as a little child I knelt and lifted up my heart in prayer for the Revolution'.

'The stage not only refines the manners, but it is the best teacher of morals, for it is the truest and most intelligible picture of life.' To read Hazlitt on acting is to realize how he loved the theatre. He saw Mrs Siddons act at Hackney. 'The gates were unbarred, the folding doors of fancy were thrown open and I saw all that mankind had been, or that I myself could conceive, pass in sudden and gorgeous review before me.' He became theatre critic of *The Times* (1816) and brought to this work an intimate knowledge of the stage. *Characters of Shakespeare's Plays* (1817) is still one of the most stimulating approaches to the study of the dramatist. Superior in many ways to the *Characters* are his *Lectures on the English Poets* (1818) and

*William Hazlitt*
(Artist: William Bewick)

*English Comic Writers* (1819). There was surely a feeling of affinity when he wrote, in the letter, of Dr. Johnson and his prejudices: 'His were not time-serving, heartless, hypercritical prejudices; but deep, inwoven, not to be rooted out but with life and hope, which he found from old habit necessary to his own peace of mind, and thought so to the peace of mankind. I do not hate, but love him for them.'

In his essay, 'My first acquaintance with poets', Hazlitt describes the impact upon him of Coleridge and Wordsworth. In sentence after sentence he makes the poets live, offering not so much an interpretation as a series of brilliant observations and guesses about them. Minutely observant, Hazlitt painted with words: witness his study of Coleridge's face. It was his ambition to be a great painter, and he became a talented one, as his portraits of Lamb and Coleridge reveal. At the exhibition of Italian pictures in London in 1799 'a new sense came upon me, a new heaven and a new earth stood before me'. He spent a few months of 1802 in Paris, studying and copying the paintings of the Louvre. He could savour the ebullience of Napoleon's France; his mood was one of 'joy unutterable', but it was one which could not be sustained. Like many enthusiasts Hazlitt found it hard to be detached about himself. His self-concern indeed bordered on the neurotic. Coleridge offered the salute of one eccentric to another: 'A thinking, observant, original man, brow-hanging, shoe-contemplative, *strange.*'

Hazlitt was unlucky with women: perhaps he expected too much and conceded too little. In 1808 he married Sarah Stoddart and went to live in her cottage at Winterslow in Wiltshire. He loved the place but tired of the woman. In 1820 he fell blindly in love with Sarah Walker, the daughter of his London lodging-house keeper and went off to Scotland to obtain a divorce; but he returned to find that this 'vision of love and joy' had gone off with someone else. We know about the affair from the *Liber Amoris*, a painfully exact self-revelation. He brooded and drank excessively but managed to recover; thereafter he would drink nothing stronger than tea. There was a masochistic tendency to punish himself. His friends deplored his self-mistrust and outbursts of violence. He tended to behave as if he had inherited the wounds of earlier dissenters and would not let them heal. He was, moreover, a perfectionist. He gave up painting though it was the passion of his early life: if he could not be brilliant then he would not be anything.

As a critic Hazlitt was often brilliant. *The Spirit of the Age* (1825) displayed him at the height of his powers. He was writing his spiritual life-story and presenting the literary characters of his age, not dispassionately but with a steady gaze. In his words, 'anger may sharpen our insight into men's defects; but nothing should make us blind to their excellences'. His criticism fastens upon the personality of the writer as it is revealed in his work — and illuminates the work in the process. His 'character writing' bears the marks of long reflection, ideas long mulled, principles long fought for, prejudices deeply ingrained. Hazlitt studied and wrote as he lived, intensely, and without thought for his health. His range is remarkable. He was the first man to give a comprehensive picture of English literature. From Chaucer to Scott, he provided critics with landmarks and perspectives, judgements to accept or to attack, but rarely to ignore.

Hazlitt's essays were collected in the *Round Table* but they were mostly written in the first place for the *Examiner* and, according to Leigh Hunt's intention, in the manner of the eighteenth-century essayists of the *Tatler* and *Spectator*. The essay, according to Hazlitt, 'is to morals and manners what the experimental is to natural philosophy, as opposed to the dogmatical method'. Less whimsical than Lamb, more concerned with the truth of the ideas that he is pursuing, his essays amount to fragments of autobiography. 'On Going a Journey' or 'The Fight' seem to be written so naturally that the literary artifice goes at first unnoticed. The vivacity of the writing helps to explain how it was that Hazlitt retained the respect and affection of those who knew him best. In the words of Virginia Woolf, 'There can be no question that Hazlitt the thinker is an admirable companion. He is strong and fearless; and he speaks his mind forcibly yet brilliantly too. ... There is scarcely an essay without its stress of thought, its thrust of insight, its moment of penetration.'

Hazlitt married again, in 1824, a handsome widow, Isabella Bridgewater, and travelled with her in France, Italy and Switzerland. She left him after only three years. Suffering from what seems to have been a form of stomach cancer, living a somewhat withdrawn life in Winterslow, or latterly London, Hazlitt continued to toil at his essays and *Napoleon*. His friends, notably Lamb, stood by him to the last and he lacked for nothing. Even so it is surprising to hear that his last words, according to his son, were 'Well, I've had a happy life.'

P. P. Howe, *The Life of William Hazlitt*, 1922.
Stanley Jones, *Hazlitt*, 1989.

**ROBERT BURNS** (1759-96), poet, wrote lyrics and songs in the Scottish dialect of English. Reckless in his living and loving, he was viewed by some as a shocking reprobate but by others with admiration, for his radical style as much as for his songs: there

were enough admirers to ensure 'the immortal memory': the
Burns of devout commemoration.

In early youth he was upset by his father's misfortunes and
embittered against a social system which he held responsible for
them. William Burns, a gardener, came from Kincardineshire to
Ayrshire to make his living as tenant farmer. He died worn out
and bankrupt in 1784. Robert too farmed for some years. He
wrote poems to express his feelings and entertain his friends,
some bawdy, some caustic. Scott thought that 'Holy Willie's
Prayer' was a masterpiece. He had read deeply among the great
English writers; his knowledge of the Scottish was limited to
orally transmitted folk songs. In 1786 he published a volume,
*Poems Chiefly in the Scottish Dialect.* It was an instant success.
Plain countrymen could enjoy them; so could genteel Edinburgh
folk. So Burns was lionised, befriended, patronised and given
much advice. The duchess of Gordon had never met a man
'whose conversation so completely swept her off her feet'. By 1787
this 'lewd, amazing peasant of genius' (W. E. Henley) had
completed most of the poems on which his fame would subsequently rest. He had found a style that matched the sentiment of
the day: natural man and noble peasant were lauded, with much
that was naive and sentimental. Fortunately that was not all.
There were some fine poems. Some would select 'The Holy Fair'
or 'To a Mouse' to represent his style at its best. He still needed
to forget his audience — and what he assumed to be their
expectations.

Meanwhile his life was as confused and uncertain as his poetic
course. Jean Armour bore his child — but out of wedlock, since
she was persuaded by her father to renounce her earlier promise.
Robert lived with Mary Campbell; she died. Then Jean bore him
twins. There were other amorous adventures before Jean became
his wife, in 1788. When he died she was expecting their ninth
child. She would be thirty eight years his widow.

The best of Burns, in art and personality, emerged in his
relationship with James Johnson, a collector of Scottish songs,
who enlisted his help in finding, editing and rewriting old songs
for his *Scots Musical Museum.* Later he became involved in a similar project for George Thomson and further songs appear in
Thomson's *Select Collection.* Burns spent much time on this
work, with much that was original, as he sought to find new

words for old airs. He wished to serve his country and would receive no payment.

In 1789 a post in the excise service, after 1791 based in Dumfries, enabled him to settle down and to resolve some of the strains inherent in his life divided, as it had been, between farming, literature and the social life of the capital. 'I am a poor rascally gager', he wrote; in fact he was a good one, energetic and bold in a hazardous profession: a foe to smugglers. He took other kinds of risk when he praised French revolutionaries or drank too much of the smugglers' brandy. A kind of courage was undoubtedly a characteristic of this cocksure, heedless man — and it would not harm the legend. But what matters is that he spoke with the voice of the Scottish people, entered into the spirit of their folk song and wrote or adapted masterpieces that would be heard wherever his countrymen gathered: that, of course, would be all over the world.

David Daiches, *Robert Burns* (rev. edn) 1966.
Ian McIntyre, *Dirt and Deity. A Life of Robert Burns,* 1996.

**SARAH SIDDONS** (1756-1831), actress, was 'born in the Shoulder of Mutton inn at Brecon, the eldest daughter of Roger and Sarah Kemble: Roger was actor-manager of a travelling troupe. At first a lady's maid, she was soon being called on for recitations in the servants' hall. Like her sister, Fanny, she became an actress. At eighteen she married William Siddons, an indifferent player and personality, but a fair judge of his wife's talent. Her first success seems to have come at Cheltenham with a performance in *Venice Preserved*. From Worcester a clergyman wrote to tell Garrick that she had a fine figure and would do especially well 'in breeches parts'. (She was in fact prudish in such matters; when she played Rosalind she insisted upon appearing in a costume that was not recognizably either masculine or feminine — and somewhat ridiculous!) At Drury Lane in 1775-6, the then ageing Garrick gave her promising parts, including Lady Anne against his Richard III, but she did not excel and was not re-engaged. Never a modest critic of her own work, she blamed Garrick for her failure; in truth she was inhibited and had not developed the grand and passionate style of her maturity. In the provinces again she was coached by Mr Pratt, bookseller of Bath, and acquired the poise which she never thereafter lost.

The Duchess of Devonshire found her another opening in London; in 1782 she returned to Drury Lane and enraptured her audience in Southerne's *Fatal Marriage*. The theatre was packed for every performance of *Measure for Measure*, in which she played Isabella. Her true *métier* she found when she played Lady Macbeth. She refused, to the consternation of the management, to carry a candle in the sleep-walking scene, as Mrs Pritchard had done. But the audience were so engrossed by her performance that they did not notice. Now she could make her own rules and terms. Several of her brothers and sisters, notably John Kemble, followed in her wake, and with them arrived a new style of acting. Less natural than Garrick and his contemporaries, less vivacious than Edmund Kean in his heyday, theirs was a stately, declamatory manner, 'high tragedy', suited to Sarah's Junoesque figure. 'If you ask me, "What is a queen?",' said Tate Wilkinson, 'I should say, Mrs Siddons.'

She was a striking woman, with high-bridged nose and imperious mouth, the delight of painters and symbol of fashionable society. Reynolds and Gainsborough immortalized her on canvas. Playwrights and politicians were at her feet, among them Burke, Windham, Goldsmith and Sheridan — though the last found difficulty in paying her salary. Dr. Johnson, whom she visited at Bolt Court, pronounced her 'one of the few persons whom neither praise nor money ... had depraved'. 'One would as soon think of making love to the archbishop of Canterbury as to Mrs Siddons,' people said. She lived mostly apart from her husband and quarrelled bitterly with her sister Fanny. She was sharp in money matters and haughty back-stage: managers winced before her demands. She had children to support, seven altogether, though four of her daughters died young. By all accounts she was a devoted mother, and would turn down invitations to dinners to be with them.

After the eighties she began to appear less regularly. Volumnia, Cordelia and Desdemona remained among the parts which she invested with that special character of which Hazlitt wrote: 'Power was seated on her brow; passion emanated from her breast as from a shrine. She was tragedy personified.' In 1802 she and her brother John took a share in Convent Garden Theatre. It was burned down and re-built, but the seats were more expensive; after re-opening there were riots for nights and a clamour for the 'O.P.' (old price). In 1812 Mrs Siddons took her final bow as Lady Macbeth. When she died in 1831, over 5,000 people attended her funeral in Paddington church, a tribute to the years when 'to have seen Mrs Siddons was an event in everyone's life'.

Y. Ffrench, *Mrs Siddons*, 1936.

**HENRY CRABB ROBINSON** (1775-1867), chronicler of his times, was the son of a tanner of Bury St Edmunds. In his youth he was an attorney's clerk. A small legacy enabled him to go to Germany. He was there for five years, 1800-5, mainly at Jena, Frankfurt and Weimar. Outgoing, friendly, liking the company of interesting people, he met most of the Germans who exercised such an influence at that time, notably Goethe, Schiller and Herder — and the famous *émigré*, Mme de Stael. From 1807 to 1809 he worked for the *Times*, latterly in Spain: he could be called the first war correspondent. In 1813 he was called to the Bar and worked hard enough to enable him to retire, in 1828, with sufficient income to enable him further to cultivate and record literary life. He was one of the founders of London University (1828) and an early member of the Athenaeum Club.

It was said of Crabb Robinson that he never lost a friend. Only with Hazlitt was there a brief estrangement — and then because that provocative writer criticised both Wordsworth, another friend, and the law — his profession. Robinson certainly never wearied in the pursuit of friendship, nor in the acts of imaginative kindness which secured it. He had a special regard for Coleridge; for Blake the devotion that the critic owes to genius. It is partly through him and through his matchless diaries that we know them, along with Lamb, Wordsworth, Southey, the Flaxmans, Miss Mitford; indeed few among the most interesting, gifted people of the day were outside his acquaintance. The value of his diaries lies in his assiduity, his fairness, in a way the ordinariness, allied to integrity, that inspired trust — and confidences. The attraction lies in the absence of malice, affectation, exhibitionism. 'The best English diaries', wrote Kate O'Brien, 'have been written by bores'. If this be a rule, he is an exception for which we, like his many friends, may be grateful.

**EDMUND KEAN** (*c*. 1787-1833) was the finest tragic actor of his day, a man who lived wildly and dissipated his great talents. The events of his boyhood are uncertain, since the main source is Kean himself — and he liked to embroider a tale. It seems that he was the son of Nance Carey, a strolling actress, who soon abandoned him. He appeared as a stage cupid, received lessons from a ventriloquist uncle and a Drury Lane actress; he went as a cabin boy to Madeira, but soon returned and fell into the life of a stroller. He played Prince Arthur at Drury Lane when about fourteen but went off to take a circus job in Bartholomew Fair. Having broken both legs tumbling in Saunders' circus he returned to less dangerous employment. Engagements included a recitation before George III at Windsor, small parts at the Haymarket and larger parts in the provinces. He married Mary Chambers, an Irishwoman some years older than himself, in 1808, and they lived precariously for some years. He was always impulsive and often drunk. On one occasion, while he was playing in Norwich, he was due to dine the next day with Bishop Bathurst. He had a battle in the street with nightwatchmen and was so disfigured that he was compelled to send his apologies to the good bishop. A large bump on his nose threatened to be permanent. 'No matter', he said to his wife, 'I shall now have a Roman nose as well as John Kemble' (his greatest rival and leader of the 'declamatory' school of acting).

Dr. Drury, the headmaster of Harrow, came across Kean playing at Exeter — and even acting Shylock and Harlequin in the same evening! He got a Mr Grenfell to write to Whitbread about Kean and the manager of Drury Lane Theatre engaged him for three years. Appearing in the rôle of Shylock he was loudly acclaimed. There followed the parts of Richard III, Hamlet, Othello and Iago. 'To see Kean act is like reading Shakespeare by flashes of lightning', said Coleridge. For Hazlitt he was 'an excellent substitute for the memory of Garrick', but no more than Kemble could he act the perfect Hamlet: 'Mr Kean's Hamlet is too splenetic and rash, as Mr Kemble's is too pointed and formal. His manner is too strong and pointed. He throws a severity, approaching to virulence, into the common observations and answers.' The criticism tells us a lot about Kean, though it should be remembered that Hazlitt thought that there should be 'as much of the gentleman and scholar as possible infused into the part and as little of the actor'. He also said that his acting was 'not much relished in the upper circles. It is thought too undisguised a display of nature.'

Kean's performances would very likely seem to us unsubtle and blustering. He was obviously powerful in stage presence, although quite small, and bandy-legged after his accident. He had a musical voice and a fine head. He was convicted, in a sordid case (*Cox v Kean, 1825*) and had to pay damages to the man with whose wife he had been having an affair. His reputation never recovered fully from this episode, though he had good receptions in Paris and New York and was elected a Huron chief in Canada. Performances and public reaction were both unpredictable. Acting, in his tempestuous manner, before excitable, impressionable audiences, taxed him physically and emotionally. He would sometimes go for solitary, hectic, midnight rides along the turnpike, returning to sleep in the stable. He built a little cottage in Bute to retreat to in depressed and remorseful moods. There once he tried to stab his wife. His Coriolanus failed, his Lear was a popular triumph. He revelled in Sir Giles Overeach and it is in this part that he is depicted in George Clint's painting at the Garrick Club, one of several which portray his classical rôles. He was capable of thrilling audiences to the end in his best rôles. He was playing Richard III in the year of his death, and his last illness overcame him when he was acting Othello.

Recklessly generous with the large sums of money he earned in his heyday, Kean offended his admirers by his debauched taste for low company, and he ill-treated his wife. He was ashamed of his origins and he sent his son Charles to Eton. He too became an actor and producer in due course: devoted to his mother, he effected a last-minute reconciliation between his parents.

Raymund Fitzsimons, *Edmund Kean, Fire from Heaven*, 1973.

**SIR HENRY RAEBURN** (1756-1823), portrait painter, called 'the Scottish Reynolds' (though Romney was a closer parallel), was born in Edinburgh, to which his father had come, as the last of a line of Border farmers, to set up in a mill in Stockbridge on the Water of Leith. Raeburn was left an orphan at the age of eight and grew up under the gentle care of his adult brother. He

was apprenticed (like several of the Renaissance painters) to a
goldsmith, who encouraged him in miniature painting. In 1778 he
married Ann Leslie, a prosperous widow; she brought him an
estate adjoining his brother's in Stockbridge, and great domestic
happiness. To visit London in 1785 was, for an artist, to visit
Reynolds; and Reynolds sent Raeburn on to Rome for two years.
In 1787 he returned to Edinburgh, which had entered on its golden
age. Of this happy period Raeburn was for thirty years the biographer in paint: in nearly 700 portraits he commemorated those
who in talents or birth were then 'the most virile and unspoilt
aristocracy in Europe'. 'I could see none of my old friends,' said
an elderly lady returning to Edinburgh in the 1870s 'until I went
into the Raeburn Gallery, and found them all there.' Of course, he
sometimes desired to loose the bonds of his provincial limnership.
He must have yearned to work in London, to refresh his own
brushwork by painting with his peers, to have Fox, Nelson or
Canning as his sitter. But he was dissuaded; and the result is a
*corpus* of the features of a single society, completer even than the
Holbein drawings of the Court of Henry VIII. Raeburn was
elected R.A. in 1815, and knighted by George IV, when the king
made his famous visit to Edinburgh in 1822. He died in the
following year, from a cold caught while visiting St. Andrew's in
the company of Walter Scott.

There was nothing bohemian about this artist. He golfed,
fished and played the archer with his friends. He took his young
son Henry on highland expeditions to gather material for his
landscape backgrounds. Not content with painting, he acted as
architect; and the names Raeburn Place and Ann Street recall
where he laid out a part of Edinburgh's new town on the family's
Stockbridge properties.

Had he been a scientist too, he might have become a parent of
the photographic camera; for as artist he was preoccupied (like
Wright of Derby) with the effect of light falling on the human
figure. Form in a Raeburn portrait is expressed in terms of
chiaroscuro, by broad areas of light and shade spread out with
crisp, decisive brushstrokes. As he worked without assistants, he
painted the whole picture himself, and he painted with assurance
and speed (his method of work is splendidly described by Stevenson in *Virginibus Puerisque*). But facility is frequently dangerous.
In Raeburn's case it too often barred him from exploring the

depths and complications of character. And in any case the sun of his own disposition cancelled all that was dark or weak or vicious in others. It seems he 'never saw an ugly face'; and he crowns his sitters with virtues to which many of them can have aspired only in their happiest moments. Qualities of nobility, benevolence and grace are dealt out pretty justly here and there, but sit uneasily — almost vulgarly — on the more homespun of his clients. Raeburn was too kind to be candid. But there they stand or sit, in novel attitudes, in romantic surroundings, looking down their noses, a race of demi-semi-gods. What masterpiece has *Lt. Col. Lyon* been caught sketching? Is there any secret of the world or the law that *Adam Rolland* is not privy to? Can benign *Dr. Adam*, Rector of the High School, really have died of apoplexy? (We know he did.) Here *Dr. Spens* draws an arrow which cannot miss its mark; here *The Revd. Robert Walker* is one with the north wind, as he skates on Duddingston Loch. On this side *The MacNab*, in full panoply, has hurried to the studio straight from a gathering of his clan; on that, the lovely *Mrs Scott Moncrieff* confounds the assertion that Raeburn could not paint a young woman. There breathe the Judges, rosy and affable. ... but in truth, as soon as you start to look, you forget how to cavil.

Theodore Brotchie, *Henry Raeburn*, 1924.

**GEORGE ROMNEY** (1734-1802), portrait painter, was born in Lancashire, was apprenticed to a local artist and, shortly after his marriage to Mary Abbott in 1756, established himself in Kendal and invited clients. In 1762 he removed himself, but not his wife or children, to London, where he had some preliminary success with history paintings submitted to the Society of Arts. He travelled abroad to France and Italy, and when he finally returned to England in 1775, he was in a fair way to engage a public somewhat tired of the pomp of Reynolds and the subtlety of Gainsborough. Although he remained a shy, vulnerable, solitary man, who refused to send his pictures to the Academy, he attracted a wide patronage and not least — for it was worth a legion of flatterers — that of the Duchess of Devonshire. Soon he was the professional rival of Reynolds himself, who, being nettled that fashion was thus preferred to art, spoke coldly of 'the man in Cavendish Square'. Romney might have been expected now to call his wife to share in his success; but, whether at her own wish or not, she continued lonely in Lancashire for twenty years, during which her husband passed through prosperity to the sole eminence to which Reynolds's death raised him; only then, with the sense upon him that the night was coming when he could not work, did Romney return to his wife. To her credit, and perhaps a little to the credit of Romney's charm, she gladly received him until his death in imbecility in 1802.

The parents of Miss Bowles were for having her painted by Romney, fearing the tendency of Reynold's portraits to fade. 'Never mind,' they were told, 'a faded picture by Reynolds is better than the best of Romney's.' What Reynolds made of the girl and her dog is there in the Wallace Collection for anyone to delight in; but in any case the comparison was just. Romney's pictures do not glow like Reynolds's, they do not explore the mysteries which Gainsborough's do. But Romney was always elegant. In him a masterly hand supported a strong and simple sense of style. He could realize the visionary prospects of an aristocratic youth on the verge of manhood (*William Pitt, Richard Newman Harding*, and some of the Eton leaving portraits); he could figure the maturity of an interesting man (*Joseph Allan, Warren Hastings*; and the portraits of *Cowper*). Unfortunately he fell for the space of four years from 1781 into a sort of infatuation with Emma Lyon or Hart, soon to be Lady Hamilton, who appears now 'in a straw hat', now 'in a turban', now surprisingly as 'Innocence'. He painted about fifty pictures of her. Lady Hamilton (however lovely) was a shallow woman, as unworthy perhaps of Romney's attentions as of Nelson's. Yet Romney seems to have taken her as the type of womanhood, and thereafter could hardly paint a woman in depth: an easy sentimentality, a failure in taste amounting to the banal, pervades his work, and intrudes even into the Eton portraits.

Romney's freshness was always attractive; it is due in part to his temperamental dislike of finishing a picture once the heat of invention had cooled. Cartloads of paintings just begun were removed from his house at Hampstead after his death, and even in his finest work the details are often only sketched in.

Ellis Waterhouse, *Painting in Britain 1530-1790*, 1969.
Leger Galleries, *George Romney as a Painter of Children*, 1984.

JAMES GILLRAY (1756-1815), artist and satirist, was the son of a veteran of Fontenoy turned sexton. When only twelve, he did a caricature of Lord North, and proved what was in his blood. He was apprenticed to a signwriter and studied at the Royal Academy. Beginning in the vein of social satire, he was soon attracted to politics, and from 1782 to 1811, by dint of his formidable imagination and rapid execution, was the leading political caricaturist in Britain. The windows of Miss Humphrey's print-shop in St. James' Street, where he also boarded for the greater part of his life, became the cynosure of those eager spirits who wished to see what new and scurrilous interpretation Gillray had put on political events. The unblushing violence of his caricatures, often repulsive to us today, was evidently acceptable to the eighteenth-century politicians; indeed, it is by considering that Gillray was never pursued for libel that one gathers how thick-skinned they were; and the licence allowed him was a source of amazement to Germans and others with a straitened experience of political liberty. Even the royal family, who received again and again the shafts of Gillray, were sorely offended, it seems, only when the Queen was depicted unclad as one of a trio with Pitt and Thurlow in *Sin, Death and the Devil* (1792). Though Pitt was cast as *Death on the Pale Horse* in 1795, he was generally treated without animosity and even with respect: Gillray was a Tory at heart and patronized by Canning. But the venom was reserved for Napoleon 'the Corsican Carcase-Butcher' and for the Whigs who espoused the cause of the Revolutionaries in France. The swarthy features of Fox being a gift for any caricaturist, his 'loyalty' is severely handled. Though Gillray engraved cartoons of astonishing complexity (and that he could do so without the least endangering their formal composition appears from *Shakespeare Sacrificed* (1789), *Promis'd Horrors of the French Invasion* (1796), and *The Apotheosis of Hoche* (1798) or when he draws a multitude of readily recognized politicians in *The Union-Club* of 1801) he preserves nonetheless the gift of a cartoonist to catch in memorable simplicity the essence of a situation — as where Pitt and Napoleon divide the globe in *The Plum-Pudding in Danger* (1805).

Gillray sired the race of political cartoonists which descends through the Cruikshanks, the Doyles, and Leech, down to the cartoonists, political but more polite, of our own day. He was said, by a man who knew him, to be 'a stranger to the feelings of friendship' — which is of course an easy indictment of one who lives by venom. His loneliness was relieved only by Miss Humphrey: once they decided to marry, and set out for St. James's, Piccadilly; but on the way they changed their minds and turned back. Gillray drank heavily, and died in imbecility.

Draper Hill, *Mr Gillray, The caricaturist*, 1965.

THOMAS ROWLANDSON (1756-1827), artist and satirist, was born in comfortable circumstances, studied at the Royal Academy Schools and in Paris while still a boy, and exhibited drawings at the Academy from the age of nineteen. Having squandered a small fortune, he supplied his needs by prodigal use of reed-pen and brush. He settled in London, from which, to refresh his experience, he travelled abroad as often as wars permitted. His huge and various *œuvre* has been described by a modern critic as an English equivalent to Balzac's *Comédie Humaine*; but the inspiration is Rabelaisian. He drew with tremendous brio, startling humour and a total absence of modesty. In his work (the items of which were multiplied by engravings) we find *tableaux* of theatres and ballrooms, amusement parks, fairs and race-meetings; views of town and country, thickly peopled, shaded by stylized trees, extracts of Merry England; scenes of rustic gatherings at inn or stable in the vein of his friend Morland; and book illustrations, as those for William Combe's *Tours of Dr. Syntax* — not to mention the great number of drawings (today we should call them cartoons) which are simply humorous commentaries on the life of his day.

In the kingdom of satire, he divides the honours of the time with Gillray. Gillray was the political, Rowlandson the social, satirist. Rowlandson's blows are aimed at general anomalies, at the scandals of electioneering, at horse-trading in high places, at the hypocrisy of the rich and the fecklessness of the poor. Here he is heir to Hogarth; but he caricatures more savagely than Hogarth and sacrifices truth of observation to a hunger for the grotesque. We do not recognize his creatures as we do Hogarth's, but we laugh at them more. Thus, since he satirized to amuse, not to convert, he was not the preacher that Hogarth was.

He is called a water-colourist, but he harked back to the older practice, and used water-colour only to tint his line-drawings. It is with line that he is the master: however complex the organization of his picture, however widespread the action, Rowlandson's fluent rhythmic line defines the parts, weaves in and out of them, and draws them into a coherent and satisfying composition.

Ronald Paulson, *Rowlandson, a new interpretation*, 1972.

**JAMES WYATT** (1746-1813), architect, came of a family which spawned architects. He rose quickly to a position of unbounded regard, in which he was officially confirmed when he succeeded on Chambers' death (1796) to the Surveyor-Generalship.

He was an artist of astonishing versatility and a genius for borrowing other people's styles. Thus he confessed that 'when he came from Italy he found the public taste corrupted by the Adams, and he was obliged to comply with it'. But his first adventure was in winning the competition (in 1770) for rebuilding the Pantheon in Oxford Street, a temple of concerts and masquerades. Wyatt's Pantheon was burnt down in 1792, but it caused a furore on its erection. The great domed interior was an amalgam of Santa Sophia and the Roman Pantheon — though, as the upper part was entirely of wood, the technical achievement was hardly comparable. But Wyatt's name was made. He had drawn on the Adam brothers for some of the ornament of the Pantheon; the brothers had complained of his plagiarism. He proceeded to build Heaton and to complete Heveningham in a style which must have confirmed their worst fears — and they were right to regret his competition, for the things were brilliantly done and in perfect taste: somehow he seemed to make decoration *mean* more. He then built mausoleums based on designs in Chambers' *Treatise*; and the severer classicism of Chambers is seen again in the interior of Wyatt's Dodington and at the Oriel College Library. But he seemed to have little to say entirely of his own in the tale of classical architecture.

Meanwhile, however, he had taken up Gothic. Perhaps his interest was aroused when he was employed to do some restoration at Salisbury Cathedral. His first essay proper was the house of Lee Priory, which, though it clearly harks back to Horace

Walpole's Strawberry Hill, shows, as perhaps no other neo-Gothic building had shown, that the architect knew what Gothic was really about. Then came Fonthill, which, until its destruction, must have been the most sensational house in England. Built in the pattern of a huge cross, with an octagonal tower in the manner of Ely Cathedral which soared to three-quarters the height of the spire of Salisbury, it was the expression in stone of the fantastic nature of its founder, William Beckford. Beckford hurried on the work; Wyatt (of whom Beckford said 'if he can get near a big fire and have a bottle by him, he cares for nothing else') was characteristically indolent in supervising the supporting arches; and the great tower collapsed a score of years later. After Fonthill, the Gothic Ashridge, built for the Earl of Bridgewater in 1806-13, must, despite its huge central hall, have seemed a mild conception.

Other architects took fire at Wyatt's Gothic, but he was the acknowledged leader of the revival, who prepared the way for Barrie and Pugin. He perished in a carriage accident in 1813.

J. M. Robinson, *The Wyatts, An architectural dynasty*, 1979.

**SIR JOHN SOANE** (1753-1837), architect, was probably the most promising figure in architecture at the turn of the century; after which he has to bear comparison with Nash, whose work was about as different from his as it could have been. Nash was an architect of enormous versatility, who preferred to work in the grand manner, to immerse detail in the over-all effect of mighty schemes. Soane by contrast was an artist of limited range — which, broadly stated, was the neo-classical — who nevertheless went to the furthest limits of that range, and, in so doing, produced some work of surprising originality and an almost twentieth-century *timbre*. It must be added that, although he was sparing in detail, it is the accumulation of clever effects of detail that makes the success of his best buildings.

Having an ambitious frame of mind, he advanced from being the son of a mason to being a pupil of George Dance II and Henry Holland, leading architects of the neo-classical school. He won medals at the Royal Academy, went to Italy on a travelling scholarship, and returned to England in 1780 to a modest diet of country-house design; from which he was rescued by his appointment in 1788 (on Pitt's recommendation) to take over from Sir Robert Taylor, who had died in office, the work of constructing the Bank of England. Now Soane seems to reach maturity in a step. The Bank Stock Office goes up. There is a whiff of Byzantine influence about it, but it breathes on the whole a spirit older than classical antiquity: in such a building Agamemnon might have dwelt. It shows the influence of the theories of the Abbé Laugier, prophet of neo-classicism, who, writing in 1753, had recommended to architects the simple logic of the hut of primitive man, 'the model upon which all the magnificences of architecture have been imagined', and advised that 'one would never put anything in a building for which one cannot give a solid reason'. This plea for economy of means serves also as a comment on much of twentieth-century architecture — from which we deduce Soane's apparent modernity.

There followed the Rotunda in 1796: the unusual grooved ornamentation was perhaps borrowed from Piranesi's Egyptian patterns — Soane was to use it frequently. Much of his building at the Bank has been obscured by late additions, but the fine screen-wall, which is of a decidedly classical design, is largely intact, and the variety of his work on the Bank illustrates his eclectic taste.

Thereafter he built some exquisite country-houses: Moggerhanger, with its curved Doric portico (a dash of Regency), and Pitzhanger (now the Ealing Public Library), fronted by Ionic columns, each with an individual entablature and a figure atop. But his two most interesting buildings are the Dulwich College Art Gallery and Mausoleum, built with a bequest, and his own house at 13 Lincoln's Inn Fields. The Dulwich building, which has been reconstructed after wartime damage, is again primitive in concept; again it bears the grooved patterns; the mausoleum is central, flanked by alms-houses, the picture gallery behind; the proportions are striking, and the whole work is restrained and economical (and not only because there was little money to spend). Of the interior of his own house, of the ingenious methods of lighting and use of mirrors, of the highly personal decoration, much could be said; on the exterior, the pilasters grow out of the top of each other, and their capitals do not support entablatures, but mark the stages of vertical proportion. In this house the fastidious old man assembled the sculptures, the

Hogarth paintings, the thousands of architectural drawings, the sarcophagus of Seti I, and the other *personalia* which he presented to the nation before his death and which can still be seen there.

He was Professor of Architecture at the Royal Academy from 1806 and was knighted in 1831. But he remained a retiring man. The uneasiness he felt in society is mirrored in his work — he often seems uncertain how far he can safely go; sometimes his proportions make the architectural equivalent of a social *gaffe*. He was not 'safe', but that was the price of his originality.

Dorothy Stroud, *Sir John Soane, Architect*, 1984.

JOHN FLAXMAN (1755-1826), sculptor and draughtsman, an artist of original genius, grew up in London in the *milieu* of his father's shop, a manufactory of plastic models and casts for sculptors as distinguished as Scheemakers and Roubiliac. The boy was unhealthy: for a time he could not walk without crutches and, being confined to the shop, he turned to copying and drawing from his father's products. By the age of twelve, he was exhibiting sculptural work at the Society of Artists; at fifteen, he entered the Royal Academy Schools, which were themselves in their infancy. But he worked at improving his mind as well as his hand: read spontaneously; was 'taken up' and introduced to the circle of 'blue-stockings' which surrounded Mrs Montagu; and thus received his baptism into the world of letters and of classical antiquity. Those interests were quickened by his friendship at the Schools with William Blake — widened too, for Blake, though he was two years younger, had long been susceptible to mystic visions, had seen angels among the trees, 'their bright wings bespangling the boughs like stars'; and Flaxman was only too ready to embrace the ecstatic influence. Christian sentiment, then, and veneration of the Antique, were to dominate his work; and he became, for us as for Blake, the 'Dear Sculptor of Eternity'.

In his twentieth year, he joined his father in working for Josiah Wedgwood, who at this time was employing even the great Stubbs. At 'Etruria' the young Flaxman designed an ingenious set of chessmen, now to be seen in the Soane Museum; but his daily task was to invent motifs to be set up in relief on Wedgwood's famous pottery and cameos. His inventions are clear, often beautiful, *pastiches* of Greek vase-painting and Roman friezes;

and the necessity of working at the same time in silhouette and in relief was evidently congenial to him.

For Flaxman's best work was done in relief. In the portrait bust he was not specially interested; as for statues in general, he could match the best of his contemporaries in carving them, as you can see from the Petworth groups, or the monuments to Lord Mansfield (Westminster Abbey) and Lord Nelson (St. Paul's). But he held that the third dimension should be as much the illusion of art as a palpable fact; the method of the relief had the classical virtue of understatement. Besides, it admirably suited the talent he shared with Blake, that for linear design. In the early monument in Gloucester Cathedral, on which Mrs Morley (who had died at sea) rises from some Blake-like waves with the aid of some Raphaelite angels, the relief is so bold that the figures hang out from the wall; later, as in the Homerically simple monument to Dr. Sibthorp in Bath Abbey (1802), the relief is nonetheless effective for being lower. Of this kind is the little monument to Agnes Cromwell (Chichester Cathedral, 1800), a superlative work of rhythm and beauty, excelled in Flaxman's *œuvre* only by the plaster model for the same monument (University College, London). Indeed, it is Flaxman's plaster models which show his genius working at full heat; like other artists of the time (Constable, for example), he felt obliged to elaborate the final work, and in so doing lost some of the spontaneity of the sketch. But also he followed the practice, now becoming general, of leaving much of the final execution assistants working with a pointing machine — an 'advance' which played the devil with individuality of texture.

Not that Flaxman was anxious about texture. In style if not in idea, he was a neo-classical sculptor — that is, he followed the rules and standards of antique sculpture. This did not oblige him to ignore contemporary dress and manners, though some of his mixtures are a trifle bizarre (e.g. the Lord Nelson). It did mean that in modelling features he was bound to prefer the ideal to the natural. He is the obverse of Roubiliac: his planes are broad, generalized and (after the fashion of Canova, the doyen of neo-classical sculptors) polished. The effect is grand when it succeeds, stiff and awkward when it does not.

In search of the Antique, he spent seven years in Italy from 1787. This visit settled his style, brought him the friendship and praise of Canova, and set his pencil to work on those illustrations to Homer which most clearly exemplify the triumphs and the limitations of his simple linear approach. On his return he accumulated a large practice: 'J. Flaxman fecit' is a seal of quality on numerous monuments in country churches; but he was seldom given the big commissions, and we may assume that his original mind contained many more ideas than were executed in marble. Perhaps he was too little a man of the world; perhaps the chastity of his art put patrons at a distance; perhaps he was disadvantaged like Richard Wilson because, while his style was classical, his mood was romantic before its time. Certainly he was a simple man, loved by his friends and honoured by his colleagues. In 1810 he was appointed the first Professor of Sculpture at the Royal Academy; and the lectures he delivered sounded a strange new note: for they taught what he had striven to show by his work, that the artist has an evangelical duty to society, 'to elevate the mind to a contemplation of truth'.

David Irwin, *John Flaxman, Sculptor, Illustrator, Designer*, 1979.

**WILLIAM BLAKE** (1757-1827), poet, artist, visionary, stands alone in his time. He can be classed as a romantic, but his work is unique and fits into no pattern. A few discerning contemporaries perceived his genius. Wordsworth thought him mad, but said: 'there is something in the madness of this man which interests me more than the sanity of Lord Byron and Walter Scott'. Artists as different as Flaxman, Lawrence and Palmer were his devotees. Victorians accepted him as a brilliant eccentric, designer, writer of lyrics and of 'prophetic books'. The symbolism and private mythology of these works have been subjected to intensive criticism in this century: though interpretations vary widely with the standpoint of the critic, the effect has been to reveal new light and depth of meaning. It is recognized that his long poems, for all their apparent muddle, are based on a harmonious and consistent range of ideas. In a time of revolutions Blake had special insight into the changes taking place around him. Imagination in him was both creative and disciplined by intellectual power. The strangeness of much of his work comes from the fact that he was trying to communicate difficult ideas in an original way. 'That which can be made explicit to the idiot', he wrote, 'is not worth

*William Blake*
(Artist: Thomas Phillips)

my care.' He chose rather to write and paint in a way that 'rouses the faculties to act'.

'Born 28 November 1757 in London and have died several times since.' So he wrote in a friend's autograph album. His father was a tradesman who gave him no regular schooling but kept him supplied with books and prints. He was apprenticed, at ten, to an engraver. In 1779 he entered the Royal Academy Schools. He was much influenced by the current mood of radicalism amongst London craftsmen. 'Wilkes and Liberty', then the American war, aroused in him ecstatic hopes of deliverance from oppression. He was a natural rebel; characteristically he fought against the establishment dominated by Sir Joshua Reynolds. He opposed tradition when it sought to preserve itself by rules. But when he first expressed himself in verse he showed that he was steeped in the great writers. 'The Poetical Sketches' were commenced, the author claimed, 'in my twelfth, and occasionally resumed ... till my twentieth year.' Already, amongst imitations and experiments, can be heard the music of words, and in his most simple lyrics can be found the deeper layer of meaning which is so plainly missing in most eighteenth-century poetry. Such freshness as —

> How sweet I roamed from field to field
> And tasted all the summer's pride

should have been acclaimed as opening the door to a new poetry. It was not, but he did not lack friends and patrons. The young Swiss artist Fuseli brought him into a radical group which centred upon the bookseller, Joseph Johnson, Cowper's publisher; here he met Paine, Godwin, Wedgwood and Priestley.

In 1782 he married Catherine Boucher, an illiterate, but sympathetic, partner for his genius. On the death of his father in 1784 they went to live in Soho, where William set up a print-shop. He was much affected by the death of his younger brother and pupil Robert in 1787. The vision that he recorded after this event, of Robert's soul rising 'through the matter-of-fact ceiling' and 'clapping its hands for joy' is the epitome of Blake's idea of the limits of the rational world. It was also the start of a period of intense activity. Through the spirit of Robert, as he thought, he hit upon a new method of 'relief etching', text and illustration being engraved on metal plates together in a single design. This 'illuminated printing' was to be the vehicle of nearly all his poetic work. He was his own printer, illustrator, bookseller, artist-craftsman. Because only a few books could be produced in this way, his readership was limited but this does not seem to have concerned Blake, who was driven along on his spiritual odyssey by the need to clarify his own insights; he was a prophet, not a publicist.

In 1788 he engraved two tracts, *There is no Natural Religion* and *All Religions are One*. His object was to attack the psychology of Locke, based on the proposition that 'Man cannot naturally Perceive but through his natural or bodily organs', which was so profoundly influential in the eighteenth century. Against Locke's view that 'the desires and perceptions of man . . . must be limited to objects of sense', Blake insisted upon the ability of the mind to perceive values, especially the value of the holy. Based upon his own experience, this idea of the intuitive power of mind, a consciousness to be found in the deeper levels of the mind, is a key to understanding Blake. When it is related to the work of subsequent thinkers, notably in this field Jung and Freud, and, in turn, their impact upon recent writers such as D. H. Lawrence, it becomes plain why modern critics are so impressed by Blake.

There is interest too for the social historian. The industrialism which was transforming society meant to Blake a domination by 'material interests'. Everybody knows his protest against the 'dark, satanic mills'. The horror is more effective by contrast with his persistent vision of pastoral beauty. The French Revolution, like the American revolt before it, lent weight to his sense of living in a time of shaking. But it was in the sights of London, the poverty of children such as the 'Chimney Sweeper', a wretched 'little black thing among the snow', unregarded by 'the cold and usurous hand' of charity — that Blake found material for his poetry of indignation. *The Songs of Innocence* (1789) and the parallel *Songs of Experience* (1793) are lyrics whose simple words and freshness of vision convey a child's world and can be read as nursery rhymes. The Lamb, key symbol of innocence, and the Tyger, who is experience, stand also for virginal imagination against the world — the law, the church, capital, governments, everything that was formal and systematic. So these lyrics are also timeless commentaries on human bondage.

His print-shop failed. After a few years at a house in Poland Street, the Blakes moved, from Soho to Lambeth and 'a pretty clean house'. After the *Song of Los*, last of a sequence of experiments in which Blake worked by mythical figures such as Orc, embodiment of the spirit of revolt, and Urizen, god of law and conformity, towards an epic development of his view of history, there was a gap of about nine years in the series of engraved books. He went, in 1800, to live in Sussex, in a cottage on the coast belonging to William Hayley, a squire of literary interests. Hayley organized Blake's defence when he was tried at quarter sessions for using seditious language to a soldier. Blake was acquitted and returned in 1803 to settle in South Molton Street. Inspired by the beauty of Sussex, confident once more in his own powers, he returned to the creation of a new mythology. 'I must create a system', he wrote, 'or be enslaved by another man's.' His system was no logical plan; rather it was a series of stories about symbolic figures, which derived from a catholic range of sources, classical, neo-Celtic, Indian (from the recent translations of Wilkins and Jones) and the Hebrew mythology of the Bible. It became very complex and the central figures changed. But the theme of all the poems, completely worked out in the 'Four Zoas', re-handled in 'Milton' and 'Jerusalem', is the disaster inherent in the separation of the reasoning power from the emotional part of the mind. Always the writing is enriched by comment on the ideas of his time. Malthusian economics, for instance, takes a swinging blow when Urizen, in the 'Four Zoas', reads lessons of Moral Duty from his Books of Brass: 'Compell the poor to live upon a Crust of bread, by soft mild arts.' Later, 'Avaunt, Cold hypocrite!' cries Orc (and Blake). Blake seems to have been impressed by Christ rather as artist than as founder of a church. 'Nobodaddy' is his name for a non-human supernatural deity; to the end, all churches were 'synagogues of Satan'. There is some irony in the use of 'And did those feet in ancient time' as a hymn, for his theme is more humanist than specifically Christian. The magnificent imagery of this section of the epic 'Jerusalem' (completed in 1820) is dulled in effect by familiarity and may be mistaken for vague emotionalism. Southey reported in 1811 that he had visited Blake and been shown 'a perfectly mad poem called Jerusalem'. The poem will not reveal its power to the literal mind; besides, Blake's scheme 'To open the Eternal Worlds, to open the immortal eyes of Man inwards into the Worlds of Thought, into Eternity', is a staggering step into a future way of thinking. On this work, which passes beyond both the lyrical charm and the rhetoric of earlier works to what Foster Damon calls a 'new, dark splendour, a vast breadth, a sense of towering structure', Blake, as if he knew that it was the climax of his achievements, lavished nearly a hundred pictorial designs of intricacy and force.

What Blake has given to English art is something very rare. In his day he was practically ignored; towards the end a small group of artists — Linnell, Palmer, Calvert, George Richmond — warmed their hands at his genius; but the time of his greatest influence may still lie in the future. He was obliged, in order to earn a living, to spend time engraving other people's work; but his own *œuvre*, in tempera and in watercolour, engraved or blocked or printed, is a sizeable one. And it is a consistent exposition of Blake's belief that art is a spiritual activity, and that the artist is a messenger sent from God to glorify God in the world — not by imitating the forms of nature, but by giving form to spiritual visions conceived in the imagination. 'I am,' he wrote, 'under the direction of Messengers from Heaven, Daily and Nightly.' He also wrote, 'Greatness of Ideas is Precision of Ideas': he knew he had abnormal powers of vision — as a boy, he had seen God looking in at the window, and angels mingling with the haymakers — and it was essential to his creed that he should be true to those powers and record his visions with the utmost fidelity. Others have turned to shadows and distortions in order to rehearse their dreams; but Blake made himself one of the great masters of line, which is the very vehicle of precision. If his forms are often outlandish (trees, for example, which never grew this side of Eden), it is because he professed to draw only with the eye of the spirit, without reference to the natural or 'vegetable' world he could see every day. But even the strongest imagination must feed on the memories of earlier sense impressions; and what Blake claimed were direct transcriptions of spiritual vision, often turn out to contain reminiscences of his own studies, in the fields of Greek sculpture and Gothic architecture, of the works of Dürer and Raphael and Michelangelo. When, in one of his drawings for *Paradise Lost*, Blake sets Adam and the Archangel Raphael on a framework which is simply a medieval choir-screen retranslated into the living plants which it had symbolized, it is Blake's memory at work as much as his imagination. Yet his originality can hardly be overstated. And it increased with age, until, with his illustrations for *The Divine Comedy*, his final work, he moves into worlds of terrifying strangeness and grandeur.

Blake is not an 'easy' artist: visionaries seldom are, and this particular visionary was also the prophet of an obscure religious mythology. But for those who miss the spiritual allusions, there is always the rhythm of Blake's 'flaming line' to enjoy, and his irrational, emotive use of colour — to see how he fulfilled his avowed purpose 'not to gather gold, but to make glorious shapes, expressing Godlike sentiments'.

Blake is said, just before he died, to have 'burst out in singing of the things he saw in Heaven'. The last six years of his life were spent in contented poverty, in lodgings in Fountain Court off the Strand. The epitaph of his friend, the painter Samuel Palmer, cannot be improved upon: 'He was a man without a mask; his aim single, his path straightforwards, and his wants few; so he was free, noble and happy.'

Mona Wilson, *The Life of William Blake,* 3rd edn, rev by G. Keynes, 1971.
David Bindman, *William Blake, His Art and Times,* 1982.
P. Ackroyd, *Blake,* 1993.

GEORGE MORLAND (1763-1804), painter of rustic subjects, exhibited his first drawings at the Royal Academy at the age of ten. His father was old when he was young; and, being himself an artist and the son of an artist, educated the young Morland, under the strictest regimen, exclusively in art. Young Morland was compelled to copy incessantly, to the perfection of his technique, but to the wearying of his spirit. At nineteen he escaped from domestic tyranny, and reacted against it as strongly as the son of any moralist is supposed to do. Thereafter his story is one of increasing degradation: of thraldom to picture dealers who plied him with drink in exchange for his art, while they multiplied his paintings by copying them behind his back; of financial extravagance indulged even in the debtors' prison, even while he painted against time and invention to relieve the debt; of low company and rewards, of strength and opportunities lost — a story relieved only by some steadiness at the time of his marriage (to the sister of the artists William and James Ward) and by the pleasures which, however transitory, he found in the most adventurous of his dissipations. (And could a man have been wholly unhappy who painted pictures of such engaging innocence?) He was released from debtors' prison under the Insolvent Debtors Act of 1801; died under confinement in a sponging-house in 1804; and his wife, falling into convulsions at the news of his death, died four days later.

The unscrupulous copying of Morland's paintings, and completion of his sketches, make it hard to number his huge output of paintings and engravings. In the last eight years of his life he is said to have painted 100 pictures a year, quite apart from his drawings, and at one time he kept his 'models' (pigs, foxes, goats and a horse) in his very house. He had not only to satisfy creditors and feed the dealers who fed him, but cater for the public demand for his pictures. It was as if the people had premonition of the plunder of the English countryside, and desired a memento of the England that was passing: they certainly liked to be assured that the English peasantry were not made on the French model, carrying revolution in their hearts. For Morland's work is rustic painting of the most comfortable kind. His animals have none of the sleek, nervous breeding of those Stubbs painted; his country people are stock characters, who gather at the stable or the village inn. This was art for the ordinary man, and must have made the fortune of the dealers. One is tempted to say that Morland put out pot-boilers: the wonder is — which is also a tribute to his art — that he hardly did so. The quality which he maintained under severest stress speaks of a mastery of paint which, had he ever paused to strike out afresh, had he ever given himself time to invent, or to refurnish his pictorial imagination, might have raised him to a high, if not the highest, rank.

Ellis Waterhouse, *Painting in Britain 1530-1790*, 1969.

**JOHN CROME** (1768-1821), landscape-painter, called 'Old Crome' to distinguish him from his less talented son, was a native of East Anglia, which has been the rich nursery of so many landscape-painters. His father was a journeyman weaver, and the boy ran errands for a doctor, was apprenticed to a house and signpainter, and had next to no schooling. He was taken up, however, by one Thomas Harvey of Catton, who was not only an artist himself but the possessor of Gainsborough's *Cottage Door* and a collection of Flemish and Dutch masters. Thus was Crome educated. Other benefactors he had, Sir William Beechey and later John Opie, both portrait painters of merit; but he never grew away from the impression made on him by his first sight at

Harvey's house of the school of van Ruisdael and Hobbema and
Cuyp — indeed his dying words are reported to have been,
'Hobbema, my dear Hobbema, how I loved you'.

In London alone were to be sought the wells of patronage for a
promising artist — even Gainsborough had found that — and to
practice in Norwich, in the days before the railway, seemed almost
professional suicide. But Crome took the risk, enjoyed the
rewards when they came, and made good his income by teaching
— he was drawing-master at the Norwich Grammar School for
most of his life. In the hope of creating a local market for paintings, he founded in 1803 the Norwich Society, an association of
artists (with Cotman among them) to which each contributed
some capital, and which from 1805 to 1833 held what were
perhaps the earliest regular picture-exhibitions outside London.
Occasionally Crome sent his pictures to the Royal Academy,
but for the most part they were shown among the work of this
Society. Thus in his day his fame was no more than local. He was
a cheerful, sociable man, with a fondness for boating on the
Norfolk waters.

In transposing the seventeenth-century Dutch landscape to
England, Crome did what Wilson had been on the brink of doing
— he bridged the classical and the romantic in English landscape
art. He shut away the Italian impedimenta and cleared the room
for Constable. But his work, though full of beauties (one thinks of
*Mousehold Heath* and *The Poringland Oak*), is yet too derivative
and modest to declare him great. He could paint the level lands of
Norfolk all dun under luminous skies — but the same restraint
which kept him from London stunted the greater growth of his
work, even as some of the willows are stunted which he painted
so well.

Derek & Timothy Clifford, *John Crome*, 1968.

**JOHN SELL COTMAN** (1782-1842), landscape-painter, left
some water-colours which are amongst the most individual of the
period. Born and bred in comfortable circumstances in Norwich,
he came to London at the age of sixteen and was introduced to
the circle patronized by Dr. Monro — of which Turner and Girtin
(his seniors by seven years), as well as John Varley and Peter de
Wint, were members at one time or another — and later to that

patronized by Sir George Beaumont, the other most discerning patron of the day. Like Turner and Girtin (whose sketching-club he joined), he travelled indefatigably through Wales and northern England in search of material for topographical drawings.

In 1806, he suffered a bout of the neurasthenia to which he was prone, and decided to return from London to Norwich. Here he joined the Norwich Society of Artists, which had been founded by Crome and others in 1803. But in Norwich it was even harder than in London to make a living by the brush alone; and Cotman, having married, was obliged to take a job as a tutor in drawing. Here again he was lucky in his patronage: for Dawson Turner, to whose family he went at Yarmouth, not only kept him as tutor, but sent him to Normandy to make drawings for a work he planned on the antiquities of Normandy. In three tours of Normandy, he greatly enlarged his scope. During the 1820s he was again in Norwich, and his last years (from 1834) were spent on a second sojourn in London, where Dawson Turner's influence had obtained for him the Professorship of Drawing at King's College. He was increasingly tormented by nervous depression, and died in 1842.

In his day, he was largely unappreciated. One of his finest romantic drawings, *The Dismasted Brig* (*c*.1823: British Museum) sold at auction in 1836 for 17*s*. But his style is unmistakable. His use of tonal variation is perhaps over-obvious, so that his landscapes tend to recede in somewhat mechanical alternations of light and dark; but there is no denying that this practice, coupled with his unerring sense of composition, gives immediate interest, by pattern alone, to even unpromising material. He deals in broad washes of colour and, whether in architecture or in landscape, indicates details of form by flakes of colour within the broader masses, or by strokes of the reed-pen, or simply by the roughness of the paper. His colour is modern in its daring, and became more brilliant as he grew older. He shares the credit for the liberation of the water-colour from its eighteenth-century traditions.

Exhibition Catalogue (Arts Council of Great Britain), *John Sell Cotman*, 1982.

**THOMAS BEWICK** (1753-1828), wood-engraver, was born near Newcastle and spent most of his life there, being apprentice and later partner in a firm of engravers called Beilby. In his illustrations for John Gay's *Fables* (1779) and *Select Fables* (1784), for a *General History of Quadrupeds* (1790), and for a *History of British Birds* (1797 and 1804), Bewick brought the woodcut to a state of perfection which it had never reached before in England and has hardly reached since. But he was naturalist even before he was artist. He observed wild animals as acutely as Stubbs did, and portrayed them with equal science and dexterity. 'The execution of the plumage in Bewick's birds', wrote Ruskin, 'is the most masterly thing ever done in woodcutting.' Thus Bewick did as much by the burin to popularize natural history as his contemporary White of Selborne did by the pen. And this is not to forget the beauty of his landscape backgrounds, nor those little 'tale-pieces' which decorate the end of the chapters, comical but often — which was strange in so ingenuous a man — macabre vignettes, such as that which terrified Jane Eyre: 'the black, horned thing seated aloof on a rock, surveying a distant crowd surrounding a gallows'.

Montague Weekley, *Thomas Bewick*, 1953.
Iain Bain, *Thomas Bewick*, 1979.


**CHARLES CORNWALLIS, 2nd EARL CORNWALLIS** (1738-1805) was a general, who had a second and greater career as Governor-General of India at a critical time. His name is most often connected with the unfortunate surrender of his army at Yorktown. Yet in the campaigns leading up to that episode he had shown energy and skill. In later phases of his life he guided the destinies of India and Ireland.

He was the son of the fifth Lord and first Earl Cornwallis, of an old Suffolk family, and of Elizabeth Townshend, daughter of the second Marquis Townshend. After Eton he served on the staff of Lord Granby, when that admirable soldier was winning battles in Germany. Like so many serving soldiers in a period when opportunity for active service was rare, he made a beginning in politics. He inherited his earldom in 1762 after only two years in the Commons, and held minor offices in several governments. After Lord North's advent to power (1770) he firmly opposed all measures against America. When war came he could not, however, refuse the command which was given him, with the local rank of lieutenant-general.

Like some other officers he seems to have begun operations in a half-hearted spirit; as if it were a police action against mistaken compatriots whose strength of purpose and military viability were yet unknown. He co-operated with Howe in the unhurried campaigns which led to the capture of New York, the victory of Brandywine River and the occupation of Philadelphia. In 1778 he went on leave and returned as second-in-command under Clinton. News of his wife's death brought him home again. In 1780 he began a campaign for the reduction of North Carolina and Virginia. He defeated Gates at Camden (1780) by a dawn attack, and Greene at the battle of Guildford Court House, but the latter victory could not be followed up. He had no contact with Clinton and no reserves; the country was hostile. In the autumn of 1781 he decided to make a base in Virginia where his army could recoup for future operations. Between the rivers York and James, near Chesapeake Bay, he encamped his 7,000 men. Washington seized the chance offered by this defensive move. He marched swiftly south to hem in the British. Meanwhile, after the encounter of Admirals de Grasse and Hood in early September, the French enjoyed temporary command of the sea; after reinforcements they outnumbered the British by nearly two to one. Clinton could not send off reinforcements at once. When the fleet at last arrived, with 7,000 men, on the 24th October, they found that Cornwallis had surrendered five days earlier. Since naval supremacy was soon regained and Clinton still had a strong force, the military situation was not calamitous. Politically, however, the surrender of Yorktown was decisive. It proved to the politicians that this war could not be won.

It says much for Cornwallis that his reputation was little impaired by Yorktown. For sound advice and difficult duties Cornwallis was the man to be approached. He was always ready to do his duty. In 1786 he acceded to Pitt's request to succeed Warren Hastings as Governor-General of India. It was to his advantage that he was his own commander-in-chief, as was allowed by Pitt's India Act of 1784. With no Indian experience, he began with no commitments, no friends to promote, no axe to grind. He brought impartiality and an objective view.

Within months of his arrival the whole Board of Trade was

suspended. Before his massive integrity 'corruption and small-mindedness withered'. Men like Shore and Duncan, professional India men, came to admire him intensely. He separated the functions of the collector of revenue from that of district judge. He was primarily concerned with safeguards against maladministrations: 'No system will ever be carried into effect,' he wrote, 'so long as the personal qualifications of the individuals that may be appointed to superintend it form the only security for the due exercise of it.' He was acting in line with accepted liberal theory, but the system was the cause of many disputes. If Cornwallis could have foreseen the calibre of the men who were to govern India in the nineteenth century, he might not have been so rigid. Elphinstone in the Maratha country, Metcalfe in central India, were to revert to a simpler system: the collector, the equivalent to the later district officer, was to be 'the philosopher king' with all power in his hands.

Cornwallis's other great work, also controversial, was 'the permanent settlement' of land revenue. He confirmed the official aristocracy of hereditary rent-collecting magnates. If it was a bad system in the first place to farm out the revenues, it was also inevitable; at least it was now controlled. The *zemindars* had fixed rents to pay (nine tenths of receipts), the cultivators or *ryots* were given protection.

The third Mysore war interrupted reform. Tipu, son of Haidar Ali, ruler of Mysore, had been bred by his father to hate the British, to covet the rich lands of the Carnatic. In 1790 he attacked. Cornwallis took personal charge of the war. He made two advances (May 1791, January 1792) into Mysore. Failure of supplies enforced retreat the first time; it was difficult campaigning in the dusty plains of south India. His second attempt brought him to Seringapatam. He then accepted terms. Should he not rather have destroyed Mysore? Memories of Yorktown may have inhibited him. What if he had failed to storm the fortress? He preferred conciliation and diplomacy. The Marathas and Hyderabad were given land to cement their alliances. Tipu, shorn of half his lands, was left to plot and fight again.

Cornwallis resigned in 1793. The issue was the future of the Company's troops. He wanted the Directors to take royal troops into their pay. The Company's Europeans were unsatisfactory in discipline and performance. The Bengal officers were obstructive and Cornwallis did not get the support he wanted from the Directors. After seven hard years in India he was glad to return to his Suffolk home. But there was to be little leisure for him. England was at war. Now a marquis, in 1795 he accepted a cabinet seat as Master of the Ordnance and improved the coastal defences. In 1798 he went to Ireland as lord-lieutenant and comander-in-chief. So after America and India he entered the third great area of stress and violence.

Cornwallis arrived just after the battle of Vinegar Hill, where General Lake had defeated the main force of the United Irishmen (June 1798). He was able to deal with Humbert's expedition without difficulty, though the Frenchman displayed the daring of a true son of the revolution. The Irish rebellion presented less difficulty than the Irish constitution. Cornwallis' outlook was not over-subtle. Like Wellington, who eventually granted the Irish Catholics emancipation, he took a pragmatic, soldier's line. He endorsed the policy of Castlereagh and Pitt: 'Until', he said, 'the Catholics are admitted into a general participation of rights, there will be no peace or safety in Ireland.' Castlereagh carried out the business of union, the detailed, mercenary bargaining. Cornwallis gave him full support, insisted upon the fulfilment of compacts — and resigned, along with Pitt, Castlereagh and their leading colleagues, when the King refused to accept emancipation. When Cornwallis' son was asked who would succeed his father as viceroy if emancipation were rejected, he answered 'Bonaparte' — undoubtedly his father's view.

Cornwallis may not have been the best choice as British emissary to Amiens to conduct peace talks with the French (1801). He was 'respected but disappointing' (J. Ehrman). Nor was Hawkesbury sufficiently experienced in diplomacy to secure the best bargain. They negotiated with good intentions and a trust that stemmed more from hope than experience. The government soon had to break the letter of the peace, hold on to Malta and the Indian posts that had been rashly ceded, and risk the resumption of war. When Wellesley was recalled from India in 1805 and a successor was required to make a peace with the Marattas, who but Cornwallis would answer?

At the age of sixty-six he sailed for India. When he arrived he was aghast at the ceremony and parade established by Wellesley; he preferred to work in simple surroundings. He was also old and tired. Within three months of landing he died. If a single man had to be chosen to illustrate the noblest features of the aristocratic ideal in the eighteenth century it might be Cornwallis. He was a true patriot.

W. S. Seton-Karr, *Cornwallis*, 1890.
A. Aspinall, *Cornwallis in Bengal*, 1931.

**JOHN SHORE, 1st BARON TEIGNMOUTH** (1751-1834) was a great Indian administrator, a man of strong Christian faith who helped to establish high standards for the British rulers of India. His father was a Company man; his mother was the daughter of Captain Shepherd, a captain in the Company's naval service. India was in his blood. He went to Bengal from Harrow, where William Jones, the great orientalist, was among his friends.

In the Company's service he rose steadily by a stoical devotion to duty. The year after he arrived at least a fifth of the population of Bengal died in a famine. He could be under no illusions as to the size of the administrative and social problems. By nature a cool, mild man, Shore stuck to duties which he found distasteful, in a climate that was barely tolerable, for a salary which he steadily refused to augment by the customary sweets of office. 'Poor I am and may remain so', he wrote to his mother, 'but conscious rectitude shall never suffer me to blush at being so.'

At the age of nineteen he became Assistant of the Revenue Council of Bengal at Murshidabad and, having an idle superior, took on most of the work. Rarely have men so young, been given such huge responsibility. From 1775 to 1780 he was on the Revenue Council of Calcutta, and later on the committee of revenue. He drew up the minute which formed the basis of Bengal's *zemindari* system of revenue collection. (The *zemindar* was a hereditary revenue collector: Shore wanted his lease to last for ten years. In 1793 Cornwallis — against his wishes — fixed the settlement in perpetuity.) From 1787 to 1793 Shore was on the Supreme Council of Bengal. Like many dutiful men he was prone to think himself a martyr. 'The life of a man in Bengal who does his duty is really that of a galley-slave', he wrote. But there was a lighter side. As a good Harrovian be played cricket. He found time to translate into English in three volumes a Persian form of the

*Jog Bashust*, a Sanskrit exposition of the doctrines of Vedanta. Letters to his friends contained verse translations from the Arabic. Foremost among his early friends was Augustus Cleveland, a local magistrate who died at twenty-nine and left a legendary name behind him. He also spoke of his love for Cornwallis, the Governor-General before him. It was Shore's brief to supply sound administration, to preside over a period of consolidation after the great advances made by Cornwallis.

Appointed Governor-General in 1792 (despite Burke's protest) he accepted the baronetcy which he had earlier refused. When after four years a mutiny in the Bengal army and the serious turn taken by the French war led to the appointment of a man of action, Shore may not have been sorry to leave. His solemn, cautious paternalism was a far cry from Wellesley's imperious pride. One cannot imagine that great pro-consul writing as did Shore: 'When I consider myself the Ruler of twenty-five millions of people ... I tremble at the greatness of the charge ... I consider every native of India, whatever his situation may be, as having some claim upon me.' He could be criticized for allowing the Marathas to invade the lands of the Nizam, and the French to penetrate with 'advisers' into several other states. In the north the Sikhs, in the south Tipu Sahib, prepared for war. Yet on occasion he could act with courage — as over the Oudh succession. The words in which he affirmed his belief in moderation deserve to be recalled: 'Our reputation for justice and good faith stands high in India and if I were disposed to depart from them, I could form alliances that would shake the Maratha empire to its very foundations. I will rather trust the permanency of our dominion to a perseverance in true principles.'

He came home to an Irish peerage. He became a privy councillor and a member of the board of control. He was closely associated with the Clapham sect of evangelicals and became the first president of the British and Foreign Bible Society. His *Memoirs of Sir William Jones* (1804) provided a solid memorial to his old school friend. He lived to a great age. Lord Macaulay wrote of him: 'Of his integrity, humanity and honour it is impossible to speak too highly.'

Lord Teignmouth (son), *Memoir of the Life ... of Lord Teignmouth*, 1843.

# RICHARD COLLEY WELLESLEY, MARQUIS WELLESLEY

(1760-1842), statesman, was the eldest son of Lord Mornington, and the elder brother of Arthur, Duke of Wellington. His career seems ultimately to have been disappointing only when measured against his pride and prospects. He might have become prime minister, and yet the qualities that made him a magnificent Governor-General of India would not have made him a good prime minister. The famous brothers were similar in appearance, in pride of family and will to serve. Richard was more imaginative, intellectually better endowed, but a man of caprice, a lover of gestures. His soldier brother was essentially a narrower person, whose sensitive and romantic feelings were subjected to the disciplines of a supremely purposeful life. If Arthur appears to be the greater man, it is mainly because of a directness, concentration and hard common sense which were perfectly suited to soldiering. They worked together in India and then their talents were perfectly complementary.

Lord Mornington was an Irish peer who flooded acres of land round his house at Dangan to improve the landscape, loved 'cool grots' and gratified his musical tastes by mustering his own orchestra. Richard was sent to Harrow and would no doubt have stayed there but for his part in a schoolboy demonstration. He was removed to Eton, where he became a very fine scholar. He recited Lord Strafford's last speech before the royal family and the prime minister at the Speeches of 1778. He went to Christ Church and then took his seat in the Irish House of Lords. In 1784 he entered the British House of Commons — as an Irish peer was entitled to do (Castlereagh and Palmerston are two other notable examples). He always stood loose to political allegiance but, if anything, he was a Whig: a free-trader, an open-minded sympathizer with most sorts of reform and, like so many Irish gentlemen of the Ascendancy, an advocate of Catholic emancipation. He sat on the India board in 1793. In 1797 he was sent out as Governor-General with the English title of Baron Wellesley.

He came by himself, leaving behind the French lady, Hyacinthe Roland, his former mistress whom he had recently married. It was as though he had decided that women had no place in the exacting life of Indian government. He approached his task with dedicated seriousness. He saw India as a theatre in the world war with France. Dundas, who combined being minister of war with responsibility for India, was of his mind. Both men seem to have decided that they could sail on past the intentions of Pitt's India Act to an expansion of British rule and trade. Wellesley saw himself as responsible rather to the government than to the directors. From the start he was opposed by those who believed that the limits had been reached. There were others, however, like David Scott of the directorate, who believed that the Indian princes were incapable of providing sound administration. Wellesley believed that a forward policy was inevitable, if India were not to remain anarchic or be lost to the French.

Wellesley presided over an informal ruling group in Government House, Calcutta. He evoked the loyalty of ambitious young men, who looked forward to carving their careers out of the conquest and administration of new lands. His magnificence did not escape comment. It was said that he wore his medals on his night shirt. The extravagance of viceregal ceremony no doubt shed a glow on those who participated. He looked the part: hawk-faced, with an air of command, repelling familiarity 'with a degree of vigour amounting to severity'. 'His great mind pervaded the whole', wrote Malcolm, 'His spirit was infused into every agent he employed ... all sought his praise, all dreaded his censure.' Like Arthur Wellesley he was minutely careful of details. Like him, too, he concentrated power in his hands. He achieved thereby the unity of purpose and action which is the hallmark of his governorship.

From the King of Oudh and the Nizam of Hyderabad, his chief allies, he demanded, in place of annual payments to maintain troops for their protection, the permanent cession of territory. The chosen land completed the encirclement of Oudh and shut off Hyderabad from the sea. Tipu of Mysore had been beaten but not subdued by Cornwallis. Wellesley had a pretext for action in some captured letters in which Tipu asked the French for military aid. Wellesley projected and his brother carried out an expedition to Seringapatam, strong in its island river site, but not strong enough to resist a brilliant assault (March 1799). Some rich areas of Mysore were kept for the company, another given to Hyderabad. A puppet ruler was placed over what was left. The ruler of the Carnatic was deposed, though his complicity in Tipu's schemes was vague. The Company assumed in the Carnatic the full control which they had long enjoyed in Bengal. So the British were paramount beyond dispute in Southern India. The Maratha confederacy of states embodied much of what was worst in India. The quarrels of the chiefs endangered the general peace. Wellesley's policy was to take advantage of these divisions. A prince in danger from his neighbours was encouraged to turn to the British for help. 'The princely fly was firmly enmeshed in the British web', as V. A. Smith put it. So the British championed the cause of the Peshwa Baji Rao against Holkar, Sindia and the Rajah of Berar. In the wars that ensued Arthur Wellesley assumed over-all command. He defeated his enemies by swift, well-planned movements. At Assaye, in 1803, he destroyed the power of Sindia; in 1804 he attacked Holkar; in Trafalgar year the Grand Mogul accepted British protection. A great territorial empire was being carved out of decomposing native India.

A Governor-General's power was a heady potion for a man of Wellesley's temperament. The 'glorious little man' behaved at times like an impresario. For not sealing his letter in proper form the king of Oudh was addressed from a great height: 'Besides indicating a levity wholly unsuitable to the occasion', he was 'Highly deficient in the respect due to the first British Authority in India.' When crossed by a subordinate he could display a degree of affronted authority that bordered, to judge by letters, on the megalomaniac. Against such outbursts one must set the strains and ultimate loneliness of his position. The Directors were displeased by the expense of his administration. He did not obey the rules. He sent his brother Henry on a diplomatic mission, though he was not employed by the company. He built a palace in Calcutta and lived royally. His admirable suggestion for the setting up of a college at Calcutta to train civil servants was looked upon with suspicion by the directors. In 1801 he had had the boldness to dispatch Baird, with an Indian force, to assist the campaign against the French in Egypt. He wished to use the British fleet to seize Mauritius from the French and Java from the Dutch. The directors could not deny great victories, nor overlook great risks. In 1804 Colonel Monson was defeated and Lake was repulsed at Bharatpur; two reverses to set against many victories, but enough for Wellesley's critics. He was recalled. The Maratha wars were left unfinished. His successor patched up a peace which benefited only the robber bands which flourished under Maratha protection.

Wellesley came home, in 1805, to threats of impeachment, but

Fox (and no doubt with memories of Warren Hasting's futile ordeal) took no steps. Wellesley still felt that he had been ill-treated, that his Irish marquisate was scant recognition. His governorship had ended in frustration. How successful had he been? It must be allowed that his judgement was mainly right; his methods, though high-handed, were effective. Against him it may be argued that he had broken what existed of authority in central India without putting anything in its place. He had pointed the way to British supremacy but in the short term he had over-strained her military and financial resources.

In 1809 Wellesley went to Spain to assist his brother as ambassador to the Junta. In December of that year he became Foreign Secretary. Prime Minister Perceval's intention was to create a government of national unity: Wellesley at the Foreign Office, Liverpool at the War Office, together represented the government's determination to pursue the Peninsular war. Wellesley was a troublesome colleague from the start. From the standpoint of men like Perceval and Liverpool his methods seemed unbusinesslike, his manner high-handed, his policy individualist to the point of disloyalty. He behaved as if he ought to be Prime Minister and was only serving in a subordinate capacity until the King and parliament recognized his claims. Unfortunately for Wellesley, it was necessary to have some following or to find a formula to which men of different persuasions might adhere. This required a political skill which Wellesley lacked. When, in the autumn of 1811, the anxiety of the Regent to find a broad-bottomed ministry offered a chance at last, Wellesley found himself almost friendless. He had alienated influential Tories, while the Whigs, even Grenville, could not agree with him on his view of the war. The Prince's attitude stiffened. The Whigs were given to understand that he preferred measures to men. Canning, Grey, Grenville and now Wellesley headed groups 'rich in debating points but poor in prospects' (Steven Watson). Before Spencer Perceval's death (1812) Wellesley had prepared a long attack on his handling of affairs. He was prevented by an indisposition from delivering it. After Perceval's death he published it and the world questioned his taste. Wellesley had one more chance then to form a government. Again, like Moira after him, he failed. The government prospered, not a little owing to his brother's victories. The rest of his political career was spent in opposition.

In 1821 Wellesley became lord-lieutenant of Ireland. Once more he found work which fitted him. In a period of difficulty, when 'oaths were of little obligation and human life of no value' (John Grattan), he fought against prejudice and conciliated where conciliation was possible. He suppressed Ribbonmen, Orangemen, Whiteboys and other terrorists, reorganized the police, reformed the magistracy and provided poor-relief. He resigned in 1828 when Wellington became prime minister. Ironically, therefore, he was not in office to see his brother, who had always opposed Catholic Emancipation, pass the measure which he had so long advocated. He did, however, briefly resume the lord-lieutenancy under Grey.

The end of his life was contented. He cultivated the classics and enjoyed the friendships of like-minded men, notably Brougham. A second marriage in 1825 to Marianne Patterson, a young American widow, brought him great happiness. He left no legitimate children. By his own request he was buried in Eton College Chapel.

Iris Butler, *The Eldest Brother: the Marquess Wellesley, 1760-1842*, 1973.

P. E. Roberts, *India under Wellesley*, 1929.

GILBERT ELLIOT MINTO, 1st EARL OF MINTO (1751-1814), Governor-General of India, had a liberal and cosmopolitan upbringing. He was the son of Sir Gilbert Minto, third baronet of Minto, politician, scholar and wit, a leader of Edinburgh society. He chose his friend David Hume to tutor his son; he also attended the Pension Militaire at Mirabeau. Minto brought an open and inquiring mind and liberal principles to his political career. After being at Christ Church, Oxford and Lincoln's Inn he became member for Morpeth in 1776. He was a hot Whig and a friend, among others, of Burke; he shared Burke's views upon India, carried a motion condemning the conduct of Elijah Impey at Fort William and shared in the impeachment of Warren Hastings. Like Burke he parted company with Fox over the Revolution. He was employed by the government as negotiator at Toulon after Hood had occupied the town in 1793. Experience in administration came in 1794 when he was made governor of Corsica. In that unlikely spot he experimented with constitutional government, set up a parliament and expelled General Paoli, 'the liberator'.

In 1798 he received a peerage and in the following year was appointed ambassador at the court of Vienna, where it was his delicate responsibility to preserve good relations with our strongest ally. He was for a short time President of the Board of Control; then the 'Talents' ministry made him Governor-General of India. He was there from 1807 to 1813. He followed the autocratic Wellesley. The Directors were alarmed by the extent of their new responsibilities after two decades of conquest. Minto's mission was to consolidate and pacify, a rôle well suited to his easy and rational temper. He was not content, however, with a passive rôle. The Russian bogey raised its head when Napoleon made his treaty with the Tsar at Tilsit (1807). Minto countered threats of Russian activity in Central Asia by a triple diplomatic move. Malcolm was sent to Persia, Elphinstone to Afganistan, Metcalfe to the Punjab, to construct alliances. The work was skilfully done. Ranjit Singh of Lahore proved a loyal ally. Shujah Shah of Afganistan was soon, however, to lose his throne. The emphasis of policy was on security against external threats. In central India the peace that Cornwallis had patched up with the Marathas had left the inhabitants defenceless against marauding Rajpur or Maratha chieftains. The Pindaris, Pathan mercenaries formerly employed by the Maratha chiefs, formed robber bands. It was left to Minto's successor to deal with them.

Minto appreciated clever and imaginative men. He was quick to appreciate the quality of Elpinstone and Metcalfe. He gave warm and practical support to Raffles, whose plans fitted in with his own desire to seal off the Indian ocean from the French and their Dutch puppet-allies. He actually accompanied Raffles on his expedition to Java (1811) and, after its successful conclusion, was able to write: 'An empire has been added to the dominion of the British Crown.' Remembering perhaps his Corsican days, he stayed for some weeks with Raffles, helping him to establish its government on liberal principles. The exertions of this year may have been responsible for his decline in health. He died the year after his return from India.

Humane and broad in his interests, Minto strengthened a good tradition. He was genuinely interested in the Indians and ready to learn from India. He went deeply into the beliefs and customs of

Hindus and Moslems. In the view of English evangelicals he was sadly tepid in support of Christian missions. But he projected the establishment of colleges for Moslems. He was no Wellesley to take bold military initiatives, no Bentinck to defy unpopularity and tackle abuses in a radical way, but he was ready to back good and active men.

John Buchan, *Lord Minto*, 1924.

SIR THOMAS STAMFORD RAFFLES (1781-1826), administrator, orientalist, naturalist and patron of science, is best known as the founder of Singapore. He was also an enlightened governor of Java during the British occupation of that island, 1811-16. A versatile, far-sighted man, Raffles was perhaps, as G. M. Trevelyan has suggested, 'the first European who successfully brought modern humanitarian and scientific methods to bear on the improvement of the natives and their lot'.

The son of a sea captain, born off Port Morant in Jamaica, he became a secretary at the age of fourteen in the East India House. In 1805 he went to be assistant secretary to the new establishment at Penang. At this time Napoleon hoped to take over the Dutch colonies in Asia; the British were resolved to prevent his doing so. In 1806 the Dutch fleet was destroyed by a British squadron in Batavia harbour; in 1808 the Moluccas were occupied. Raffles meanwhile had mastered the Malay language and delved into their history. When in 1810 he went to Calcutta to offer his services to Lord Minto, the Governor-General, he had already made his mark as an expert in that little-known region. In a letter to his wife Minto described him as 'this very clever, able, active and judicious man, perfectly versed in the Malay language and manners'. Minto commissioned him to prepare the way for a military expedition to Java, where the Dutch governor had declared for France. Besides the most thorough preparations for invasion, including extensive propaganda for the benefit of the Rajahs of Java, Raffles was busy collecting specimens, insects, moths, fungi, shells, and manuscripts and poems about the Malays. In June 1811 he left his headquarters at Malacca, with Lord Minto; in August the troops landed, under the command of Sir Samuel Auchmuty: in a month 3,500 troops had destroyed a Franco-Dutch army of 10,000. Java had capitulated. Lord Minto decided to hold the island, though his instructions were only to render it militarily useless, and he appointed Raffles governor.

He dealt with native resistance by a successful attack on the Sultan of Djogjakarta. His power once secured, he made good use of it. A convinced free-trader, he ended the Dutch system of monopoly and introduced free trade — with small duties to raise sufficient revenue. He looked forward to the growth of trade between Java and Britain. He worked out a new system of land rents: essentially this meant the end of the Dutch system of forced labour and compulsory cultivation of certain crops such as coffee. Rents were to be fair and some initiative was left to the peasant. Raffles showed in all his projects a respect for freedom and for the individuality of the six-and-a-half million people under his government. His approach was sensitive and scholarly, his interests varied, but he was no dilettante; on the contrary, he was as practical as he was energetic. He revived the old Batavian Society of Arts and Sciences and made it a centre of research. From India came the director of the Archaeological Survey to study the remains of Hindu temples. The temple of Borobodur emerged from its cocoon of black lava. Dr. Horsfield, the future keeper of the Company's museum, one of the foremost botanists in the world, worked with him. As a young clerk in London Raffles had been inspired by the anti-slavery movement; he kept an interest in this cause until his death. In Java the main social problem was not slavery but the apathy of people long used to feudal conditions. Raffles sought to give more power to the people.

Raffles' governorship was to prove but an interregnum since the island was handed back to the Dutch, with most of their other possessions, in 1815. Some indication of his feelings can be gathered from what he later told a deputation from the Asiatic Society. 'There was Java, an island of rice; and Borneo, an island of gold; and Banca, an island of tin; and the Celebes, islands of spice' — enough, as he said, 'to supply the rest of the world for all ages, all recklessly abandoned to the Dutch by a government that knew neither *why* nor *what* they were giving.' Raffles at least had the satisfaction of knowing that the Dutch accepted his institutions and methods. 'A modern colonial administration', wrote a Dutch historian, 'was forced on us from outside.' On his way back in 1816 he interviewed Napoleon on St. Helena. When he arrived in England he married his second wife and devoted himself to the monumental *History of Java*. In two volumes he described the history, society and literature of Java, with engravings and line drawings. The book was deservedly well reviewed; Raffles was honoured bv a levée at Carlton House and a twenty-minute speech by the Prince Regent. He was knighted and made a Fellow of the Royal Society. His scientific pursuits did not satisfy Raffles's ambition. He had experienced the pleasures of administration and he had a vision of liberal imperialism which the indifference of governments could not impair. He was appointed governor of Bencoolen in Sumatra which had remained British. Before he left he wrote a state paper to Canning arguing that a new base should be found as 'an *entrepôt* for our merchandise', Bencoolen and Penang being too far away from the Malayan archipelago. But Canning was not then foreign minister and Castlereagh was preoccupied with Europe: he did not wish to offend the Dutch. The directors of the East India Company regarded Bencoolen with disfavour since it was of little value as a trading station. Raffles and his wife found themselves in a 'den of ravenous dogs and polecats'. Raffles set about making this unpromising place a centre of British trade and influence. He freed the slaves and set up a school for the children of slave parents. There were protests from traders and other injured interests. This energetic, idealistic governor was becoming a nuisance.

It was Raffles's habit to go to the man in power. In 1818 he secured from Lord Hastings, Minto's successor in India, instructions to secure 'the establishment of a station beyond Malacca such as may command the southern aspect of these straits'. Hastings soon revised his orders: Raffles was to desist from the attempt to found a settlement — but when this postscript arrived, Raffles had already planted the British flag upon the ancient Malayan city of Singapura and was planning its development. 'With this single station alone I would undertake to counteract all the plans of Mynheer.' So Lord Hastings and the governors of the Company were presented with a *fait accompli*. The Company's council denounced him — but some individual directors acclaimed his vision and Hastings stood by him. Raffles spent three more years at Bencoolen cultivating pepper and collecting specimens. In October 1822 he returned to Singapore and spent six months working intensively on the planning of the city:

harbour, roads, administrative quarter, Chinese quarter. The port was to be free of duty, open to all. There was to be a Malay college where Malays could advance in their own language and others could study it.

It is almost incredible that so much was done in six months; it was the hectic work of a sick and distressed man. Three of his five children had died of fever in Sumatra. He endured violent headaches. Fortune was persistently cruel: on his way to England he lost all his possessions by fire on board ship — his notes for a history of Sumatra, thousands of drawings and a menagerie of wild animals. He was treated ungratefully by the Company. He was appreciated, however, by the leaders of the anti-slavery movement. He had shown that it was feasible to abolish slavery. In the Abbey his monument by Chantrey stands alongside those of Wilberforce and Buxton. There is also a bust of Raffles in the Lion House at the London zoo. This commemorates the founder and first president of the Zoological Society 'for the introduction of living animals, having the same relation to zoology as a science that the Horticultural Society does to botany'.

Raffles died at Hendon less than two years after his return to England. In post-colonial Singapore his name and memory live. In Java, too, he is 'the great Raffles'. He taught Malays, Chinese and Javanese to think of the Englishman as just, liberal and sympathetic. He ranged in mind and action beyond the conventions of his time and the limits of the system he served.

R. Coupland, *Raffles: 1781-1826*, 1926.
Emily Hahn, *Raffles of Singapore*, 1948.

**CHARLES THEOPHILUS METCALFE, 1st BARON METCALFE** (1785-1846) was the younger son of a major in the Bengal army who later rose to be a director of the East India Company. His mother, in the forthright words of his biographer, was 'grim' but 'a woman of strong understanding'. Charles was neglected and snubbed. At Eton, he was once seen riding a camel, from which his tutor deduced that he was 'orientally inclined'. And he found satisfaction in a life of service in India — 'happiness' would be too strong a word for this withdrawn, somewhat enigmatic figure, who has been called the greatest Indian official of his generation.

Though he bemoaned 'an ugly phiz', he made his mark early. 'The ugliest and most agreeable clever person — except Lady Glenbervie — in Europe or Asia', Lord Minto once wrote of him. He was called 'the little stormer' after he had volunteered to lead an assault against an Indian fortress. He gained the alliance of Ranjit Singh, the Muslim prince of the Sikhs, which Lord Minto believed was vital to British security. He returned from dealing with the most formidable prince in India, with an alliance which endured — and a Sikh mistress who gave him three Eurasian sons. At the age of twenty-seven he was given charge of Delhi. In theory he was but Resident at the court of the Mogul emperor. In reality the emperor ruled over nothing but his court. Metcalfe was responsible for a great area, besides relations with other nominally independent princes whom he had to cajole and persuade as best he could. Thompson no doubt exaggerates when he calls Metcalfe's administration of Delhi 'the greatest single administrative work put through by a single British ruler.' Comparable results were achieved elsewhere. But his work was distinctive. He ended hanging and flogging and the selling of slaves. He forbade *suttee* — widow-burning — and set an example which the Governor-General would one day have to follow. He carried out a great work of pacification. Indian boys caught pilfering were sent to a special camp where they could be taught a trade. He was also severely practical: his revenue rose nearly fourfold in six years. He rejected the Cornwallis scheme and treated the tax-collecting *zemindar* strictly as an agent of government. Furthermore his collectors were also magistrates; he would have none of Cornwallis's division of executive and judiciary. His recommendation that there should be small districts, in each of which a European should have general authority with Indian aides, was broadly embodied in the Act of 1833.

Metcalfe subsequently worked with the Governor-General as secretary in the secret, foreign and political departments. Then he went as Resident to Hyderabad (1820-27). He found there an eighteenth-century situation where the Resident and an enterprising gentleman 'not of pure European blood' were managing the Nizam's affairs to their own monetary advantage. Hastings, the Governor-General, was content (for peace and quiet) to overlook the peccadilloes. Metcalfe took a lofty line and acted with his usual vigour. Though rebuked by Hastings he had the support of the supreme council. He himself became a member of the council in 1827. He was Bentinck's right-hand man during most of his forward-looking government. For a year, 1835-6, he acted as provisional Governor-General, between the administration of Bentinck and Auckland. The Directors held him to be unsound. They passed him over for the governorship of Madras — and he sailed home. He had been in India for thirty-seven years without break.

His career had postscripts. In 1839 he was made Governor of Jamaica. In 1843 he became Governor-General of Canada. He resigned after two years. Essentially he is to be judged, as he would wish, as a servant of the British *raj*, one of those men who gave meaning and substance to the ideal that is expressed in Ellenborough's famous statement: 'We have a great moral duty to perform in India.'

E. Thompson, *Charles, Lord Metcalfe*, 1937.

MOUNTSTUART ELPHINSTONE (1779-1859) was the fourth son of the eleventh Baron Elphinstone, and of Anna, daughter of Lord Ruthven. He was one of the ablest administrators in India, who worked to give peace and sound law to their Indian subjects. At the critical time when British order was being imposed upon the turbulent Marathas, he exercised a decisive influence. He was also a selfless and lovable man, one who made no enemies except in the course of duty.

Born in Dunbartonshire, educated privately and at Edinburgh High School, he went out to India in 1796. He began as a writer at Calcutta. His first years were given to pedestrian employments, but he made some interesting friends: the Sanskrit scholar, Samuel Davis; Colebrooke, a conscientious magistrate and authority on Sanskrit law and Hindu history and literature; and Edward Strachey, who was to be one of Wellesley's picked aides. He served at Poona under Sir Barry Close, a courageous political officer, who had a great influence on him. He was attached to Arthur Wellesley's staff and rode by his side at the great victory of Assaye. A characteristic of Indian service at this time is that young men were given big responsibilities, if they were judged fit for it. Elphinstone was active and spirited, but he had also a measure of detachment: He was essentially a civilized man. He wrote about the storming of a fort at sword-point that it reminded him of some verses of the *Iliad*.

In 1804 he was made Resident at Nagpur. In 1808 Lord Minto sent him to Afghanistan. He could do little there. Shujah Shah, to whom he was accredited, was soon to lose his throne. But he found time to write a history of the kingdom of Kabul. He returned to be Resident at Poona, where he was at the centre of the formidable confederacy. His local ruler was the Peshwa Baji Rao, indolent but vicious. It was Elphinstone's task to keep him neutral. He was left, in 1817, with but a handful of troops. Had the Peshwa attacked when expected to do so, when a relief battalion was still on its way to Poona, Elphinstone must have been defeated. When he did assault, the residency was evacuated and burned. 'I beg you will excuse this scrawl', he wrote, reporting the event, 'but all my writing implements, with everything I have, except the clothes on my back, form part of the blaze of the Residency which is now smoking in sight.' He had his revenge for, with Colonel Burr and General Smith, he had the satisfaction of routing over twenty thousand Indian troops with but three thousand of his own. He took romantic pleasure in the sight of the Indian onslaught: 'Grand beyond description, but perfectly ineffectual.'

After the war the Peshwar's country was annexed and settled. Elphinstone made simple arrangements for justice. The collector had all power except that of capital punishment; under him were the *mamlutdars*, Maratha officials, collectors of revenue and deputy magistrates. In the village the headman was given some authority. Punishments were summary: severe flogging, short spells of solitary confinement in dungeons. Elphinstone once ordered that the ringleaders of a plot to murder all the Europeans be blown from guns, a method 'painless to the criminal and terrible to the beholder'. In 1819 he was made governor of Bombay. He presided over the codification of the laws. He was unusual in his time in having no pronounced religious opinions (though later in life he became a unitarian). His idea of education was not so much evangelical as practical. He advanced money from public funds to a society for educating Indians. He thought it 'difficult to imagine an undertaking in which our duty, our interest and our honour are more concerned'. He envisaged a class of assistants filling 'a large portion of the civil stations and many of the subordinate employments of the army'. It was an exact forecast of the eventual form of British rule in India.

Elphinstone lived thirty years after his retirement from Bombay, giving him time for travel, scholarship, writing — and for his friends. He once retired for months to a village inn to devote himself to the study of Greek. He embarked upon a history of India, a masterly account, sadly left incomplete. All accounts agree upon the interest and charm of his conversation. An ardent scholar and a devoted administrator, in private life he was the soul of courtesy, a fine product indeed of his class and culture.

J. S. Cotton, *Elphinstone*, 1892.

**FRANCIS RAWDON-HASTINGS, 1st MARQUIS HASTINGS** (1754-1826), Governor-General of India, was the eldest son of John Rawdon, first Earl of Moira. He was educated at Harrow. It is said that when he went back there, a renowned statesman, he 'tipped' every boy in the school. After a time at University College, Oxford, he went into the army and served with credit in the American war. In 1778 he was made adjutant-general to the forces in America. In April 1781, in a small fight at Hobkirk's Hill, he defeated the American General Greene. He gained in America a reputation for strategy remarkable in one so young, and his experience in irregular warfare was to be useful to him later in India. He was a martinet and his severity aroused comment: he even set a price on the heads of rebels. What a soldier he might have become can be gauged from his victory at Hobkirk's Hill, described by Cornwallis as 'by far the most splendid of this war'. He received a peerage in 1783. At first he was a supporter of Pitt, but friendship with the Prince of Wales drew him into the Whig camp. In 1793 he succeeded to his father's Irish earldom. In 1794 he successfully led a supporting force through Belgium to join the Duke of York. The ultimate failure of the Duke's campaign obscured the tactical skill of that operation, carried out in the teeth of a large French army.

He was a strong supporter of the Catholic cause in Ireland and one of the main opponents of the Act of Union. His military career advanced by way of home appointments which gave him practice in administration. In 1803 he became commander-in-chief in Scotland. In 1806 he was made Master of the Ordnance and sat in the Cabinet of 'the talents'. He was active on behalf of the Prince of Wales in investigating the conduct of the Princess. He took a leading part in the negotiations of 1810-12: first over the revived question of the Prince of Wales's regency; later, in the abortive attempts to found a coalition in which at one stage he tried, with Wellesley, to form a ministry. In outlook he resembled Wellesley. Of all the Governors-General who succeeded the 'little lord' he came nearest to him in style and achievement.

He went to India in 1813. His predecessor, Lord Minto, had pursued a policy of appeasement in accordance with the wishes of the Directors. But territorial advance could not be halted so easily: intervention which, in theory, as a good Whig, Hastings deplored, became inevitable when neighbouring states were misruled. In this land, where 'gold is won by steel' (Walter Scott), annexation was sometimes a safer way than alliance with corrupt or unstable states. The frontiers of British rule were strategically unsound. For seven hundred miles along the valley of the Ganges the frontier was open to northern hill tribes who would not learn peace except by conquest. India's political decay had left many petty sovereignties: régimes of conquest, sustained by plunder, innocent of administration. Maratha chiefs in the country north-east of Bombay backed or acquiesced in the Pindaris, robber bands who terrorized central India. Treaties with such men were of little use: rulers succeeded rulers with bewildering frequency.

Hastings' time was spent in the consolidation of British rule. In November 1814 he set about the Ghurkas of Nepal, difficult neighbours and great warriors. The British commanders fumbled at first; there were reverses. The patient tactics of General Ochterlony brought success in the end. Simla was left in British possession, the hill town that generations of British officers were to know so well; henceforward it was part of army training to go up to the hills in the Indian summer. The Ghurkas, moreover, were to prove valuable allies and soldiers. In 1817 Hastings decided to attack the homelands of the Pindaris. He had to keep the Marathas quiet while the Pindaris were dealt with. Gwalior was bound by a treaty, Baroda dared not move, three other Maratha chiefs rose and were defeated; meanwhile the robbers were encircled, killed or dispersed. His two armies performed nobly despite floods in the Deccan and an outbreak of cholera. The peace established in 1820 made the British government the sovereign power south of Sind and the Sutlej, and brought nineteen small Rajput states under British protection.

In matters of government Hastings' approach was sometimes that of a soldier rather than an official charged with the well being of the inhabitants. When Metcalfe was trying to reform the government of Hyderabad where he was Resident, Hastings censured him for actions which would 'estrange and irritate the better classes'. In this case, where an experienced administrator was battling against a corruption which 'tainted the whole atmosphere', Hastings seemed content to advise: leave well alone. In 1821 he resigned on a trivial issue. He had made the mistake of allowing a native bank in which he had an interest to lend money to the state of Hyderabad. The Directors accused him of corruption; he was cleared, but his action in making the loan was censured. Like so many of the upper classes of his generation he was casual about money matters; he was also generous. He spent large sums on establishing schools and missions; he also lived in splendid style. He once lent his country home to some French *émigrés*: in his guests' rooms he left signed, blank cheques which they could fill up at pleasure. It is not surprising that when he left India he was a poor man and that he was content to accept for his old age the governorship of Malta, where he spent the years 1824-6.

Consistency was not his prime virtue. He had once denounced the British government of India in unbridled terms: 'It was founded on injustice and had originally been established by force.' He had now proved himself a strong and imaginative administrator. A tall, athletic man with a stately and impressive manner, Hastings could have been a great soldier, possibly a Prime Minister. In India he was able to use his talents to the full.

Major Ross, *The Marquess of Hastings*, 1893.

**LORD WILLIAM CAVENDISH BENTINCK** (1774-1839), Governor-General of India, was among the most notable of a generation of English statesmen who conceived it to be their duty to eradicate abuses and govern the country upon western lines. The salient decision of his administration was to make the English language the official and literary tongue of India. In his time a great metamorphosis was completed: from trading company to reigning government. It was a change of structure and· scope, above all of principle. As Charles Trevelyan said in 1853: 'To Lord William Bentinck belongs the great praise of having placed our dominion in India upon its proper foundation in the recognition of the great principle that India is to be governed for the benefit of the Indians.'

Bentinck was the second son of the Duke of Portland who was Prime Minister, 1807-09. He made his career in the army, served under the Duke of York in the Netherlands and was attached to the staff of Suvoroff in 1799. In 1803 he was made governor of Madras but was recalled in 1807 after a bloody mutiny of Indian troops at Vellore. He led a brigade under Moore at Corunna and in 1811 was made commander of British forces in Sicily. He served in Spain in 1813 and commanded a successful expedition against Genoa in 1814. He was appointed Governor-General of Bengal in 1827 and became the first governor-general of India under the Whig act of 1833. He brought a clear mind to bear on the problems he encountered, and undertook great reforms. Critics have doubted whether his work was conceived in the spirit of compassion or of service to the native population. Writing about this period John Malcolm said that 'our administration, though just, is cold and rigid. If it creates no alarm, it inspires little, if any, emulation. The people are protected but not animated or attached'. The keynotes of policy were conviction and courage. Bentinck exemplified both. He had provoked mutiny in 1807 because he ordered the sepoys to shave their beards and remove their turbans. He now showed mature sense in his choice of targets.

The story that Bentinck wished to pull down the Taj Mahal in order to sell the marbles may be apocryphal, but it suggests what people thought of 'the clipping Dutchman'. The Burmese war had cost £13,000,000 and he was bent on economies and also imbued with the spirit of rationalization. He reduced the charges of the civil and military services and recovered part of the land revenues that had been alienated by fraud. He simplified the judicial system, increased the number of native judges, and ordained English in the higher, and local languages in the lower courts. He began the long work of organizing the system of taxation of over twenty million inhabitants of the northwest provinces. It was his policy not to interfere with the native princes, but he deposed the rajah of Coorg for excessive cruelty, annexed Cachar (soon to become famous for its tea-gardens) and took over the government of Mysore because of the misgovernment of the rajah. He approved the diplomatic contacts of Alexander Burnes and made a treaty with Ranjit Singh and another with the Amirs of Sind, opening the Indus to British merchants and traders. Bentinck abolished transit duties, planned a network of roads and the development of steam transport on river and sea. His administration saw also the beginnings of tea and coffee cultivation and projects for drainage and irrigation canals: economic and social progress in the Roman style.

Bentinck is rightly famous for the suppression of *thuggee* and *suttee* during his administration. *Thuggee* was murder, carried out by bands of *thugs* for the goddess Kalih and for the booty which she granted as reward. Sleeman was put in charge of a police operation which was thorough, drastic, but scrupulously fair when it came to the conviction of suspects. *Thuggee* had become widespread: one estimate is that twenty or thirty thousand travellers were killed every year. Between 1831 and 1837 three thousand *thugs* were convicted. One man boasted that he had killed seven hundred and nineteen people; like the rest he believed that he was fulfilling the divine will. *Thuggee* was an aberration from orthodox Hindu belief; but *suttee* or widow-burning was a central rite. An enactment in 1813 that a widow might not be burned without permission suggested that the government acquiesced — and the numbers of official burnings rose steadily. Bentinck abolished *suttee* in 1829 in Bengal; Madras and Bombay followed six months later. Isolated cases continued to occur. In the independent territories the government could only influence, not command. The rajah of Idar was followed to the pyre in 1833 by seven queens, two concubines, four female slaves and a manservant!

Firm, impartial authority based upon a blend of Christian ethics and common sense was what Bentinck offered; it was supposedly what the Indians needed. Bentinck was fearless in dealing with abuses, because he believed in native progress. Therein lies the point of the words with which Macaulay completed his essay on Clive, anticipating 'the veneration with which the latest generation of Hindus will contemplate the statue of Lord William Bentinck'.

D. C. Boulger, *Bentinck*, 1892.
J. Rosselli, *Lord William Bentinck*, 1974.
John Keay, *Honourable Company*, 1991.

MUNGO PARK (1771-1806), pioneer of African exploration, was born at Foulshiels in the Yarrow valley. He was the seventh son of a family of thirteen, but his father managed to send him to the grammar school at Selkirk. Only intelligence and enterprise could make a career for a farmer's son; there was no room on the land except for the eldest. He studied medicine at Edinburgh, but without distinction, and was lucky, on coming to London in 1791, to secure an introduction through his brother-in-law, the botanist James Dickson, to Joseph Banks, who was a member of the 'African Association'. In 1795, he accepted the Association's commission to explore the interior of Senegal.

Earlier attempts sponsored by the Association had failed. It is likely that Houghton, Park's immediate precursor, had been murdered, because he carried too much merchandise. Park therefore travelled light, accompanied by a man and a boy, both negroes, with a handful of trade goods, some survey instruments and a smattering of the Madingo dialect. He lived frugally on the milk, corn and ground nuts of the natives. He was captured and kept prisoner for three months by Arab slave-traders. Houghton had established the fact that the Niger flowed eastwards. But its course and destination remained uncertain; did it join the Nile or the Congo, or did it evaporate in the Sahara? Few accepted what proved to be correct — that it flowed into the Gulf of Benin. Park struck the Niger at Segu, followed it far enough to confirm its eastward flow, then managed to walk back most of the way, until he fell in with a trading caravan. He returned to England and published an account of his journey which ran into several editions (1799). Objective and bald, this is a classic traveller's tale. In its restraint of manner and absence of moralizing it is very much of the eighteenth century. We learn more of the country than of the author, but a picture emerges — stoical, deeply religious in a simple, Calvinist way, full of curiosity and capable of patient endurance.

Park married Alison Anderson, the daughter of his former master at Selkirk, and they had three children. He became a doctor at Peebles. Amongst his friends there was Sir Walter Scott, who was much taken with his knowledge of border ballads. Africa had entered his blood, however, and he seized the opportunity offered, this time by the government, to lead an expedition to follow the whole course of the Niger. He set out at the beginning of May 1805, with his brother-in-law Dr. Anderson, Lieutenant Martyn — a hearty fellow, given to shooting natives — some naval artificers and thirty-five volunteers from the garrison of Goree. His instructions, as laid down by the Secretary of State for the Colonies, were 'to pursue the course of the river to the utmost possible distance' and 'to establish communication and intercourse with the different nations on the banks'. Unfortunately he started only just before the rainy season (in April 1805). 'Now the rain had set in I trembled to think that we were only halfway through our journey.' Most of the soldiers died on the march to Segu. Anderson had died of dysentery. Park had managed to cure himself by a dose of calomel so strong that his mouth was ulcerated and he could not sleep for a week. At Segu he parleyed with Chief Mobidine and constructed a forty-foot flat-bottomed boat. He sent his servant Isaaco back to the coast with his letters and journal, then continued down the Niger with his few remaining companions.

Park simply vanished into a mist of folk tales and speculation. It seems, by the account of the devoted Isaaco about six years later, that he and the remaining three white men were killed by natives as they tried to negotiate their canoe past a rock obstacle by the village of Boussa. (A chief of that region is said to wear Park's ring at the present day.) They were then only some 250 miles from the mouth of the river, having travelled over a thousand miles. Park's last journals were never recovered and there survives from this second journey only a diary up to November. His was the sort of bravery that puts him in the class of Anson, Cook, or Scott of the Antarctic. His own laconic account is his best memorial: he knew what the hazards were, but his notes were calm and orderly to the end.

W. H. Hewitt, *Mungo Park*, 1923.
E. W. Bovill, *The Niger Explored*, 1965.


**SIR CHARLES MIDDLETON, 1st LORD BARHAM** (1726-1813), naval administrator, prepared the navy for its crucial rôle in the Revolutionary and Napoleonic wars. On the main staircase at Exton Hall in Rutland there hangs a picture of the fleets at the close of the battle of Trafalgar, painted for presentation to Lord

Barham who was First Lord of the Admiralty in the year of the battle of Trafalgar.

Born in 1726, Middleton entered the navy as a 'Captain's servant' at the age of fourteen. He had no special chance of distinguishing himself in the Seven Years' War and for twelve years afterwards he lived on half pay. He was recalled for active service again in 1775 and commanded in turn the *Ardent* and *Prince George* battleships. In 1778 he was appointed Comptroller for the Navy. His mother was a cousin of Lord Advocate Dundas and his immediate sponsor was Lord Sandwich, the First Lord. Middleton rose by the conventional path of patronage, but his appointment came at a critical moment in England's affairs: jealousies amongst senior officers, exacerbated by the Keppel and Palliser courts martial, and incompetence and graft at the lower level of administration and supply, threatened the efficiency of the navy just when it was called on to fight France, Spain and the Americans with a fleet which had undergone two decades of peacetime economies. The timber shortage was all the more acute because of the cessation of supplies from America. An alternative source was found in Nova Scotia, better terms were offered to ease the transport of domestic timber. By all means possible, reserves of hemp, pitch and masts were built up, while an urgent programme of building was mounted in the dockyards. Coppersheathing became general practice when, at Middleton's suggestion, a preservative was applied which made it possible to use the sheathing with iron bolts without corroding them. The use of the carronade, a short-range gun made at the Carron ironworks, gave British ships superiority in close actions.

After the war the fleet was systematically re-equipped and rebuilt; timber was given time to season and reserves of material were built up. At the same time Middleton tackled the complex weaknesses in naval administration. The political climate was favourable to reform. In 1785 a commission was set up to inquire into the fees and gratuities received in public offices. Besides prohibiting fees, the Commission accepted his plan that the Board, essentially unchanged since the Restoration, should be divided into three committees: Correspondence, Stores and Accounts. A Deputy Comptroller should be appointed to assist him, a Secretary and Surveyor of Civil Architecture added to the Board. Unfortunately these proposals were not implemented by the government until 1796. Middleton, an avowed reformer amongst colleagues, some of whom stood to lose by his reforms, was in an exposed position. In March 1790 he resigned.

It was to Middleton's credit that he was able to leave a well-equipped navy. Compared with 1775 or 1755, the transition from peace to war was easy. But things went awry again under the lax comptrollership of Sir Andrew Hamond and Lord St. Vincent stirred up a hornets' nest when he became First Lord in 1801. He himself was much to blame for his misjudgement when he cut down stocks after the Peace of Amiens, and Middleton inherited an awkward situation bedevilled by complaints and inquiries, when he was recalled in January 1805 to be chairman of yet another reforming Commission. Three months later he became First Lord himself, when Melville was forced to resign after criticism of his handling of naval accounts while he was Treasurer of the Navy. In this way, with the debris of administrative scandals all round him, Lord Barham, as Middleton now became, rose to be head of the Navy. After anxious months came the glorious day, when England 'saved herself by her exertions' and Nelson destroyed the French fleet, and the vestiges of Napoleon's invasion with it, at the battle of Trafalgar. It is uncertain how much Barham was responsible for Nelson's strategy. But it was lucky that the country had this man, with his large experience, at the head of operations.

His voluminous papers are a fascinating source for this rich period of naval history. He was the confidant of such men as Hood and Kempenfelt. His real influence was far greater than his official work would suggest, for he was consulted by seamen and politicians on the many points on which he had expert knowledge. Austere, religious — he was a friend of Wilberforce and an early opponent of the slave trade — outspoken, he was sometimes an awkward colleague, but he was always a great public servant.

J. K. Laughton, *Letters and Papers of Charles, Lord Barham*, 3 vols., 1907-11.

**ADAM DUNCAN, VISCOUNT DUNCAN OF CAMPERDOWN** (1731-1804) was commander-in-chief of the North Sea squadron entrusted with the task of blockading the Dutch in the Texel in the summer of 1797. England's state was then alarming.

The wooden walls proved unsound when mutinies broke out at Spithead and the Nore. His fleet lay inactive at the Nore, while Duncan bluffed the Dutch by constant signalling to imaginary ships beyond the horizon. Then, in October, with his chastened fleet back on station, he won the victory of Camperdown which destroyed the Dutch fleet as surely as his blockade had spoiled their commerce.

Duncan is an isolated figure in the eighteenth-century navy, a craggy Scotsman, Presbyterian and Whig in a navy which was dominated increasingly by sons of squires and parsons, Anglican and Tory. He was born in a house at the end of Seagait in Dundee. He had little influence, though his mother was a Haldane, but he eventually inherited some property. He distinguished himself in the Seven Years' War, especially at the capture of Havana in 1762, but between 1764 and 1795 he was employed for only two years. The authorities seem to have taken a tepid view of his professional qualities. His was a remote personality. Nelson, who much admired the method and manner of his victory at Camperdown, had never met him. But he was admired by the seamen who served under him. He seems to have been a strikingly fine figure, six foot three, with a crown of snow-white hair. He took care of the interests of men who were usually neglected, the officers in the small ships: cutters, sloops and luggers; though a firm disciplinarian on board ship, he detested the press gang. The comment of one anonymous seaman may be representative of many: 'They can't make too much of him. He is a heart of oak; he is a seaman every inch of him.'

The battle of Camperdown, 11 October 1797, proved these qualities and rewarded Duncan for his anxious vigil of the summer. The tactical handling of the fleets showed little subtlety on either side. The way in which Duncan cut through the enemy in two parallel line-ahead columns has encouraged historians to see Camperdown as the forerunner of Trafalgar. In fact Duncan was not acting according to a pre-conceived plan. He saw that the Dutch, with a slightly inferior force, were likely to take refuge in shallow water where he could not follow. So he acted impulsively to gain the leeward (and landward) position, relying upon the fighting qualities of his ships to win the battle in the ensuing mêlée. That is what happened: he secured nine out of sixteeen Dutch battleships and two frigates; no British ships were sunk though British casualties were nearly as heavy as the Dutch. 'It is a marvellous thing', the Dutch admiral Winter (also six foot three) is supposed to have said as he stood a captive on the deck of the *Venerable*, Duncan's flagship, 'that two such gigantic objects as Admiral Duncan and myself should have escaped the general carnage of this day.' On that day Duncan had restored England's confidence in her navy and the navy's confidence in winning the war at sea.

Christopher Lloyd, *St. Vincent and Camperdown*, 1963.

**SIR WILLIAM CORNWALLIS** (1744-1819), admiral, commanded the Channel fleet in the years 1803-5 when Napoleon threatened invasion and only Britain's storm-tossed ships stood between the French army and England. By sound strategy and stout-hearted seamanship Cornwallis helped to save his country. Nelson's pursuit of Villeneuve and the final triumph of Trafalgar would not have been possible without his relentless blockade.

The fourth son of the first Earl Cornwallis, William first served in the Seven Years' War under Boscawen at Louisburg, and under Hawke at Quiberon Bay. In the American war he was with the victorious Rodney at St. Kitts and Dominica (1782). While his elder brother was conducting the Mysore campaign he was in command on the East India station; on the outbreak of the Revolutionary war he seized Chandernagore and Pondicherry. In 1794 he was sent to serve in the Channel, but after a dispute with the Admiralty, a court martial and mild censure for a breach of discipline, he was unemployed for the rest of the first half of the war. In 1801 he was restored to command in the Channel. When two years later the second and more deadly phase of the war began, he was assigned by St. Vincent to his historic mission.

'The Devil stands at the door,' said Nelson as he made ready to embark on the *Victory*. Cornwallis, as he took up his station at Brest, would no doubt have expressed himself more prosaically. Old Billy-go-tight, as his men called him, florid of countenance, with the bluff features and speech of a country squire, was not given to rhetoric. As Napoleon prepared for invasion it was Cornwallis's part to watch, Nelson's to chase — when the French break from Toulon eventually gave him the chance. Savaged by winter storms, sails tattered, masts sprung and spars broken, Cornwallis's ships were somehow kept at sea through the gales of winter and spring. The men were weakened by living on a diet of tough salt beef and mouldy biscuit; maggots and weevils consumed their share; only liberal admixture of brandy and wine made the brackish water drinkable. St. Vincent's recent economies had reduced the seaworthiness of some of the ships. Yet they stayed at sea in storms that severely damaged Napoleon's waiting transports. Mahon hardly exaggerated when he said that it was those distant ships, upon which the Grand Army never looked, that stood between it and the dominion of the world. In part that army had Napoleon to blame — for building barges when he should have been building men of war to combat the British ships. Cornwallis, Pellew, Collingwood, Calder and Keith saw to the rest. The battle of Trafalgar was only a postscript — though a conclusive one — to the failure of the French to concentrate their naval forces and provide support for the invasion. A month before, Napoleon had abandoned his invasion plan and marched for Germany.

The part played by Cornwallis in the events leading up to Trafalgar can hardly be criticized — though they brought him disappointment. When news of Villeneuve's return from the West Indies was brought to England, Barham, St. Vincent's successor at the Admiralty, at once ordered Cornwallis to send Sir Robert Calder to intercept him. Calder inflicted relatively little damage in the thick weather of 22 July. Villeneuve was allowed to slip away. Calder was severely blamed — and perhaps unfairly. There was to be no more hesitation among the British admirals: when Ganteâume sailed out of Brest on 21 August 1805 Cornwallis eagerly accepted the chance of a fight — only to be thwarted when the French withdrew to the cover of their shore batteries. Cornwallis was wounded by a shell splinter: he did not mention the matter in his report. When Villeneuve eventually sought and found the open battle of 21 October with Nelson and Collingwood, Ganteâume was still in Brest, immobilized by Cornwallis's stern blockade. It was his last service for he subsequently retired.

A. T. Mahon, *The Influence of Sea Power upon the French Revolution and Empire, 1793-1812*, 2 vols., 1892.

## HORATIO, VISCOUNT NELSON, DUKE OF BRONTÉ

(1758-1805) was born at Burnham Thorpe Rectory in North Norfolk, the third son to survive but the fifth to be born to the Reverend Edmund Nelson, a quiet man, distantly related to the Walpoles. He died in the cockpit of the *Victory*, at the moment of a memorable triumph in the greatest battle in British naval history. His personality is hard to convey through the facts of his life, romantic and heroic as these are. Nelson's greatness was recognized by many who had to deal with him, as well as by people to whom he was but a name. He had always a strong sense of his destiny. Like other great men, he had an actor's flair for improving upon the occasion. He was intensely imaginative, in his writing and conversation, in his professional duty and in the manner in which he enacted the important scenes of his life. It is not surprising that, as he himself complained, every portrait of him showed a different man.

His career began as it was to continue, with a restless eagerness to be doing great things. On a winter's morning, with his brother William, he found the way to their school at North Walsham blocked by snow. Their father urged them to make one more attempt. When William thought the time was come to give up, Horatio insisted upon pressing through: 'Remember, brother, it was left to our honour.' He wanted to follow his uncle Maurice Suckling to sea. This uncle, captain of the *Raisonnable*, upon which Horatio sailed as midshipman in 1771, and subsequently Comptroller of the Navy, was able to launch him on his career. On Suckling's suggestion he went on a merchant vessel to South America to acquire practical seamanship. Then, in 1773, he accompanied a North Pole expedition for scientific research, under the Hon. Daines Barrington. In 1775 he joined the *Seahorse*, frigate, on a voyage to the East Indies, but this unfortunately brought fever which recurred at intervals through his life. His slight, fragile-seeming build might have been the legacy of this illness, which nearly killed him. So, he confided later in life, was his resolution to be a hero: 'confiding in Providence, I will brave every danger'.

In 1777 he went to Jamaica on the *Lowestoft* frigate as lieutenant; with war came quick promotion and in 1778 he became Commander, in the following year Post-Captain. In 1780, commanding the frigate *Hinchingbrooke*, he led the naval force in the

*Horatio Nelson, Viscount Nelson*
(Artist: Lemuel Francis Abbott)

expedition against Port Juan. Strenuous exertions in nightmarish conditions were followed by a further visitation from 'Yellow Jack' and he was invalided home. In 1781 he was appointed to commission the *Albemarle*, a converted French merchantman and poor sailer. In this vessel he served on the American station and there made the acquaintance of Hood, whom he greatly admired, but he did not take part in the major fleet actions. In March 1787 he married a young widow, daughter of a planter in the Leeward Islands, Fanny Nesbit. With her he settled down to five years on half pay, the regular lot of a naval officer in peace-time, at Burnham Thorpe. The company of a lady, invalidish and tending to low spirits, who bore him no children, the mild amuse-ments of Norfolk society, coursing and birds-nesting, were not enough for him. After much frustration he got command, in 1793, of the *Agamemnon*, 64 guns, at the outset of a war which was to provide unparalleled challenges and opportunities to the navy and its young captains.

Nelson went with Hood to the Mediterranean. With him sailed a neighbouring rector's son, William Hoste. In the letters of this young midshipman, who followed him from the *Agamemnon* to the *Captain*, we learn of the respect, amounting to adoration, that Nelson inspired amongst those he commanded. 'Was there ever such a man in our Navy before, or can you imagine that there ever will be one to equal him?', he was later to write. Nelson now showed his heaven-sent gifts of command, quick imaginative strokes, a longing for glory, the ability to transmit his ardour to his men, an unusual generosity in his interest for others and readiness to praise them. In 1800 he was to write to Lord Spencer from the *Foudroyant*, 'Not for all the world would I rob any man of a sprig of laurel — much less my children of the *Foudroyant*. I love her as a fond father, a darling child, and glory in her deeds.' This was unusual language for a sailor to employ in writing to the First Lord. In a reticent service, Nelson's uninhibited, warm personality made its mark because it went with superb technical virtuosity. He expected to succeed; with his men stirred by his confidence, happy in his trust, it is not surprising that he did.

Nelson was employed in the blockade of Corsica and then commanded the naval brigade at the reduction of Bastia and Calvi; here a blow from a stone, thrown up by shot, destroyed his right eye. In 1795 he was present at Hotham's two small victories outside Toulon, but thought them insignificant, though he captured the *Ça Ira* in a memorable duel; already he conceived of battle in terms of destroying the enemy. His chance came in February 1797 at the battle of Cape St. Vincent, where he was commodore under Jervis; it was his boldness in breaking the line that transformed a line battle into sharper action of a more destructive sort. When the *Captain* was laid alongside *San Josef* to board, he followed the soldiers in to receive the swords of the Spanish officers. Though Jervis' dispatch was reserved, he appreciated that the victory owed much to Nelson. In the fleet, enthusiasm was boundless; at home his reputation was made. He was promoted Rear Admiral and received the Order of the Bath. His fame was not lessened by the gallant failure of his attack upon a richly laden Spanish ship at Santa Cruz in July. But he lost his right arm, shattered at the elbow as he was about to draw his sword, in a boat just off the mole of Santa Cruz.

His fortieth year brought greater glory. In March he hoisted his flag on the *Vanguard* and took a small squadron into the Mediterranean to watch the French. Damaged by a storm, the *Vanguard* was forced to put into San Pietro while the French squadron was bound for Egypt. During the weeks of searching, his fleet actually sailed so close to the French, at night in a fog, that the French Admiral heard their signal guns and hastily altered course. How history would have been changed, if Nelson had met Napoleon that night, we are left to guess. Eventually he learned that they had gone to Egypt and tracked them down in Aboukir Bay where, against Admiral de Brueys with seventeen ships against his twelve he won a classic victory, as daring as Quiberon Bay — and even more complete. De Brueys made the mistake of relying on the reefs which protected his position. Nelson risked going into a strange bay at dusk, without charts or pilots. The wind blew along the French line, so he concentrated his attack on the weather end, then creeping down the line, captured or destroyed the whole fleet, except for two frigates. The scene, with the darkness lit up by the fire of the drifting ships, was unforgettable. The high moment came at ten p.m. when the flagship, *l'Orient*, 120 guns, blew up in an explosion which was heard ten miles away. Nelson was wounded in the head but remained active. Morning dawned, heavy with smoke upon a scene of carnage; the French had lost over 5,000 — taken, drowned, burned or missing. Nelson sailed to Naples and into the arms of Lady Hamilton.

The wife of the English ambassador, she was a low-born beauty, much painted by Romney. Nelson was enslaved by her and the liaison that followed lasted until his death. His letters reveal a complete infatuation. His cold and scornful attitude to his wife, on top of desertion, is the most unattractive feature of the affair. Lady Hamilton became somewhat blatant and her flattery disgusted Nelson's friends, but the affair is redeemed from squalor by Nelson's naïve, unquestioning devotion to the woman who destroyed his reputation, and very nearly his career. When Nelson, who had been made Duke of Bronté by the King of Naples, evacuated the King from Naples to Palermo and subdued the insurgents, he was ordered by Lord Keith, commander-in-chief in the Mediterranean, to sail to Minorca. Nelson refused; when the order was repeated he sent his second-in command, Duckworth, himself remaining to control the blockade of Malta from Palermo. He was censured by the Admiralty for his conduct, resigned his command and came home, with the ambassador and Lady Hamilton. Arriving in England in November 1800, he saw his wife for the last time; the interview was unhappy.

The strain of long years at sea upon an imaginative nature, the innate tendency to dramatise situations, the ambition suddenly and brilliantly realized at the Nile — all help to account for the almost bizarre personality of these years. With his insensitivity to society's views, his habit of plain speaking and his reputation in the service for arrogant disobedience, it is not strange that he was looked on coldly by some of his superiors. Nelson acted on the principle that he once outlined to his father: 'I always act as I think right.' When he had bought a property in Surrey at Merton where he could live with Lady Hamilton, he wrote to her: 'Have we a nice church at Merton? We will set an example of goodness to the under-parishioners.' In the same way he was probably unaware of the feelings he aroused in Sir Hyde Parker, to whom he was Vice-Admiral in his next employment, a punitive expedition to the Baltic.

On 2 April 1801, Nelson took twelve ships of the line and the smaller vessels into Copenhagen harbour. Hyde Parker, who was always cautious, following up Nelson's attack according to plan, was disturbed by the hot reception Nelson was receiving and signalled for withdrawal. Nelson had just remarked that this was 'warm work' — then 'but mark you, I would not be elsewhere for thousands'. The signal was reported to him. He walked about, working the stump of his right arm in agitation. Then, after saying that he would be damned if he would leave off the action, he said 'You know, Foley, I have only one eye. I have a right to be blind sometimes'. He raised his spy-glass to his right eye and announced, 'I really do not see the signal'. Heedless of the fact that three ships had run aground, he persevered in the face of heavy fire from the shore batteries till he had sunk, burned or taken all the seventeen Danish ships. He was shocked by the carnage of the action — but it was entirely successful. The Northern League was dissolved; a code was agreed to govern the searching of ships and the definition of contraband — the causes of the dispute. Nelson, who had been made Baron after the Nile, now became a Viscount and succeeded Parker as commander-in-chief, but a bout of influenza caused him to return to England. Ordered to look after the defence of the coast, on the prospect of a French invasion, he planned an attack upon the flotilla at Boulogne, which failed with some loss.

When war was declared again in April 1803, Nelson went back to the Mediterranean in the *Victory*, which had served as flagship for Keppel and Kempenfelt, Howe, Hood and St. Vincent. For the next eighteen months he cruised about Toulon; he was briefly absent for the first time when in March 1805, Villeneuve slipped out of port and sailed for the West Indies. Meanwhile Napoleon had 90,000 men and 2,000 transports ready at Boulogne. He ordered the admirals to assemble and return to Europe to clear the channel of such English ships as remained. But when Austria declared war on France, his invasion plan was put off. Trafalgar was thus a postscript. But the sequence of events that led up to it was dramatic. Nelson searched for Villeneuve blindly, following intuition: at first, wrongly, to Sardinia; thence to Egypt; then, on the second break-out, correctly, to the West Indies. The courage that dictated his decision to follow Villeneuve there, leaving the Channel unguarded, is typical: 'If they are not gone to the West Indies I shall be blamed: to be burned in effigy, or Westminster Abbey is my alternative.' He passed Gibraltar on 7 May, a month behind Villeneuve. He returned, having taken only twenty-four days to cross the Atlantic, hard on his tracks. For two years he had not set foot outside the *Victory*. He was still concerned about the Mediterranean. Fortunately Barham had ordered Calder to block the French *en route* for Brest. On 22 July, the day after Nelson reached Gibraltar, Calder fought the French off Finisterre. He did not destroy them, but they retreated back to Ferrol under cover of fog. In August they went on to Cadiz. Nelson arrived there on

28 September with *carte blanche* from the Admiralty to fight as he wanted.

On 20 October the French came out, with thirty-four ships of the line. The next day the British, with 27 ships, came up with them off Cape Trafalgar. The enemy were extended in a half-moon. Nelson's original plan was carried out to the extent that his ships split one third of the French line from the rest. But it developed into the pell-mell battle that he liked to see, relying upon the gunnery of British ships and the competitive fighting spirit of the crews. They did not need his celebrated signal, 'England expects that every man will do his duty', to spur them into action. Eighteen of the French ships were sunk or taken; none of the remainder ever fought again. The enemy lost in killed and wounded nearly 6,000 men. But Nelson did not live to enjoy this consummation of his tactics and spirit. At about 1.30 p.m. he was hit in the spine by a sharp-shooter from the *Redoutable* while he stood on his quarter deck, unmistakable in his decorations. At about three, Hardy came below to tell him that they had 'twelve or fourteen of the enemy's ships in our possession'. At about 4.30 he died.

The glory and pathos of the scene — the dying Admiral in Hardy's arms, his delirium, his words, 'Kiss me, Hardy' — can move us still, so we are not surprised to read, in a sailor's letter, his feeling of agonized loss: 'I should like to have seen him, but then, all the men in our ship who have seen him are such soft toads, they have done nothing but Blast their Eyes and cry ever since he was killed. God bless you! chaps that fought like the Devil, sit down and cry like a wench.' When, after terrible storms had delayed the sending of dispatches, the nation heard about the victory, on 6 November, the news was received with a sense of national loss. Men could only say 'Alas poor Nelson'. Later, they were able to express their respect in a state funeral of unprecedented pomp. The only sound from the crowd beside the procession was like a 'low murmur', which arose from their removing their hats. Sailors of the *Victory*, his 'band of brothers', tore apart one of the ship's flags to secure mementoes of their captain. Later, Nelson's elder brother was made an Earl, money was voted to him and to his sisters. But Lady Hamilton and his daughter Horatia, so confidently entrusted to the nation in his last note, written on the morning of battle, were left without provision.

Carola Oman, *Nelson*, 1948.
Oliver Warner, *A Portrait of Lord Nelson*, 1958.
T. Pocock, *Horatio Nelson*, 1987.

**CUTHBERT, LORD COLLINGWOOD** (1750-1810), admiral,
was born at Newcastle-upon-Tyne in September 1750, of an old
north country family, somewhat reduced in circumstances. All his
life he exhibited traits of the north-countryman: he was dogged,
loyal, undemonstrative, unimaginative, but competent, a fine
fighting sailor whose greatest service was performed after the
victory of Trafalgar, when he maintained strict blockade upon the
remains of the French fleet and rubbed in the lesson of sea-power
which had been so dramatically asserted by Nelson.

Collingwood entered the navy at eleven as a volunteer in the
*Shannon* frigate, commanded by his cousin. He early made the
acquaintance of Nelson and they became fast friends; the more
volatile Nelson valued the steady fidelity and interest of Collingwood, burly, red-faced, as different in physique and appearance as
he was in temperament. In 1780, commanding the *Pelican*, he was
wrecked in a hurricane. He played a prominent part at Howe's
victory of the 1 June 1794, and was indignant at being passed over
in the distribution of honours after that engagement. At Cape
St. Vincent, in 1797, he came to Nelson's aid at a timely point
in the action, after Nelson had drawn upon himself the fire of
two Spanish ships. His comment on this move is typically reticent:
'It added very much to the satisfaction which I felt in thumping
the Spaniards that I released you a little.' He had himself received
the surrender of one Spanish battleship; another was about to
strike her colours when he sailed over to Nelson. His watch over
the Franco-Spanish fleet in Cadiz, in the summer of 1805, with only
three ships, was a superb feat of seamanship. 'I do not know an
officer I would so soon go on service with' wrote Captain Duff,
soon to be killed at Trafalgar. At that battle, on 21 October, Collingwood, appropriately, was second-in-command. 'See how that
noble fellow Collingwood carries his ship into action!' were
Nelson's last recorded words before the battle started, for Collingwood was the first into action, breaking the enemy line as he
engaged the vast *Santa Ana*, drawing upon himself the fire of
half-a-dozen others. The death of Nelson left him in command
of the battered fleet, his own *Royal Sovereign* as peppered and

splintered as any; the next week of gales was a grim ordeal after the battle and it was not even possible to send home dispatches until 26 October. Collingwood was given the title of Baron.

The rest of Collingwood's life reads like anti-climax only if it is imagined that the naval war was ended by Trafalgar. In fact there were still several French and Spanish squadrons capable of operating dangerously. With responsibility for the seas from Cape St. Vincent to the Dardanelles, Collingwood had to protect British communications and keep the enemy divided and immobilized. This entailed maintaining a close blockade. Detaching one squadron to patrol the central Mediterranean, and a few ships to watch Toulon, he took charge of the most important operation — the blockade of the Atlantic port of Cadiz. Patrolling on a lee shore with dangerous shoals, he kept station in all weathers. The vigil was terribly demanding. Collingwood was a just and humane commander, but he expected the same self-denying qualities of endurance from his captains and crews as he displayed himself. Discipline remained high and the health of the crews surprisingly good. He had his disappointments: in 1808 he failed to bring Admiral Ganteâume to action, though he was able to bottle him up in Toulon. In this year Collingwood moved to the Mediterranean to watch the large French fleet in Toulon, since the war in Spain made it necessary to command the gulf of Lyons. In October 1809 Collingwood defeated a French force that had at last ventured to sea. Skilful cruiser handling and a fast chase brought reward: two ships of the line and the whole of the enemy's convoy were sunk or taken.

Suffering from painful stomach trouble, the result of long confinement on board ship, Collingwood had asked the Admiralty to replace him in the summer of 1808. 'I know not', wrote the First Lord, 'how we should be able to supply all that would be lost to the service of the country, and the general interests of Europe, by your absence from the Mediterranean.' Collingwood had not seen his home for four years. He had to spend two more winters on arduous duty. On 6 March 1810 his flagship at last sailed for home; the next day he died. His weather-beaten ships had enacted an epic of naval history. During years of continuous French aggression he had prevented Napoleon from securing the Mediterranean. British trade flourished, the enemy's wilted. This strong and selfless man was indeed, as Creevey wrote, 'the prime and sole minister of England, acting upon the sea, corresponding himself with all surrounding states, and ordering everything upon his own responsibility'. He was buried beside Nelson under the cupola of St. Paul's. His work had perfectly complemented the victories of England's greatest admiral.

P. Mackesy, *The War in the Mediterranean, 1803-10*, 1957.
G. Murray, *The Life of Admiral Collingwood*, 1936.

**SIR WILLIAM SIDNEY SMITH** (1764-1840), known always by his second name, was one of the more unconventional seamen of his time. He was a less stable character than the fictional Hornblower, but if Mr C. S. Forester had ever found himself short of material for his stories of the sea he need only to have borrowed from the career of Sidney Smith.

He joined the navy at the age of thirteen and served in the American war under Rodney. In 1793 he joined Lord Hood's fleet at Toulon, without appointment and in his own ship. When Hood was forced to evacuate the town Smith was entrusted with the demolition of the French fleet; the operation was botched and only half the ships were sunk, for which the blame was placed on the Spanish sailors who carried it out. His approach to war was that of an Elizabethan buccaneer with a taste for fighting against odds. In 1796 he was captured during a raid on Le Havre and imprisoned. The French would not allow exchange to a man who had so damaged their shipping. From his prison in Paris he managed to supply the British government with important information. In 1798 he escaped and secured himself a command of an 80 gun ship, the *Tigre*. He quarrelled with most commanders, for he was an incorrigible individualist, quarrelsome and vain. But in 1799 he was sent with a small squadron and a roving commission to the Mediterranean. There he earned the fame he craved by his defence of Acre.

Napoleon underestimated the strength of the crusader fortress when he began its siege in March 1799. It was brilliantly defended by the *émigré* officer Phélypeaux and 3,000 Turks. But it would have fallen without the efforts of Smith and his squadron of three ships. He cut off Napoleon's small boats laden with siege stores and maintained the garrison's own supplies. At the critical point, as the desperate French launched their last assault, British sailors helped to man the breach. Napoleon, who had announced that the whole fate of the East hung on it, now abandoned the siege, leaving a third of his force dead. 'If it had not been for you English', he was later to say, 'I should have been Emperor of the East. But wherever there is water to float a ship we are sure to find you in the way.'

Without orders, on his own ship, Smith concluded a treaty providing for the evacuation of Egypt which his government had to repudiate. But his will to win could not be neglected by the Admiralty: in 1805 he was promoted to admiral's rank. He was to be found wherever there was danger or service of an unusual sort. In 1807 he organized the timely evacuation of the Portuguese royal family from Lisbon. Later he served mainly in South American waters. He never experienced again the glory of his defence of Acre. His boastful panache — for a time he affected long mustachios — came perilously near to buffoonery. His greatest asset was imagination. He was an early advocate of the use of torpedoes against the French invasion flotillas at Boulogne. Fittingly, and typically, he was present as an interested spectator at the battle of Waterloo. In his later years he lived mainly in Paris, amusing himself with a fictitious order of 'Knights Liberators', whose aim was to liberate Christian slaves from Barbary, but who seem to have existed mainly in his correspondence.

J. Barrow, *Life of Sir William Sidney Smith*, 2 vols., 1848.

**SIR DAVID BAIRD** (1757-1829), general, came from the old Scottish house of Newbyth and entered the army in 1772. During his service in Macleod's Regiment of Highlanders, later the 71st, he was imprisoned for four years by Hyder Ali and barbarously treated. He returned to India, however, for the Second Mysore War, 1791-2, and served as a Brigadier in Cornwallis's army. He was in command of a brigade at the Cape, 1797-9, before returning once more to India. In 1799 he led the attack upon his old prison, Seringapatam, with outstanding valour, but he went unrewarded either by the Company or the general in command. Baird was a huge man, but he had the gentleness often found in the unusually strong. He shielded the sons of Tipu after the attack and saved them from a vengeful death, an act of chivalry long remembered in India.

In March 1801 Baird executed a little-known feat of war, when he led Indian troops, dispatched from Bombay to the Red Sea, in a march across 120 miles of desert to the Nile. There was only one lot of wells on the route, the heat was extreme, and this was long before the days of 'tropical clothing' or salt tablets, but only three men were lost out of 7,000. They arrived too late to take part in Abercromby's victory, but in time to help Hutchinson capture Alexandria.

Baird's subsequent career was unlucky. He went back to India, only to be snubbed by the Wellesleys, who seem to have had little use for him. He was knighted in 1804, then sent out to recapture the Cape from the Dutch, no difficult operation (1806). Unfortunately he was persuaded by Admiral Popham to lend his regiment for an expedition to Buenos Aires; subsequently he went there himself, but too late to prevent a débâcle for which he was much blamed. Competent soldiers were not plentiful, however, and on his way home Baird was used to assist in an expedition directed against the Danish fleet (1807). The fleet was captured, Copenhagen bombarded; Baird was wounded. In the following year he was sent to Corunna as second-in-command in Moore's Spanish expedition. He joined Moore just before the great retreat to base; it was not his *métier*, the commissariat was bad and his division got out of hand; thwarted of battle, they were sullen, drunken when they could be, and mutinous. More from the example of Moore than from the planning of Baird, the army survived to fight at Corunna, but there Baird fought bravely, had his arm shattered and endured its amputation with his customary fortitude.

J. Fortescue, *History of the British Army*, vols. iv-x, 1906-20.

**SIR RALPH ABERCROMBY** (1734-1801), general, was the son of a laird of Clackmannanshire and was a Dundas on his mother's side. He was sent to Rugby School and was first intended for a career in law. At the age of twenty-two, however, he became a cornet in the Third Dragoon Guards. The Seven Years' War had broken out and he followed his inclination to be a soldier. He served through five campaigns in Germany under Granby and ended as *aide de camp* to a divisional commander. When the American war broke out he was colonel of his regiment.

Disapproving of that war he gave up the Scottish seat in Parliament to which he had been recently elected. When the French came into the war he felt justified in retaining his commission; in 1783, however, he retired on half pay and for ten years lived a studious, retired country life.

Nearly sixty years old and rusty in military matters but keen to serve his country, he received one of the first important commands of the Revolutionary War in 1793 as major-general of a brigade of the line in Flanders. Everything was against the success of the British operation. Abercromby's men were mostly raw and untrained. The political direction was amateurish. The Austrians were dilatory allies and the local population did not give the expected support. The Duke of York was a brave but somewhat wooden commander. The campaign was ultimately a costly failure and it was a reduced and demoralized force that was eventually shipped back to England in the spring of 1795. That a total disaster was avoided was greatly to Abercromby's credit. He had trained his troops assiduously and they had shown in battle and retreat a steadiness that showed what could be done in happier circumstances.

Abercromby served next in the West Indies, where yellow fever was a greater menace than French or Spanish soldiers. His successes included the capture of Saint Lucia and Trinidad in 1796 and 1797. He failed to capture San Juan, Porto Rico in April 1797 and sailed, no doubt thankfully, for home. On his suggestion native regiments were raised to garrison the British islands, where a white soldier's expectancy of life was under two years. Appointed commander-in-chief in Ireland, Abercromby found the troops there in poor state and issued a general order stating that 'the Army was in a state of licentiousness which must render it formidable to anyone but the enemy'. Pitt did not support him and Abercromby resigned. He was an unassuming man, but he was now thoroughly disillusioned with politicians. Historians have largely followed the adverse verdict of soldiers like Abercromby and Stuart upon the policies and methods of Pitt, Dundas and Windham, though they stress the difficulties that faced those hard-pressed men. Divided efforts, casual preparation and lack of co-ordination are the main charges. Pitt undoubtedly thought that Abercromby made unnecessary difficulties. But the latter's experience in the Helder expedition of 1799 is revealing.

The basic assumption behind the expedition was that the Dutch would rise against the French; they did not stir. To succeed, the British force must have enough flat-bottomed boats, horses for the artillery, supplies and other field services; above all the troops must be trained for their work. The expedition was despatched in August 1799, before the militiamen had been given time to train under their new officers; there were insufficient boats and not enough horses even for the artillery. In the circumstances commander and men did well. A landing was effected against heavy fire, the Dutch fleet was captured. Brune's counter-attack was firmly repulsed. Under York, who arrived in September to command the whole force (joined by a Russian contingent), the troops fought stubbornly in constant rain. The army was evacuated by agreement with Brune, who would have asked harder terms, if he had known that its supplies were exhausted.

Abercromby's greatest achievement was the Egyptian campaign and the subsequent victory of Aboukir. The preliminary operations were not encouraging. Dundas allowed General Stuart's plan for an attack in Italy to be spoiled by dispersion of effort. When Abercromby was appointed Commander-in-Chief of all Mediterranean forces in May 1799 it was too late. The Austrian commander Melas was defeated at Marengo in June. Dundas ordered Abercromby to concentrate upon Gibraltar and thence to attack Cadiz. This operation was cancelled at the last moment after disagreement between Abercromby and Admiral Keith. When Dundas now ordered Abercromby to sail with fifteen thousand troops to concert operations with the Turks for the expulsion of the French from Egypt, the general plainly felt that the time had come to win or die. The principal difficulty of the operation lay in providing a water-supply. Again he had no land transport. If the fleet were driven off the coast by bad weather the army might die of thirst before it could take Alexandria. It is not surprising that he wrote to the minister 'that there were risks in a British warfare unknown in any other service'.

Troops and sailors were drilled in disembarking so that they could at once take up their exact position on shore. The approach, on an open beach below a defended sand-hill, a block house and the formidable Aboukir castle in regular formation of boats, the landing under intense fire and the subsequent dash against the sand-hill led by General Moore, have been justly recognized as a classic of war. The army pushed inland for four miles through deep sand and drove the French from defensive positions. Their position was nonetheless alarming: within ten days of landing there were two thousand men in hospital. Fortunately the French commander Menou, with ten thousand men, decided to try to drive the British into the salt lake of Aboukir. In the battle that followed, Abercromby's force was penetrated by French cavalry and he was taken prisoner — though soon delivered. He directed the last moves from an earthwork, in pain from a chest wound but saying nothing about an earlier thigh wound which was to prove fatal. A blanket was placed under his head for a pillow. Abercromby asked what it was. 'Only a soldier's blanket', was the reply. 'Only a soldier's blanket!' exclaimed Abercromby: 'a soldier's blanket is of great consequence, and you must send me the name of the soldier to whom it belongs, that it may be returned to him.' On 28 March, a week after the battle, he died.

The excellent conduct of the British troops at Aboukir, their concentrated and deadly missile-fire, inflicted casualties of more than three to one and gave the French a foretaste of the later exploits of the infantry in Spain and Portugal. That some of the force were militiamen, originally contracted to serve only in Europe, was another hopeful indication. The fine old soldier, respected by all for his courage and sagacity, loved by his troops, 'a very good-natured man', in the phrase of one who fought under him, had served his country better, perhaps, than his country deserved.

John Fortescue, *Six British Soldiers*, 1928.

THOMAS GRAHAM, BARON LYNEDOCH (1748-1843), the only surviving son of the laird of Balgowan and of Lady Christian Hope, was one of the toughest and most competent of Wellington's Peninsular commanders. Yet he did not begin in the regular army. In early adult life he was a country gentleman, a sportsman who played in the first Scottish cricket team (1785), an improving landowner who introduced Cleveland horses and Devon cattle into his country and an expert horseman. He was travelling in France when his wife died there (1791); while he was bringing the coffin back through France a Jacobin mob insulted him and broke into it; he was mistaken for a spy and nearly lynched. The experience scarred him for life.

A gentle and cultivated man, a fine linguist, in politics a Whig, he now devoted his life to fighting the French. He served at Toulon as *aide de camp* to Lord Mulgrave in 1793. He was member of Parliament for Perthshire from 1794 to 1807, but he neglected no chance of active service. In 1796 he served with the Austrians in Italy and distinguished himself by carrying dispatches for the starving garrison of Mantua through Bonaparte's lines, dressed as a peasant. He was second-in-command under Stuart at the capture of Minorca in 1798: a fine operation, carried out without loss, to which Graham contributed by cutting the Meradal pass in the middle of the island and with it all communication between Port Mahon and Ciudadella. Early in 1799 he was in Sicily organizing the defence of that island and arming peasants for resistance. In 1800 he was at the capture of Malta.

By the influence of his friend Sir John Moore, Graham at last obtained permanent military rank: he went with Moore to the Peninsula in 1808 and shared in the advance, retreat and evacuation. He was a major-general with a brigade at the fiasco of Walcheren. In 1810 he was given command of a force of 9,000 British and Portuguese which, with a large Spanish force, held Cadiz against Victor. In March 1811 at Barossa he won a stirring victory against odds and in difficult country. A suicidal frontal attack by his light infantry up a hill gave him time to change his front and drive home a flank attack. But for the incompetence of his Spanish colleague, General Lapena, the victory would have been decisive. Napier described Graham's attack as 'an inspiration rather than a resolution, so wise, so sudden was the decision, so swift, so conclusive was the execution'. Afterwards the defeated General Ruffin spoke of 'the incredibility of so rash an attack'. Rashness, in this case, had saved the day. The sixty-two-year-old Scottish laird proved himself a master of war. Had he been better supported by the Spaniards he might have capitalized on his victory; as it was he took the pressure off Wellington at a crucial time. Besides Hill, Graham was perhaps the man in whom that much tried commander most confided. For some of 1812 he was absent sick, but he returned to lead Wellington's left wing on its great outflanking march of 200 miles through the Tras-os-Montes which preceded the victory of Vittoria (1813). His first attack on San Sebastian failed, his second succeeded. He led the advance into France in October 1813. In 1814 he missed the final victories of Wellington's army, because he was sent with newly-raised troops, whom Wellington badly needed, to Holland to take Bergen-op-Zoom and Antwerp. For Graham the expedition provided an anti-climatic end to a glorious career when his raw soldiers were repulsed in a night attack on Bergen.

At the peace he received a peerage but refused a pension. To the end of an astonishingly vigorous life he was hunting, travelling, breeding horses and cattle. He was a great leader, a man of strong passions but gentle manners. He hated the French as a race, but dealt humanely with them as individuals.

A. M. Delavoye, *Life of Lord Lynedoch*, 1880.

**CHARLES STUART** (1753-1801), general, was the fourth son of the third Earl of Bute, George III's prime minister. He was a successful commander in the Revolutionary wars. But for his early death, in Fortescue's opinion, he might have earned the name of a Marlborough or a Wellington. He saw active service first in America. 'Exceedingly intelligent, takes great pains and is as bold as a lion', ran a superior's report. For two years he was in command of a battalion of Cameronians. After his return from America he could find little employment. The name of Bute still aroused prejudice. He travelled, however, a great deal and acquired a knowledge of languages, especially Italian. In 1794, acting in conjunction with Nelson, he executed a masterly attack upon Calvi, the formidable French stronghold in Sicily. Roads had to be made and guns hauled over rocky hills to a height of nine hundred feet. The town, with its numerically superior garrison, surrendered in August.

In 1798 Stuart was given the assignment of capturing Minorca. 'No one', wrote Admiral St. Vincent, recommending him, 'can manage Frenchmen as him, and the English will go to hell for him.' Dundas, the Secretary of State, may have had misgivings for Stuart was proud, a true son of the Butes, and held politicians in contempt (though he was himself member of Parliament for Bossiney). When he had been sent to Portugal to stiffen that country's resistance he had written to Dundas, 'I am determined to be guided by your instructions so long as they are within the reach of

my comprehension'! In the view of ministers he was a cantankerous fellow who delighted to scorn orders and to argue with his
superiors.

As a commander of men Stuart was inspiring: fiery, strikingly
handsome in a thoroughbred way, pleasant-mannered, but a furious worker. He had turned a rabble of French loyalists into a well-
disciplined force. With the staunch aid of Graham he secured
Minorca without losing a man. He had no field guns, since their
carriages fell to pieces on the roads, but by sound planning and a
marvellous piece of bluff he brought the French garrison to sur
render to a smaller force. He refused (and was surely right in
doing so) the pleas of Dundas for a raid on the fortress of Cartagena. He used his time better by fortifying Minorca: every landing
place was made an impregnable maze of earthworks. When Nelson appealed for troops to help hold Sicily, however, he responded
at once and went there himself with two regiments. He drafted a
masterly plan for the island's defence. 'Essential military operations', he wrote, in words which anticipate the events of the
Peninsular wars, 'are too often avoided, neglected and mis-
arranged from the false idea that they can only be effected by
disciplined troops, whereas in many cases, in many countries and
particularly in Sicily, the joint efforts and exertions of armed
peasants are more likely to prove effectual.' How many regular
soldiers have been so imaginative? Somehow this unusual man
made patriots and soldiers out of suspicious Sicilian peasants.

After his Minorca triumph Stuart had proposed forming a
Mediterranean force to operate against the French flank. The
government preferred to mount an invasion of the Netherlands in
conjunction with the Russians. When eventually the cabinet came
round to Stuart's Mediterranean plan, ministers had been shaken
by the failure of the Helder expedition. Dundas supported Stuart,
but the Cabinet was divided and half an already small force was
sent to Brittany to aid the royalist insurgents. General Pigott
brought 5,000 men to Minorca in April 1800. By then Stuart had
resigned. He had refused to implement the decision of the
Cabinet to hand Malta over to Russia. Dundas, defending a bad
decision — for the Russians were already planning to leave the
coalition — was at least right to say 'If officers are to control our
councils there is an end to all governments.'

It is hard to resist the conclusion that his country had wasted his talents. As an administrator he was recognized by the Duke of York, an authority at least in that field. He asked for information about Stuart's system of regulation of commissariat, pay and medical departments, 'a system that everyone is loud in praise of'. As a strategist he offered analysis and planning of a high order. He understood the need for naval and military co-operation and his friendly association with Nelson showed what could be done in this way. His Italian plan could have made a decisive difference by giving the Austrians support at the point at which the French were, at that stage, most vulnerable. Napoleon might then have lost the battle of Marengo. Fortescue accepts his failings, his 'imperfect sense of discipline', his lack of physical strength and of that 'divine patience which characterized Marlborough'. And yet he was the soldier who came nearest to Marlborough in the combination of 'personal charm, ascendancy over men, diplomatic skill, bodily courage, resolute will, administrative ability and strategic insight'.

John Fortescue, *Six British Soldiers*, 1928.

**SIR JOHN MOORE** (1761-1809), general, was the son of a Scottish doctor and writer, whose novel *Zeluco* suggested to Byron the idea of *Childe Harold*. He took his son, who had been at Glasgow High School, on a long tour to learn foreign languages and ways. At Berlin the boy saw the ageing Frederick the Great and the celebrated Prussian manoeuvres: forty thousand men engaged in the field exercises of the kind that the methods of the French army were soon to make obsolete. At Vienna he was offered a commission in the Imperial army by Joseph II himself. He joined the British army at the age of fifteen, and thereafter the army was his life.

Moore was a complete professional soldier, an intelligent student of war and of the men who were lucky enough to come under his command. He saw his first service in the American war. On his return home he entered Parliament for a Scottish constituency; he was a Pittite during his short career in the Commons (1784-90). When the French war started he was a lieutenant-colonel and was soon employed in the attack upon Corsica; there his skill in the training of troops was noticed, and he became adjutant-general to General Stuart. In 1796 he went under Aber-

*Sir John Moore*
(Artist: Sir Thomas Lawrence)

cromby to the West Indies; when his general was ordered to go to Ireland to suppress the rising there he took Moore with him. In the following year, 1799, he was Abercromby's right-hand man in the invasion of Holland and was badly wounded in that abortive operation. In Egypt, in 1801, it was his brigade that led

Abercromby's army to victory at Aboukir. He was again wounded, and his commander, the valiant old Scot, who taught Moore much about caring for troops, was killed. On his return home, he was given the chance to put his ideas into practice.

In 1799 an experimental rifle corps had been formed and trained in mobile tactics. It was reconstituted in October 1802 and sent to Shorncliffe for special training under Sir John Moore, as he now was, along with the 14th Light Dragoons and two regiments of the line. The brigade thus formed was to be the spearhead of the force that was being mobilized to resist invasion. Moore made it into an *élite* body, so distinctive in discipline, morale and tactics that today his name is honoured as the founder of the light infantry. The essence of his system was that every soldier should know his own part, and to this end he insisted that his officers treat their men as human beings. The drill was practical rather than merely ceremonial: by insistence upon physical fitness, by rewards for good conduct, by example and encouragement, he sought to make his men proud, though they were recruited at the alehouse door, from Irish cabins and the London slums. That this worked is a tribute to the high standard of Moore's officers, inspired by the example of a selfless commander who had a craftsman's eye for the handling of his material. The men were made to march fast, 'to bring down the feet without shaking the body' — the words will appeal to all who have stamped on a parade ground. Above all they were trained to be crack shots, to kill at 300 yards, to use cover and not to waste a round. They were told 'to inflict death upon the enemy rather than to confound, astonish and intimidate'. They were expected to be self-reliant as well as tough, to cook and to mend; the officers were made to race their commander up hills.

Such tactics might cause offence, especially since Moore was brusque with what he regarded as false parade. When asked once if the hussars were to wear their pelisses, he replied, 'Oh, yes, and their muffs too.' But most were enthusiastic, like the future historian Napier, who was a subaltern under Moore and who said that at Shorncliffe 'officers were formed to command and soldiers acquired such discipline as to become an example to the Army and proud of their profession'. Another soldier wrote, 'The 52nd is at this moment one of the first corps in the Service' although 'the cat-o'-nine-tails is never used.'

It was tragic that Moore and many of the troops that he had trained so skilfully were spent in a campaign that was nearly a disaster. Moore had a soldier's suspicion of politicians, and was at odds with Castlereagh during the Spanish operations, but it was not the government's fault that these operations began with misfortune. Neither the collapse of a promising Spanish resistance, nor the fact that Napoleon would be free to move with a quarter of a million troops were anticipated, when Moore was told to take command of the army in Portugal and to support the Spanish as best he could. Wellesley's troops had shown at Vimiero that the French could be beaten. In October 1808 Moore found enthusiasm for his command among the troops, who had been sickened by the convention of Cintra; but he realized that he must take a great risk, to unite with Baird's force in northern Spain before Napoleon could crush the Spanish revolt. He marched; at the same time the Spanish armies caved in before the French. He waited for news of them in mid-November, when he reached Salamanca. Not realizing how serious their situation was, he decided to risk a coup against Napoleon's line of communication between Madrid and France.

That, he probably realized, would draw upon him the whole French army. Did he sufficiently weigh the risk to his own army, the only British army at that time in fighting trim? After Moore had joined Baird and struck east towards Burgos, Napoleon turned. Moore retreated precipitately by the direct route, across the mountains to the sea: 250 miles of terrible country in bitter cold. His troops drank, looted, and alienated the inhabitants; but they remembered how to fight. A fine sustained rear-guard held Soult at bay, and significantly the rear-guard lost less men than any other division. When the battered force reached Corunna they defended the town and on the 16th January 1809 repulsed the French with loss. 24,000 out of 30,000 were then evacuated but not their commander. He was mortally wounded in the fight which saved the army from shame. 'Not a drum was heard, not a funeral note' as his shrouded body was consigned to its grave.

There is room for dispute about his handling of troops. Should he have turned to fight more often? Need he have pushed on so fast? He himself deplored the collapse of discipline, but could anything else be expected of troops who felt cheated of battle? His bold march seriously disrupted Napoleon's plans. The campaign provided valuable battle experience and Wellington, essentially cautious in his strategy, gained much from it. Politicians criticized Moore's strategy but his men had nothing but praise for him. He was a great trainer of troops, from whom in recent times Montgomery and Paget borrowed ideas and methods. The laments of his troops, their sense of loss, are witness enough to the character of the man.

Carola Oman, *Sir John Moore*, 1953.

**WILLIAM CARR, VISCOUNT BERESFORD** (1768-1854) was entrusted in 1809 with the reorganization of the Portuguese army. The one-eyed general created a fine fighting force, capable of holding its own alongside British regiments and making a valuable contribution to the Peninsular War effort.

Illegitimate son of the first Marquis of Waterford, Beresford learned his soldiering at the military school at Strasbourg and was commissioned ensign in the 6th Regiment of Foot (1785). In Nova Scotia he lost the sight of an eye in a shooting accident. In 1795 he was given command of the Connaught Rangers and went with them to the West Indies in Abercromby's expedition of 1795-96. He served in India and under Baird in Egypt, taking part in the famous march across the desert to the Red Sea (1801). In 1807 he commanded at Buenos Aires; he captured but could not hold the colony and had to capitulate. He was imprisoned, but escaped to England after a few months. The end of the year saw Beresford in Madeira occupying the island in the name of the King of Portugal. He stayed there as governor and learned Portuguese before joining the British army in Portugal. He accompanied Moore on his advance to Spain; the retreat to Corunna added new dimensions to his military experience. In 1809, at the request of the Portuguese, he took on the rehabilitation of their army. They made him a Marshal and gave him a whole wing of the palace of Mafra. A big man, with a regal look of 'cold command', despite his blinded eye, he liked to ride about Lisbon in state, accompanied by a large staff. The Portuguese soldier, he wrote, was 'naturally indolent', some of the officers 'a dead weight'. He worked hard to create a useful force from the regular army, though the militia, the *Ordenanza*, was fit only for garrison duty. He got British volunteers, officers and N.C.O.s, to help him; the

officers were tempted by an automatic step up in rank; on
the whole they seem to have done their work of training well.
Beresford was sensitive to Portuguese pride, though mindful of
the need to have his units properly officered. Where a Portuguese
commanded a brigade he insisted on two British colonels — and
*vice versa*. 'The better class of native officers', says Oman, 'were
piqued into emulation' while 'the worst was gradually elimin-
ated.' Beresford's force did not appeal to Wellington when he first
saw it, but he recognized the valuable part it played in harrying
Soult during the retreat from Oporto (1809).

In the spring of 1811 Wellington appointed Beresford to replace
Hill in temporary command of the southern Peninsular army. At
the battle of Albuera he checked Soult (16 May 1811). Napier
asserted that his tactical dispositions were bad and that he was
hesitant at crucial moments of the battle. We also have Wellington's verdict in a private letter: 'We had a very good position and
I think should have gained a complete victory without any
material loss, if the Spaniard could have manoeuvred.' The other
main cause of the heavy British casualties was the impetuosity of
General William Stewart, who counter-attacked without allowing
for his infantry's proper deployment. There were few more
appalling incidents in the history of the Peninsular War than
the attack of the Polish lancers, in a blinding hail-storm, on
Colborne's exposed Light Brigade; nor anything more splendid
than the fighting of the infantry of Colborne's, Abercromby's and
Hoghton's brigades. On receiving Beresford's sobering account
Wellington told him: 'This won't do; it will drive the people in
England mad. Write me down a victory.' Victory it was: the invest-
ment of Badajoz was resumed and Soult lost the strategic initiative; 'They were completely beaten, the day was mine, and they
did not know it and would not run', he complained. When the
torrential rain washed off those terrible slopes 'in streams dis-
coloured with blood' and the survivors of the two armies re-
grouped in expectation of another fight, it was the French who
were the more battered, in casualties (7,000 against 5,900 British
and Spaniards) and in morale. The memory of Albuera 'haunted
them thereafter in the presence of the British infantry like a blow
across the eyes' (Bryant).

Beresford was present at the siege and successful assault upon
Badajoz and he was wounded at Salamanca. He was back in time

for Vittoria and the battles of the Pyrenees. After the war's end he returned to England, a barony and a pension of £2,000 a year. In 1820 he was sent to Brazil to help suppress the rebellion there; but his return to Portugal was obstructed by the Portuguese authorities. He finally settled in England in 1822, was elevated to Viscount in 1823 and became Master-General of Ordnance in 1828-30 under Wellington. Beresford was no Wellington — as his men were keenly aware. Yet Wellington appears to have thought Beresford the most suitable man to take command in the Peninsula in the event of his own death.

Sir Charles Oman, *History of the Peninsular War*, vol. iv. (1906).

SIR THOMAS PICTON (1758-1815), general, was the son of a country gentleman of Pembrokeshire. He entered the army at the age of thirteen, he died on the field of Waterloo. He was unusually tall and strong, and stories collected round his name in profusion. In 1783 he checked a mutiny by striding into the ranks, grabbing the ringleader by the scruff and marching him away. Unconventional about clothes, he fought at Busaco in a red nightcap, at Waterloo in a top hat. He was alleged to be rough, even cruel, but he was trained in a hard school. In 1797 he was made military governor of Trinidad, in 1801 civil governor of that wealthy island. He built roads and developed trade. His brisk methods made enemies, however, and in 1802 commissioners were sent out by Addison's government to inquire into alleged injustice. When he returned in 1803 he was arrested and held to a large bail. Three years later the action of *Rex v Picton* was begun. The charge was that he had allowed the torture of a mulatto woman accused of robbery, under the existing Spanish law; the juristic question was whether, when a country came under the sovereignty of Britain, the Common Law immediately replaced any previous system. Found guilty on a technical point, Picton was tried again in 1808 and acquitted. Nevertheless the charge stuck to his name and Picton had no active service until 1809 when he went with Chatham as Major-General in command of a field brigade in the Walcheren expedition.

In 1810, on Wellington's request, he was appointed to command the Third Division in the Peninsula. In the daring escalade at Badajoz, in cool retreat at El Bodon, in gallant attack at

Vittoria, Toulouse and Ciudad Rodrigo, in a dozen scrapes and sallies, always in the thick of the action, Picton inspired his troops. Foul-mouthed but genial, at his best in danger, he was too independent to please his superiors. Wellington was often cold towards him, the government niggardly. Twice he received the thanks of the House, but he was refused a peerage. His statue at Carmarthen commemorates Britain's Marshal Ney, 'the bravest of the brave'. In 1815 he was appointed to the command of the Fifth Division; he joined the Duke the day before Quatre Bras. There he had some ribs broken, but only his servant was told. He was so wounded at the outset of Waterloo that he would probably have died, even if he had not received a musket ball while leading a victorious charge against the French.

Michael Glover, *Wellington's Peninsular Victories*, 1963.

**ROWLAND, 1st VISCOUNT HILL** (1772-1842), general, was the son of Sir John Hill, of an old Shropshire family, and of Mary Chambre. He was born at Prees Hall, one of sixteen, of whom five served in the army. His statue in Shrewsbury surmounts 'the Column', as it is called there, 132 feet high, an incongruous monument to the most modest of men. 'Daddy' or 'Farmer' Hill was greatly loved. Mild and benevolent in appearance, he was both daring and reliable in action. Of all Wellington's senior officers he was perhaps nearest to the Duke in ability and comradeship. 'The best of Hill', he once said, 'is that you always know where to find him.' He was also one of the few Peninsular generals to whom Wellington felt he could give independent command.

Hill was educated at a private school in Chester and entered the army in 1790. The rapid expansion of the army brought promotion to many young officers. While a subaltern he studied for a time at Strasbourg military school. Two of his uncles, Richard and Robert, were noted evangelisers and all his life he was an earnest Christian. In Rowland religious feeling and a natural pugnacity went with a serene and unselfish temper. He was imaginative in his command of men, a worthy contemporary of Moore and Wellesley. He is credited with the innovation of the Sergeants' Mess; he also provided a school for his regiment, the 90th Foot. The 90th was brought to a high pitch of training. It was men like Hill who prepared the way for the magnificent achievements of the infantry in the Peninsular War. Apart from his own work his example was infectious. Egypt, in 1801, brought his first chance of distinction; he was also wounded there. He tasted victory at Vimiero (1808). He then served under Moore, fought in the rearguard at Corunna and did not leave until the last of the wounded had been disembarked.

Apart from sick leave in the winter of 1810-11 he served throughout the Peninsular campaigns. He took a leading part in the brilliant actions of Oporto and Talavera. He was lucky to escape before the latter battle when surrounded at night by French skirmishers — one of the only two occasions when he was heard to swear. At Torres Vedras he commanded the right-hand corner of the defences. When he returned from England he made a great march and a bold attack to beat the French at Arroyo de Molinos (October 1811). His troops marched twenty to thirty miles a day in lashing winter rain to surprise the French force. They bivouacked in the mountains in a gale, six thousand feet up, soaked, frozen, then marched again before dawn to catch the French at breakfast. Eight hundred French were killed, fifteen hundred taken prisoner; the British losses were seven. In May 1812 he stormed the bridge at Almaraz and cut the line of communication between Soult and Marmont; the prelude to the victory of Salamanca. Unable to hold the Tagus, he joined Wellington in the retreat from Madrid, a masterly operation in appalling conditions. At Bayonne, Orthez and Toulouse he performed great feats. At the first battle he was attacked by Soult with overwhelming force, but he held on, though at the end the field was so thick with corpses that Wellington said he had never seen the like.

At Waterloo, now a peer, he saw his last fighting. Under his command was Adam's brigade, which made the last decisive charge against the Imperial Guard. On this occasion, however, he had little to do on his own as Wellington took personal charge in his sector. In the final advance he was knocked over and 'mislaid' for a time. Afterwards he was second-in-command of the army of occupation. In 1828 he succeeded the duke as commander-in-chief and held that office until a few months before his death. On his death-bed he declared that he did not believe that he had an enemy in the world. He had survived unscathed the professional jealousies and quarrels which were endemic in the army. As one of his officers wrote in Spain: 'He never, under any excitement whatsoever, forgot that he was a gentleman.'

G. L. Teffeteller, *The Surpriser: The Life of Rowland, Lord Hill*, 1983.

**ARTHUR WELLESLEY, 1st DUKE OF WELLINGTON** (1769-1852) is one of the indisputably great figures of English history. Opinion may differ as to whether he was a finer soldier than Marlborough or Napoleon. Such questions will always be debated. It is enough to place his name alongside those masters of war. As a politician he had severe limitations. Like Coriolanus he was at different times the most popular and the most hated man in his country. He embodied some of the finest as well as some of the more insufferable traits of the aristocrat. He would always do what he believed to be right, regardless of party or public clamour.

He was the third son of the first Earl of Mornington and of Anne Hill-Trevor, the daughter of Lord Dungannon. Theirs was an old Anglo-Irish family: the name Wesley or Wellesley had only been added to that of Colley in 1728. Arthur spelled his name Wesley until 1798. He was most likely born in Dublin: the event did not seem important enough for an exact record. From his father, dilettante, musical and spendthrift, he inherited, no doubt, his love of music. He was a graceless, rather lonely boy; he was later stonily reticent about his boyhood. A portrait that survives shows a delicate face; the nose that was to be so famous already has a slight downward curve; the eyes were light blue, hair fair to brown. He was at the Diocesan School, Trim, then at Brown's preparatory school in Chelsea. He was not well prepared for Eton, nor did he flourish there. A schoolfellow describes him as 'quiet, dejected and observant'. Was this possibly a Churchillian reluctance to enter into activities in which he would not shine? He left Eton at fifteen, a dim figure after the brilliant school career of his eldest brother, Richard, to make way for the brighter younger brothers, Gerald and Henry. Neither at school nor afterwards was he a devoted Etonian. It seems, however, that he found his feet at Angers, where he attended the military school, learned some French and made the acquaintance of local nobles. Friends observed that it made a man of him; it also made him a soldier. At eighteen he was gazetted ensign in the 73rd Highland Regiment; his first action, reputedly, was to have one of his soldiers weighed in full kit.

In Ireland, where he served as an aide to the Duke of Buckingham, lord-lieutenant, he hovered between the frivolous life of social Dublin and serious pursuits. He gambled heavily — but in his spare time he read Locke. Was he not struck by Locke's demonstration that all knowledge derived from experience? During his time in Ireland he met and wooed Kitty Pakenham, aged seventeen. His offer was rejected by her parents, since his prospects were uncertain. Yet he was making his way. In 1790 he had been elected member for Trim in the Dublin parliament. In 1793, the year of his proposal, he advanced by purchase to a lieutenant-colonelcy in the 33rd Foot. War was declared and the army expanding. In a serious mood he burned his violin; he would be a soldier without distractions.

His first active service was in the Low Countries under the Duke of York. When asked, forty-five years later, what he had learned there, he answered: 'Why, I learned what not to do, and that is always something'. He had seen the effects of divided command and a winter campaign undertaken without adequate preparation in food or clothing. The army was at its worst, after hurried recruitment following years of cheese-paring: there were casual, inexperienced officers, and men whom Fortescue was to call 'the offscouring of the nation'. The 33rd was ordered out to India. Wellesley sailed with a library of books: law, economics, military history, theology. Like Napoleon he was hungry for knowledge. Before he left he consulted Warren about his ailments. 'I have been attending a young man', said the doctor, 'whose conversation is the most extraordinary I have ever listened to … if this young man lives, he must one day be prime minister.'

India brought strenuous service in the best available school. In July 1797 Wellesley's eldest brother was appointed to be governor-general and began at once upon the forward policy which could only succeed if the army played its part. Arthur was presented with a unique chance of distinction. There was jealousy. Baird was upset when the younger man was appointed to the command of Seringapatam after Baird had led the assault. But he silenced his critics by his ability. After Tipu he dealt with Dhoonhiah Waugh. In April 1802 he was promoted to major-

*Arthur Wellesley, 1st Duke of Wellington*
(Artist: Robert Home)

general. At the end of that year Lord Wellesley made his alliance with the Peshwa of Poona, who had been driven out of his land by Holkar: this quarrel between the Maratha chiefs gave him the chance to deal with them separately, to humble their predatory power and to dispatch their able French advisers. Arthur wanted to harry them at once, before they could group. He began with the brilliant capture of Scindiah's great hill fortress, Ahmednug-gur (August 1803). 'These English', said a Maratha chief, 'are a strange people. They came here in the morning, surveyed the wall, walked over it, killed the garrison and returned to breakfast.'

At the battle of Assaye (24 September 1803) General Wellesley destroyed the military power of Scindiah. At odds of six to one, with troops who had already marched twenty-four hours, on ground that would not have favoured him had he not appreciated that he could outflank the enemy by crossing the River Kaitna, he won a classic victory. About his inspired guess at a ford that no one could see, but the key to the battle, he declared: 'When one is strongly intent on an object, common sense will usually direct one to the right means.' Asked long afterwards what was 'the best thing' he ever did in the way of fighting, 'Assaye', he replied, without adding a word. In November he rubbed in his ascendancy with the smashing victory of Argaum. Then he captured the seemingly impregnable hill fortress of Gawilghur. He showed that guns and troops could move in precipitous mountains.

He left India in March 1805 an experienced commander, and unbeaten. 'A sepoy general', Napoleon was to call him, but he understated the value of the Indian experience. He had learned to handle large forces in hot, dry country. He had learned to be firm with officers whose reckless drinking and quarrelling impaired efficiency. His Indian dispatches were meticulous in description. How did he find time for them? 'My rule was always to do the business of the day in the day.' He returned from India hard and fit.

He had remained single. Now he married Kitty Pakenham after proposing formally by letter before he had seen her again. The act was chivalrous, fatalistic, perhaps typical in its lack of under-standing of the warmer, more spontaneous human feelings. From the start they were incompatible. He was imperious, easily irri-tated by disorder; she fluttery to the point of seeming feeble-minded.

For about a year (1807-8) Wellesley was chief secretary of Ireland under the Duke of Richmond. In the middle of this period (August 1807) he left to command a brigade under Lord Cathcart in Canning's stroke against Copenhagen. This operation, boldly conceived, executed with brisk precision, registered his claims at the Horse Guards, where Indian experience counted for little.

A greater chance came with the Spanish revolt of May 1808. In a Europe dominated by a single nation as never before, at last there was an opening to be exploited. Wellesley was busy assembling a force to invade Spanish America: now he was to take his 9,000 men to Portugal. His object was to eject the French from Lisbon; in the long term 'the absolute evacuation of the Peninsula by the troops of France'. In this task he was to succeed triumphantly. Vimiero, Busaco, Torres Vedras, Talavera, Badajoz, Fuentes de Onoro, the Arapiles, Vittoria and the battles of the Pyrenees — these names, so glorious in British military history, were but the greater landmarks in six years of campaigns; there were to be arduous trials and sharp setbacks, but no defeats. There was, however, a false beginning when, after winning the Battles of Tolica and Vimiero, he was superseded in command, as arranged beforehand, by Burrard and Dalrymple. He put his name to the Convention of Cintra by which those cautious generals negotiated the evacuation of Portugal by the French. Party venom obscured the good sense of this treaty. Wellesley received an object lesson in the factiousness of politicians and the fickle sympathies of the mob. He returned briefly to Ireland after being exonerated by a court of inquiry. In the winter of 1808-9 Moore was forced to retreat through Spain to the sea. His force was evacuated from Corunna, but he died there. Against all objections Wellesley persisted in his belief that Portugal could be held. One politician believed in him: Castlereagh persuaded sceptical cabinet colleagues that Wellesley should be sent to Portugal. So he left his plans for the draining of Irish bogs to establish a military presence in Portugal (April 1809).

Napoleon announced that he would drive the English 'leopards' into the sea but he did not supervise the operation in person. His contemptuous attitude encouraged his marshals to campaign recklessly. Wellington (to use the title he chose when he became a viscount after Talavera) demonstrated repeatedly the superiority of British fire-power in defensive positions. It is mistaken, however, to see him only as a defensive commander. This is to concentrate on the central campaign of the war, the defence of the lines of Torres Vedras to which he retired before Massena's invasion in 1810. His conception of defensive strategy was always dynamic, not a matter of waiting to be attacked; as he once wrote to a subordinate in India, 'You should attack any party that may come within ... your reach.' Napoleon professed to believe that the British were brave but could not manoeuvre. Throughout, Wellington used the ground better than his opponents. Moreover, when he was sure of his ground, he could be swift and audacious. The brilliant crossing of the river Douro which discomfited Soult and won Oporto is a case in point. Another is the strategic surprise he secured by his two-pronged invasion of Spain in 1813, which led by way of great flanking movements to the battle of Vittoria and the final extrusion of the French.

Wellington was able to rely on sea power. Above all the Peninsular War depended upon supplies. Here was a subsistence economy with little left over for an army. His logistical planning rested upon the principle that 'Articles of provision are not to be trifled with or left to chance.' A flow of supplies came in from outside. Their distribution was the general's own concern. 'Minute and constant attendance to orders' is a regular theme. Delegation was not his strong point. He treated some of his officers as bumbling amateurs — but that is what they were. The difficulties of his army reflected an anarchic situation: overlapping jurisdictions at the top, purchase of commissions, and the gentlemanly approach to war which went with it. 'Nobody in the British Army', Wellington complained, 'ever reads a regulation or an order as if it were to be a guide for his conduct or in other manner than an amusing novel; and the consequence is that when complicated arrangements are to be carried into execution ... every *gentleman* proceeds according to his fancy.' The men they commanded were attracted by drink and plunder, disciplined by the lash. Wellington had no illusions about his army. He saw it break into a hellish orgy after the capture of Badajoz, disintegrate in the retreat from Burgos. He was only being realistic when he declared that he had to rule with an iron hand. Deeply imbued as he was with the spirit of aristocracy, he was also a single-minded professional. He could rely upon two things: the bravery of the British soldier when he is well led, and a new seriousness of mind among many of his officers. His own aide-de-camp, Lord Fitzroy Somerset; the ever-dependable 'Daddy' Hill; John Colborne, colonel of the superbly efficient 52nd; Major Edward Somers-Cocks, Wellington's ideal of the officer and leader — these men may stand as representative of the best of his army.

Wellington was essentially an infantry soldier. He did not mass his guns, but sited them singly to support his line. Much of Spain and Portugal was unsuitable to cavalry. He had, indeed, little confidence in this arm, whose officers embodied some of the worst faults of the army. They relied too much on mere dash; nor did regimental officers control the advance. Where a charge was well conducted, as was that of le Marchant and his heavy dragoons at Salamanca, the effect was tremendous. The story of the cavalry is in the main, however, one of wasted opportunities, like Slade's futile action in 1812, which stung Wellington to words for which cavalrymen never forgave him. 'One would think that they cannot manoeuvre, excepting on Wimbledon Common.' The core of the army was therefore the infantry. Moore's Shorncliffe training had raised standards of fire-power and manoeuvrability. In the famous Brown Bess they had a better musket than their opponents. They were probably the most efficient troops in the world. Wellington believed that 'a disciplined infantry that keeps its order and reserves its fire has little to fear from cavalry'. Infantry attacks he met by adroit handling of the lines: with flanks secured, the front sheltered if possible behind a crest from the enemy's artillery. Often, as at Busaco, the French columns would come through the fire of cannon and skirmishers only to encounter the main British line.

Wellington's coolness under fire was proverbial. 'When I come myself, the soldiers think that what they have to do is the most important as I am there ... and they will do for me what perhaps no one else can make them do.' After the battle of Sorauren he wrote to his brother William: 'I escaped as usual unhurt, and I begin to believe that the finger of God is upon me.' He was everywhere in the thick of battle, reconnoitring, lying in a ditch with the infantry and directing their fire, rallying shaken troops. 'Never was courage so conspicuous; never was it so necessary' wrote a brigadier after Waterloo. In that battle Wellington exerted continuous tactical control. With his instinct for the crisis of the battle he recognized the attack of the Imperial Guard as such a moment, its repulse as the moment for decisive counter-attack. 'No cheering, my lads, but forward and complete your victory.' This was rhetoric indeed for the Duke, famed for his laconic but clear orders.

Wellington stood on French soil on 7 October 1813, after the crossing of the Bidassoa. There ensued the battle of the Nivelle which showed Soult, as the Arapiles had shown Marmont, that he could be bold and imaginative in attack. The campaign that ensued was called by Oman 'the great game'. But the battle of Toulouse, on Easter Sunday, 1814, was 'a very severe affair'. In Toulouse Wellington heard that Napoleon had abdicated. He came home to a hero's welcome after a farewell order to his troops which was too spare and simple for his critics. The mischief lay not in the lack of high-flown phrases but in the dispersal of his army. His men believed that he could have held them together. When Napoleon returned to France and Wellington had to take to the field again, he had cause to bewail the lack of his seasoned troops. 'An infamous array' was his description of the allied force assembled in Belgium in March 1815. It was just good enough to resist Napoleon, aided by Napoleon's mistakes before and on the fatal day of Waterloo. The battle and the fighting that preceded it cannot be recounted in detail. He almost lost Quatre Bras, and Waterloo was a 'close-run thing'. For his outnumbered army it was a supreme test of endurance. Wellington had appeared not to doubt the outcome. 'Damn the fellow,' he remarked, as Napoleon launched charge after charge; 'he is a mere pounder after all.' Later, 'It was now to be seen which side has most bottom, and can withstand killing longest.' At 6.30 he was reported to have said: 'Night or the Prussians must come.' He had already won his battle before the Prussians attacked, by the repulse of the Old Guard. The Prussians turned defeat into rout.

Wellington wrote the Waterloo dispatch in a state of emotional shock from the loss of so many friends. There was resentment at his failure to mention every regiment, every exploit. How could he have done so without a team of staff officers? We may marvel at the strength of this man who had been in the centre of battle all day: after a few hours' rest, having received reports of casualties which, as his doctor reported, made tears splash down, making furrows in the sweat and grime, writing a dispatch which covered four days of fighting from 15 to 18 June and filled four columns in *The Times*.

Wellington was made a Duke in 1814. Chief of many foreign titles bestowed on him were those of Prince of Waterloo and Duke of Ciudad Rodrigo. In July 1814 he had to thank the House of Commons for a grant of £400,000 and the estate of Stratfield Saye in Hampshire was given to him by the nation. For three years he served as commander-in-chief of the army of occupation in Paris. It was he who induced Louis XVIII to accept Talleyrand and Fouché as advisers. He opposed resolutely, with Castlereagh's agreement, the dismemberment of France or reprisals. He also persuaded the House of Baring to advance a loan to the French government which enabled them to discharge their indemnity within three years. The recovery of France, so necessary to the equilibrium of Europe, owed much to his moderation; he despised meanness. He found that a French watch, with a map of Spain on the case, originally ordered for Joseph by Napoleon had been withheld by the emperor after Joseph's defeat. 'A *gentleman*,' he said scornfully, 'would not have taken the moment when the poor devil had lost his *châteaux en Espagne*, to take away his watch also.'

He returned to England in 1818 and became Master of Ordnance in Lord Liverpool's cabinet. He was not, of course, a simple soldier entering a political novitiate. He brought unique authority, in Europe no less than in England. With some historians as with some of his contemporaries, his military reputation has constituted an instant prejudice. 'The Duke is a soldier', wrote Scott in 1826; 'a bad education for a statesman in a free country.' 'A man educated in camps and ignorant of the British constitution', wrote Lord Ellenborough in 1823. When Wellington formed his government in 1828 the cabinet insisted upon his giving up command of the army. It was widely said that he would insist upon martial law, yet the evidence of his cabinet career refutes the view that he was simply a dutiful soldier who sought military solutions.

From youth Wellington had been a politician as well as a soldier. It was then normal for a soldier or a sailor to have a parallel political career — and natural for the victor of Waterloo to wish to serve his country in the political sphere. He was authoritarian in political philosophy and practice, but he revered the constitution. During the last years of the Regency and the first years of his reign George IV harassed his ministers by insisting upon his divorce. Canning resigned, Liverpool wanted to; Wellington and Castlereagh remained firm. Wellington eventually got the king's permission to broaden the base of his administration and so averted the prospect of an 'ultra' ministry built around Sidmouth and Eldon. His moderate and practical outlook contributed, therefore, to the successes of Tory government in the more prosperous conditions of the early twenties. It was unfortunate that the unity for which he worked should have been marred by his quarrel with Canning. He opposed Canning's most important decisions on foreign policy: recognition of the independence of the Spanish American colonies, for example. There was a strong personal antipathy, too. 'It was not what the Duke said', wrote Arbuthnot in 1825, 'but what he *looked* when Canning was mentioned.' He was sufficiently loyal to Liverpool and to his own ideal of government not to join with the 'ultra' peers to undermine Canning's position. But when Canning was chosen instead of him to succeed Liverpool as prime minister in 1827, Wellington had had enough. Supported by Peel, he refused to serve under him.

Ostensibly the reason was Catholic emancipation — but the real cause was personal. Uncharacteristically, Wellington had allowed himself to act in the spirit of faction. He was the only man at that juncture who could have preserved the unity of Toryism. It was, in Feiling's words, 'the end of a party'. Goderich succeeded Canning as head of the Canningite-Whig alliance. He proved too weak and in January 1828 the king sent for Wellington. He formed his cabinet in such a way as to restore the balance of Liverpool's government. Huskisson and three other Canningites were included. They objected when he wished to adjust the new Corn Law to favour home-produced grain. He therefore manoeuvred them out of office, knowing that they could no longer turn to the Whigs and were therefore politically impotent.

He had rebuilt a sound position — but could he govern soundly? He wanted time — but Ireland would not wait. Wellington was faced by midsummer of 1828 with the choice: emancipation or civil war. He chose emancipation and stood firm, with Peel, against an emotional storm which would have overturned a lesser man. Not only at Oxford, where Peel lost his seat (or at Trollope's Ullathorne!) but among responsible Tories such as Winchelsea — with whom Wellington fought a duel! — there was a sense of betrayal. 'It is a bad business', he told Sidmouth, 'but we are aground.' Conducting the measure through the Lords he showed familiarity not only with Ireland, but with the concordats of the Catholic countries; he resisted the die-hards and wrested consent from the king. 'The people of England', he once told a friend, 'must be governed by people who are not afraid.' Unfortunately more than firmness was required of a prime minister. He must be sensitive to other men's views; he must be prepared to delegate. Wellington tended to regard opposition as disloyalty and he took on too much himself. 'It can never be right', said Mrs Arbuthnot, 'that the First Lord of the Treasury should be consulted as to who should be Colonel of the Life Guards.' His enormous strength was over-taxed. We see the strength of Lord Eldon's complaint that the Duke was a man not of reason but of determination.

Slowly during 1829 Wellington won back the dissidents. George IV had been upset by Wellington, but he would not have Grey at any price. In 1830, the king died. The political battle was renewed upon new terms, but Wellington failed to adjust his position. He rejected the idea of taking Grey into his cabinet. Then he made his greatest blunder. When the new parliament met in the autumn of 1830, he declared unequivocally against reform. No ministry could survive if it did not make some change in that direction. At first he was moderate in opposition. In February the Belgian question troubled the government: the Duke instructed his political lieutenants not to raise the matter in the Commons. He would not exploit a question of national security for party advantage. 'The Duke thinks of nothing but the country', wrote Ellenborough. But after the Whig success at the general election of April 1831, he was apparently saying 'The revolution is begun and nothing can save us.'

It was because of his unreasoning intransigence more than anything else that the Lords rejected the Bill in the autumn. It is hard for us to recapture the fever of those months. Wellington was not alone in ascribing to the old constitution a sacred character. He had an instinctive understanding, we must remember, of the a ristocratic ideal. As he later told Peel: 'It is not so easy to make men feel that they are of no consequence in the country, who had heretofore so much weight and still preserve their properties ... and their seats in the House of Lords.' Privately he continued to be gloomy, even hysterically so. But in politics he regained his balance. In May 1832, when the king tried to rid himself of the Whigs, the Duke prepared to take office, even to introduce a Reform measure himself, to repeat his Emancipation move. His colleague Peel did more than Place — or the mob who broke his windows at Apsley House on a night when his Duchess lay dead in an upper room — to deter him from this hopeless attempt. Wellington resigned himself to the Whig reform and saved his king from having to implement his promise to create new peers by persuading enough of the old ones to let the bill become law.

After the bill, Wellington handled the Tory peers with tact, complementing Peel's efforts to instruct the party in the Commons. A few months of power in 1834 and increased representation in the Commons bolstered Tory morale. Peel did not return to office until 1841. Meanwhile Wellington found himself on the defensive against a phalanx of peers who had found in Lyndhurst a capable 'ultra' leader. In the circumstances the Duke did well to prevent the peers from using their majority to paralyse Whig government. Wellington affirmed his principle that the peers should not oppose the government on a major question, in 1846, when he persuaded the peers to pass the Corn Law repeal — though he did not personally approve of it. He held no departmental office in Peel's administration, though he was in the Cabinet. He was growing deaf and liable to seizures. He had made a great mistake when he resumed command of the army from his old subordinate Hill in 1842. For the greater part of the year he would with difficulty mount his horse and ride past admiring crowds to the Horse Guards: a painful dismounting was followed by irritable, sleepy hours at his desk. Officials at the ministry despaired. He obstructed necessary reforms. The army that fought and blundered in the Crimean War was essentially his army.

Wellington was as indifferent to adulation as to hatred. He hated pomp and heroics, flatterers and humbugs. He preferred to live simply in the midst of grandeur. The austerities he practised in war became second nature in peacetime. His study in Apsley House had five doors — and five draughts. His mind was too keen to suffer fools gladly, he liked to express himself tersely and the impression we gain from his many recorded sayings is of sound horse-sense. How could they solve the problem of sparrows fouling the exhibits in the Crystal Palace? Queen Victoria sent for the Duke. 'Sparrow-hawks, ma'am' was his answer.

Anybody who doubts his intellectual power should read his military dispatches; they are often masterpieces of economy and aptness of expression. De Quincey spoke of them as 'A monument raised to his reputation which will co-exist with our language.' His ability to clarify a complex problem, and to put his finger on the vital spot amounts sometimes to genius. The honesty of his judgements offended some. He did not shrink from hard truths — and undoubtedly liked to improve them sometimes by a caustic and ironic turn of phrase. 'The scum of the earth ... fellows who have all enlisted for drink', he said of British troops, comparing their recruitment with those of the French army. War had left him with few illusions. 'Take my word for it, if you had seen but one day of war you would pray the Almighty God that you might never see such a thing again.' Essentially he was not a hard man. He wept after the bloody storming of Badajoz. When his friend Arbuthnot was buried at Kensal Green, 'the hero of a hundred fights sat wrapped in his mourning cloak, with tears streaming down his cheeks'. Enriched by the nation, he felt he had an obligation to assist all who asked him. Arbuthnot found him one day stuffing banknotes into envelopes and asked him what he was doing. 'Doing? Doing what I am obliged to do every day. It would take the wealth of the Indies to meet all the demands that are made upon me.

It is easier, perhaps, to appreciate the Iron Duke than to warm to him. The Iron Duke's public virtues are well known. He stood for efficiency, honesty and dignity in the conduct of affairs. He always did his duty and rarely let personal considerations affect his choice of action. He ennobled the life of his time by what he was, as much as by what he did. Laden with honours and titles, familiar with courts and kings, uniquely trusted and revered, he remained entirely uncorrupted. Disraeli declared at the time of his death that he had left his country a great legacy: the contemplation of his character.

Ed. N. Gash, *Studies in the Military and Political Career of the First Duke of Wellington*, 1990.
Ed. A. Brett-James, *Wellington at War, 1794-1815: A selection of his wartime letters*, 1961.
M. Glover, *Wellington as Military Commander*, 1968.
Elizabeth Longford, *Wellington*, 2 vols., 1969 and 1973.

**SPENCER PERCEVAL** (1762-1812), who had been Prime Minister for three years, was shot dead in the lobby of the House

*Spencer Perceval*
(Artist: George Francis Joseph)

of Commons on 12 May by a bankrupt merchant, John James Bellingham. His shocking end is perhaps better known than his steady life. Yet it is likely that, but for a madman's bullet, he would have earned a large place in political history, as the Prime Minister who rode out the storm — and brought the ship safely into harbour. He was only fifty when he was killed, physically robust and active, politically secure and respected. Napoleon was preparing to march on Moscow, Wellington to take the initiative in the Peninsula. Indeed, in Fortescue's words, he had 'endured the dust and heat of the race without earning the immortal garland'.

He was the younger son of the second Lord Egmont, who was celebrated for his glum appearance; he died when Spencer Perceval was eight. The boy was sent to Harrow which was just then attracting the notice of parents away from Eton and Westminster and entering its golden age as a nursery of politicians. Under Heath and Drury he became a competent classical scholar, made some life-long friends, among them Dudley Ryder, the future Lord Harrowby and a staunch political ally, and acquired a lasting affection for the school. At Trinity College, Cambridge, he became a confirmed evangelical, living in a world apart from the majority of undergraduates, a world of earnest manners and set opinions. He could be thoroughly eccentric in his religious concerns — as when he indulged in his taste for prophetic calculations about the end of the world. He did not hesitate to use his parliamentary influence to promote legislation on moral questions such as adultery and divorce. Yet there was little of that priggishness that men noted about the 'Saints'.

For lack of means. Perceval had to go straight to a career. Decisive, tough-minded and methodical, he rose rapidly in his Bar practice. In 1796 he became member of Northampton after a fiercely contested election in that notoriously radical borough. He enjoyed the support of the Castle Ashby interest, but his constituency, with its thousand electors, was no pocket borough. He was a conscientious member and had no trouble in keeping this seat for the rest of his life.

It was about this time when he was making his way, that Romilly wrote of 'his excellent temper, his engaging manners and his sprightly conversation'. Like many small men (he was little more than five feet tall) he was also thrusting and tireless. He wooed Jane Wilson and married her against the wishes of her father, who did not see a future Attorney-General in this impecunious barrister He received a pleasant sinecure, the Surveyorship of the Maltship and Clerkship of the Irons, and he was orthodox on such sensitive questions as the revolution and the constitution. But all was founded on hard work and good advocacy. From the start he was a fervent Pittite and spoke effectively for the ministry in critical debates. At the same time he was entrusted with the prosecution in important state trials. In 1801 he became Solicitor-General in Addington's administration. He had no qualms about taking office under Pitt's supplanter, since he did not hold with Pitt's policy of Catholic emancipation. He overrated the threat of the Pope as the instrument of a hostile power. But his views were grounded on his faith in the Church of England. Unlike many evangelicals he was utterly opposed to the liberal idea that any body of Christians is a church in itself and entitled to full social and political rights in the state. It was in the name of the Church of England — envisaged as a positive moral force in the nation — that he opposed the Roman Catholic claims, framed his education policy and also projected reforms which would purify his church and make it more effective. Though he was widely regarded as a fanatic, his was a positive and idealistic view.

When Pitt was on his way in 1798 to fight the duel with Tierney that might have ended his life, and was asked about a possible successor, he told Ryder, his second, that 'Mr Perceval was the most competent person, and that he appeared the most equal to Mr Fox.' It is a remarkable judgement upon a man who was dismissed with memorable unfairness by Sydney Smith, who could not bear the 'sepulchral Spencer Perceval', as having 'the head of a country parson and the tongue of an Old Bailey lawyer'. In fact Perceval's qualities did not amount to genius, but they were largely what was needed in the situation created by the exigencies of war, the weakness of the Whigs and the intransigence of the king on the question of Catholic emancipation. He was therefore promoted from Solicitor-General to Attorney-General in 1802, in which office he remained under Pitt after 1803. After Pitt's death he was considered to be the leader of 'Pitt's friends'. A brief period in opposition was followed by two years at the Exchequer, from March 1807 until he succeeded Portland in October 1809. Because of Portland's inability to transact any business in the latter months of his administration, Perceval acquired independence and authority. When he became Prime Minister, few were surprised and George III was delighted. But the position was deplorable in all respects. The reckless behaviour of Canning had removed not only himself, but also for the time being Castlereagh from the political scene. Rivalries went so deep that the main question in choosing new ministers was less that of fitness for the job than willingness to work with colleagues. In the end his cabinet was less than impressive. Lord Chancellor Eldon laid twenty to one that the government would not even face Parliament. A typical Whig reaction was Grey's: he was torn between admiration for Perceval's courage and indignation that he should dare to form a ministry at such a time. Wynn found a disturbing feature: 'In the whole of the list there is not one man of old property, weight and influence in the country but that idiot Lord Westmorland.' Auckland argued that none of the ministers, except for Perceval, was able enough to devise a strategy to contain Napoleon, to find means to implement it, and to combat the French economic campaign without crippling the country's own economy. Fortunately Wellington was capable of holding his own in Spain, Liverpool proved a capable war minister, Napoleon contributed to his own defeat and Britain's economic strength enabled it to survive the continental decrees.

At the start, however, the government's prospects were bleak. That it survived, and with some credit, was due mainly to Perceval. His resilience was exactly what was required. The ministry survived the inquiry into and debates on the Walcheren expedition. Somehow money was found to pay for the Peninsular War. Wellington saw mainly the shortcomings of the Treasury but ministers deserved praise. These were, in Gladstone's phrase, 'the heroic days of war finance'. In the detailed business of the exchequer Perceval owed much to talented subordinates, notably Huskisson and Herries. He tended to act as he thought his mentor Pitt would have done. All the responsibility and much of the work was, however, his. He remained chancellor of the exchequer after becoming Prime Minister, despite prolonged efforts to find someone to relieve him of a burdensome post, and his five budgets are models of sound finance. Between 1808 and 1812 the supplies needed exceeded those of any comparable period and a greater proportion than ever before was raised by taxation. The total of new debt contracted between 1803 and 1807 was £156,000,000; from 1808 to 1812 it was but £123,000,000. After Perceval's assassination it rose again steeply. The chancellor had stood firm against the defeatism of those who believed that it was impossible to finance continuous operations on the Continent, and against the caustic attacks of the bullionists.

Perceval's ministers made some capital out of George III's fiftieth jubilee in 1810. They were justified in hoping that some of the old king's popularity would rub off on them. The king's sons were nothing but an embarrassment. The Duke of York had been forced out of the Horse Guards after revelations about the sale of commissions by his mistress, Mrs Clarke. Perceval, who defended him stoutly at that time (1808) insisted upon his reinstatement in 1811. When in the summer of 1811 George III relapsed into insanity, the question of regency was raised again. Perceval followed the precedents of Pitt, went on with his work, and had the satisfaction of being confirmed in office. As Perceval survived crisis after crisis his reputation advanced to a point at which 'plucky Perceval' could be described (by J. W. Ward) as 'the most popular man in England'. He worked incessantly and felt the strain, though, said Long, he was 'as hard as iron'. Only Sunday morning service at St. Margaret's, Westminster, with his large brood of children in attendance, and occasional informal parties, provided relaxation; but a tranquil home provided the ideal background for his labours. He would often slip quietly into the nursery to see his children, for 'he was never so happy as when playing in the midst of them'.

In 1812 Wellesley resigned after prolonged intrigues. Talk of coalition was largely a screen for his own ambition to be Prime Minister. The Regent very properly stood by Perceval who was able to strengthen his administration by bringing back Castlereagh to the Foreign Office and Sidmouth as Lord President; Castlereagh brought talent, Sidmouth votes. In the country at large, however, these manoeuvres looked insignificant beside dangerous outbreaks of popular violence. A trade depression in 1811 had brought unemployment; the Orders in Council were widely blamed, machines and stocking frames were smashed. One of Perceval's last acts was to set up a special commission in Lancashire to deal with the Luddites.

Bellingham, who had suffered imprisonment in Russia, where he had represented a firm of Liverpool merchants, may have thought that Perceval was the member for Staffordshire, and former ambassador to Russia; he was certainly deranged and it is only the loosest link that connects his murderous act with the distresses of merchants and weavers. But mobs assembled that night in London to exult, bonfires were lit and flags waved in

Nottingham and Leicester. Some were convinced that an English revolution was beginning. In fact the country was quiet. The administration survived under Lord Liverpool, whose capacities were at least equal to those of Perceval. But the old Toryism had received a mortal blow. 'The most reactionary Prime Minister of the century' (Aspinall) was certainly a defender of the *status quo* in church and constitution. Liverpool, also opposed to Catholic emancipation, may have been a better man to lead the Tories into the politics of transition after the end of the war.

In another view (Roberts) Perceval was 'hardly equal to the responsibilities of his post'. This is surely to overlook the particular needs of these years. That slight figure, that good-tempered spirit, that clear-sighted pursuit of England's essential goals, above all the unselfconscious probity, appealed to independent country members and to declared opponents. He was that rarest of political leaders, one who is entirely trusted. He died practically penniless, though his family were generously compensated by parliament. George III said of Perceval that he was 'perhaps the most straightforward man he had ever known'. Wilberforce's tribute sounds uncomfortably in modern ears: never had he known any individual die 'of whose salvation he entertained less doubt'. Wilberforce touched, none the less, upon the heart of the matter. The faith was the man.

Denis Gray, *Spencer Perceval*, 1963.

## ROBERT BANKS JENKINSON, 2nd LORD LIVERPOOL

(1770-1828) was first Lord of the Treasury and head of a Tory administration for fifteen years, from 1812 to 1827. To Disraeli he was the 'Arch-Mediocrity', but Gladstone believed that 'England was never better governed than between the years 1822 and 1830', and in the words of his biographer, Yonge, he was 'the very last who, in the strict sense of the word, can be said to have governed England'. His accomplishments were solid rather than exciting. In a period of menace and novelty he preserved a calm and fortitude that evoke respect. In a fluid political situation he maintained a coherence in government that witnessed to his political skill and personal integrity. His ministry contained at different times six future prime ministers: Canning, Goderich, Wellington, Peel, Aberdeen and Palmerston besides the talented Huskisson and

Castlereagh, who did not become Prime Ministers. Essentially a manager in outlook and method, Liverpool showed little inclination to lift his eyes above the details or to examine the principles upon which policy rested. From the beginning he showed that mistrust of general ideas which is characteristic of a certain type of Tory. He may be remembered as the prime minister of the Six Acts. But he was also the man who encouraged the liberal measures of Canning, Huskisson and Peel.

Liverpool's father, one of a line of Oxfordshire baronets who had been rustic and obscure since Anthony Jenkinson, the explorer of Queen Elizabeth's reign, became a specialist in patronage. Without rising in office beyond the Board of Trade he acquired a fortune and an earldom. He meant his son to be a paragon and watched closely every stage of his development. Robert Jenkinson's career was grafted on to his father's solid stock. It was later said of him that 'he always quoted his father'. At Charterhouse and Christ Church he was solemn and consequential; good nature, and a sharp intellect were not always proof against envy and ridicule. Long-necked, heavy-looking, in manner he was awkward rather than absurd. His great friend at Oxford was the brilliant and caustic Canning, storm petrel of Tory politics throughout Liverpool's political career. Canning's barbs were to fly more venomously after 1801 when he resigned with Pitt, and Liverpool went on to serve under Addington. Eventually, however, Liverpool was to be instrumental in bringing Canning back into government.

After Oxford Jenkinson travelled abroad. The grand tour could translate an academic acquaintance with the classics into a living experience of the continuity of European culture. He was present at the taking of the Bastille, which only confirmed his suspicion of the French. While he was abroad he had been returned for Sir John Lowther's borough of Appleby, though still under age (1790). In 1791 he made his maiden speech, on the Russian question, and earned Pitt's compliments. Pitt could recognize an old head on young shoulders. He rarely rose to this level again, but he remained a cogent parliamentary speaker; for many years he bore the main burden of debate for the government in the Lords. In 1793 he secured a seat on the India Board. In 1793 he changed Appleby for Rye and freed himself of patronage. He became colonel in the Kentish militia. He was serious about his

*Robert Jenkinson, 2nd Earl of Liverpool*
(Artist: Sir Thomas Lawrence)

soldiering and equally so in his approach to marriage. Despite his father's pompous opposition he married Lady Louisa Hervey, daughter of the Earl of Bristol, a steady girl who made him an admirable wife.

After Pitt's resignation upon the Catholic emancipation issue he became foreign secretary under Addington. A strong anti-Catholic himself, he felt no need to go out with his chief. He devoted himself none the less to reconciling Pitt and the Canningites to Addington. He supported the war with the optimism of a man who did not believe that revolutionaries could win wars. 'Jenky's march', the march on Paris which he had predicted in 1794, was later held against him. He was associated with the intransigents, anti-Jacobin, anti-French. A cartoon of Gillray in 1796 showed him tied with Canning to the *lanterne* by the Whigs of Brooks's. As Prime Minister in the year of Waterloo he may be said to have answered his critics!

He was properly sceptical of Napoleon's intentions in the Amiens peace negotiations and insisted on holding on to the island of Malta. When Pitt returned in 1804, he became home secretary. Since 1802 he had sat in the House of Lords, with the title of Lord Hawkesbury. George III thought better of him. On Pitt's death he sent for Hawkesbury, who advised him to bury the hatchet and summon Fox: public-spirited but perhaps also calculating advice. Fox was ailing and Hawkesbury only thirty-five: the Whigs had belatedly accepted the war — let them now try to run it. The field was left to 'the talents' but Hawkesbury was given the valuable wardenship of the Cinque Ports which had been Pitt's. Next he served under Portland in an administration which was virtually a committee of four: Castlereagh, Canning, Spencer Perceval and himself. The quarrel between Castlereagh and Canning brought Portland down; and ensured that future Tory administrations would be weakened by the absence of one or the other. Defeatist about the war, the Whigs were stiff in their political demands: they would come in as a party or not at all. So Spencer Perceval grasped the reins. He had established himself by energy and pluck when he was assassinated in May 1812.

Under Perceval, Liverpool (he had inherited the earldom in the previous year) became Secretary for War and the Colonies. Austria was at last subservient to France, the Continental system was being tightened by the co-operation of Russia and Sweden and English mercantile interests were suffering accordingly; with the opposition seeming to consult Whig traditions rather than the nation's interests, with ministers united only by their own unpopularity, the situation called for strong nerves and good planning. Wellington had some harsh criticisms to make of the government, but to Liverpool he owed support through all parliamentary storms, unfailing supplies — and a free hand. When Liverpool became Prime Minister the Peninsula policy had been vindicated and Wellington was on the high road to victory. Napoleon was bound for Moscow and calamity; but the nation was in the throes of an economic crisis for which war with America and the Orders in Council, the government's retaliation to Napoleon's economic warfare, were held responsible.

The Prince Regent had to accept Liverpool who wooed the Canningites with the promise that the Catholic question would remain 'open' — without success. The new government began with a vote of no confidence in the Commons and resigned. Wellesley and Moira tried in turn to form governments. Moira seemed to have succeeded but either lost his nerve or yielded to the pressure of the Regent, his friend, to stand down for Liverpool. In June 1812 Liverpool resumed, second-best for all but his closest colleagues. He had wide experience in the great offices of government. He was transparently honest. He would work in the spirit of his family motto '*Palma non sine pulvere*'. In practical terms of government he was the indispensable co-ordinator of men and measures.

To see the war through, to hold a firm course in the depressed commercial climate of the post-war years, to encourage and help to steer the liberal and reforming measures which seemed desirable in the twenties — these were to be his tasks. At first Liverpool was assisted by the diplomatic ability of Castlereagh and the unique authority of the victor of Waterloo. In the second phase he had Huskisson in the key post of President of the Board of Trade, and Peel, high Tory with a taste for pragmatic reform, as Home Secretary. Canning returned in 1822, the year of Castlereagh's suicide and Sidmouth's resignation from the home secretaryship; and this year has been seen as the dividing line between the two phases of Liverpool's premiership. The obituarist of the *Annual Register* reminds us, however, of the importance of continuity in these years. 'The alterations in the Silk Trade, the Navigation

Laws, the Corn Laws, in the whole system in short, of the duties and prohibitions, had taken place under Lord Liverpool's authority and with his approval. His character at the same time was to the public a sufficient pledge that love of novelty and theory would not be allowed to run into extravagance ...'.

The legislative record was not so barren before 1822 — nor so fertile after 1822 — as to justify a firm distinction between the two periods. Canning and Robinson were brought into the cabinet in 1816 and 1812 respectively. Huskisson had Liverpool's ear from 1814. He supported the Corn Law of 1815. Canning, like Wilberforce, supported the Six Acts, in 1819. In 1812 protestant dissenters had been freed from the relics of penal legislation. In 1814 a generous peace was made with the United States. In 1819 final steps were taken towards resumption of cash payments. In the same year the Factory Acts gave some protection to children in cotton mills; in 1820 the first Truck Act was passed. Economic revival contributed as much as new ministers to the reforms of subsequent years (though Peel's reforms as Home Secretary are largely an exception). It is true that the government in the immediate post-war years sometimes appeared to be timidly repressive. Disraeli's charge, that Liverpool 'was peremptory in little questions, and great ones he left open', is not unfounded.

Ministers had recourse to what they called strong measures. Two of the Six Acts have passed into permanent law. In view of the turbulence of the new towns and old cities like London and Bristol; the Cato Street conspiracy whose object was to murder the whole Cabinet; machine-breaking; above all a lack of civil police which compelled the use of troops in affairs like that of St. Peter's fields — those much abused Acts may seem more like reasonable precautions than instruments of bigoted repression. Despite clamorous appeals for extraordinary government action, even for the formation of 'armed associations of the well-disposed' — a sure way of fomenting civil war — Liverpool held calmly to a middle course, equally resolute against agitators of the left and worried magistrates and mill-owners of the right.

For a successful politician Liverpool was unusually sensitive; he seemed to be genuinely upset by criticisms. 'Blinkinson', as Canning called him, was notorious for the twitches and fidgets which betrayed the strains he underwent. Periods of depression were more likely to be caused by friction in cabinet than by public upsets and problems. But colleagues admired him, even warmed to him. The opinion of an opponent is worth quoting. Lord Dacre, who presented Queen Caroline's petition in the Lords, said that Liverpool, who had the embarrassing task of defending the interests of George IV in this matter, was 'very able and the honestest man that could be dealt with.' Like Baldwin in the abdication crisis of 1936, Liverpool was at his best in a messy case like this, when the issues were not clear-cut, when public personalities were cruelly exposed. His essential respectability was reassuring. He stood above scandal or suspicion of personal gain. Canning realized the extent to which ministry, king and country depended on Liverpool at this time. 'Nothing but plain management, or rather absence of all management, will suit the crisis; and happily Liverpool stands in a situation in which *his own* word will carry him through.' Pitt and Peel were greater men than Liverpool; neither did more than he to reconcile the English of the important, soon to be enfranchised middle classes, to the politician. The elder Pitt had thought it worth while to parade his honesty as a political virtue; a hundred years later it was taken for granted.

Liverpool 'had no habits of any but official employment'. He could be benign, even unreserved with close friends, but when he unbent it was usually with an effort. He lacked spontaneity in company and when he tried to be jolly he risked being ridiculous. Princess Lieven, the wife of the Russian ambassador, made a conquest of him or so she boasted. One evening 'after a long and solemn dinner, he amused us by the odd fancy of jumping over the back of a big sofa, on which I was seated, and establishing himself on a little footstool in front of me. The great Liverpool hovered and then settled on the ground, looking very comic.' Canning encountered him at Bath in 'a huge pair of jack-boots, of the size and colour of fire buckets'. The laughter was rarely malicious, and he continued to be respected. There was sufficient thought behind his actions to set him apart from the mere technicians of politics. To read him, for instance, on the subject of the old representative system is to discover a conservatism that was not blind but deep, even wise. We learn that 'the landed interest is the stamina of the country'. He held that the House of Commons was primarily a deliberative assembly. 'If public opinion is necessarily to affect their decisions on every occasion, it will cease to be a deliberative assembly.'

In 1821 he intervened to prevent the members of the disenfranchised borough of Grampound being given to Leeds, and to give them to the county of Yorkshire instead: to confer upon the 'populous manufacturing towns' the right of election 'would subject the population to a perpetual factious canvass ... I do not wish to see more of such boroughs as Westminster, Southwark and Nottingham. I believe them to be more corrupt than any other places when seriously contested ... and the persons who find their way into Parliament from such places are generally those ... who are least likely to be attached to the good order of society.' The principles of representation mattered less to him than the end product. In the boroughs he was concerned about violence and corruption, in Parliament about the sort of man who arrived to debate and vote. Parliament — and this was the classic Tory defence — represented interests rather than numbers. In giving due weight to the landed gentry, the Church, the universities, Liverpool did not neglect the interests of finance, commerce and manufacturing. In the unreformed Parliament there were at least a hundred who came into one of the latter categories.

Liverpool's part in the evolution of economic policy was no small one. In 1812 he said: 'When it was asked what should be done to make commerce prosper, the answer was *laissez-faire*.' He was for 'leaving capitalists to find out the way in which their capital could best be employed' and held that 'on all commercial subjects the fewer laws the better'. At the same time he understood that it was important to preserve the balance of economic interests in the country. To his credit he defended the bill of 1818 to regulate the hours of children in cotton factories, pointing out that 'to have free labour there must be free agents'; children were not free agents and they were undoubtedly harmed by excessive labour.

Under Liverpool the duties of the First Lord of the Treasury were not nominal. The Chancellor of the Exchequer was still regarded as his assistant. Liverpool guided, even if he did not dictate, post-war fiscal policy, and after Robinson succeeded Vansittart in 1823 his direction became if anything firmer. He also acted as a link between the fiscal and commercial policies of the nation. Huskisson had been an intimate since 1814, and the introduction of free trade measures into Robinson's budgets reflects not only the influence of Huskisson over Robinson, but also Liverpool's personal interest.

In matters of foreign policy Liverpool was lucky to be served by Castlereagh and then by Canning. He was responsible, however, for bringing Canning back into government; indeed he would have preferred Canning, of the two, in 1812. He had little sympathy with Castlereagh's European outlook, or his close association with Metternich, though he supported him loyally; after 1822 he identified himself closely with Canning's liberalism. The majority of the cabinet had been in sympathy with Castlereagh. Canning was inevitably regarded with suspicion, though more because of the tone of his pronouncements than what he actually did. Liverpool had therefore to come out as a partisan, in open support. His nerves were frayed by the furious exchanges in cabinet between Wellington and Canning. He knew that England's interests required that Canning should remain foreign minister; but that effective government relied upon the support of the 'ultras'. Liverpool's success in reconciling the factions; in creating, if not a lasting harmony, at least a situation in which positive measures of government could receive general consent, is emphasized by the course of events after his retirement. 'Ours is not, nor ever has been, a controversial cabinet upon any subject', said Wellington in 1821. This was hardly true after 1822. Yet the crucial policy statement, 'that it is the opinion of the Cabinet that any further step to be taken towards the South American states should be decided without reference to the opinions and wishes of the Continental allied powers', was taken with only one dissenting voice. After the government decision of December 1824, to recommend that the King recognize the South American republics, Canning acknowledged what he owed to Liverpool: 'Spanish America is free and, if we do not mismanage our affairs sadly, she is English and *Novus saeclorum nascitur ordo*. You will see how nobly Liverpool fought with me on this occasion.'

It is only rarely that we find measures which were Liverpool's alone and reflect his special interests. One such was the grant of a million pounds in 1818 for the building of new churches; another half-million was allocated for this purpose from the repayment of the Austrian loan in 1824. From the same source came £60,000 towards the purchase of pictures from the Angerstein collection for a National Gallery. It is appropriate that Lawrence's portrait of Liverpool should show him holding the charter of the National Gallery. Earnest in a mildly evangelical way, civilized as well as learned, Liverpool may not have acted decisively enough to leave the idea of a great man, with contemporaries or in the history books. By any standards, however, he was a good man, and a sound Prime Minister. After his stroke on 17 February 1827, he lingered for nearly two years in semi-consciousness. He died in December 1828. By then Canning too had died. Robinson, now Lord Goderich, had tried, and failed, to govern. The Duke of Wellington, Prime Minister, and Peel had already decided that Catholic emancipation must be granted. Predictably this split the Tories, already weakened by the departure of Huskisson from the cabinet and the loss, therefore, of Canningite support. It is hard to resist the conclusion that the death of Liverpool was also the death of old Toryism. Fortunately for his country, Liverpool had done enough to ensure that some of its best features survived, to re-appear in later governments, notably those of Peel and Disraeli. The strength of English Conservatism has ever been to adapt to circumstances while standing firm on essential principles. Of this Conservatism Liverpool was a strong representative.

W. R. Brock, *Lord Liverpool and Liberal Toryism, 1820-27*, 1941.
N. Gash, *Lord Liverpool*, 1984.

**ROBERT STEWART, VISCOUNT CASTLEREAGH, 2nd MARQUIS OF LONDONDERRY** (1769-1822) was born in the same year as Napoleon and Wellington. A statesman of exceptional ability, Castlereagh helped to bring about the final defeat of Napoleon in the world war and to create the durable order which followed his fall. For a hundred years his reputation has suffered at the hands of historians who lived in an age of relative stability and could hardly understand the alarming international environment of Castlereagh's time; who could not therefore respect, in Morley's words, 'a European settlement, that set nationality at defiance'. In the light of the two world wars of this century his principles and politics can be more fairly appraised. He brought his country's authority, and his diplomatic skills, to the first great experiment in international peacetime co-operation.

His father was Robert, later first Marquis; his mother Sarah

*Robert Stewart, 2nd Marquis of Londonderry*
(Artist: Sir Thomas Lawrence)

Seymour-Conway. His family was of Scottish origin but settled since James I's day at Ballylawn in County Donegal; they also possessed the estate of Mount Stewart in County Down. His half-brother, General William Stewart, a notable soldier and diplomat, later succeeded to the marquisate since Robert died childless.

Robert was educated at the Royal School at Armagh and at St. John's College, Cambridge. He travelled abroad for a year or so and took the chance of hearing a debate in the Constituent Assembly in Paris. From 1790 to its decease he had a seat in the Irish parliament, and in the British House of Commons, for the pocket boroughs of Tregony and Orford, from 1794-7. From 1801 he sat in the united parliament for County Down, always refusing the English peerage which would have compelled him to transfer to the House of Lords. He married in 1794 the daughter of Lord Buckinghamshire; she was beautiful and he remained devoted to her; they had no children. Castlereagh was extraordinarily handsome in the patrician manner so well caught by Lawrence.

In 1798 he was made Chief Secretary on the demand of Lord Cornwallis, the new Lord-Lieutenant. His task was to suppress a dangerous rebellion and to conduct through the Irish parliament the legislation for the Act of Union which he knew to be essential. The crushing of the rebellion led to brutal atrocities, while persuading Irish members to accept the Union involved systematic jobbery in titles and money. Castlereagh denounced the way in which the rebellion was crushed; in fact it was outside his control. He may have disliked the methods necessary to carry out the Union, but it should be remembered that parliamentary seats were regarded as a species of property; like Pitt, Castlereagh would have thought it wrong to abolish them without compensation. He was a firm advocate of the emancipation of the Catholics and he resigned, with Pitt, when this was refused by the king. He did not have a strong feeling of party obligation, however, and took office under Addington when he was offered the Presidency of the Board of Control. When Wellesley wanted support for his forward policies, Castlereagh provided it, in parliament and with the directors of the East India Company. Nor did he ever, for political or personal purposes, utilize the vast patronage of the Indian empire. He did, however, urge caution upon Wellesley. His belief that it would be dangerous to be too closely involved in the affairs of 'that turbulent (Maratha) Empire' was proved to be well-grounded.

In July 1805 Castlereagh was made Secretary of State for War and the Colonies. He was Pitt's chief lieutenant in the Commons; the rest of the Cabinet were all in the Lords. In the months when

England faced invasion he showed a great composure and an ability to plan operations with meticulous care. Unfortunately the expedition which was to have gone to north Germany to support Prussia had to be recalled to England when Napoleon's too rapid moves and his victory at Austerlitz made it plain that there was nothing for them to do. In January 1806 Pitt died and Castlereagh was left without office by the oddly-named 'Ministry of All the Talents'. When the Portland ministry was formed, however, in 1807, Castlereagh returned to the War Office. The new administration contained five future prime ministers; Castlereagh was never to hold that office, but he was for many years, with Metternich, the most influential statesman in Europe.

He made intelligent preparations for a new and greater army. Behind the regular army of 200,000 there was to be a regular militia of 120,000 which was intended to supply gaps in the army and take home service off its shoulders. Beyond these forces stood the 'sedentary militia', based upon the counties, another 200,000; 'volunteers of the best description', 180,000, and finally a body of trained men, not yet organized in battalions but available to fill the gaps in the militia. The entire scheme gave the country a military force far better than anything that had existed before. Was it properly used? In the long run success in the Peninsula justified Castlereagh's work but at first there were cruel disappointments. Wellesley's victory at Vimiero was undone by the dilatory conduct of his seniors, Burrard and Dalrymple. Sir John Moore was compelled to retreat precipitately before the French. Castlereagh, with that magnanimity which seldom failed him, accepted responsibility for the operation. In Moore, Castlereagh had picked a fine professional soldier; it was unfortunate that Napoleon had been enabled by the Convention of Erfurt with Alexander I to concentrate his troops in Spain. In 1809, however, it seemed that he was in trouble with the Austrians. Castlereagh's plan to land a large force at Walcheren to destroy the French invasion flotilla at Antwerp and to exploit any further reverses the emperor might receive was therefore sensible. This time his choice of commander was at fault. Chatham was dilatory and the expedition accomplished nothing beyond the capture of Flushing, having lost half its 40,000 men.

Castlereagh had to cope with all the problems that came with the leadership of the government in the Commons under an ailing prime minister. He was undermined by the ambitious rivalry of Canning. When he discovered that Canning had been making his own membership of the government conditional upon Castlereagh's dismissal, he called him out to a duel. Canning's punishment for months of intrigue was a light wound in the thigh — and exclusion from high office again until after the war. Castlereagh was able to continue in active support of Perceval's administration and before the latter's assassination in 1812 he was recalled to office. From February 1812 until his death he was foreign minister, for all but a few months of that time under Liverpool. These years which saw the defeat of Napoleon, the peace settlement of Vienna and the operations of the Quadruple Alliance tested to the full his diplomatic gifts. He proved himself a statesman of a high order, perhaps the greatest foreign minister that this country has ever had. A modern authority, Lord Strang, has seen him as the founder of the British tradition of firm but conciliatory diplomacy.

Almost alone he had to speak for the government in the Commons, against a captious opposition, and upon a wide range of questions. He showed a mastery on different occasions of constitutional law and monetary policy. He was formidable in argument but more matter-of-fact than eloquent. Hobhouse thought he spoke best when under sharp attack, like a top 'which spins best when it is most whipped'. But he must often have been very tired. It should be remembered that his staff was ludicrously small and amateurish by modern standards; most memoranda, dispatches and letters he penned himself. Government then was personal in a way that is hard for us to grasp. The physical and emotional strain was immense. He had little leisure for the enjoyments of private life. Instead he was immersed in great events. They were exciting enough. He grasped the significance of Napoleon's defeat in Russia and played a big part in the formation of the new alliance, encouraging the Russians and Prussians, on whom its success depended, to come to a closer understanding. When the forces of the great powers had defeated Napoleon at Leipzig. Castlereagh had to prevent the alliance falling apart as others had done; after weeks of personal negotiation at allied headquarters he persuaded them to sign the Treaty of Chaumont, by which they bound themselves to make no separate peace, and to remain in alliance for twenty years after the end of the war. He promised that Britain would pay twice as much for the final efforts of the war as any other power. Castlereagh's personality weighed more, however, than British gold. Metternich was impressed. In his memoirs he later recorded his considered view: 'Absolutely straight, a stranger to all prejudice, as just as he is kind, Lord Castlereagh knew at a glance how to distinguish the truth in everything.'

Castlereagh's initiative and resolve were rewarded. In April Napoleon was expelled to Elba. For Castlereagh the 'Hundred Days' was but an interval, anxious enough, in the complex work of peace-making. The terms of the settlement of Vienna provide the framework for the history of the century that followed. Suffice it to say that a redrawing of the map which was in many ways generous and far-seeing, which produced an order of things more stable than the peace of 1919, was to a large extent his work. At no time in our history has the influence of Britain in Europe been more impressive. It came partly because it was seen to be disinterested, partly because of Castlereagh's moral ascendancy. A clause upon which England insisted was the guarantee of France to abolish the slave trade within five years. The mild treatment of France, even after the Hundred Days, by which that country was able so soon to re-enter the concert of the great powers, reflected Castlereagh's temper. 'Equilibrium' was one of his favourite words. He believed that, as a result of the peace settlement, 'calculations of prudence' had been simplified for there remained 'but few Pieces on the board to complicate the Game of Publick safety'. He once explained his hopes of a system which would give 'the counsels of the Great Powers the efficiency and almost the simplicity of a single State'. He condemned a French intrigue in Buenos Aires as 'flowing from some of the dregs of that old diplomacy which so long poisoned the body politic of Europe ...'. England's duty was to prevent the revival of 'a more contentious order of things', since 'our insular situation places us sufficiently out of reach of danger to admit of our pursuing a more generous and confiding policy'. The treaty, for all its faults (one, the union of Belgium and Holland, was soon to be exposed), embodied these principles and produced a remarkably stable order.

At home, where he was associated with the government's resistance to all suggestions of radical reform and where he played a large part in enacting the Six Acts of 1819, Castlereagh was generally regarded as the embodiment of blind reaction, the willing accomplice of the legitimists. He adhered loyally to the principle that the powers must act together and supported the congresses that met from time to time to put their co-operation into effect. He was, however, temperamentally opposed to what he privately called 'the sublime mysticism and nonsense' of the Czar Alexander's Holy Alliance and regretted the confusion that ensued between the repressive aims of the *exaltés* and the more negative intentions of the Quadruple Alliance. He was also sensitive to the isolationist spirit that always takes Englishmen after a great war: as danger recedes it becomes once more indecent to be a European! His view was that England should use her influence to restrain the monarchs from unwarranted interference, as in 1820, in the case of the Spanish insurrection and Russia. He later denounced the principle of Troppau, that the powers had a right to act together to suppress revolution, in a way that gave much encouragement to nationalist feeling. Over the Greek question that occupied the last months of his life he laid down principles from which Canning did not deviate. Indeed it may be guessed that if he had lived Castlereagh would have acted much as did the supposedly more liberal Canning. Sure in his own judgement, knowing that he had steady support from the majority of ordinary members of Parliament, Castlereagh did not care about public opinion. He cultivated an air of aloofness and even said that it was more gentlemanly to be unpopular. There was also a natural shyness: Princess Lieven found him short of words at dinner parties except when he could talk of his sheepbreeding at North Cray. There he was a charming host. In public he was imposing — like Mont Blanc, said Croker. 'It is a splendid summit of bright and polished frost which, like the travellers in Switzerland, we all admire; but no one can hope and few would wish to reach.' His real *forte* lay in private negotiation. Wilberforce found him so persuasive in such meetings that he tried always to deal with him by letter. He could wear down an opponent by persistence, knowledge and charm. In 1818 he produced forty-three objections to European proposals that the Quadruple Alliance should intervene in troubles between Spain and her South American colonies. His moral and intellectual ascendancy was better known to the Czar Alexander and to

Talleyrand than it was to the mass of his own countrymen. Metternich thought him to be the only Englishman to understand Europe.

In the summer of 1822 Castlereagh began to show signs of the strain of continuous high office. Besides his supervision of foreign affairs he had to bear much of the brunt of the depression and unrest at home. The unpopularity of George IV made matters worse for his harassed ministers. Castlereagh was a solitary worker and he had few confidants. To the end all this official correspondence was in his own handwriting. He became the victim of an obsession that he was threatened by the exposure of some charge of immorality. The king, noticing Castlereagh's uncharacteristically hysterical manner, warned Liverpool and medical precautions were taken. Lady Castlereagh refused to give him the key of his pistol case but he found a small penknife and stabbed himself to death on the morning of 12 August. It has been conjectured that he was suffering from paraproteinaemia, an imbalance in the blood that could damage the brain, so giving rise to delusions.

He was buried in Westminster Abbey. A few ruffians jeered at his coffin but there was no large demonstration of hostility. That he was universally execrated was a crude Whig myth, promulgated by men such as Byron: his epigrams are too well known. The appreciation of a parliamentary opponent is better worth quoting. Brougham wrote to Creevey: 'Put all their men together in one scale, and poor Castlereagh in the other — single, he plainly weighed them down.' Friends and foes alike recognized his courage, straightness and coolness. Had he lived a year or so more, had he been more articulate, more of a phrasemaker, he might have been able to prove that, as the French historian, Albert Sorel, recognized, his principles 'to which he adhered with unshakeable constancy ... were all comprehended in one, the supremacy of English interests; they all proceeded from this high reason of state'. Castlereagh, impassive, lofty, energetic without false display, practical in everything, succeeded, as few English ministers have succeeded since, in being a good European while remaining a steadfast patriot.

J. A. R. Marriott, *Castlereagh*, 1936.
C. J. Bartlett, *Castlereagh*, 1966.

GEORGE CANNING (1770-1827) devoted the best of his extraordinary talents to the pursuit of power. Yet he was in high office for a relatively short time. He was Foreign Secretary twice, from 1807 to 1809 and from 1822 to 1827: seven years altogether in which he enunciated principles and did business with a style which left a permanent mark on our foreign policy. He became Prime Minister in April 1827 and he died in August. Throughout his stormy career he had scorned half-measures. He was a man of extremes who liked to challenge and to provoke, of imperious will and scintillating wit, and of brittle sensibilities. He was in many ways the most un-English of politicians and yet a more fervent patriot never breathed. He was treated with suspicion by grandees of both parties. Yet none argued more powerfully than he against the excesses of Jacobin and reformer. He made many enemies; he was undoubtedly his own worst enemy.

His father, the disinherited heir to a family of Ulster gentry, died when he was one. His mother, Mary Anne Costello, took to the stage to support herself and a growing family; first there were illegitimate children, then she married again; there were more children and she set up as a linen-draper. An uncle, Stratford Canning, a city financier, took care of George and sent him to Eton and Christ Church. Canning was distressed by his mother's way of life and longed to help her. When he achieved office he was able to secure for her a pension on the secret list. He once said that it was to his mother that he had devoted his first years in politics. Whatever feeling was uppermost, whether pride, compassion or the natural fondness of a son, this relationship offers clues to a touchy, intensely hard-working man with a single-minded passion for politics. At the same time he was clever and self-sufficient: his ambition needed no spur that his own spirit and his friends' acclaim could not provide. At Eton he excelled in classics, became head of the school and helped to edit *Microcosm*, a weekly magazine that circulated outside the school — and made a profit! Precocious and witty, he was made to be admired. Gainsborough's portrait of him as a boy of seventeen, a freshman at Oxford, shows long cavalier hair, a bold face, fine dark eyes and a curving lip. He won the Latin verse prize at Christ Church, acquired a reputation for parodies and prepared himself for the political career that seemed inevitable, even though he made a show of reading for the bar and joined Lincoln's Inn. His

*George Canning*
(Artist: Sir Thomas Lawrence)

uncle was a friend of the leading Whigs, whose speeches and style appealed to the exhibitionist in Canning. Sheridan hailed a brilliant recruit; fashionable hostesses spoiled him with praise.

It was, however, a time of shifting allegiances. Canning was impressionable but classical studies had trained him to be conservative in taste and views. Dryden was his poet and Johnson his philosopher. The Revolution which was so exciting to Fox, so disturbing to his Christ Church friend, the solemn Jenkinson, was to Canning at first an interesting, indeed valuable experiment, since 'a pure representative Republick' had never been tried. So he defended the right of the French to carry on in their own way. Moreover he rejoiced in the defeat of Brunswick in 1792, as the philosopher Walker would rejoice, he said, in the punishment of any Eton boy 'who should attempt to spoil any of the electrical experiments by breaking one of his great cylindrical glasses'. According to the same right of rational self-determination which was to remain a steady principle with him, he denounced France for declaring revolutionary war. The event confirmed him in his allegiance to Pitt. He accepted a treasury borough (Newport, Isle of Wight) in 1794 and entered Parliament as a strong government man, a fire-eating anti-Jacobin. Disappointed Whigs, caustic print-engravers seized upon an ambition that he took no pains to hide. His friendship with Pitt was based all the same on a true attraction of mind and principles.

From the start he may be distinguished both from the official type — of which Jenkinson was a notable example — bent on administrative experience, and the 'amateurs' for whom politics were less of a business than a way of life. Canning is hard to place. His oratory sounded contrived and insincere even when most brilliant but his ability was undeniable. In 1796 Pitt made him an Under-Secretary for Foreign Affairs. In 1797, with several others, he started the *Anti-Jacobin*. Aptly named, sharply satirical, this paper taught the Whigs that they had no monopoly of wit or propaganda: it was effective journalism — but it only confirmed the suspicions of those who saw him as 'a light, jesting, paragraph-making man'. About the war Canning was deadly serious. He believed that there should be no negotiation until the oppressed should be delivered from French tyranny. It was always to be his master principle that Britain had a special responsibility, by virtue of her superior institutions, her rights and liberties enshrined in law, for opposing the dangerous theories of revolutionary France. Government he held to be 'a matter not of will but of reason'. Again 'a simple democracy is tyranny and anarchy combined'. Guard the constitution against Jacobins at home and abroad — this was his message. Britain must be great in order to be happy.

He was confirmed in his beliefs by the breakdown of the peace talks of 1797, by the *coup Fructidor* which set the Directory on a new path of conquest. In 1799 Canning became a member of the India Board. In 1800 he married an heiress, Joan Scott, became the Duke of Portland's brother-in-law and gained financial independence. In 1801 he resigned with Pitt over the question of Catholic emancipation. He then attacked colleagues, like Jenkinson, who had joined Addington's ministry, with such venom that his motives were suspect even to those who enjoyed his aphorisms and shared his concern. 'Pitt was to Addington as London is to Paddington' but Pitt was resolved not to harass his successor. He would not follow Canning's 'ungovernable ambition', as he called it. When 'Britain's guardian gander' did resign and Pitt returned, Canning was made Treasurer of the Navy. The quarrel between Addingtonians and Canningites disrupted a ministry that was already weak enough. Canning held no office in 'The Talents' but in 1807 he became Foreign Minister under Portland. As Canning said in Parliament, only 'commanding, overawing talents' could save the state.

He was part-author of the brilliantly timed dissolution which followed the resignation of Grenville in 1807. The subsequent election on a No Popery cry, cynical enough in the mouth of Canning, who favoured Catholic emancipation, strengthened the government against the Whigs, Grenvillites and Addingtonians, and emboldened ministers to take firm measures. The seizure of the Danish fleet in 1807 was a typical Canning stroke. He had learned from British intelligence services about the secret clauses of the Tilsit treaty and he acted to prevent the French from using the Danish fleet. It was an arbitrary but economical way of countering Napoleon's schemes. He was equally far-sighted in securing the rescue of the Portuguese royal family and acquiring the Portuguese fleet. His ardent promotion of total war pleased many Tories. But he would not confine himself to his own department; he criticized his cabinet colleagues. He did not want to be associated with the failures of the war. He disapproved of the Walcheren expedition and criticized Castlereagh after its failure. Castlereagh learned that Canning had been negotiating for months to oust him from the government. In three folio sheets he challenged Canning to a duel. 'I would rather fight than read it,' declared Canning. On 21 September 1809, at 6 a.m. on Putney Heath, at the height of this great war, two of His Majesty's most important ministers fought their duel. It was a high, mad moment in the age of faction. Castlereagh lost a button, Canning a piece of his thigh. Both men had to resign.

For the time being they were irreconcilable: of the two men this damaged Canning the more. He rebuffed Perceval's attempts to reunite 'the separated Members' of Pitt's party, saying that he would not 'wait the good pleasure of any individual'. It must be the Foreign Office or nothing — but when he was offered it in 1812 he turned it down rather than serve under Castlereagh as Leader of the House. The negotiations of that year were tortuous. Canning was undoubtedly mistaken — and Huskisson right in trying to dissuade him — in demanding 'a fair and stateable equality', which meant in effect that he should have complete free-dom in policymaking. The Prince Regent's comment that 'he was too fond of writing and too touchy' is fair.

In 1812 Canning was elected member for Liverpool as candi-date for the liberal merchants. After a noisy campaign to which Brougham contributed 150 speeches, Canning and the Tory Gas-coigne pushed the radical Whig into third place. Elsewhere in this general election Canningites suffered; already the 'party' was small and ineffectual with several adherents of little consequence — like 'Dog' Dent, who campaigned for a tax on dogs. It was said that they 'dined fourteen and voted twelve'. In July 1813 Canning made a gesture towards Tory reunion by formally 'disbanding' his party. Huskisson was given office, Granville a peerage, and Canning charge of a special mission to Portugal: in 1814 he became ambassador at £14,000 a year. Liverpool had always held the door open to Canning, whom he genuinely admired. Canning thanked him 'not from politician to politician but with the genuine warmth of old Christ Church feelings'.

In June 1816 Canning went to the Board of Control. In the four and a half years that he spent in charge of Indian administration he showed again the concentration, rapidity and stretch of mind that made him such an outstanding administrator. He also brought his debating talents to defend the government's case against reforms of all descriptions. With an ingenuity that some thought perverse he defended the old political order. 'He flashed such a light around the constitution', said Coleridge, 'that it was difficult to see the ruins of the fabric around it.' He is often accused of sophistry. It is fairer to see him as the greatest and most convincing of followers of Burke. 'Ancient habits', local entities, 'the spirit of corporation and neighbourhood': these were the living truths that made up a nation. He rejected the 'cold, presumptuous, generalizing philosophy' which would render people 'dead to the glories of Waterloo but tremblingly alive to the imperfections of Old Sarum'. Of course he appreciated that there must be concessions. No one understood better than the member for Liverpool the case for enlightened self-interest in politics as in trade. If practical reforms led to an improvement in material conditions then theories of reform would lose support. This was 'liberal' Toryism as it was understood by Canning, Huskisson and 'prosperity' Robinson, and successfully promoted during the years 1822-7.

Canning resigned in December 1820 because he disagreed with the government's plan to deal with Queen Caroline. He had long been friendly towards her; he defended her case in the Commons and urged the Cabinet to drop the divorce clause of Liverpool's bill to take away the Queen's title. He probably expected that the government would fall if they persisted; like Brougham he certainly underestimated her ability to overplay her hand and spoil her cause. In 1821 his prospects at home seemed bleak though Liverpool wanted him back. He accepted with misgivings the offer of India. We are left to speculate what sort of Governor-General he would have been — how magnificent, how rash — because in August 1822 Castlereagh killed himself. Canning was about to sail on the *Jupiter*, East Indiaman; instead he stayed to be foreign minister. Huskisson moved to the Board of Trade, Robinson thence to the Exchequer. Liverpool's administration took on a new lease of life. Canning had a free hand at last to mould British foreign policy.

Canning had agreed with most of Castlereagh's decisions while criticizing his methods. He distrusted the practice of diplomacy by conference; he had not experienced its value at the time of the great peace-making. By Castlereagh's death collaboration between Britain and the Holy Alliance powers had already broken down. Canning's arrival did not so much signify a change of direction as a new emphasis and style. Canning was a conservative, an anti-Jacobin. But he was able to interpret British interests in a way that Manchester mill-owner and Shropshire squire could both understand. He would not interfere on behalf of revolution; nor would he hear of military action against constitutionalists. When the French proposed to enter Spain on behalf of King Ferdinand, Canning warned them that Britain would not allow a permanent occupation of that country. When the French invaded and overcame the constitutional party Canning began to deal with the emerging American states (August 1823). In December President Monroe enunciated his celebrated doctrine, that the American territories were not to be considered 'as future subjects for colonization by any European powers'. Under welcome pressure from London merchants the British government recognized the republics of Buenos Aires, Mexico and Columbia. Later Brazil too achieved independence by British mediation (1825) after complicated transactions. When the former 'constitutional emperor' of Brazil, Dom Pedro, succeeded his father as King of Portugal and granted a constitution, Spain gave aid to Dom Miguel and his absolutist party. Thereupon Canning sent a fleet and 4,000 troops to Lisbon, Miguel's following were dispersed and the Spanish withdrew. It was defending this action in Parliament that Canning made his most celebrated statement. 'Contemplating Spain, such as our ancestors have known her, I resolved that if France had Spain, it should not be Spain with the Indies.' 'I called the New World into existence to redress the balance of the Old.'

Decisive actions and brave words, as the *Annual Register* said, 'had completely fallen in with the feelings of the public, and had identified him, in some measure, with the dignity and character of the empire'. Greece, where rebels had proclaimed, in January 1822, a constitution for independent Greece, provided further chances for the assertion of liberal principles. But the situation was dangerous. England could not look with indifference upon the advance of Russia into a disintegrating Turkish empire. There was sympathy for the Greeks but, as Lord Byron found to his chagrin, the rebels were hardly the sturdy democrats envisaged by

Englishmen trained on Thucydides. Byron died at Missolonghi and English schoolboys dressed in Greek national costume. Ibrahim recovered the Morea for the Sultan and Canning decided that he must act to forestall the Russians and their plan to set up three separate Greek principalities. The Greeks asked Britain to mediate. Alexander died and was succeeded by Nicholas I, a rigid soldier; Wellington was sent to St. Petersburg to make an agreement with the Russians. The Treaty of London (July 1827) subsequently brought France into an Anglo-Russian agreement to enforce an armistice upon the Turks. Allied naval squadrons sailed for Greece. The Turks refused the armistice and Ibrahim refused to sail home. The allied fleet under Codrington destroyed his fleet in Navarino Bay. When the Treaty of London was made, Canning was Prime Minister; when the battle of Navarino (20th October) was fought he had been dead two months.

It was appropriate that Canning should have succeeded Liverpool; having retained his friendship he had won his confidence. Canning reached a wider public than anyone since Lord Chatham: he was the first foreign minister to explain his policy in platform speeches. He did not succeed, however, in overcoming the hostility of his colleagues. When he was eventually commissioned to form a government, Wellington, Peel and four other cabinet ministers refused to serve in it. There were resignations from government and household. He constructed a coalition with the good-will of most of the Whigs. The old Tory party was irreparably split. Once again he had disrupted the party, with the assistance of Wellington. There was little consolation in power. By combining the rôles of Foreign Secretary and Leader of the House he had exhausted his powers. He was always an exceptionally intense and rapid worker. 'He could not bear to dictate', said one of his secretaries, 'because nobody could write fast enough for him.' He was known, however, when incapacitated by gout in the hand, to dictate two dispatches at once to different secretaries. When he became Prime Minister he was already dosing himself with laudanum. He had caught a chill at the Duke of York's funeral; he caught another in Lord Lyndhurst's garden in July. Resistance was low. Personal attacks had 'rent that proud heart'. As surely as Castlereagh was killed by overwork, so was he, 'just as much as any poor horse that drops down dead in the road', wrote Dudley.

Before Canning died he knew that he had failed to persuade the mass of his party to accept his leadership. He understood that Whig support was temporary and would become conditional. He saw more clearly than most that there was coming, in his own words, 'a great struggle between property and population' which was 'only to be averted by the mildest and most liberal legislation'. Without Canning, cleverest of them all, the Tories could not avoid — or win — this struggle. He was buried in the Abbey, next to Pitt. It was his rightful place.

P. J. V. Rolo, *George Canning*, 1965.
W. Hinde, *George Canning*, 1973.

**WILLIAM HUSKISSON** (1770-1830), politician and economist, was the son of an impoverished Warwickshire squire. After some early schooling in England he was brought up by a relative in Paris where he witnessed some of the scenes of the revolution. To this unusual start in life may be ascribed an independent but somewhat awkward temperament. He was generally regarded as a valuable man to have in office because of his intellectual gifts and especially his understanding of matters of trade and finance, but he never shed a certain prickliness. His appearance did not impress: 'Tall, slovenly and ignoble-looking' was how Greville described him. He aroused that mistrust which sometimes accrues to a man who makes his colleagues feel unsure of their own abilities.

Huskisson became private secretary to Lord Gower, the ambassador in Paris, and returned to England on Gower's recall in 1792. Canning found him useful, since he was bilingual in dealings with *émigrés*. In 1795, before he entered Parliament, he became Under-Secretary at War. He became member for Morpeth in the following year. Thereafter he sat for a succession of close boroughs until in 1823 he was elected as a suitable successor to Canning, member for Liverpool. He was in his element as secretary to the Treasury under Pitt (1804-5) and Portland (1807-9). He resigned with Canning and took his part in the feuds which split the Tories for the rest of Canning's life. This was unlucky, since he was by nature an administrator and would have done best in a post where he could work out long-term policies. He had learned from Canning the supreme virtue of competence in government. In 1814 he returned to office as Minister of Woods and Forests. He contributed regularly to debates on his own special topics: the corn laws, currency, banks and trade. Thus he built a solid reputation as a leading expert on some of the most sensitive questions of the post-war period. He was understood to be a liberal in economic questions. As a member of the finance committee set up in 1819 he had recommended a return to the gold standard. In 1821 he drafted the report of the committee on agricultural distress. In 1823 he was given a seat in the cabinet as President of the Board of Trade and Treasurer of the Navy.

He was as important as Canning or Peel in bringing new life to Liverpool's administration. He won the support of businessmen by his free trade views. The commercial interests of countries were best served, as he had written in his pamphlet *The Depreciation of the Currency*, 'by leaving to every part of the world to raise those productions for which soil and climate are best adapted'. Petitions of merchants from the big cities against restraint of trade now had an active supporter in government. Since Parliament had rejected the idea of an income tax, import duties were necessary to maintain the revenues. Robinson, President of the Board of Trade before Huskisson and now Chancellor of the Exchequer, had already secured some relaxation of the Navigation Laws (1822) to attract the trade of the former colonies and to afford to British colonists in Canada and the West Indies direct access to European ports. Huskisson worked closely with 'Prosperity' Robinson, as Cobbett called him. He carried out the most extensive general reduction of duties since the peacetime administration of the younger Pitt. In 1824, for instance, the duty on raw silk was reduced from 4s. to 6d., on wool from 6d. to 1d. a pound. Adam Smith's economic liberalism was no longer controversial. There were only ninety members present in the House of Commons when his measure, excluding from their application European goods put into bond and offering equality of shipping dues to other countries who would make similar concessions, was passed.

Canning's death in 1827 was a great blow to Huskisson, who was now understood to be the leader of his group. He was ill-suited to the delicate balances and compromises of a coalition government. He took office under Goderich (as Robinson had now become) as Secretary for War and the Colonies and remained in the same capacity under Wellington. There ensued prolonged disagreements about the Corn Bill.

Huskisson had long been suspected of being opposed to the agricultural interest. He was unlucky, however, to encounter Wellington at his most unhelpful. He had earlier proposed a sliding scale of duties, pivoting on a normal point of 60s. a quarter. The Duke had carried a protectionist amendment in the Lords. Canningites thought that he was unwise thus to prepare the ground for a struggle between peers and people. The government dropped the measure. After Canning's death and Goderich's resignation, Huskisson and Wellington compromised, and the bill eventually carried (but not without resignation offers by Huskisson) was similar to the original. Huskisson may have been over-sensitive: his colleague Charles Grant, President of the Board of Trade, was even more difficult. But Wellington was primarily responsible, since he treated even reasoned opposition within the cabinet as a form of mutiny. When ministers first dined together at Apsley House in January, Ellenborough noted that 'the courtesy was that of men who had just fought a duel'. Huskisson was ever on the defensive. He eventually resigned, on the question of the redistribution of the disenfranchised seats at East Retford and Penrhyn. He proposed the transfer of these franchises to Manchester and Birmingham. After a compromise had been reached, with Penrhyn's franchise going to Manchester and East Retford's to its hundred, the Lords rejected the enfranchisement of Manchester. Huskisson and friends then voted against the government and Huskisson offered to resign. He was undoubtedly upset when Wellington promptly accepted and would not let him change his mind; whereupon the Canningites went out *en bloc*.

The departure of Huskisson's group undoubtedly weakened Wellington's administration. But in 1830, at the time of the opening of the Liverpool–Manchester Railway, reconciliation was in the air. Huskisson was to attend the celebrations as well as Wellington and Peel. On the morning of the 15th September a procession of trains brought the notables from Liverpool towards Manchester. They halted for water for the engines at Parkside and Holmes, the government whip, brought Huskisson along to Wellington's carriage. They had shaken hands and started to talk when the Rocket came up at speed on the parallel track. Holmes flattened himself against the carriage but Huskisson dithered, scrambled clumsily up to Wellington's carriage, slipped and fell back into the path of the oncoming locomotive. He was terribly injured and died that evening. It was a sad end to the useful life of a man whom Melbourne called 'the greatest practical statesman' of his time.

C. R. Fay, *Huskisson and his Age*, 1951.

FREDERICK JOHN ROBINSON, VISCOUNT GOD-ERICH, 1st EARL OF RIPON (1782-1859) was Prime Minister for five months: 'a transient and embarrassed phantom', Disraeli called him. Unable to master his colleagues or to secure even the semblance of harmony from the reluctant coalition which passed for a cabinet, he eventually resigned in despair. Financial abilities, a sensitive and philosophic mind, and a pleasant, witty, House of Commons manner had carried 'Prosperity Robinson' too far. In less demanding offices he would have a further useful career.

He was the second son of the second Lord Grantham and of Lady Mary Yorke. At Harrow he was the schoolfellow of two future prime ministers, Aberdeen and Palmerston, and of Lord Althorp. After serving for two years as private secretary to the Lord Lieutenant of Ireland, his kinsman, the third Earl of Hardwicke, he was elected to Parliament for Carlow in 1806 and in the following year for Ripon, where he sat for twenty years. He was soon promoted to minor offices in the Tory administrations of 1809 and 1812. In September 1809 he resigned from the first (he was Under-Secretary for the Colonies) in sympathy with Castlereagh. He strengthened this alliance when he accompanied Castlereagh to Vienna in 1814. In March 1815 he introduced the 'Corn Law' which prohibited the importation of corn until the home price had reached 80 shillings a quarter — with 'the greatest reluctance'. He suffered from the bill's unpopularity when a mob attacked his house in Old Burlington Street and destroyed some valuable pictures. In January 1818 he was appointed President of the Board of Trade. In May 1820 he declared in the House of Commons that 'he had always given it as his opinion that the restrictive system of commerce in this country was founded in error, and calculated to defeat the object for which it was adopted'.

In January 1823 Robinson was given a chance to go further in the direction of reform when he became Chancellor of the Exchequer, for his successor at the Board of Trade was Huskisson. The two men worked together under Liverpool's skilful direction in the 'economic cabinet' in the interest of fiscal liberalism; they were assisted by a general revival of trade and a climate of opinion which was increasingly favourable to the axioms and policies of the classical economists. He was lucky, like any chancellor who is in a position to make reductions of taxation, but he used his position skilfully, combining the lowering of such taxes as the window tax (halved in 1823: there was great rejoicing) with the reduction of the debt, and judicious grants for such objects as the purchase of the Angerstein collection 'to lay the foundation of a national gallery of works of art', the erection of buildings for the British Museum and the restoration of Windsor Castle. In his free trade budget of 1824 he proposed to use his surplus 'as a means of commencing a system of alterations in the fiscal and commercial regulations of his country'.

Robinson's free trade policy did not lack courage, and it succeeded. His style may be studied in his third budget, of 1825, when he congratulated the House on the prosperity of the country and invited members to 'contemplate with instructive admiration the harmony of its proportions and the solidity of its basis' before reducing duties on iron, hemp, coffee, sugar, wine, spirits and cider. Expansive chancellors have often had to swallow their boasts: before the end of the year a commercial crisis caused primarily by the over-issue of paper money forced Robinson to prevent the issue of notes under £5. Evidence of mounting distress in 1826 did not deter him from a sanguine assessment of the country's situation in his budget of that year. It was indeed remarkable, as Martineau pointed out, what different conclusions 'Prosperity Robinson' (Cobbett's name for him) and 'Adversity Hume' could draw from identical statistics. Robinson wanted Liverpool to promote him to the House of Lords and a less onerous post; when Canning became Prime Minister he was created Viscount Goderich and Secretary of State for War and the Colonies. His failure to uphold the government's position in the House of Lords against Wellington and his high Tory phalanx should have disqualified him for higher office. But when Canning died George IV chose Goderich to form a cabinet.

He began badly by yielding to the king, as it appeared to his colleagues, over the appointment of Herries to the exchequer. Herries quarrelled bitterly with Huskisson over the chairmanship of the finance committee. Robinson was surprisingly defeatist. In cabinet meetings 'Goody Goderich' was ill at ease, his sudden tearful collapses in odd contrast to the bland face he normally presented. It was perhaps fortunate that he never met Parliament. On the 8th January, 1828, he resigned — but seems to have been surprised that he was offered no place by his successor, Wellington. He supported the Catholic Emancipation Bill, however, and the repeal of the Corporation and Test Acts. 'A good and useful speech' on the national debt (1830) showed him at his best. His appointment to be Secretary of War and the Colonies in Lord Grey's government (1830) and his commitment, after 'a sacrifice of many pre-conceived opinions' to parliamentary reform, probably represented his true position — a mild and guarded liberalism. His proposals for the abolition of slavery were, however, unacceptable; so Stanley succeeded him and he became Lord Privy Seal and Earl of Ripon. With Stanley and Graham he resigned over the appointment of the Irish Church Commission (May 1834). Peel made him President of the Board of Trade in 1841. In May 1843 young Mr Gladstone succeeded him; he went to the Board of Control. It was fitting that he should move the second reading of the Bill for the abolition of the Corn Laws — and subsequently resign with Peel in June 1846.

Ripon died at his house on Putney Heath in January 1859. He was buried at Nocton in Lincolnshire. He had always seized any chance of escaping to his Lincolnshire estate. The indifferent health of his wife (they married in 1814; she was Albinia Hobart, daughter of the fourth Earl of Buckinghamshire) may have been another inducement. Unfortunately he gave the impression of wanting the fruits of office while shrinking from the toils. He had expressed his dread of 'the labour and confinement of the situation' when made chancellor; a friend congratulated him on being promoted to a position 'where *work* you must and *speak* you must'. As a speaker he usually pleased, since he had the art of 'enlivening even dry subjects of finance with classical allusions and pleasant humour' (Le Marchant). 'His political convictions', said Lord Crewe, 'were limited to those announced by the diverse governments of which he was a member.' His only surviving son inherited his abilities and his liberalism and became Governor-General of India.

W. D. Jones, *Prosperity Robinson*, 1967.

JOHN SCOTT, 1st EARL OF ELDON (1751-1838) was the younger of two brothers, sons of William Scott, a Newcastle coal merchant, and Jane Atkinson; both brothers became famous lawyers. The elder, William, was the finer scholar and an equally good lawyer in his own sphere, the Admiralty and ecclesiastical courts. He is commemorated by Oxford in the Stowell law fellowship, from the title that he acquired in 1821. He also represented the University in Parliament for twenty years. The friend of Dr. Johnson in his old age and a member of 'the Club', he was a stout Tory all his life though he played little active part in politics. John Eldon, by contrast, was drawn early into high politics. He was Lord Chancellor, with only a year's break, for twenty-six years. During that time, as Sydney Smith put it: 'Lord Eldon and the Court of Chancery sat heavy on mankind.'

He was an enterprising young man. From Newcastle grammar school he went to University College, Oxford. At the age of 21 he eloped with Bessy Surtees, daughter of a rich banker: a wild start to a sedate and happy marriage of nearly sixty years' duration. Called in 1776, he acquired a large practice in the equity court. In 1783 he took silk and entered parliament, under the wing of Lord Thurlow, as member for Weobley, a decayed borough in Herefordshire. He conceived himself to be a Pittite for life. But it was only in his hatred for the Revolution and Napoleon that he resembled Pitt. Solicitor-General in 1788, he became Attorney-General in 1793 and took a leading part in the measures of those years against sedition and conspiracy. This part was not disagreeable to him. But he was scrupulous in his concern for precedents and points of law. He inclined to hold strictly to the letter of the law and he was willing to see it reinforced by statute, but he was always impartial. In 1799 he became Chief Justice of the Common Pleas and a peer; in 1801, under Addington, he first sat upon the woolsack.

If Eldon's conservatism is to be judged from his more extreme statements, it appears to be almost grotesque. About Russell's bill of 1828, for instance, to repeal the seventeenth century Test and

Corporation Acts: 'Bad, as mischievous and as revolutionary as the most captious Dissenter would wish it to be.' Of the growth of societies for the education of working people, the 'march of intellect' movement, he declared that it would direct 'a hundred thousand tall fellows with clubs and pikes against Whitehall'. On the question of parliamentary reform he was predictably adamant. Writing to his brother in April 1830 he declared that the reform agitation was of 'a more frightful kind than the prospect of 1791'. Furthermore 'the sacrifice of the Test Act, and the passing of the Roman Catholic Emancipation Bill have established a precedent so encouraging to the present attempts at revolution under name of Reform, that he must be a very bold fool who does not tremble at what seems to be fast approaching'. 'My Lords', cried the old man in a House of Lords debate, 'sacrifice one atom of our glorious constitution, and all the rest is gone'. His rigorism could have far-reaching consequences. A judgement of 1805, for instance, declared that the statutory limitation of subjects in grammar schools was binding. Until an act of 1840 empowered courts to change the statutes, some Elizabethan grammar schools could teach nothing but Latin and Greek.

Obscurantist, alarmist and immovable in the face of argument, Eldon was in high favour with George III, who came to regard him as indispensable. He acquired a similar ascendancy over George IV. The tough, industrious lawyer and the self-indulgent prince shedding tears together over the prospect of Catholic emancipation make an affecting scene. Lord Sidmouth, his brother's son-in-law, was his natural ally and in the years from Waterloo to 'Peterloo' Eldon joined with the Home Secretary in a firm alliance against new ideas and popular movements. They liked to refer to themselves as 'the last of the old school'.

He was not, of course, unique. His power came partly from the fact that he voiced and lent prestigious authority to the views of numerous squires and parsons. His own career commended his outlook to the new rich as to the old. 'Pompously patrician as only a self-made man can be' (Steven Watson), he also represented the conservatism which was then to be found in its richest and most eccentric forms in clerical, unreformed Oxford (which venerated Eldon as its high steward), and in law courts where the name of Blackstone was still more important than that of Bentham. The courts were Eldon's life. He acquired a deep and subtle knowledge of the law and with it that backward-looking tendency which is the vice as well as the virtue of the English lawyer bred on precedents. The anonymous author of his *Life* (1827) wrote that Lord Eldon 'had no acquaintance with the state of the institutions of other countries, and he had no notion of the rapid improvements that were going forward in his own. His studies in modern literature were confined to the Gentleman's Magazine.' In short, we see supreme professional competence and a closed mind in formidable combination. Lord Eldon's staunchness had its admirable side. 'He never ratted', an Oxford man called out on one of his visits to that city. There was a sort of oaken consistency about the man. It is a quality that emerges more attractively from his legal work than from his political career, which was devoted to 'dishing the whigs', keeping men whom he regarded simply as traitors out of office, even as in 1812, in a coalition; to preventing the removal of religious restrictions and, most harmfully perhaps, against the Tory Peel as against the radical Romilly, to defending every detail of the criminal law from rationalization of its often barbaric punishments and procedures.

The delays of the chancery court in Eldon's time were the subject of constant complaints. Dickens has immortalized the delays and vexations of litigation about wills and property that were its principal business. It was essentially of Eldon's court that he was writing. It was during his time that the delays became intolerable. This man, who was so decisive in his ordinary judgements, balanced legal points in a way that critics found unfeeling and pedantic. But there was a good side to Eldon's long deliberations, his reserved judgements and his not infrequent reversals of his deputy's decisions. No one knew better than he that his judgements would become part of the fabric of the law, to be treated with the same respect that he accorded to past judgements. He was therefore determined not to be rushed. The judgements he made were hardly ever reversed. A parliamentary commission on the delays of Chancery could do little about it, for Eldon himself presided and, in the words of *The Times*, its report was 'an apology for all the abuses of the Court'.

Eldon was prepared to work like a horse but it was not enough. What he did achieve, however, was more important than the improvement of the machinery. He crowned the work of Lord

Hardwicke, to whom alone among Chancellors he can be compared in this respect, by giving permanent form to the principles
of his science. In his time Equity became 'a fixed body of legal
doctrine'. In the case of Gee v. Pritchard (1818) he defined his
view thus: 'The doctrines of this court ought to be as well settled
and made as uniform, almost, as those of the Common Law,
laying down fixed principles, but taking care that they are to be
applied according to the circumstances of each case'. Equity after
Eldon was much more than a miscellany of remedies more elastic
than the Common Law allowed; it was part of the law of the land,
in its administration and protective functions, and thus complementary to the Common Law. It is for this that Eldon should be
remembered — as a great public servant.

In his private life Eldon was kind, cheerful, and not abstemious.
He confided to Brougham that he would have been dead had
he left off his wine, 'viz, nearer 2 than 1 bottle of port a day'.
Greville, who thought him 'a contemptible statesman', describes
him 'beguiling the tedious hours' during which the Prince Regent
used to keep the Lords in Council waiting at Carlton House, with
amusing stories of his early professional life and well-told anec-
dotes of celebrated lawyers. Perhaps there was a salty, saving
touch of realism about the man, a human being beneath the wig
of justice. He could view his own career with detachment — and
he knew that times were changing. 'If I were to begin life again,'
he said once, 'Damn my eyes but I would begin as an agitator'.
But it is slightly forbidding to be told that his idea of humour was
to translate *Chevy Chase* into the style of a bill in chancery.

Lord Campbell, *Lives of the Lord Chancellors*, 1847.
Lord Brougham, *Historical Sketches of Statesmen*, 1839.

**JOHN WILSON CROKER** (1780-1857), politician and journalist, played a larger part in the public life of his time than his
talents or virtues warranted. He was a tireless, devious intriguer,
a political mole; he burrowed ceaselessly in the soil, left his mark
everywhere but was hard to catch. He was an Irishman, a graduate of Trinity College, Dublin, and member of parliament, after
some legal training at Lincoln's Inn and advocacy on the Munster
circuit, for the seat of Downpatrick (1807). He began, in 1809, the
series of articles for the *Quarterly Review* (ninety-nine in its first

hundred numbers) which made him, for the next forty years or more, an oracle of Tory policy. For twenty years he was Peel's confidant until a quarrel which leaves us wondering which was worse: Croker's effrontery or Peel's icy rejection of a devoted adherent. As secretary to the Admiralty he found scope for his talents: he was given the post as reward for his part in defending the Duke of York in the case of Mary Ann Clarke. He offended the Duke of Clarence by exposing corruption. He held the post from 1809 to 1830 and retired with a pension of £1,500.

He was a fluent and cogent writer and an imaginative administrator. He had the Admiralty lit by gas, backed railway development, and supported proposals for a decimal coinage. Unfortunately, as critic and as a party man he spoiled good cases by exaggeration and defended bad cases in a way that suggested cynicism. Feiling suggests a cause in 'the congealed, time-restricted dogmatism characteristic of the Irish Protestantism whence he rose'. Whatever the cause it is hard to forgive the strident insensitivity of his article upon Keats' *Endymion* (1818), or the travesty of Toryism which he expounded through the pages of the *Quarterly*. He was not as bad as Macaulay made him seem: 'coldboiled veal' and 'a very bad man, a scandal to politics and to letters'. It has to be remembered that Croker had fallen upon Macaulay's history for its one-sidedness — and had scored some sound points. He professed an astringent sort of honesty. His definition of party is, for example, a classic in its way: 'Party is much the strongest passion of an Englishman's mind. Friendship, love, even avarice, give way before it.'

Croker was a man of many kindnesses, and generous to lame ducks. One of his many literary productions was *Stories for Children from English History*. Sadly his own and only child died at the age of three. He founded the Athenaeum Club. Many of his machinations were well-meaning. But it was his misfortune — as of all men who reduce politics to a struggle between personalities — that the more he sought confidence, the less he obtained it. In *Coningsby* and in the character of Rigby, the wirepuller and party hack, Disraeli gave him a dubious immortality. Rigby was 'confided in by everybody, trusted by none'.

Ed. B. Pool, *The Croker Papers, 1808-57*, abridged edition, 1967.
Keith Feiling, *Sketches in Nineteenth Century Biography*, 1930.

GEORGE IV (1762-1830) was the eldest son of George III and Queen Charlotte. Born before the end of the Seven Years' War, on 12th August, the anniversary of the accession of the House of Hanover, he died when agitation for the Reform Bill was approaching its climax. His life-span coincided with the most intense phase of the Industrial Revolution. During this time the population expanded vigorously; an immense war tested the resources of the nation, left it strong abroad but beset with social and economic problems. The mechanism of government was ill-adapted to meet the challenges of a fast-changing society. Monarchy was represented by an old man, falling into madness; then from 1820 to 1830 by a decayed fop. It is remarkable that the institution survived.

George IV's life affords entertainment but pathos is never far from the surface, for he was an intelligent and sensitive person. In his most shocking moments, in cowardice, debauchery or spite, he is not unlovable. Indisputably, he damaged the cause and image of monarchy in the eyes of hard-pressed ministers and a resentful people. With a better upbringing — and with his sense of occasion — he might have been a beloved monarch, a popular symbol, an Edward VII. But he was marred by the self-indulgent, hectic society of the Whig friends of his youth. They flattered the man and spoiled the prince. The flabby king of 1820 was only the hulk of the fine ship of the eighties, his mind and moods undisciplined beyond redemption.

He was carefully tutored, on the model, as George III insisted, of an ordinary English gentleman's son, and he showed an ability to learn rapidly. He became a fluent linguist. When he 'came upon the town', however, he plunged recklessly into dissipation. He received a separate establishment when he was twenty-one at a time when the ministers, especially his friend Fox, wanted to stress the subjection of the crown by exacting a large allowance from his reluctant father. He got £50,000 a year, with another £12,000, the revenues of the Duchy of Cornwall, on condition that Parliament paid his gambling debts — another £50,000. With this behind him George set out to lead the fashionable world. From Carlton House he patronized the Whigs. There he fêted Fox after his famous victory of 1784 against the king's candidate at the Westminster election; there he installed Mrs Fitzherbert, six years older than himself, twice widowed and a Roman Catholic, after a secret marriage. When the king objected he took her ostentatiously off to Brighton, which then sprang to life as the centre of fashion. He subsequently denied the marriage to placate Parliament, putting his spokesmen Fox and Grey in an embarrassing position by so doing.

Meanwhile George's debts had soared; in 1787 he had the question raised in Parliament. The king gave an extra £10,000, Parliament paid off £100,000 of the debt and gave a further £60,000 for the rebuilding of Carlton House. When 'the flying gout' (or porphyria) incapacitated George III, in October 1788, the prince alternated between distress and expectation: for two nights he sat up waiting for the summons, fully dressed and gaudy with decorations. Then, through Fox, he claimed the full prerogatives of the crown in regency. The king recovered before the battle was decided, and George was hissed and pelted in the London streets for his unfilial behaviour.

George was in fact acting in the Hanoverian tradition in warring with his father; it was becoming a constitutional convention. He was deeply attached to Fox, whose principles were untested by power because of the unfailing grip of Pitt. After the Revolution and during the ensuing war those principles became more rigid and remote. The prince, who never had the single-mindedness to pursue political questions in depth, lived in a political vacuum; he was conspicuous enough to be unpopular, but too much excluded from administration to gain experience of affairs. One episode affords a clue to his political isolation, splendid but inane. In 1803, when invasion threatened, 'Prinny' tried to obtain a higher command in the army than his present colonelcy in a regiment of dragoons. Addington, intimating to him the king's refusal, wrote that 'the king's opinion being fixed he desired that no further mention should be made to him on the subject'. The prince wrote in melodramatic strain, asking to be allowed 'to shed the last drop of my blood in support of your Majesty's person, crown and dignity; for this is not a war for empire, glory or dominion, but for existence'. The king praised his 'zeal and spirit' but said that his services would not be required unless Bonaparte actually landed: then he might fight at his father's side. Had the prince been given practical training from the start, in soldiering and government, things might not have come to this sorry pass. His private life afforded him consolations, though in the most important respect there was a catastrophe. His marriage in 1795 was undertaken partly to secure a further repayment of debts, partly to furnish an heir. In the person of Caroline of Brunswick it brought personal political embarrassment for the rest of her life. Years later a courier hastened to inform him of the death of Napoleon: 'Sire, your greatest enemy is dead'. He was met with an excited cry of 'By God, is she?'

He built and entertained in the grand manner. His programme was costly. Parliament's increasing generosity, even to the point of setting up a sinking fund for his debts, could do no more than hold the sums in check; they were still over half a million in 1815. Posterity, however, derived benefits from this mania, unique amongst English sovereigns though common abroad. 'Mahomet's Paradise', as the visitor called Carlton House, the Pavilion at Brighton, the Royal Lodge at Windsor, the remoulding of Buckingham Palace, the Gothic restoration of Windsor Castle: add to this list the adornments to London which he patronized — Carlton House Terrace, Regent Street (now defaced), Regents Park and the Nash terraces — and the contribution is seen to be impressive. But contemporaries outside his small circle of men of wealth and taste contrasted this splendour with the aching needs of the people. Indeed, it is astonishing that the building and banqueting went on unchecked during the Napoleonic wars. The cost fell largely upon the tax-paying middle and upper classes; amongst sober people there was a wide distaste for the prince's way of life. But the publicity that he and his brothers attracted — and most of the denigration and satire settled upon him — found its readiest audience in the hovels of the poor. Radicals questioned the need for a king. Moralists despaired of an example coming from above. In 1817 an attempt was made upon the Regent's life.

By then George was a firm Tory. In 1812, when he had assumed virtually royal powers after the last madness of George III, the Whigs had looked for his patronage; they demanded a free hand in both measures and men. But in this year victory was in sight and the Regent was reluctant to destroy an administration which could conduct the country to glory. He offered them a coalition which they, predictably, refused. Thereafter George had little power to manoeuvre. He disliked Canning, but he was unable to prevent his being made foreign minister and later pursuing a liberal foreign policy. Indeed he came to admire Canning and selected him, over the head of Wellington, to be Prime Minister in 1827. He tried to stand out against Catholic emancipation, recalling somewhat inappropriately the principles of his 'revered and sainted father'. Eventually he caved in before the inflexible will of Wellington and the ministers; after dismissing Wellington from office he recalled him the same evening. On this day the ministers had been treated to five hours of blandishments, threats and tears.

George's reign began badly with the ludicrous affair of the divorce bill against Queen Caroline and the public contest that this provoked. His magnificent coronation did little to improve his image. He did, however, achieve something by his progresses and visits to his dominions; Ireland, Hanover and Scotland received him well. He allowed himself to be kilted and tartaned for his triumphal ride through Edinburgh; the highlander began a second and romantic life, under royal patronage. But his constitution, undermined by brandy and the laudanum which he took when he was in the slightest pain, was unequal to the stress of public appearances. He fell back on a quiet domestic life at Windsor with Lady Conyngham, the last of several women who were as much comforters as mistresses. The ebullience faded. He began to tell senile tales of battles that he supposed he had attended; he took a belated interest in religion. For years his size had been such that he preferred to loll in specially designed dressing gowns. In 1830 he had to be tapped for the dropsy. Soon afterwards he died.

George IV's life had been that of a selfish exhibitionist. His taste, which tended towards excess, to heavy gilding and strong colours, with much of crimson and gold, came fortunately under the restraining influences of discriminating men — Hertford, Holland and Nash. He was a good judge of art, and he persuaded the government to buy the Angerstein collection that became the nucleus of the National Gallery. Some people admire the exuberant *chinoiserie* of the Brighton Pavilion; it may be the most revealing memorial of the pleasure-loving prince.

Somewhere in this fat man lurked, however, a more fastidious taste: after a boxer was killed during one of the prize-fights he loved to attend, he ceased to patronize the sport; he disposed of his stud when some suspicion arose concerning his handling of a race. He admired Jane Austen and read the works of Scott as they appeared. When Raffles came home from his governorship of

Java, the prince gave a reception in his honour and spoke for twenty minutes about his work. He had read enough of Raffles's history of Java to appreciate the man's imagination and ability. No monarch before or since has played such a part in the encouragement of the arts. What he could have become if he had not squandered his talents we may guess from the fact that he had a remarkable memory. He could remember the date, style and colour of each of the many thousands of suits that he had worn.

A. Aspinall, *The Letters of George IV, 1812-30*, 3 vols., 1938.
C. Hibbert, *George IV*, 2 vols., 1971-3.

**PRINCESS CHARLOTTE-AUGUSTA** (1796-1817) lived turbulently and died young: her story illustrates poignantly the difficulties of a royal upbringing. Her parents were the Prince Regent and Caroline of Brunswick; from her mother the princess may have inherited her hoydenish manners and a tendency to hysteria. Because of his quarrels with his wife, the Prince Regent was reluctant to regard Princess Charlotte-Augusta as heiress to the throne. She, however, was acutely conscious of her status and her father's attitude made her take her mother's side. She was a handsome girl, beloved by George III when he was sane enough to recognize her. But she was wayward and high-tempered. When she was engaged to the Prince of Orange in 1813 and found she did not like the prospect of marrying him, she broke it off, to the fury of her father and the embarrassment of the government. In 1814 she was kept at Windsor in disgrace. In 1816 she married Leopold of Saxe-Coburg, afterwards Prince of the Belgians. The Prince Regent disapproved, but the couple lived happily at Claremont for a year and a half. There the Princess gave birth to a still-born child and died, in November, 1817. There were spontaneous expressions of grief in the country, for Charlotte's career had appealed to many who could find little of romantic interest in the rest of the family. Her death was significant, too, because it led to the immediate marriage of the Duke of Kent, and to the subsequent birth, in 1819, of the Princess Victoria.

Ed. A. Aspinall. *Letters of the Princess Charlotte, 1811-1817*, 1949.

**FREDERICK AUGUSTUS, DUKE OF YORK** (1763-1827) was the second, and by and large the most impressive, son of George III. He enjoyed the distinction of being titular Bishop of Osnabrück at six months. In 1784 he was made Duke of York. By then his bent was clearly towards soldiering. Like his great-uncle Cumberland, he was entirely serious in his study of arms; his promotion was accelerated by his rank, but he was no amateur. He was a Colonel at seventeen after a year's study at Berlin and might have been made commander-in-chief, if the Prince of Wales had become Regent in 1788.

At the start of the Revolutionary War he was appointed to command the British contingent which fought under Coburg in Flanders. The duke was inexperienced and Coburg was inept. The campaigns were unsuccessful to the point of shame: York's courage was undoubted, but his cautious tactics were lampooned. In one of the defeats which the allies incurred during 1793-4, on 18th May 1794 he only escaped the enemy's dragoons by the speed of his horse. After the retreat into Holland at the end of 1794, York was recalled. He was promptly raised, however, to be Amherst's successor as 'Field-Marshal on the Staff', in effect commander-in-chief, to which actual appointment he was gazetted in April 1798. He was more successful at the Horse Guards than he was in the field, for be was honest and sensible and had a true Hanoverian's gift for military administration. The army was in indifferent shape after Amherst's passive rule. York campaigned against corruption and the abuse of patronage and doled out justice without fear or favour. Eight years before Napoleon himself created a system of transport he instituted the 'wagon-train'. He founded the college that was to grow into Sandhurst and started the characteristic two battalion structure of the infantry regiment. The army that he commanded in the Holland campaign of 1799, his last active service, was already much improved.

York was married to a Prussian princess who was tolerant of his amours. But in 1809 a scandal broke which brought him and his work into notoriety. A Mrs Clarke, who had been formerly his mistress, encouraged by her present protector, Colonel Wardle, charged him with trafficking in army commissions. He stood fast in the face of blackmail and forgery and in the parliamentary inquiry that ensued he was acquitted of corrupt practices. He had, however, to resign his post and did not resume it until 1811; thereafter he was in command until 1827, when he died. For all his limitations he was a responsible and sincere man; a stronger character than his elder brother whom he liked, but despised. He died just before George IV or he would have succeeded him. We may guess that he would have fought against Catholic emancipation and parliamentary reform, but that he would still have cut a more impressive figure on the throne than did William IV.

Roger Fulford, *Royal Dukes*, 1948.
J. Fortescue, *History of the British Army*, 1899-1930.

**WILLIAM IV**, (1765-1837) was the third son of George III and Queen Charlotte. Since he was not thought of as a potential king he was allowed a normal upbringing and a chance to prove himself in a career. As a naval officer he was notable chiefly for his fussy approach to discipline. Criticism of his conduct was largely confined, however, to the navy. Such was the public contempt for George IV that his brother's accession in 1830 was hailed with joy. Ministers might be concerned about his impetuous temper and naïve judgement. But Greville's private assessment (and he was no admirer of the family) probably represents what most politicians thought of their new sovereign, a fairly robust sixty-five-year-old: 'Altogether he seems a kind-hearted, well-meaning, not stupid, burlesque, bustling old fellow and, if he doesn't go mad, may make a very decent king, but he exhibits oddities.'

William Henry, Duke of Clarence, entered the navy at the age of thirteen and acquired a fair knowledge of seamanship. He served on the *Royal George* under Rodney in the Mediterranean, then under Hood on the West India station. He received his first command, a frigate, in April 1786, again in the West Indies. He had become friendly with Nelson and gave away the bride at Nelson's marriage at Nevis. His besetting fault as a commander was that he would quarrel with his subordinates. He was not so much harsh as irritatingly meticulous. He was promoted Rear-Admiral in 1790 and did not serve again. He begged for a chance to serve in the war, but this was refused him. It would have been an embarrassment to the Admiralty, since officers were reluctant to serve under him. So he settled down, disgruntled but not really bitter, to the life of a country gentleman at Bushey, with Mrs

Jordan, an actress. Her new *ménage* was almost respectable by the standard of the royal dukes, though it aroused some derision; it seems to have been a happy one and she bore the Duke no less than ten children. She also helped to support the extravagant household by continuing with her acting whenever she could. In 1811 William was reluctantly forced to give her up; he continued to be kind to her, and provided for their children, but she died abroad, and poor.

In 1817 the death of the Princess Charlotte brought him within two steps of the throne; he immediately took a wife, Adelaide of Saxe-Coburg-Meiningen; she was a tender and unselfish companion to him. When the death (1827) of his elder brother, the Duke of York, made him heir to the throne, Canning unwisely made him Lord High Admiral: the title was revived for him, an archaic and, as Canning no doubt assumed, empty distinction. But the Duke was no less a Hanoverian for having been a naval officer — and he promptly took command of the Channel fleet. He began to promote his friends and assert his authority in the wildest manner and was made to resign. He was indignant but he got over it. There was a certain bluff honesty about the man which helped him to recognize his limitations.

His accession coincided with the Reform Bill crisis. Had he behaved as obstinately or rashly as some feared, he could have destroyed the monarchy. On the other hand the prolonged crisis gave the king a chance to prove the value of monarchy as the stable element in a changing world. It cannot be said that he was a model constitutional king. He understood too little and spoke his mind too freely for that. He believed, however, that it was his duty to support the prime minister, regardless of party: in this he was wisely tutored by his secretary, Taylor. He admired Wellington but was equally ready to accept Grey. He felt the strength of Tory opposition and argument, but he accepted, under pressure, what Lord Grey gave him to understand was necessary. He did not use his right of preliminary veto, as he was entitled to do. To prevent the threatened resignation of his Whig ministers in April 1831 he consented to dissolve Parliament; when it became clear that it was essential to act quickly to forestall a motion against dissolution, he went at once. 'I'm always at single anchor', he declared, sweeping aside officials' objections that the coachman and horse-guards were unready, the horses' manes unplaited! 'My

Lord, I'll go, if I go in a hackney coach', he told the apologetic Grey. He drove through cheering crowds to an angry chamber: as he ascended the steps of the throne it was seen that his crown, hastily donned, was balanced precariously on one side of his head. But his words were dignified: 'I have been induced to resort to this measure for the purpose of ascertaining the sense of my people.' He maintained his trust in Grey, awarded him the Garter, resisted all Tory influences in court and family (Queen Adelaide favoured Wellington) and even consented at last to a new creation of peers, sufficient to secure the passage of the bill through the Lords. He later wrote a letter to the opposition peers advising them to give up their resistance. In the negative ways that were open to him he did right. The monarchy survived.

Think of William as king and he is odd, if not grotesque. Think of him as a retired naval gentleman of limited education, unused to contradiction and to sophisticated argument, and he becomes credible, even likeable. A fly sheet illustrating 'The Grey Horse and the Union Coach' showed a bystander asking the question: 'Pray, who drives the coach, neighbour?' The neighbour answers: 'Why, friend, she runs by steam now, but old Bill King, a sailor chap, drove her first.' The transition had to be made. William, 'true king of the Tories' though he might be in the eyes of a Grenville, helped to make it in a modest and honest way for which he deserves to be kindly remembered.

William was fond of his niece Victoria and bitterly disliked her mother, the Duchess of Kent, for keeping the girl away from his court. Indeed, one of his last public speeches contained such a rude attack upon her and so outspoken a wish that he should live long enough to prevent her being regent that some thought him quite mad. He had his wish. Queen Victoria acceded to the throne a month after she had come of age. How gratified he would have been, if he had foreseen how long and glorious her reign was to be.

P. Ziegler, *King William IV*, 1971.

## ADELAIDE OF SAXE-COBURG-MEININGEN (1792-1849)

was an unremarkable woman and queen, but her character and conduct were admirable at a time when the reputation of the Crown was low. She married William, Duke of Clarence, in 1817 and bore him two daughters, who both died in infancy. During the reign of George IV she and her husband, by then heir-presumptive, lived at Bushey. She was crowned with William in 1831. They were warmly attached to each other; she saw the best side of a foolish but amiable man, while we know from Queen Victoria's journal that she was a kind and gentle person. William, whose earlier life had been far from decorous and who had ten illegitimate children, settled under her devoted care into a benign old gentleman. The kindness and good-heartedness that made the Court a pleasanter and better place reflected her nature, as it was described by one courtier: 'Sensible, sympathetic and religious'.

M. F. Sanders, *The Life & Times of Queen Adelaide*, 1915.

**CHARLES, 2nd EARL GREY** (1764-1845) was the son of General Grey, the younger brother of Sir Henry Grey of Howick. Sir Henry was childless and invited Charles to take over his estate: Howick, pleasantly sheltered by woods, between the Cheviots and the North Sea, became the centre of Grey's existence; his love of family life in this remote country house was to be a byword with colleagues and a sometimes exasperating fact of political life.

Grey is deservedly famous as the prime minister at the time of the Great Reform Bill. No political measure has aroused greater popular excitement than this bill, yet no politician had less of the popular about him than Grey. 'The very type of the *grand seigneur*', he had begun his political life as an ardent advocate of reform; he ended it, presiding over the most aristocratic ministry the country has known, taking the chance that he never thought would come, obtaining power — and strengthening his party — by reforming the House of Commons. The Whigs did not create the reform movement. But by the clear-sighted, firm handling of the Reform crisis they averted political and social catastrophe. They carried a measure that in any other country would have shaken every institution by which an old community was held together. The manner in which the bill was passed was crucial. Grey was well served in this respect by Russell, Althorp and Brougham; but the ultimate responsibility was his.

When Grey was six he was sent to private school at Mary-lebone where he was wretched. After one illness he was taken out by his nurse to see some Jews hanged for forgery at Tyburn, and

*Charles Grey, 2nd Earl Grey*
(Artist: Unknown)

mounted on a grenadier's shoulders lest he should miss any details of a spectacle which haunted him for the rest of his life. He went to Eton. He later showed a marked coolness towards Eton and to its type of schooling and sent none of his numerous sons to any public school on the grounds that he had himself been nothing at Eton! And yet if anyone exemplified the virtues and graces that were products of the system at its best at Eton and Harrow — a system which, as J. R. M. Butler reminds us, was 'aimed at the training of statesmen, at a time when statesmanship consisted largely in winning and retaining the confidence of an assembly of some six hundred gentlemen' — it was Grey. Butler continues, in words which go to the heart of this period and class: 'Special attention was therefore paid to oratory ... large, dignified, lofty, appealing to the sense of honour and responsibility of a particular class ... Similarity of education combined with similarity of social position to produce a close society favourable to high spirit and intensity of life rather than breadth of sympathy. For effective debate it is necessary that speakers and audience should share a common fund of experience and a common *hinterland* of thought.'

At Eton, as at Cambridge, his closest friends were Whitbread and Lambton, the father of his future son-in-law, 'Radical Jack'. Grey entered the House of Commons for one of the Northumberland county seats, without having to contest the election or to interrupt the grand tour to which he devoted nearly three leisurely years, and from which he returned steeped in the ancient culture of southern Europe. His first political associations were formed before the French Revolution came to turn preferences into principles. The eloquence of Fox fortified him against Tory blandishments and the Duchess of Devonshire was for a time his mistress. Lady Holland later said of his political beginnings: 'The fashion was to be in opposition; the Prince of Wales belonged to it, and he was not then disliked; all the beauty and wit of London was on that side, and the seduction of Devonshire House prevailed.' Grey's maiden speech against Pitt's commercial treaty with France was an exercise in classical oratory in a manner that was both prejudiced and illiberal. That political questions could not always be resolved by speeches he learned from the embarrassing affair of the Prince of Wales's marriage when, to save his face and to ensure that he was not excluded from the Regency the Whigs, represented by Sheridan and Grey, explicitly denied the existence of the Prince's marriage with Mrs Fitzherbert. 'Grey at least always tells the truth', wrote Creevey. But in this early period of his political life this essentially straightforward man seems to have been out of his element, spoiled by early success perhaps and the seductions of a rich society and a complacent clique.

Lord Holland believed that 'a certain disposition to reform of Parliament' was 'essential in a good Whig'. Grey went further than most Whigs approved of when, in 1792, he entered the Society of the Friends of the People. But he was no republican. Electoral reform was conceived by the Whigs, along with 'oeconomical reform' in which progress had already been made, as a means to their constant ends: of weakening the position of the Crown in politics, and consolidating the position of men of property. It was both less daring and more self-interested than it appears if taken out of the political context — an apparently unbreakable coalition of conservative interests.

Grey was prepared, however, to maintain at least nominal contacts with radicals like Cartwright and Thomas Hardy, who represented 'the industrious lower and middle classes of society'. He attended the trial of Hardy for treason, as he told his fiancée Elizabeth Ponsonby, 'in order to learn how to conduct myself when it comes to my turn'. He stood firm in the face of anti-Jacobin hysteria and stiffened Fox to stand by his principles. In 1797, ninety-three Foxites supported Grey in a reform motion which went so far as to include a rate-payer franchise, triennial parliaments and a large redistribution of seats. The incident shows the strength and limitations of these men. They had made a stand on principle at an unfavourable time. They then seceded from Parliament and spent an agreeable recess of about three years, visiting each other's houses, enjoying political talk, hunting, dining — and toasting 'our sovereign the people'! They recognized the necessity of keeping their principles intact and the futility of embodying those principles in legislation when so large a majority opposed them. They saw no need apparently to provide a regular opposition to the government.

On the death of Pitt the Foxites came at last into power in uneasy alliance with the Grenville group, pledged to fight the war which most of them had formerly denounced, and to secure a measure of relief for Catholics. In the Ministry of 'all the talents' (February 1806 to March 1807) Grey was first at the Admiralty, then on Fox's death became foreign minister and took over the leadership of the party. In the process he repudiated Whitbread and the more radical Whigs. He had already argued that

Whitbread, his school-fellow and brother-in-law, was ineligible for Cabinet office as a dissenter and a brewer! When in 1809 the reform movement was revived with a flurry of meetings and petitions, though he was in opposition again and free to act upon principle, Grey remained aloof. He did not support Brand when the latter got 115 votes in the Commons for a measure less drastic than his own of 1797 and he approved the imprisonment of Burdett in 1810.

It seems that he tried to mislead the king upon the subject of Catholic emancipation. The measure of relief introduced by the Whigs was, however, only a small one. George then insisted upon a pledge that the matter should be dropped for good which, he knew, would divide the Whigs. Grey offered to abandon the measure for the time being. But he had neither the conviction nor the competence to lead a ministry in such difficult circumstances. He had already lost his county seat by the 'No Popery' cry and the adverse interest of the Duke of Northumberland, and acquired the rottenest of rotten boroughs, Appleby, before he succeeded in 1807 to his father's new earldom. Thereafter Westminster saw him but seldom, and Ponsonby, Whitbread and Tierney led an opposition to the governments of Portland, Perceval and Liverpool, of which Roberts says: 'Their criticisms were purely destructive: their objections frequently cancelled out each other; and they could not agree in championing any intelligent strategical plan.'

On three occasions Grey could have led his party back into office in a coalition. Perceval's overtures in 1809, on the death of Portland, were rejected by return of post from Howick, which caused mutters in Brooks's. In 1811 and 1812, when the Prince Regent was seeking half-heartedly for a combination which should include the 'old and tried friends of Mr Fox', Grey refused to be tempted. He believed the Regent to be insincere and his proposed combinations unworkable. He scorned the bibulous Sheridan and courtly Yarmouth, and held the prince to be 'the worst anchoring ground in Europe'. He had been an adroit courtier in his youth; he was now a better man and wiser politician. If his pessimism was becoming depressing, it was in some respects realistic. He was ill-equipped for the grind of administration in wartime; he lacked the tenacity and patience of a Lord Liverpool. Only a great issue, and a great opportunity, would now tempt him back into active politics. His value in the period from

1812 to 1830 was simply that he was sufficiently detached to have no need to compromise, sufficiently unambitious to be trusted and respected.

In the post-war years Grey broke with Grenville (1817) and tried to preserve a middle position between those who were uninterested in reform and those who seemed ready to adopt violent means to secure it. He denounced the Six Acts, but stood firm against the Radicals. He sought to maintain the identity of the Foxites, in the belief that their day would eventually come, and would have nothing to do with anything less than a comprehensive measure; his policy therefore was to wait until it was feasible. Such patience came easily to a man who was content at home with his adored wife, fifteen children, his library, horses and beautiful estate. It was exasperating to impatient spirits such as his son-in-law Lambton (Durham) but Grey was adamant. In 1822 he wrote: 'I can now consider myself as little more than a bystander'. He maintained an Olympian interest in affairs but he lacked a challenge. He began to suffer from recurring depressions and declining health: '... and no wonder', said Creevey, 'with all he eats and his little exercise'. Grey took a keen interest, however, in the struggle of the Greeks for independence and in 1829 suggested the boundary which was eventually adopted. 'I little thought', he wrote to Holland, 'that living here at the bottom of Northumberland I should be marking out the limits of new kingdoms'.

At that stage Grey seemed willing to support Wellington, who had carried Catholic emancipation and promised retrenchment and economy. The next year he was drawn out of Northumberland by the Whig successes in the general election caused by the accession of William IV. He was surprised by the extent of these successes; his conviction that reform was desirable was strengthened by the July Revolution in France; then the duke's absolute rejection of the idea, and the rise of a popular front on the issue convinced him that it was necessary. This was his hour, and it was to be his bill. As Butler wrote: 'Lord Grey's statesmanlike conviction of the need and advantage of an extensive measure was the prime source of the Bill; the wisdom of Russell and the will of Durham embodied this conviction in a bold and simple form.' Without such a combination of the experienced and bold, the compromisers, the nervous and 'bit by bit reform' men of the majority would surely have so emasculated the bill that it would have roused, without satisfying, the country.

Grey found new energy in the challenge of his office. In Creevey's diary for the spring of 1831 he is the hero of the day, relaxed and jovial. One entry contains a memorable picture: 'March 26. I wish you could have been with me when I entered the Premier's drawing room last night. I was rather early, and he was standing alone with his back to the fire — the best-dressed, the handsomest, and apparently the happiest man in all his royal master's domains.' His government had problems besides reform. The agricultural riots of 1830 were dealt with by sentences so savage that they tarnish the government's entire record: Melbourne as Home Secretary was primarily responsible, but Grey could have seen to it that there was some mitigation. Althorp's budget of 1831 ran into difficulties and had to be largely recast; the failure saddled the Whigs with an undeserved record for economic mismanagement. A cholera outbreak made hideous the winter of 1831-2. Grey's handling of his large cabinet was easy-going. In Durham's words: 'every member of the Cabinet, old or young, able or decrepit, thought himself at liberty to discuss the whole state of Europe'.

By the terms of the bill of March 1831 a quarter of the seats were to be transferred from small boroughs to the larger unrepresented towns, and the new uniform franchise was almost to double the existing number of voters. During the next fourteen months Grey won the fight to preserve the bill intact between popular frenzy (the riots of Bristol at the end of October 1831 were the worst example) and the obstinacy of die-hards, who were reduced to arguing that the constitution, though it had palpably changed in convention and usage, must never be altered by legislation: constituencies must be fixed for ever irrespective of social and economic change. Rather than risk inevitable collision, the Whigs had to secure, in Brougham's words, 'the support of the people as distinct from the the populace'.

Standing above the protracted battle in parliament, Grey saw the issue clearly and calmly. He was saved most of the fatigues which those who had to pilot the bill through the Commons endured. He was particularly successful in dealing with the king. They started from very different points of view but they shared two things: the wish to act correctly, according to 'the sense of my people' (in the words of William's dissolution speech of April 1831) and a preference for stability. Each recognized the honest purpose of the other. This mutual trust was vital when Grey made, and the king crossly accepted, his sensational request for the creation of new peers to secure the passing of the bill. Grey had the strength of standing, in Butler's words, 'direct on the support of the people'. It 'raised him for the moment to a pinnacle no minister had reached since the days of Pitt, and which it is doubtful if Peel or Palmerston, or even Gladstone, ever attained after him.' William IV was a little afraid of the people, this new force. Grey himself did not relish close contact with its leaders. He only met Place once, at midnight, when a deputation of London tradesmen came uninvited to Downing Street. Grey's short, perhaps sleepy, replies gave Place a false impression that he meant to whittle down the reform proposals and brought about a temporary rupture between the Whigs and their radical allies. In the end firmness prevailed.

Grey could not avoid being fêted as a popular hero. After the passing of the bill he enjoyed the election of Christmas 1832 which gave the Whigs a predictably large majority. 1833 saw the great act which abolished slavery in the colonies. Scottish burghs were made open to election and the first Factory Act was passed. In 1834 came the new Poor Law, ruthless, controversial, a thoroughgoing utilitarian measure. Before it passed the Upper House Grey had resigned. In May 1834 Russell had 'upset the coach' by hinting at the disendowment of the Irish church: Stanley, Graham and Richmond promptly resigned and joined Peel. A muddle and division over the renewal of the Irish Coercion Act produced the resignation of Althorp — and Grey took the chance, thankfully, of stepping down. He had been plagued by cantankerous Lord Durham; illogical Irish and sensitive churchmen were too much for an old man of seventy. He retired to pleasant sunset years at Howick where, as a guest recorded, 'the very servants are of a breed that makes one feel at home'. Creevey describes him at the end of the day: 'He looks about for his book, calls his dog, Viper, and out they go, having been all day as gay as possible, and not an atom of that *gall* he was subject to in earlier life. ... A curious stranger would discover no out-of-the-way talent in him, no powers of conversation; a clever man *in discussion*, certainly, but with no fancy and no judgement (or very little) in works either of fancy or art. A most natural, unaffected, upright man, hospitable and domestic; far surpassing any man one knows in his noble appearance and beautiful simplicity of manners, and equally surpassing all his contemporaries as a public speaker. Take him all in all, I never saw his fellow, nor can I see any imitation of him on the stocks.'

G. H. Trevelyan, *Lord Grey of the Reform Bill*, 1920.
E. A. Smith, *Lord Grey, 1764-1845*, 1990.

JOHN CHARLES SPENCER, VISCOUNT ALTHORP, 3rd EARL SPENCER (1782-1845) is better known by the first title. He had it until the death of his father, who had been Pitt's First Lord of the Admiralty. His mother was Lavinia Bingham. He was Chancellor of the Exchequer in Grey's reform ministry and leader of the House of Commons during that momentous time. He was educated at Harrow, where Byron and Peel were among his schoolfellows, and at Trinity College, Cambridge. He used to talk modestly about his attainments at school and university, but he was notably conscientious, as in everything he tackled in life. At Cambridge he took a degree, which was not then obligatory upon a nobleman. He also incurred debts at Newmarket which encumbered his purse and property for the rest of his life. His fervent devotion to hunting and his rustic manners dismayed his parents. His father spent his years of retirement amidst the splendid paintings of Althorp and a library which he made among the greatest in the land (created by the second Lord Sunderland, in 1892 it went to form the nucleus of the Rylands Library in Manchester). He could not understand his son's reluctance to travel abroad or look at pictures.

Althorp began his political career conventionally enough, becoming member for Okehampton as supporter of Mr Pitt. From 1806 to his elevation to the earldom he was member for Northamptonshire. In that year he was given a junior Lordship of the Treasury under Grenville and became devoted to Fox, then in his last year of life but still able to fascinate a young man of simple idealism. He attached himself to 'the Mountain', as Romilly, Whitbread and the advanced Whigs were called, and traces of the radicalism of this period remained for the rest of his life. In these early days, however, he took his hunting more seriously than his politics and he was a renowned master of the Pytchley. He made the happiest of marriages in 1814 to Esther Acklom; four years later he was left broken-hearted by his wife's death in childbirth. He remained thereafter lonely and unconsoled. It was typical of him and of feelings deep beyond expression that he at once gave up hunting. The squires of Northamptonshire thought he would never be so famous again.

Thereafter he buried himself in the study of contemporary social and economic problems to make himself a more useful politician. The knowledge he gained was to prove useful to him at the time of the Factory Act of 1833. It was he who proposed the amendment to that act providing for regular inspection of factories employing child labour — and making the act therefore a genuine protection to those for whom it was designed. Meanwhile he maintained a steady opposition to Liverpool's administration. Well-informed and practical, this 'very model and type of an English gentleman', in Greville's phrase, Althorp was early a free-trader and always a champion of economy. His mind worked slowly, but his deficiencies as a speaker did not displease the House, since he made a point of being brief and direct. 'There is a better speaker than Althorp in every vestry in England', wrote Campbell. When he was Chancellor he rose to answer the Tory Croker's spirited attack, saying that he had made some calculations, which he considered as entirely refuting Croker's arguments, but had unfortunately mislaid his notes; but if the House would be guided by his advice, it would reject Croker's amendment. That they did so as a matter of course suggests respect for scrupulous honesty and sound judgement.

Althorp read his Bible regularly for strength and guidance as to his duty and policy. Out of struggle, solitary reflection and a conscientious habit of puzzling things out came a stock of wisdom on which his colleagues came to rely. He preserved links with radicals and liberals of the younger generation, men like Russell, Buller and Macaulay, whom proud Grey hardly reached. His radical affiliations, liberal sympathies and impeccable Whig pedigree combined to make him the central figure: after 1830 he was the man, above all, who preserved party unity in the hectic manoeuvres of the Reform crisis. As Chancellor of the Exchequer he was sound if unimaginative. As leader of the Whigs in the House he acquired a unique authority. Early in 1830, in a room in Albany, a group of about forty Whigs had asked Althorp to take the leadership, nominally but ineffectually exercised by Tierney, who had died in January. Peel suddenly noticed in the Commons that Whigs referred to themselves as 'we'. Althorp was more than a figurehead in this new-found unity of purpose and planning.

During the tense, hot, reform debates in 'the ill-ventilated, ill-lit, uncomfortable, sacred room' (Trevelyan), Althorp was a rock of steadiness and cheerfulness. It was in July and August of 1831, when the bill was being fought over in committee, that stamina and nerve were really tested. Of this session Macaulay wrote that he believed there were 'fifty members of the House of Commons who have done irreparable injury to their health by attendance in the discussions'. Russell was keen and game — but 'done up with fatigue'. The opposition was repetitive, pedantic, violent and obstructive. Althorp remained so unruffled and good-tempered that even his opponents could not be angry with him. It was common knowledge that he was not in this business, 'where so much property, such great principles were at stake', for his own gain. He had no personal reason to be dismayed at the first defeat of the ministry. When a messenger brought news of Wellington's failure to form a ministry, Althorp was found 'in a closet with a groom, busy oiling the locks of his fowling pieces and lamenting the decay into which they had fallen during his ministry' (Lord Cockburn).

With people Althorp was usually conciliatory; on issues he could be obstinate. Against strong pressure and the temptation of a popular gesture he stood out for the maintenance of pensions to those who already had them, although he admitted that he had not the support of 'the great majority out of doors'. There was a principle at stake; contracts had been entered into. When Cabinet differences came to a head over Ireland, where he opposed the policy of coercion and believed that it was essential to try to work with O'Connell, he insisted upon resigning. Grey also resigned: he wanted to retreat to Howick. He persuaded Althorp to stay for a few months more to help Melbourne. In the autumn of 1834 Althorp took up his earldom and Melbourne at once went to the country.

'He came out of the fields and woods and to the fields and woods he returned'. The new Earl Spencer gave up politics for good and devoted himself to the nurture of his neglected estate, to stockbreeding and the general encouragement of agriculture. He became the first president of the Royal Agricultural Society and founded the agricultural college at Cirencester. The man who always opened his bailiff's letters before his political correspondence, Melbourne's 'tortoise on whom the world rests', had no qualms about refusing the lord-lieutenancy of Ireland and the governor-generalship of Canada. He had once described his entry into politics as the great fault of his life. Yet there, for a few critical years, he achieved greatness. 'No one', said Greville, 'neither of the Pitts, nor Canning nor Castlereagh, could govern with the same sway the most unruly and fastidious assembly which the world ever saw'.

Sir D. le Marchant, *Memoir of Lord Althorp*, 1879.
M. Brock, *The Great Reform Act*, 1973.

**HENRY PETER BROUGHAM, BARON BROUGHAM AND VAUX** (1778-1868) had a career in public life which was only disappointing when measured against his exceptional talents. Although for most of his political life he was associated with the Whigs, he was always an individualist. He was sometimes what a later generation might call 'a bounder' or 'too clever by half' and he inspired mistrust amongst colleagues, rivals and opponents alike. No party could have contained him for long, except perhaps as leader. The promotion of education, reform of law, abolition of slavery and free trade were among the causes he made his own. He was fluent with the pen as in speech and a great mass of letters survive to provide an intimate portrait of his restless, jealous, self-assertive personality. The 'steam intellect' of Peacock's telling phrase, 'Foaming Fudge' as Disraeli lampooned him in *Vivian Grey*, scholar, lawyer, philosopher, economist, wit, orator and clown, Brougham was compulsively serious and busy about many things but seemed to lack a central seriousness of purpose. He let his energy be dissipated in conflicting projects. Althorp was chosen leader of the Whigs in the Commons at the outset of the crucial reform campaign over the head of Brougham and it is not difficult to see why. As Greville said: 'Brougham is ... a very remarkable instance of the inefficacy of the most splendid talents, unless they are accompanied by other qualities, which scarcely admit definition, but which must serve the same purpose that ballast does a ship.'

Brougham (pronounced *Broom*) was born in Edinburgh. His father was a gentleman of Westmorland, his mother a niece of the historian Robertson. It was only vanity that prompted him later to claim descent from the noble Norman house of Vaux. He was educated at Edinburgh High School and University. A master of his school, Alexander Christison, wrote a book in 1802 called *The General Diffusion of Knowledge One Great Cause of the Prosperity of North Britain*. The title provides a text for Brougham's career. One part of him remained always the Scots dominie, wagging a learned finger, talking from a great height. He was to be the slave of his own virtuosity. Campbell, his biographer, declared that if Brougham were locked up in the Tower of London for twelve months without being allowed a single book, the year would not elapse before he had written an encyclopaedia. Lord Holland told him that if a new language were discovered in the morning he would be able to speak it before night. Rogers conveyed well the mingled awe and amusement that he evoked: 'This morning', he said as Brougham was leaving a country house, 'Solon, Lycurgus, Demosthenes, Archimedes, Sir Isaac Newton, Lord Chesterfield and a great many more went away in one post-chaise.' And yet, brilliant as his talents were, he had to work hard. He was admitted in 1800 to the Scottish bar, but did not flourish in the Tory atmosphere of the courts. How much he valued the training he received there can be gathered from his devotion to Lord Granton, upon whom he claimed to have modelled himself in forensic and political oratory. But he had other interests from the start. In 1802 he helped to found the *Edinburgh Review*, with Horner and Jeffrey, to promote liberal ideas. He wrote more than fifty articles in its first twenty numbers, and generally acted as a sub-editor. He continued thereafter to use the *Edinburgh* as a vehicle for his ideas. He was responsible for giving it the party bias which even some Whigs deplored.

In 1806 Brougham secured a post as secretary to a mission in Lisbon. In 1808 he was called to the English bar. He entered Parliament in 1810 for Camelford. He rewarded Wilberforce for his patronage and interest by carrying an act making participation in the slave trade a felony. He went on a campaign against the government's policy of economic retaliation. There was already a wide-spread movement of protest in the country: petitions flowed in to parliament. Brougham saw to it that every petition presented was made the occasion of an attack on the government. 'Mr Brougham was always in his place', wrote Bagehot. 'Hardly an hour passed without detecting some false statement or illogical argument.' He succeeded in securing a committee of the House of Commons to inquire into the state of trade: it sat for six weeks and examined over a hundred witnesses from manufacturing towns. He learned to appreciate the power of the mercantile and manufacturing interests and it was this that made him so formidable an advocate of political reform when he came to speak, as in 1831, of 'those hundreds of thousands of respectable persons — the most numerous and by far the most wealthy in the community ... who are also the genuine depositaries of sober, rational, intelligent and honest English feeling'. Intense application, an eye to the public beyond the House of Commons, indifference to the gentlemanly rules of political society, and what Bagehot called 'a knocking mind' advertised his arrival. Like Burke he could transform a debate and dominate a scene; he could also embarrass by excesses of rhetoric.

In 1812 he contested Liverpool and was defeated after a memorable campaign. When he was returned for Winchelsea (1816) he at once joined in the attack on the government which led to the repeal of income tax. Meanwhile he had acquired a fair practice on the northern circuit. He specialized in semi-political cases, such as the successful defence of thirty-eight Manchester radicals charged with administering an unlawful oath. By accepting the 'sedition line' as it was called, he turned professional work to political use. He was deeply versed in law. One of his principal interests was in reform of the penal code. His rational and impatient mind could cut through the accretions of centuries of statutes and judges' decisions. Yet as advocate and as chancellor the question hung over him: was he sound? 'He strikes hard, sir,' said one attorney, 'but he strikes wrong.' He lacked discretion and restraint. As Chancellor he provided swift judgements, cleared off arrears. But lawyers have not reckoned him a great chancellor. There was no background of patient reflection to his judgements. He was never sufficiently absorbed in his profession to be a great lawyer, in the way that Eldon, for all his faults, undoubtedly was.

What he did possess was the power to stir men about a great

cause. The Westmorland election of 1818, in which Brougham had the temerity to challenge the overweening Lowther interest, provided one such issue. He attacked the notion that a great landowner could treat county representation as a hereditary right. He lost the seat but he advertised a principle, and himself, by his campaign.

In 1820 the cabinet's bill to dissolve the king's marriage made necessary an inquiry into Queen Caroline's conduct. Brougham defended her with vigour and basked in the public enthusiasm. It looked as if the trial would wreck the ministry; before it began he offered to try to keep the queen out of the country in return for a silk gown. He played with the idea of turning out the government and becoming prime minister. When the ministers offered Caroline a large sum if she would live abroad, Brougham advised her to reject the offer. It is not surprising that the establishment, crown, ministers, Whig leaders alike, regarded him with suspicion. 'He has always some game or underplot out of sight ... some extraordinary connexion with persons quite opposite to himself' wrote Creevey. Brougham had seen himself in 1816 as Grey's choice for the leadership, the man who could reconcile aristocratic whiggery to popular radicalism. He had managed, however, to alienate both radicals and oligarchs, Francis Place as much as Lord Holland. He had conspicuously failed to build up a political connection of his own.

Brougham failed in his grand scheme of a national system of education. Lord Stowell spoke for conservatives of all ages when he warned: 'If you provide a larger amount of highly cultivated talent than there is a demand for, the surplus is very likely to turn sour.' There were still those who thought that education would upset 'the great law of subordination'. Small beginnings could, however, be made. Brougham supported effectively the establishment of London University, the Mechanics' Institutes, and the Society for the Diffusion of Useful Knowledge (1827). It is hard for us to appreciate the feelings roused by the last. Cobbett predictably attacked 'Scotch feelosophy': to that robust countryman Brougham's schemes were irrelevant to the people's needs. Brougham was vulnerable on economic questions. In 1822 a speech he made about the plight of agriculture was torn apart by Huskisson and Ricardo from opposite sides of the House. His views on Poor Law reform were based on the harsh axiom that the poor will always prefer to live idly than to work. When out of office he had protested against the government's treatment of the Luddites. As Lord Chancellor in 1831 he defended the savage sentences meted out upon the rickburners and machine-breakers. They were of course impeding 'progress'. The movement for popular education expressed the hopeful spirit of the 'age of improvement'. It also polarized various social prejudices, against industrialism, against the new doctrines of political economy, against all who wished to bring scientific inquiry to bear upon ancient institutions. Coleridge prayed to be delivered from 'a popular philosophy and a philosophic populace'.

Brougham was 'the most able friend of the Mechanicks now living', said a preface to the *Mechanic's Magazine* in 1824. His book *Practical Observations upon the Education of the People* quickly went through twenty editions. Of course his was only one among many influences. In his own phrase, 'the schoolmaster was abroad in the land'. In almost every town by 1830 there was a group, predominantly middle class and nonconformist, that believed in 'the diffusion of the principles of rational and constitutional freedom'. More than any other politician Brougham was qualified to lead and interpret this new political instrument, the people.

For a time Brougham had looked for political salvation from joining Canning and his followers. If he can be said to have had any natural allegiance it was with this group of liberal tories Brougham knew that he was not *persona grata* among the whig oligarchs. They mistrusted his ambition and deplored his taste. He was upset by Canning's return to the ministerial ranks in 1822. He then tried to split the two wings of the Tories. After the departure in 1827 of the reconciling authority of Lord Liverpool, Brougham tried to create a new force, a Whig-Canningite coalition. The eventual union was a makeshift affair: the Whigs had three cabinet seats but Grey, Russell and Althorp all opposed it and radicals were contemptuous. Brougham had added to his reputation as a schismatic without the compensation of office. He was a disturbing ally to Canning, and to his successor Robinson. 'There are now no Whigs, no Tories', wrote Francis Place in January 1828. In that month Wellington became prime minister. Brougham adopted a new tack and led the opposition. The Tories split over Catholic emancipation and the Whigs closed ranks.

They lacked an active leader. Brougham was their most active commoner, but Althorp was chosen. In the eyes of the country Brougham was the man of destiny.

In the general election of August 1830 he won a Yorkshire seat after a campaign which, for eloquence and public enthusiasm, may be compared with Gladstone's in Midlothian. Macaulay wrote of him in 1831: 'He is, next to the king, the most popular man in England.' He did as much as any man to turn out the duke and open the way for a reforming ministry. Grey acknowledged his claims and made him Chancellor, though with 'anxiety and annoyance'. As Durham said, he had frightened 'so many people by his wild speeches'; by country Tories his name was associated with revolution. He helped to ensure that Grey was followed by Melbourne. Did he imagine that he could manage Melbourne more easily than Grey? He was twice shocked. First Melbourne resigned and the king sent for Peel. When Melbourne formed his next administration Brougham was excluded.

He had brought the disaster upon himself. Touring Scotland in the summer of 1834 he had spoken so wildly that some even doubted his sanity. 'At Dumfries', wrote Hobhouse, 'he got extremely intoxicated, sat up all night, and was carried to the racecourse next morning in a sedan chair, dressed in his wig and gown'. But it was excess of words that destroyed him. During that 'vagrant and grotesque apocalypse', as Disraeli called his tour, the press were kept busy with sarcastic comments upon his colleagues, even upon the king. When Brougham demanded to know of Melbourne what he had done amiss he was told: 'You domineered too much, you interfered too much with other departments; you encroached upon the province of prime minister, you worked, as I believe, with the press in a manner unbecoming your station, and you formed political views of your own and pursued them by means which were unfair towards your colleagues.' The outraged sense of conventions flouted gives these charges a pungency which is not lessened by Melbourne's conclusion: 'Nobody knows and appreciates your natural vigour better than I do. I know also that those who are weak for good are strong for mischief. You are strong for both.'

*The Times* set his obituary in print as if there were nothing to add. But his later years were not inactive, though he was kept at arm's length by both Tories and Radicals. Corn Law repeal saw

Brougham begin his last serious attempt to regain influence. However his attempt to rehabilitate himself in the context of a united Toryism deteriorated into a last phase of his vendetta against the Whigs. He was not taken seriously any longer. It is pleasant, however, to record that his personality grew gentler, more genial with age. Political animosities were forgotten at the dinner table. Wellesley and Palmerston were among his close friends.

He is often a figure of fun: the long, up-tilting, flat-ended nose and the jutting lower lip were a gift to the cartoonist. *Punch* never lost a chance to mock. But the mockery became almost affectionate. He is not a figure of pathos in his declining years because he remained generous at heart, unselfconscious in his ways and, to the end, original and broad in interests. Cannes was his winter home. He built there the Chateau Eleanor-Louise, so called after his daughter, whose early death in 1839 was perhaps his deepest personal loss. After the February Revolution of 1848 he made an abortive application for French citizenship. With his restlessly active mind, his theorizing and his taste for rhetoric and intrigue he would have been more at home in French political life than at Westminster. His taste for universality was in the tradition of the *Philosophes*. He devoted much time to composing his autobiography and publishing his speeches, besides writing valuable short studies of statesmen and writers. Spiritualism occupied him largely in his later years and he spent many days with Robert Owen, communicating by means of a boy medium with the departed spirit of the Duke of Kent, the father of Queen Victoria. Racy, learned talk went with a good humour and kindness that few could resist. 'Even his greatness', wrote Whitwell Elwin, a Tory friend, 'was surpassed by his kindness. His warmth, tenderness, and constancy of friendship were wonderful.'

C. W. New, *The Life of Henry Brougham to 1830*, 1961.
Robert Stewart, *Brougham, His Public Career*, 1986.

## JOHN GEORGE LAMBTON, 1st EARL OF DURHAM

(1792-1840), 'Radical Jack', was one of the architects of parliamentary reform and contributed significantly to the idea of responsible government in the empire. He was the son of William Lambton, a Durham landowner whose coal royalties were to make his son the richest commoner in the country. John Lambton was reared a Whig, though influenced less by his father, who died when he was five, than by his tutor Beddoes. To Beddoes, whose revolutionary sympathies had cost him an Oxford professorship, Lambton may have owed his committed and wholehearted liberalism as well as a breadth of thought and reading which marks him off from some of the narrower Whigs — Grey, Althorp or Melbourne, for example. He married as his second wife Lord Grey's daughter and served Grey's interest keenly, although not always tactfully. He shared with Russell, Althorp and Graham the work of shaping and steering the reform bill of 1832. He was chairman of the committee which drafted the bill. Russell introduced it to parliament.

Concerned about the well-being of miners on his estates, he offered his pits to Humphrey Davy for his safety-lamp trials, founded a collieries association to provide old age, sickness and accident benefits, and provided schools and libraries; he even allowed the miners some share in the running of their association. Fifty thousand workmen turned out to follow the coffin at his funeral. We learn, however, from Greville what mistrust Durham aroused in fashionable drawing-rooms. He denounces the vulgarity of the democrats 'who are not only wild to have a Lord for their leader, but must also have that Lord who is the especial incarnation of all those odious qualities which they ascribe, most unjustly, to the order of which he is a member, to wit ... an overweening sense of his greatness and rank'. Creevey, too, found an objectionable pride in the man whom he called 'King Jog' because in 1821 he had been heard to remark that he considered £40,000 a year a moderate income, such as a sensible man should have no difficulty in 'jogging on with'.

Beyond doubt there was a meretricious strain in Lambton. Delicate, emotional, prone to moods of intense irritability and flashes of wild temper, he echoes Byron in the wilful behaviour of his youth. After Eton, his guardians wished him to go to the university; instead he joined the 10th Dragoons. On New Year's Day he eloped to Gretna Green with Lord Cholmondeley's illegitimate daughter. Recklessly hospitable, flamboyant, a lover of the turf, he was a true son of the Whig plutocracy. Beddoes had remarked of his handsome charge, aged nine: 'He has the greatest sensibility I have ever observed in a child' and declared that he was 'as capable of going as far in good or bad as any human being I have ever beheld.'

Lambton only held one ministerial office: he was made Lord Privy Seal under Grey in 1830. He held tenaciously to the reform proposals against all temptations to compromise. The support of the radicals and the political unions strengthened his position. A speaker at the mass meeting of the political unions of the Midlands in Birmingham, in May 1832, said that 'if from treachery or from any other cause, the Bill was lost, he hoped the country would call on Lord Durham to take the seat of power'. Would he then have assumed the leadership of such a revolutionary movement as might have come about in the summer of 1832, if Wellington had returned to office? He never lacked boldness. He had long been laying the foundations of his alliance with the radicals, and he had kept in touch with men like Place. He was probably right in his contention that the unions were of value in canalizing and giving respectable form to forces which might otherwise turn to violence.

During the last years of his life Durham was generally out of the country. In 1834 he was excluded from Cabinet office by Melbourne, who decided that a diplomatic post would best suit a man disturbingly keen upon change. His conduct in the later stages of Grey's ministry had been hectic and often intolerable, even to his father-in-law. His avowed grievance seems to have been that he was not given a post with great responsibilities; he also demanded an earldom. He was undoubtedly convinced that his had been the main part in ensuring the passage of the Reform Bill. He suffered from painful neuralgia and he had suffered agonizing blows in the deaths, in 1832, of his elder son (the 'Master Lambton' of Lawrence's tender picture) and his daughter Harriet, from consumption. It explains much to add that his father, his first wife, four altogether of his children and ultimately, he too, died of this disease. How should a man, with so many possessions, and such doubtful expectation of life, be patient?

Lambton had encountered the Tsar Nicholas II when sent to secure his neutrality in the matter of Belgian independence. In 1835 he went to St. Petersburg as ambassador. He returned in 1837. The election that followed the accession of Queen Victoria left an attenuated Whig majority: the balance was held by the radicals. Lambton was sent out to Canada to practise his constitutional ideas on the Canadians. The French of Lower Canada and the British of Upper Canada were restless under administrators appointed by Whitehall. At home some English radicals demanded the severance of ties between Canada and the mother country. Durham was reluctant to go abroad again; his health was declining and he dreaded the cold. Perhaps he resented having to leave England when the political situation was so delicate — and promising — at home; none the less he responded to the Queen's appeal. Durham reached Quebec in May 1838; at once he dealt tactfully with the threat of American intervention by sending Colonel Charles Grey, his brother-in-law, on a personal mission to President van Buren. Rather than risk acquittals by sympathetic juries, Durham selected eight of the 161 prisoners awaiting trial for rebellion, secured confessions in return for a promise to spare their lives, and banished them to Bermuda. He had no proper jurisdiction and it was on this ground that he was attacked at home, and his ordinance disallowed. Durham then resigned. Brougham had exposed the weak point in his decree in the House of Lords. Melbourne had given way before the radical storm and abandoned the man whom he had sent to Canada with a promise of 'the most firm and unflinching support'.

Durham had made himself liked in Canada. His journeys about the country showed his wish to find out conditions at first hand. He had founded police forces in Montreal and Quebec, set up an efficient land registration system and appointed commissions to look into immigration. He now intended to further their interests at home. He left Quebec amid expressions of sympathy and respect; a procession of three thousand followed him to the quayside at Quebec.

Durham arrived to find that public feeling had turned against Melbourne. Once again he could have been the leader round whom radicals and liberals could gather for the assault upon the old Whigs. He did not accept the challenge. He probably saw his first duty as lying with the Canadians — and he was a sick man. It has been wrongly alleged that he did not write the report that appeared under his name and was laid before parliament in February 1839. Undoubtedly he was materially helped by his friend Buller. His ideas reflected closely the views of the philosophical radicals, Grote and Molesworth. But the report was essentially his; so was the boldness which characterized the document. He was not entirely original in his recommendations. The union of Upper and Lower Canada had been suggested to the cabinet in 1821. The theory that the mother country should be forbearing in the use of imperial authority was at least as old as Canning, if not Chatham. The prime value of the document was the firm commitment to an extension of responsible government to Canada by a man who had grappled with the problems on the spot and was at the same time versed in the constitutional practice of the mother country. Its main weakness lay in its assessment of the French Canadian situation. He let himself be persuaded that the French community would lose its distinctive character and culture and be absorbed naturally as the legislative union of the two Canadas bore fruit. So the chance was lost of creating a federal union of all the provinces such as was eventually brought about in 1867.

In May 1840 Lambton set off for Carlsbad to cure his worsening consumption, but he never crossed the channel. He died in July. Inevitably there is an unfinished look about his career. But it was no small thing to have established the future of colonial self-government when so few men beyond his own circle were interested in the idea.

C. W. New, *Life of Lord Durham*, 1929.

**DANIEL O'CONNELL** (1775-1847), 'the Liberator', Irish lawyer and popular leader, was responsible, more than any other man, for the act of Catholic emancipation. To reverse the Act of Union was beyond his powers, but his campaigns for the betterment of his countrymen made him for many years 'the uncrowned king', if not of all Ireland, certainly of the Catholic peasantry of that impoverished land. He was the eldest son of Morgan O'Connell of Cahirciveen, in Kerry, and the nephew and adopted son of Maurice O'Connell of Darrynane. He was educated at Cove near Cork and then abroad, at St. Omer and Douai. As a devout Catholic he was appalled by the irreligious spirit of the French revolutionaries. Back in Ireland he was called to the Bar (1798) and soon made his name in the courts as a pleader and cross-examiner. In Lecky's view he had repeal of the union in mind from the start: he brought new dimensions to the argument.

Grattan had never appealed directly to priests and people. O'Connell deliberately did so. He was a tall man, of splendid appearance and voice, and he spoke to the people in their native Gaelic. He saw that the priests, mostly of peasant stock themselves, often ignorant men but the natural leaders of their villages, must be mobilized in the cause. And the masses had to be taught the value of emancipation: for the educated it meant an *entrée* to commissions and civil posts, for the peasant an end to oppression.

In 1802 he married his cousin, who gave him five sons and three daughters. He acquired a vast practice on the Munster circuit: swaggering confidence, a caustic wit and a quick eye for his opponent's weakness made him a formidable advocate. Sometimes his bold tongue got him into trouble. His attacks on 'the beggarly corporation' of Dublin (an Orange stronghold then) brought a challenge from a Mr D'Esterre; in the subsequent duel he shot his antagonist. Peel, then secretary for Ireland, called him out later in the year, but O'Connell's wife informed on him and had him bound over to keep the peace. O'Connell comes badly out of this story. He provoked the duel, seeking political capital out of a personal challenge. His behaviour was crudely aggressive. He was known to be a good shot, who was reputed to keep his eye in by shooting stray curs when he was out riding on circuit. In Peel, the good Protestant, his behaviour aroused the greatest distaste. The incompatibility of the two men was significant. They clashed again when Peel was home secretary, most seriously when he became prime minister. It is to O'Connell that we owe that devastating and very Irish remark about Peel — that his smile was like the gleam of silver plate on a coffin lid. He was later to attack the young Disraeli (who had already attacked him) as 'heir-in-law of the blasphemous thief who died upon the cross'. Such was his style of controversy.

In 1823 O'Connell set up the Catholic Association to press for emancipation and repeal of the Act of Union. In 1824 he began to levy his 'Catholic rent' of one shilling a year on the members of his association. In that year he was prosecuted, and acquitted by Attorney-General Plunket, for having expressed the hope that 'another Bolivar might arise to vindicate the rights of the Irish people'. The association was suppressed in 1825, whereupon it was reconstituted in new form as 'the Order of Liberators'. The government could no longer shelve the emancipation question:

the population was rising fast and pressed grimly on land resources. There were reports of arson and brigandage from many areas; secret societies flourished and civil war seemed likely. An election in 1826 showed that tenants were beginning to assert themselves against landlords: at Waterford Lord George Beresford, whose family owned a large part of the county, was defeated by the liberal Potestant Villiers Stuart. In May 1828 Wellington had to reconstruct his cabinet after the withdrawal of the Canningites and he put Vesey Fitzgerald, member for Clare, at the Board of Trade, which meant that he had to seek re-election. As he was an emancipationist no difficulty was anticipated. But O'Connell chose to make this the time and place to issue a historic challenge. He stood as a Catholic candidate, received a majority (2,057 votes to 982) and thereby served notice upon the British government that, unless they were prepared to see the same thing happen in other Irish seats, they must concede Catholic emancipation.

Wellington and Peel acted to prevent the breakdown of government. Many of their followers felt betrayed. The king threatened to retire to Hanover; 142 members voted against the bill, but it was passed, in March 1829, and the king tearfully accepted it. The government was hardly generous: the forty shilling freeholder lost the vote and the franchise was raised to £10. But except for the offices of king, regent, lord-lieutenant of Ireland and chancellor of England, the constitution of Great Britain was opened to Catholics. The Ascendancy did not, of course, lose its hold overnight. Nor did the reformers of the thirties appease Irish discontents. In 1831 Chief Secretary Stanley introduced a system of national education to meet the need for religious instruction. English alone was used in the new elementary schools. O'Connell approved, since he, like many of the priests, regarded Irish as an obstacle to progress. Nationalism became a more coherent political force, ironically enough, just as the distinctive Irish culture was being destroyed.

In English politics the result of the Reform Act was to create an 'Irish Party', led by O'Connell and able to hold the balance between the two parties. He personally nominated about half the candidates returned; three of his sons and two sons-in-law composed his 'household brigade'. Forty-five of 105 Irish members were 'repealers'. He fought fiercely against the Coercion Act of

1833, but tried to restrain his more impulsive followers from acting prematurely to get repeal. Melbourne won O'Connell's support by the 'Litchfield House Compact'; in return for parliament votes, he pursued a policy of conciliation. Mulgrave, the viceroy, and Drummond, his under-secretary, with O'Connell's support, attacked terrorism by means of the newly enrolled Royal Irish Constabulary. The Tithe Act of 1838, which merged tithe in rent, removed one bitter grievance. After Peel succeeded Melbourne in 1841 O'Connell waited until he had finished his year of office as lord mayor of Dublin, then redoubled his efforts to restore 'the Old House on College Green'. Vast meetings met and marched and listened spellbound to violent oratory. O'Connell believed in the weight of numbers as a political argument, but he eschewed violence. The lord chancellor of Ireland wrote: 'The peaceable demeanour of the assembled multitudes is one of the most alarming symptoms'. The garrison troops were reïnforced; at one time there were more than in India!

On the hill of Tara a quarter of a million are said to have heard O'Connell. On 8 October 1843, the greatest meeting of all was to be held at Clontarf, where Brian Boru had routed the Norsemen eight hundred years earlier; belatedly the government prohibited it and barred the approaches with troops. O'Connell ordered the people to disperse and they did so peaceably. In his words, 'human blood is no cement for the temple of liberty'. He was tried for conspiracy with five others, by a Protestant jury in Dublin, and condemned. The verdict was reversed in the House of Lords in September 1844. But O'Connell lost his hold. He left prison after fourteen weeks' incarceration to find that he was being outflanked by the militants, the 'Young Ireland Party' of Davis, Duffy, Mitchell and Fintan Lalor. Some were Protestants who resented the Catholic bias of his campaign, others looked back regretfully to the principles of Grattan and Tone and sought inspiration in the Gaelic past. Many were prepared to countenance physical force in the manner of 1798. The government had been unwise to arrest O'Connell: his words had aroused the masses, but he had the courage to try to direct their protests into constitutional channels.

In January 1847 he withdrew suddenly from political life. By then he had witnessed the distressing ravages of the potato blight and the 'Great Hunger': a million of his compatriots were dead.

He had seen and deplored the growth of a secular spirit: one of his last campaigns was directed against Peel's provincial non-sectarian colleges — 'Godless colleges' he called them. His superb physique collapsed at last. He sailed to Italy to recover his health. Five months later, on 15 May 1847, he died at Genoa, on the way to Rome. His heart was taken to Rome and buried in St. Agathe's. O'Connell had taught the people to feel their power. It is hard to distinguish between his patriotic sentiment and love of his own voice and power. But some of the worse faults of the democratic politician cannot be attributed to him. He believed imaginatively in Ireland and in his church; he was lion-hearted and generous, a man of heroic stature.

O. MacDonagh, *O'Connell*, 1991.
R. B. McDowell, *Public Opinion and Government Policy in Ireland, 1801-46*, 1952.

**FRANCIS PLACE** (1771-1854), radical politician, was the son of Simon Place, a baker who became bailiff to the Marshalsea and keeper of a 'sponging house' in Vinegar Yard, Drury Lane. At fourteen the boy was apprenticed to a leather-breeches maker. At nineteen he married Elizabeth Chadd, two years younger than himself. They set up house in one room in a 'rookery' off the Strand and Place set himself, energetically and frugally, to make a living out of a declining trade.

When, in 1793, the leather-breeches workers struck work, Place was chosen to be their organizer. The strike was sponsored by the Breeches Makers' Benefit Society, which had managed to collect £250 to back their action. Place, who had started to work on cloth breeches to make more money, found that the breeches makers were making common cause: indeed, he learned about the strike, when his master refused to give him any more work, alleging that the cloth-breeches makers were supporting the others from their earnings. He resolved, therefore, to counter the masters' strategy by broadening the struggle. Some of the London men were induced by seven shillings a week strike-pay to tramp into the provinces, armed with their Society's certificate, to secure hospitality from local societies. Place also opened a shop to sell 'Rag Fair Breeches' at a special price. Thus he circumvented the employers, prolonged the strike and exposed himself to reprisals, when at last the men accepted defeat. He was given no work for eight months and had to pawn his belongings. In 1795, with trade temporarily brisk and a reformed society, of which he was secretary, the workers managed to get the conditions — for which they had struck before — this time without a struggle. Persistence, co-operation and boldness had shown the way.

Place had meanwhile become a member of the London Corresponding Society and was active as unofficial adviser of clubs. He was much influenced at this time by Tom Paine's *Age of Reason* and its anti-authoritarian message. In 1796 we find him arranging for the production of a cheap edition of the book. He stayed for some months in 1817 (leaving his business in the care of his eldest son) with Bentham and Mill at Ford Abbey, and busied himself there with learning Latin grammar. Romilly met him there and declared him 'a very extraordinary person' as well as a disciple and admirer of Bentham's. 'He is self-educated, has learned a great deal, has a very strong natural understanding, and possesses great influence in Westminster — such influence as almost to determine the elections for members of Parliament.' He used this influence to help independent reformers like Hobhouse, winner of the Westminster election in 1820, and Joseph Hume, who drew heavily upon Place's parliamentary records for his political campaigns. He was also a voluminous writer; there are seventy-one volumes of manuscripts and materials in the British Museum: he tended to be prolix in argument and laboured in style.

In later life Place supported many causes, birth control among them. In 1823 he was responsible for the distribution of handbills on this subject. He had two great triumphs. In 1824 he succeeded in getting the law against combinations of workmen repealed. In the following year he prevented their re-enactment: the Amending Act of that year left combination lawful. With Hume he had managed to pack the parliamentary committee, presented it with carefully collated evidence from employers and workmen, and rushed the act through before the government realized its significance.

His motives should be understood. As a Benthamite, who believed in 'cheap and simple government', he hoped that trades union action would be discouraged because workers would learn, in their new freedom, the futility of combining in the face of the inexorable 'laws' of political economy, and the better course of collaborating with employers in increasing the 'wages fund' that depended on employers' profits. At the same time he approved of the activity of the small unions whose concern was with conditions of labour. On the whole, however, he was careful not to become involved in any directly subversive activities. He saw the rôle of working-class reformers as accessories to those who could obtain a hearing in parliament. He had been a member of the Corresponding Society since 1794 and an official since 1795. He seems to have wanted a sober, orderly *conversazione* with other 'inquisitive, clever, upright men'. He later idealized this side of the society. It taught men 'to think, to respect themselves, and to desire to educate their children'. There was also a rowdier, impatient element; in 1796 he resigned his post and in 1797 he left the society altogether.

When some of his colleagues were languishing in gaol, Place was laying the foundations of a business. In April 1799, with a fellow workman as partner, he set up a tailor's shop in Charing Cross Road. Within two years he was on his own and employing more than thirty workmen. He did not lose sight of political issues or political friends. He managed the collecting of subscriptions for the prisoners' families. But he believed that agitation was hopeless at that time; when he intervened it would be from the base of a flourishing business. The cause of reform was best served by mobilizing public opinion so as to bring pressure on Parliament — and he could do nothing effective in this way until he had secured his own position as a prosperous tradesman. He had a large family — ten out of fifteen survived infancy — and he provided for them well.

In 1807 Sir Francis Burdett stood for Westminster and Place helped to direct a campaign which, because it was devoted to the bread-and-butter business of canvassing and registering, was cheaper than previous campaigns in this turbulent constituency. Burdett came top of the poll, radicalism obtained a loud voice in the commons — and Place was established, in the niche which he occupied until the passing of the Reform Bill, as organizer and oracle of Westminster radicalism. He quarrelled with Burdett in 1810 when the latter refused to lead the procession which Place had arranged to celebrate Burdett's release from the Tower. Like other radical leaders of these pioneer days, Place was sensitive about his status in the movement. He was by temperament a committee man, a student of the art of getting things done.

After the introduction of the Reform Bill in 1831 Place's library became again the meeting place of the extreme reformers. Years of research and study of the mechanics of popular politics now bore fruit. The various leaders of radical and liberal opinion made common cause. By May 1832 Place was making active preparations for the expected civil war. Placards, devised by him, bore the slogan 'To stop the Duke, go for gold', which produced a run on the banks. Had this not achieved its effect he planned a collective refusal to pay taxes. There was talk of barricades and pikes, but moderate counsels prevailed. Cocksure and self-important as he was, Place was no revolutionary.

Place's triumph, ironically enough, reduced his political influence, since Westminster was partially disenfranchised by the ten shilling clause and no longer held its peculiar position as a popular constituency. Place lost most of his money by the mistakes of a solicitor and was forced to exchange Charing Cross for a house in Brompton Square. He was still active in the back rooms of politics. He helped Joseph Parkes prepare the municipal corporations report in 1835 and drafted the 'People's Charter' for his friend William Lovett in 1838. But the Chartism of O'Connor and O'Brien owed little to Place: he was altogether too bourgeois for them. In 1840 he became chairman of the Metropolitan Anti-Corn Law Committee. But in 1844 a tumour on the brain incapacitated him, though he lived for ten more years. In 1851 he was separated from his second wife. In his lengthy autobiography (unpublished) Place overestimates his importance in the reform movement as a whole. But in Westminster, for two decades, he was keeper of the radical conscience and the most effective promoter of the cause.

M. Thale (ed), *Autobiography of Francis Place*, 1972.
Dudley Mill, *Francis Place*, 1988.

**ROBERT OWEN** (1771-1857), self-made manufacturer, factory reformer, educationalist and utopian socialist, spent much of his life in the search for a 'new society'. His writings and experiments were of little consequence when measured against his exalted hopes. He was so original in his plans that he may be termed a revolutionary, yet he was more assiduous than dynamic; he was neither upset nor stimulated by practical setbacks — as if nothing could gainsay the validity of his ideas. He was among the first English thinkers to recognize the moral and social benefits that industrialism could bring, and he was modern in his concern with what might be called the psychology of environment.

New Lanark was an experiment of seminal importance. Yet Owen was stubborn and blind in whole areas of life. His understanding of human nature was limited, his political sense deficient. His experience of succeeding in life by his own enterprise, and of managing large numbers of workmen in the new disciplines of the mechanized mill, with his interpretation of the eighteenth-century philosophers and their view of human nature, combined to produce an idea of a society which could be improved and transformed by the application of rational rules. This view never evolved significantly. Once he had discovered the principles of social regeneration the facts of social life became less important to him.

Owen was born at Welshpool, Montgomeryshire, the fourth surviving son of Robert Owen, a saddler. He was a clever schoolboy and at the age of seven was already assisting the local schoolmaster. At nine he left school to work in a draper's shop. He went to London, the next year, to join his saddler brother. Thence he soon took himself to Stamford and the draper's shop of Mr McGuffog who was so impressed by his assistant that he later offered him his daughter — and a partnership. Owen rejected both. He learned the cotton business: in 1791 he set up as a master-spinner. Then he became manager for a Mr Drinkwater, who had a large and well-run mill in Manchester. He showed an enlightened interest in science, as a member of the Manchester Board of Health and the Literary and Philosophical Society. What he was in Manchester he would always, in essentials, remain: a self-made paternalist who believed that workers' efforts and morale depended on their environment. When he bought the New Lanark mills from David Dale (he soon afterwards married Dale's daughter) he could create a new kind of environment that was both disciplined and wholesome for his 1,500 workers.

He stopped the employment of pauper apprentices and refused to take any child under the age of ten (six or seven was usual before). New Lanark was a virtually closed society and the workers lived on the site in specially constructed houses. Owen wanted his men to develop 'habits of attention, celerity and order'. He improved houses, streets and sanitation, built company shops and schools, and organized every detail of the employees' lives. Fines imposed for immorality and swearing went to a fund for medical care. 'Silent monitors', coloured boards beside each bench, recorded the worker's behaviour and progress. (His wife was meanwhile being encouraged to look after her home by the award of prizes.) Owen cared that workers should be contented and should have a pride in their work, their labour bearable within the requirements of factory discipline. There was no question, however, of consultation — indeed no formal representation of the men's interests. They were virtually his serfs and he was master of their lives. In 1823 his men complained about his attitude: they were 'compelled by Mr Owen to adopt what measures so ever he be pleased to suggest on matters that entirely belong to us' which was 'degrading to our characters as free-born sons of highly favoured Great Britain'.

New Lanark convinced Owen that education was the key to social progress. Education for him was training for life. He wished 'to remoralize the lower orders'. In his *New View of Society* (1813) he expanded upon the idea that children had a plastic quality and could be moulded. The curriculum of his schools was severely practical, contained 'elementary social and economic facts'; emphasis was also placed on such activities as knitting, sewing and botanical walks; both sexes were to be formed into companies for marching practice which, Owen believed, fostered discipline and harmony of body and mind. He was also original in advocating nursery schools where the first rule was to make the children happy. Inspectors of Owen's schools reported a 'general spirit of kindness and affection' and the appearance of 'one well-regulated family'.

At the end of the French war Owen thought that the government should spend money on 'a national system of training and education for the poor and uninstructed'. Nothing of the sort was done, so he turned to his own plans for 'villages of co-operation'. These were self-supporting rural colonies: their purpose, to provide employment and the setting for a good life. They were constructed on a square, with lines of public buildings, school, library, a 'place of public worship' and a communal restaurant. Cobbett spurned these 'parallelograms of paupers' but the Duke of Kent declared his interest, Napoleon is supposed to have read the *New View* in exile, and Owen toured Europe and had an audience with the future King Louis Philippe. The messianic strain became more pronounced. He promised 'to let prosperity loose upon the country'. On the analogy of the advances accomplished by inventions in industry he forecast that knowledge and moral improvement would leap forward as well. He argued vaguely for a new religion of truth (which meant living in conformity with the demands of the laws of nature). He took his idea of the formative influence of environment to the point of denying, not only responsibility before God, but even the sovereignty of the individual will.

Owen was soon abandoned by his grander patrons when his naïve views became known. He would have alarmed politicians, if they had taken him seriously. He was disillusioned by politics. His proposals for a factory bill were unrecognizably reduced by the time they reached the statute book in 1819 (the elder Peel's Act). Leading radicals had rejected his advances when he addressed them in 1817. His newspaper, *The Crisis*, with its revealing subtitle *The Change from Error and Misery, to Truth and Happiness*, its motto 'If we cannot yet reconcile all opinions, let us endeavour to unite all hearts', and its cover design of a rectangle of buildings, 'a community of 2,000 persons, founded upon a principle commended by Plato, Lord Bacon, T. More and R. Owen', blandly ignored the political excitements of the time. Owen was concerned with psychological change: a new spirit of rationality would make political moves irrelevant. The criterion would then be what was good for the human race.

He was naturally attracted to America. In 1824 he visited the United States and met many famous Americans. In 1825 he opened his Community of Equality at New Harmony, Indiana. He hoped for 'the industrious and well-disposed of all nations'; inevitably drop-outs, criminals and drunkards arrived as well. Neither a democratic assembly nor Owen's fussy attempts at autocratic rule met the community needs; nor did it pay its way. In 1827 Owen conceded failure, blaming the strength of 'the individual system, founded as it is upon superstition'. He was still ready with advice and schemes and planned a chain of Owenite communities in Texas. He was discredited — and impoverished — by the New Harmony débâcle. He had to sell his remaining shares in New Lanark. But his own confidence was unimpaired. Owenite societies borrowed his name and ideas: he had already used the term 'co-operative' and, when he returned from America, societies had been formed, in support of co-operation, with co-operative shops and 'labour exchanges' for the marketing of goods; the word 'socialism' was being widely used. Owen was not greatly interested in the co-operative movement: buying and selling were not in his scheme of things. He was enthusiastic, however, about the National Equitable Labour Exchange, opened in London in 1832, since it was based on the ideas already propounded in his *Report to the County of Lanark* (1820). The Exchange failed. Characteristically, Owen dismissed the experiment as if it were irrelevant: 'It was a mere pawnbroker's shop in comparison with the superior establishments which we shall speedily have it in our power to institute'.

Owen played, however, a large part in the formation of the Grand National Consolidated Trades Union (1833). His hope was to abolish the distinction between masters and men: the idea of co-operation along these lines had already interested him in the proposals of the Operative Builders' Union. His idea of the Grand National was one of co-operation on the national scale, with every craft and trade incorporated in one body. He convinced himself that the lower orders were not the passive objects of improvement that he had hitherto known but active, energetic and ready to assume responsibility. That they should therefore want to promote their own craft at the expense of others, that they should want to use the strike weapon at once to initiate the golden age, he did not allow for. Premature strikes weakened many unions; in several cases office-holders absconded with the funds. The movement disintegrated amidst confusion and recrimination, while Owen turned to constructing an organization which should reflect his purer ideals: the British and Foreign Consolidated Association of Industry, Humanity and Knowledge. He did ride at the head of a great procession of London workers (April 1834) protesting against the barbarity of the Tolpuddle sentences. But he soon returned from action to the idea, more important to him than any organization. He would not compromise and he could not share or sympathize with the material hopes of the workers whom he addressed so loftily — as they saw it, condescendingly.

The last part of his long life was spent in travelling about the world, reaffirming obsessively, in word and print, the principles of his rational society. He became a spiritualist. He had always presented a broad front to admirers and critics. Men could choose their own inspired interpretation of his new Jerusalem in England's blighted land; or they could see him as an amiable crank — or even a self-important prig. For all his moral earnestness he was not big or clever enough to see or admit his own shortcomings. His wife Caroline gave him eight children and had the spirit to hold to her Presbyterian convictions. He let her drift out of his life. It seems that he could feel more for people as abstractions than as human beings. But he took trouble to answer the letters of simple men when they wrote for guidance. He was an incomparably zealous propagandist. His confidence could be infectious: 'I therefore now proclaim to the world the commencement, on this day, of the promised millennium, founded on rational principles and consistent practice' was his message, on May Day 1833, to the National Equitable Labour Exchange. Engels, who rejected his thesis, paid him the tribute of describing him as 'a man of almost sublimely child-like simplicity of character and at the same time a born leader of men'.

Margaret Cole, *Robert Owen of New Lanark*, 1953.
Ed. Sidney Pollard and John Salt, *Robert Owen*, 1971.

**THOMAS ROBERT MALTHUS** (1766-1834), political economist, was the second son of Daniel Malthus of Albury in Surrey, a gentleman of scholarly tastes and a firm believer in 'the perfectibility of man'. As befitted a friend of Rousseau he undertook Thomas's education himself; thereafter it was entrusted to tutors. Richard Graves was followed by Gilbert Wakefield, whom Malthus accompanied to Warrington Dissenting Academy when Wakefield was appointed its classical master. The views of the adult Malthus, logical and systematic but stronger, perhaps, in statistical calculation than in human understanding, must surely be related to this careful education. When he went to St. John's, Cambridge, he read widely, won classical prizes and was ninth Wrangler in the mathematical tripos. He became a fellow of the college and was ordained. A curacy at Albury was followed by a living in Lincolnshire but the villagers of Walesby were left to a curate's care. His religious views were utilitarian, unenthusiastic.

'Parson Malthus' was to become a natural bogey-figure to warm-blooded traditionalists. His theories seemed to be at variance with his Christian vocation. Yet, in the face of declining real wages and a system of poor relief that threatened to pauperize the agricultural labourer, his concern about the rise in population was not extraordinary. The population of Europe had risen in the twelve centuries before 1800 to a total of 180 millions. Between 1800 and 1914 its population increased from 180 to 460 millions.

In 1796 Malthus wrote a pamphlet entitled *The Crisis*. In deference to his father he did not print it, but he continued to study questions of population and poor relief. A discussion of Godwin's *Political Justice* led him to clarify his own views. So he wrote the *Essay on the Principle of Population* in 1798. Godwin dreamed of social equality in a society from which vice and misery had been banished. Malthus declared that, even if the ideal society could be established, it would soon be ruined by excess of people. Population, he said, tended to double itself every twenty-five years, increasing by geometrical progression, while resources, at best, increased only by arithmetical progression. He later modified his argument in a second edition of the book (1803) in which he explained that the 'checks' of famine, epidemics, natural disasters and 'vice' to which he ascribed such an important rôle, were not insuperable obstacles to social improvement; rather they were dangers to be overcome, if society were to be bettered. His own panacea was 'prudential restraint', which should delay marriages to a later age than had been customary among the poorer classes.

Malthus was certainly influential. He claimed Pitt among his converts. In 1805, after marrying the year before and resigning his college fellowship, he acquired a regular audience for his views as professor of history and political economy at the new East India Company's college at Haileybury. Those who were going to govern India's teeming millions might be expected to listen attentively to 'Pop' Malthus. His lectures led him to consider the theory of rent: he published his conclusions in two pamphlets and the tract *The Nature and Progress of Rent* (1815). Ricardo largely accepted his doctrine and it proved less controversial than his theories about population. These were attacked on grounds of common sense and humanity by men of such different views as Cobbett and Coleridge. Godwin damaged the statistical case (with the assistance of Booth, a respected mathematician) by demonstrating (in *Population*, 1820) that the growth of population in America, the main source of Malthus' evidence, was largely due to immigration, while in a settled country, such as Sweden, the population had but doubled in a century — and there the standard of living had risen as well.

Malthus, though 'one of the serenest and most cheerful' of men, as his friend Harriet Martineau wrote, and acutely sensitive to the abuse which his doctrines provoked, was beyond doubt more dogmatic and 'feelosophical' (to borrow Cobbett's word) than the facts warranted. He did not allow for the effects of industrialization, the exploitation of the waste and underdeveloped areas, or the effect of education and the acquisition of property in cultivating a sense of personal responsibility. There was also something grimly patronizing about his advice to the poor. But it was scarcely inhumane. Cottage budgets of the time showed that every succeeding child after the third plunged the family into deeper distress. Malthus could argue that his was a more constructive contribution to the problem of the poor than soup or blankets from the manor house. Maynard Keynes once pointed out that the world would have been wiser and richer if it had taken its economics from Malthus rather than from Ricardo. Francis Place stressed the urgency of the matter: 'All were opposed to the Malthusian doctrine ... All disregarded the fact that the people had increased and were increasing and over-running the means of subsistence.' Country tombstones tell the tale of nature's means of birth-control in Malthus' time. Today once more the debate which Malthus initiated is relevant and alive.

Ed. A. Flew, *T. R. Malthus, An Essay on the Principle of Population* and *A Summary View of the Principle of Population*, 1970.
Patricia James, *Population Malthus: His Life and Times*, 1979.

**DAVID RICARDO** (1772-1823) was a leading authority on economic questions in the generation after Adam Smith. He was a man of versatile ability. Though rightly famous for his masterly work, *Principles of Political Economy and Taxation* (1817), it is perhaps unfair to see him only as the principal propounder of the classical political economy whose laws and logic were treated with such exaggerated respect by his followers and adopted so keenly by manufacturers. Ricardo was primarily an analyst and it was unlucky for his reputation that he was treated as a prophet.

He was the third son of a large family. His father was a Dutch Jew who had come as a young man to England and made money on the stock exchange; he was reputed an able and honest man. David's education was largely practical; from the age of fourteen he was employed in his father's business. He married Priscilla Wilkinson when he was just twenty-one and he upset his father by giving up his Jewish faith. He made a lot of money on the Stock Exchange at a time when war finance offered great opportunities to an alert speculator. All the same he earned a name for probity and also found time for other interests. He fitted up a laboratory, made a collection of minerals and was an original member of the Geological Society (1807).

In 1799, while staying at Bath with his ailing wife, he first encountered *The Wealth of Nations* and became interested in Smith's scientific treatment of economic questions. The depreciation of the currency was causing alarm in 1809 when Ricardo wrote some letters on the subject for James Perry, editor of *The Morning Chronicle*. They were later gathered into a pamphlet. The analysis and proposals of the bullion committee (1810) followed Ricardo closely. It recommended the resumption of cash payments in two years to correct a depreciation which was the result, in the committee's view, of excessive issue by the Bank of England. In the subsequent debate Ricardo added to his reputation. Malthus was among his admirers, though the two men differed on the question of agricultural protection. Malthus wanted some degree of protection, while Ricardo argued that this was inconsistent with the theory of rent which Malthus had himself propounded (it is more usually named after Ricardo). In 1819, after he had become the representative of the twelve voters of the Irish borough of Portarlington, he rose, after being 'loudly called upon from all sides of the house', to support Peel's measure for the resumption of cash payments.

Ricardo was a reluctant speaker, 'frightened by the sound of his own voice', as he confided to McCulloch. He was also but an indifferent writer. His *Principles of Political Economy and Taxation* was influential mainly because of the simple force of his main arguments and the fervent advocacy of his cleverest disciples, James Mill and McCulloch. He was listened to as an oracle by radicals and utilitarians, with whom he usually agreed upon such matters as parliamentary reform and free trade. Politicians were slowly being educated in the principles of the new 'science'. Cobbett was not among them. Of 'the change-alley people' and their influence he wrote: 'Faith! They are now become *everything*. Baring assists at the Congress of Sovereigns and Ricardo regulates things at home'. Ricardo's whole outlook was generously liberal: he voted against the Six Acts, the Foreign Enlistment and Alien Acts, and he denounced religious prosecution, notably that of Carlile. He was naturally, however, most cogent in economic questions. He supported a scheme for enabling the poor to buy annuities, opposed every kind of subsidy and tariff, and voted for every reduction in taxation. He grew bolder with age. He convinced himself, if not others, that it would be possible to pay off the national debt, in a year, by an assessment on all the property of every county.

Maria Edgeworth gives a pleasant account of Ricardo at home among his family at Gatcombe: he was ever starting new topics of conversation and arguing urbanely for the fun of it. He enjoyed charades and long walks. Letters describing a family tour to the Continent in 1822, to visit some of his Dutch relations and to meet fellow economists, were later privately printed. There was no hint in the strenuous programme of that year of his sudden collapse in health in 1823. He was widely mourned. James Mill displayed what Mrs Grote called an unexpected tenderness of feeling. McCulloch, subsequently his biographer, said that Ricardo had supported nearly every London charity, as well as an alms-house and two schools in Gatcombe. A traditionalist like Lord Grenville could praise him: 'Radical as he was, I consider Ricardo's death as a great loss both to the country and to government.'

The 'iron law of wages' was supposed to be derived from his principles, though it is likely that for Ricardo the law was no more than a postulate for logical purposes of argument. He was often less extreme than has been supposed: on free trade, for example, he never demanded more than 'gradual recurrence to the sound principles of an universally free trade'. What may fairly be laid to Ricardo's door is that he was too abstract. By making assumptions of a quasi-scientific sort about 'economic man', by using impersonal concepts such as 'labour', he and his disciples fostered the idea that there were certain immutable 'laws' which determined the operations of man in his capacity as producer and earner. No wonder that 'the gloomy science' came to be hated as a new weapon in the hands of the employer of labour. There is a certain rough justice in the fact that Ricardo's theory of value — that it is proportionate solely to the labour embodied — was taken up by Karl Marx, with consequences which Ricardo would, of course, have repudiated with horror!

SIR JOHN SINCLAIR (1754-1835), first baronet, was the first president of the Board of Agriculture and the author of a great survey of Scotland. Learned, versatile, energetic and public-spirited, he typifies the 'improving' spirit of the age and adds a distinctive Scottish flavour. All his life he combined real and good achievements with a humourlessness and complacency — and a love of the grandiose — which invite ridicule. Walter Scott dubbed this benefactor of his country 'Cavaleiro Jackasso'. One of his first acts on inheriting, at the age of sixteen, a great Caithness estate, was to build a mountain road across Ben Cheilt. It was to be the first of many enterprises on behalf of people who lacked the spirit or means of self-help.

Sinclair was educated at Edinburgh, Glasgow and Oxford Universities. He read for the bar and entered Parliament, first for Caithness, then for Lostwithiel. He was able to make good use of his position as an independent member at a time when Lord North needed all the votes he could muster — and secured the grant of £15,000 for famine relief in the north of Scotland. In 1785 his first wife, Sarah Maitland, died after nine years of marriage and he went on a prolonged tour of northern Europe. In 1788 he married again, to the daughter of Lord Macdonald; they had a large family. Pitt gave him a baronetcy, found him an awkward man to deal with but, in 1793, appointed him to be President of the Board of Agriculture. His *Statistical Account of Scotland* began to come out in 1790 and ran to twenty-one volumes. It was compiled from reports furnished by parish ministers and not its least interest is the picture it gives of this useful and versatile class of men. Sinclair first introduced the word 'statistical' into the language.

Large areas of Caithness were cultivated on a 'rig and rennel' (or open field) system of a primitive sort. Feudal services survived, including 'thirlage' (thraldom). Sinclair encouraged the rotation of crops and sowing of rye-grass and clover. He introduced the Cheviot sheep which were to come to the aid of the landowner in many parts of the Highlands, with consequences which have been seen as unmitigated tragedy, or as a sad, but inevitable and even healthy change. For Sinclair sheep were only part of a larger scheme. He planted trees, founded a herring fishery at Wick, began to rebuild Thurso and established manufactures in those towns.

In 1798 he lost his office to Lord Somerville, who was put forward by Pitt after Sinclair, as the story goes, had suggested that the president would be a peer! There was much criticism of the way he had handled the county reports in England. But he returned in 1806 and remained president until 1813. By then he had accepted a lucrative sinecure, and left parliament. 'Sir John Sinclair has gotten the golden fleece at last', wrote Scott. Perhaps he deserved it. He was, in one foreign observer's view, 'Britain's most indefatigable man'. One of Raeburn's portraits depicts an upstanding, noble-looking laird in the uniform of his own regiment of 'Rothesay and Caithness Fencibles'. In later life he dwelt mainly in Edinburgh, proving, to his own great satisfaction, that the pen was mightier than the sword. The *Quarterly Review* struck a fair balance. 'While we smile at his harmless egoism, we are free to acknowledge the debt of gratitude we owe him'.

**ARTHUR YOUNG** (1741-1820) was the most prolific of the eighteenth-century writers about agriculture. If not the soundest upon technical questions (where most would prefer William Marshall), he is certainly the most colourful, while as an historical source he is in a class of his own. For students of the French Revolution, for instance, his survey of the French countryside (*Travels in France and Italy, 1787-90*) provides invaluable evidence. In the course of his varied career he was pamphleteer and author, Parliamentary reporter, farmer, estate steward and Secretary to the Board of Agriculture. An unkind critic labelled him as the failed farmer who preached what he had found difficulty in practising. But his failures came when he was young. When later he inherited the family property in Suffolk he managed it successfully.

He was the son of Arthur Young, squire and rector of Bradfield in Suffolk. His mother was Anna Coussmaker. While still at school at Lavenham he began to write a history of England. Apprenticed to a counting house at King's Lynn he found time to write political pamphlets and four novels. In 1759 his father died, heavily indebted; Young gave up the idea of a business career and went to London, where he started a monthly magazine, *The Universal Museum*, whose reception was as depressing as its title. Young retired to the country and began working a small farm on the Bradfield estate, now his mother's. In 1765 he married Martha Allen. She bore him several children but he complained of her temper. Justifiably or not he was a neglectful husband. On the odd, cold memorial tablet he set up after her death in 1815 he simply records that she was 'the great grand-daughter of John Allen esq., of Lyng house in the county of Norfolk, the first person, according to the Comte de Boulainvilliers, who there used marl'.

In 1767 Young wrote the *Farmer's Letters to the People*, a premature effort as he later recognized. At the same time he was experiencing the practical difficulties of farming. He took 'a very fine farm' of three hundred acres in Essex, experimented, lost money, and paid £100 to a farmer to take it over. Setting out to view other farms he collected observations for *A Six Weeks Tour through the Southern Counties of England and Wales*. For nine years he farmed a hundred acres at North Mimms in Hertfordshire. 'A hungry, vitriolic gravel', he said, 'I occupied for nine years the jaw of a wolf.' From this infertile base however he sallied out on further tours (in 1770 appeared his northern *Tour*, in 1771, the eastern). He wrote pamphlets as diverse as *The State of the French Nation* and *The Management of Hogs*. 'No cart horse', he declared, 'ever laboured as I did at this period [1770], spending like an idiot, always in debt, in spite of what I earned with the sweat of my brow ...'. In 1772 he thought of emigrating — but instead he undertook the reporting of Parliamentary debates for the *Morning Post*, walking home seventeen miles to North Mimms every Saturday and back on Monday morning. In 1774 came *Political Arithmetic*, an immediate success, and election to the Royal Society.

In 1776 he went to Ireland; a servant stole his trunk on the way back and his journal and soil specimens were lost. He was for a time (1777-9) an agent in County Cork for Lord Kingsborough's estates. He returned to take another farm. In 1784 he began his *Annals of Agriculture*, a monthly publication which was to last till 1809 and provide a forum for progressive views and news of experiments. Among his contributors were George III (under the name of his shepherd Ralph Robinson), Bentham and Coke of Holkham. From Bradfield, which he had inherited in 1785 on his mother's death, he visited Bakewell, the great breeder of Leicestershire. He had already been influential in securing the abolition of the bounty on land carriage of corn to Dublin. Now Pitt consulted Young on further measures. In 1787 he accompanied the comte de la Rochefoucauld on a journey across France; he had been introduced by the count's tutor who had 'given some attention to agriculture' and sought out the now famous writer. Out of this journey and those which followed came the celebrated *Travels*. After travelling for a hundred miles on his second journey his mare fell blind; but he finished his journey and brought her safely back to Bradfield — with, amongst other things, some chicory seed which he sowed successfully. In 1789 he took a post-chaise to bring back interesting soils and manufactures and extended his travels to Italy. He was an eye witness at Paris and Versailles of some of the first scenes of the Revolution. An illness, in 1790, brought him near to death. With recovery came sober reflection and a somewhat introverted account of his past life in the *Annals*. Young took himself very seriously.

In 1793 Pitt made him Secretary of the new Board of Agriculture. He was soon at loggerheads with the President, Sinclair, criticizing him for an amateurish approach and inept appointments. Of the important series of reports on counties Young wrote the *General View of the Agriculture of the County of Suffolk*; his son Arthur did the same for Sussex. He continued to be active in pamphlet writing. Pitt was pleased by their patriotic tone (Young proposed a 'horse militia corps' as early as 1789; in 1793 he enrolled in the yeomanry at Bury) but rejected his plan for 'regulation by parliament of the price of labour'.

In 1791 Young's youngest daughter, Martha Ann, or 'Bobbin' as he called her, died, aged fourteen. He seems to have been quite broken by the tragedy. Something of his sadness can be imagined when we read their letters — for he wrote to her the most detailed accounts of his French travels when she was only six! — and from his instructions for her burial, 'in my pew, fixing the coffin so that when I kneel it will be between her head and her dear heart'. The pessimistic strains, the over-wrought moods now grew into a settled despondency. For the last years of his life he was blind. In 1811 he was operated on for cataract. Wilberforce visited him and spoke so movingly of the loss sustained to agriculture by the death of the duke of Grafton that Young wept; the last chance of saving his eyesight was therefore lost.

With his enthusiasm for improvements of all kind, his somewhat haphazard method of working and his reliance upon personal contacts with farmers and landowners rather than upon analytical or statistical approach, Young lays himself open to the charge of inconsistency. He took advanced positions upon such topics as leases, tithes and open fields which he was later forced to modify. In particular he came to revise his early opinion concerning enclosures, though it was of the methods rather than the principle that he disapproved. He was dismayed by the actual deterioration of labourers' conditions in some enclosed villages. He was confronted of course with a trend outside the control of legislators — a soaring population. But he was sensibly constructive in his proposals. He believed that the cheapest way of providing for the poor would be to put labouring families on the areas of waste that still remained uncultivated on the fringe of enclosed villages, with a cottage and three acres apiece. Property, he held, gave the poor the incentive to work hard, live frugally and save, not only their own pride, but the parish rates as well. In some counties there was no wasteland. That fact inspired a justly famous passage: 'Go to an alehouse kitchen of an old-enclosed country, and there you will see the origin of poverty and the poor rates. For whom are they to be sober? For whom are they to save? For the parish? If I am diligent shall I have leave to build a cottage? If I am sober, shall I have land to buy a cow? If I am frugal, shall I have half an acre of potatoes? You offer no motives, you have nothing but a parish officer and a workhouse. Bring me another pot.' Young did not of course lose his faith in the efficacy of enclosures. The following passage from his *General View of Oxfordshire* (1809) is eloquent with the scorn of the improver for the 'goths and vandals of farmers' who would not change their ways: 'liberal communication, the result of enlarged ideas', such as he might expect from the modern farmer, 'was contrasted with a dark ignorance under the covert of wise suspicion; a sullen reserve lest landlords should be rendered too knowing ... The old openfield school must die off before new ideas can become generally rooted.'

G. E. Mingay, *Arthur Young and his Times*, 1978.
Ed. Matilda Betham-Edwards, *The Autobiography of Arthur Young*, 1898.

**THOMAS WILLIAM COKE, 1st EARL OF LEICESTER** (1752-1842), was famed beyond his native Norfolk for good farming and benevolent landownership. In the pine-fringed estate of Holkham, set amongst solid farm buildings of the period, the great house of the Cokes is a perfect survival of the eighteenth century style. Between the elegance of his father's building and the homely virtues of 'Coke of Holkham' lies a contrast that is of the essence of the period. The fields that now look so trim were sandy, if not waste, when Coke inherited the estate. 'All you will see will be one blade of grass and two rabbits fighting for that'. No more than his precursor, 'Turnip' Townshend of Raynham, was Coke entirely original in his methods. Marling to enrich light soils, the local four-course rotation of wheat, turnips, barley and clover, and long leases were all established before him. Coke, who derived cultural interests from Eton and a long stay in Rome, was also a Member of Parliament for more than fifty years, an ardent Whig at first, a steady protectionist later, but always in favour of franchise reform; however he spent his energy and capital on improvements to his estate.

He began typically with a meeting of local farmers to get advice and co-operation. Some were slow to change their ways; even the Holkham villagers looked askance at the potato. Undeterred, he improved the content of his leases, was instrumental in improving the breeds of Southdown sheep and Devon cattle, encouraged irrigation and planted screens of conifers as breaks against the winds off the North Sea. He visited Leicestershire to study Bakewell's methods and attracted thousands of visitors from home and abroad, with a hundred house guests at a time, to his 'sheep-shearings': they were really private agricultural shows.

He came to be much loved by his tenants as they shared in his prosperity. Though stern in the protection of game he was in a minority of landowners in supporting Lord Suffield's bill to end the lethal use of spring guns against poachers. La Rochefoucauld, visiting Holkham, concluded that 'farming is regarded as an honourable estate because the highest in the land engage in it.' If there had been a revolution in England we may be sure that Holkham would not have been looted by a resentful peasantry; that there was no revolution was in part due to the sound and responsible character of such men as Coke. In 1837, after he had been for some years 'father of the house', he was raised to the peerage with the extinct title of Leicester.

J. D. Chambers and G. E. Mingay, *The Agricultural Revolution, 1750-1880*, 1966.

**JAMES MILL** (1773-1836), Indian administrator and economist, was the son of a shoemaker, near Montrose. He studied for the Presbyterian ministry at Edinburgh and was licensed to preach in 1798, but in 1802 he came to London to earn his living by his pen. He soon lost his interest in theology and took up a sceptical position. His acute and practical mind found in Bentham a stimulating tutor and in India a great subject.

After editing and writing for various periodicals, in 1806 Mill began work on his great *History of British India* (published in 1817). His aim was to give India 'a good system of judicial procedure' on Benthamite lines. As Bentham said, 'Mill will be the living executive — I shall be the dead legislative of British India'. His huge volumes are a remarkable essay in scientific history but they suffer from serious defects. Typically Mill argued that his never having been to India was an advantage: while the historian must understand 'the laws of human nature' in abstract and must study the principles of human society and 'the machinery of government', he must also eschew the detailed and picturesque. His approach was explicitly western, insensitive to the differences between one Indian and another, the subtleties of caste and the tensions that arose from the conflict of races. The book has become a memorial to the strengths and weaknesses of the 'utilitarians'. Macaulay called it the greatest historical work since Gibbon but Maine said that its inaccuracy was equalled only by its bad faith. Mill's 'emphatically polemical' intellect (his son's words) may have been less suited to history than to the political and social analysis in which he excelled. He was writing, primarily for a British readership, a critique of current attitudes towards colonies — a source of patronage and power for ruling *élites*, producing bad government.

In 1819 Mill, radical though he was known to be, was made assistant examiner by the Directors of the East India Company; in 1832 he became chief of the examiner's office: effectively he controlled all departments of Indian administration. He continued to study and write. In 1821 he published *Elements of Political Economy*. The greatest of Bentham's disciples, Mill showed in this work, and in his *Essay on Government* (ed. Barker, 1937), that he had his own great contribution to make. 'Philosophic Radicalism' was only for the few. Indeed, as Coleridge said, 'to the immense majority of men, even in civilized countries, speculative philosophy has ever been, and must remain, a *terra incognita*: the minds that govern and influence society are always few.' Some of the few were captured. 'There is now nothing definite in politics except Radicalism', wrote Mill's son John Stuart to Thomas Carlyle, in May 1832. Radicals were to find the aftermath of the Reform Bill disappointing; it was rather as a third force than a third party that they were to be effective. Turning to what John Stuart Mill called 'the root of the evil' they tackled education, colonies, the problems of poverty and of public health.

There was a fearless quality about James Mill. In his notorious 1824 essay on Colonies for the *Encyclopaedia Britannica* (where many of his most important articles appeared), he hinted broadly at the desirability of birth-control — at a time when the subject was taboo. He advocated independence for Canada and the West Indies at a time when liberals could look no further than free trade. He was nothing if not public-spirited, and took a leading part in founding University College, London. He idealized his son and trained him to be a paragon. Under the sole tutelage of his father, the boy began Greek at three! He 'never was a boy'. At twenty he had a nervous breakdown. Of this we read in his autobiography: it presents a revealing portrait of his father. We learn of the hours spent on the teaching of his children, his fanatical insistence upon a life of ordered usefulness, his truly Scottish delight in struggle, and praise of men who overcame adversity.

Every walk was an opportunity for catechism on the day's learning, every book contained a moral or political economic message — and through all ran the insistence upon logical analysis. He carefully shielded his son from contact with other boys — 'the contagion of vulgar modes of thought and feeling'. Decisive, overbearing, confident, he sought to reproduce his character and philosophy in that of his son.

John Stuart Mill recovered. He achieved greatness. His *Essay on Liberty* is better perhaps than anything his father wrote. It represents a triumph of the human spirit and intelligence over an oppressive training. His proud tribute to his father deserves also to be remembered. 'During his later years he was quite as much the head and leader of the intellectual radicals in England as Voltaire was of the *philosophes* of France.'

Alexander Bain, *James Mill*, 1882.
E. Halévy (translated by M. Morris), *The Growth of Philosophic Radicalism*, 1928.

JOSEPH HUME (1777-1855) was one of the leading radicals in Parliament before and after the Reform Bill. His zeal for reform sprang from wide experience and generous sympathies. He was often dogmatic in particular cases; but it would be wrong to call him doctrinaire. He was the youngest son of a Scottish lady, early widowed by the loss of her seaman husband and forced to turn shopkeeper to educate her children. Joseph repaid her care by his hard work. At twelve he was apprenticed to a surgeon-apothecary, at twenty admitted a member of the College of Surgeons in Edinburgh.

His first post was as a surgeon with the East India Company. Always keen to improve his position, he learned to speak the native language. He made himself useful to the military authorities when he solved the problem of drying gunpowder. Rich patrons and a variety of work, administrative as well as medical, provided him with a solid fortune, upwards of £30,000, sufficient to provide the basis of a political career. After his return to England in 1808, notwithstanding the Napoleonic War, he spent some time in foreign travel, mainly in Spain and the Mediterranean. He entered Parliament as a Tory for Weymouth in 1812 but in the following year he was defeated. When he returned to Parliament (for Aberdeen in 1818) he was a radical. In 1830 he changed his constituency and was returned for Middlesex: he represented the electors of that county of small-holders for seven years before being narrowly defeated in 1837. He was thereafter briefly member for Kilkenny; then he sat for Montrose from 1842 until his death in 1855.

Hume was a tireless, radical critic of established institutions and a constructive political reformer in many fields. Many pages of Hansard record his long and cogent speeches. Not the least important speech of his career was delivered to a Mr Burnley of Guildford, a share-holder of the East India Company, when Hume was canvassing for his own election to the council of the East India Company. Miss Burnley, too, listened to the reformer's persuasive speech: at the end her father gave Hume his votes — and her hand in marriage.

India was a central interest, as might be expected from his experience of life there and his friendship with his fellow-Scotsman and historian of India, James Mill. Another was political reform: he played an important part in the passing of the Great Reform Bill. Some idea of the range of his interests can be gathered from a list of his more celebrated causes. He campaigned for the abolition of flogging in the army, of the naval press-gang and of imprisonment for debt. He assisted Place in securing the repeal of the Combination Laws by manoeuvres which showed to advantage his knowledge of parliamentary tactics. Successful packing of the committee set up to consider the question was followed by an act, in 1824, which passed quietly in a thin house.

He helped towards the repeal of the acts prohibiting the export of machinery abroad and preventing workmen from going abroad. Colonial and local misgovernment alike attracted his critical attention. Election expenses and fiscal duties were among his targets. He was naturally among those who wanted the emancipation of Catholics and the reform of Parliament. He denounced the plan of the Orange orders to make the Duke of Cumberland king on the death of William IV — but it was not only radicals who were appalled at that prospect. His efforts made him both noted and popular. A parliamentarian recorded in 1821, 'During the last Session, a committee of about six Members sat constantly to obtain all the financial information they could.

Hume, one of them, used the fruits of their labours in opposing the extravagance of Ministers.'

The field was indeed wide; for a 'lynx-eyed Radical expert' (Maccoby) the opportunities for parliamentary skirmishing were enormous. Sometimes his views were short-sighted, as notably with regard to India and Canada where, like Mill, he could not see the imperial wood for the offending trees of patronage. But his rôle as radical *franc-tireur* was an invaluable one. He contributed to lively debates and prodded ministerial lethargy. As the *Morning Chronicle* said of him when he died: 'He was the unrelenting persecutor of sinecurists, drones, and old men pretending to do the work of the young in the state.'

Valerie Chancellor, *The Political Life of Joseph Hume, 1777-1855*, 1987.


THOMAS SPENCE (1750-1814) has been variously described as a forerunner of Communism, the Babeuf of England, or as a crank, a harmless and peripheral figure in the radicalism of his time. Babeuf plotted in 1796 the overthrow of the existing régime in France and the creation of a new society with community of property and absolute equality among citizens. The outlines of the conspiracy were revealed to English readers of the *New Annual Register* in 1796. Thomas Spence, an impoverished schoolmaster from Newcastle upon Tyne, had come to London in 1792. He was at once arrested for selling Paine's *Rights of Man*, but acquitted. He made a meagre living by publishing and selling tracts from a series of shops and, in the end, from a barrow. With his tracts he might sell saloop (a popular coffee-like drink made from medicinal bark) and, for a time, political token dies of half-penny and farthing size. Place gives us a delightful description of this resourceful man: 'Not more than five foot high, very honest, simple, single-minded, who loved mankind, and firmly believed that a time would come when men would be virtuous, wise and happy. He was unpractical in the ways of the world to an extent hardly imaginable.' He invented a phonetic alphabet and used it for an account of his own trial in 1801. But with his hand-bills and slogans — SPENCE'S SYSTEM was a familiar message on London walls — and his periodical *Pig's Meat* (1793-6), he did not appear to ministers to be as 'harmless and simple' as he did to Place. He was imprisoned for the second half of 1794 under the suspension of Habeas Corpus and again in 1801, after trial for writing seditious publications. Ministers saw him as one of the 'hidden hands' behind the popular agitations. What was his true rôle?

He seems to have developed his own distinctive theories of land nationalization as a young man at Newcastle. He regarded land-lords as beneficiaries of the conquerors and robbers of the past. He urged social revolution. Parish by parish, the ownership of land must be resumed into the hands of the inhabitants. A quot-ation from his *Restorer of Society to its Natural State* (1800) goes far to explain why a wartime government was concerned about the activities of Spence and his friends of the Cock and the Mulberry Tree. 'The public mind being suitably prepared by reading my little Tracts and conversing on the subject, a few Contingent Parishes have only to declare the land to be theirs and form a convention of Parochial Delegates. Other adjacent Parishes would immediately on being invited follow the example and send also their Delegates and thus would a beautiful and powerful New Republic instantaneously arise in full vigour.' Not only in the countryside, but also in the teeming back-streets of London there was distress enough to commend desperate meas-ures. Spence had no large following. But he and his Spenceans provoked and sustained discontent with their chalk and charcoal. They agreed to organize themselves as loosely as possible, with 'field preachers', which made it hard for the government to detect them.

Spence's death was not the end of his ideas. He was buried with ceremony by 'a numerous throng of political admirers' according to a contemporary newspaper. 'Appropriate medallions were distributed, and a pair of scales preceded his body, indicative of the justice of his views ... Upon Mr Spence's principles, a sect was founded called the "Spenceans"'. After the Watsons, Thistlewood and their group had tried to turn Hunt's Spa Fields meeting into a rising of London, the Spenceans were given official recognition. One of the 'Gag Acts' of 1817 suppressed 'all societies or clubs calling themselves Spenceans or Spencean Philanthropists'. But when Thistlewood and his gang planned to assassinate the cabi-net (1819) we may be sure that they went beyond what the master would have approved. This was not how the millennium would come about, the Spencean dream:

'No more distress, all happiness,
From landlords once set free,
The bells shall ring, we'll dance and sing
On Spence's jubilee'.

Ed. Arthur W. Waters, *Spence and his Political Works*, 1917.
D. Rudkin, *Thomas Spence and his Connections*, 1927.

**ARTHUR THISTLEWOOD** (1770-1820) was a prime mover in a plot to murder the entire cabinet. His origins are obscure. He is said to have been the illegitimate son of a Lincolnshire farmer. He had some pretensions to be a gentleman and in 1798 he was commissioned an ensign in the Militia. He had certainly visited America and France and, by one account, served with the French army. Jacobin ideas provide some clues to his career. From about 1797 it is evident that there was an element in the political underworld of London that put its hope in a violent coup which would rouse the mob to effective action. The government took the threat seriously enough to watch suspects, penetrate tavern meetings with their spies, and arrest on mere suspicion. In 1799 most of the leaders of this school of extremists were in gaol. One of them, Despard, was to die on the scaffold in 1803 after being found guilty of high treason. After the death of his wife Thistlewood drifted from Lincoln to London and joined the Spencean Society. Among the Spenceans were men like Dr. Watson and John Gale Jones, big men in the smoky, secret world of the London alehouses, where the talk was not only of principles but of revolutionary tactics.

In December 1816 a small Spencean committee including Watson and his crazy son, Preston, Hooper, Thistlewood — and Castle, the spy — called for a demonstration in Spa Fields. There had been a meeting the month before at which Henry Hunt had spoken, and secured signatures for a petition. He had not been allowed to present it to the Prince Regent and the second meeting was called ostensibly to protest against the government's attitude. But when Hunt arrived he found, in the wagon in the middle of the crowd, Dr. Watson and Thistlewood. Young Watson, London's Camille Desmoulins, called for a march, behind the tricolour flag, to the Tower! One man, Preston or Thistlewood, managed to climb on to a wall of the Tower and summon the guard to surrender 'the Bastille'. With arms from a gunsmith's shop and some boisterous sailors at large, the mob could have been dangerous — but order was restored by nightfall. The physical force school, 'five fanatics hounded on by a spy', had made themselves ridiculous. Most of the crowd had stayed to hear Hunt. The government decided to proceed with a charge of treason against Thistlewood and his associates. Was treason the right charge? The sinister and farcical elements are equally balanced.

Moderate reformers were frightened away from the popular radical movement. Ministers meanwhile looked for another pretext to act against the reformers. As Cobbett saw it: 'They sigh for a PLOT ... they are absolutely pining and dying for a plot!' Thistlewood and his friends had already given them an excuse to discredit the popular movement. In 1819, they gave them their plot.

Thistlewood had been acquitted at his first trial, amidst general merriment. To such a man as Thistlewood, anguished by poverty, unstable and deluded, ridicule was hard to bear. In February 1818 he was imprisoned without trial for disturbing the peace: he had demanded 'satisfaction' from the Home Secretary. To keep him out of the way Sidmouth thought it worth paying his maintenance out of his own pocket! He came out after a year and joined Watson, Preston and Jones in the London 'Committee of Two Hundred'. Thistlewood and Hunt wrangled bitterly about tactics. Hunt feared with reason that Thistlewood's underground communications links were designed to provoke and control an open insurrection while Thistlewood believed that the radical leaders were throwing away the advantage afforded them by Peterloo. In the shoemakers' union there existed a revolutionary cell: the majority of his fellow-conspirators were of this trade, radical by long tradition. Whatever his motives, whatever the nature of his support, his plan was a desperate one. It was suggested, as Thistlewood later alleged, by Edwards, brother to a former secretary of the Spenceans, who had first wanted to blow up the House of Commons. 'Edwards was ever at invention; and at length he proposed attacking them at a cabinet-dinner.' Meetings were held in the loft at Cato Street. James Hugo, a butcher, planned a dramatic entrance: 'My Lords, I have got as good men here as the Manchester yeomanry — Enter, citizens, and do your duty.' The heads of Castlereagh and Sidmouth were to be placed on pikes and a provisional government was to be proclaimed.

The cabinet dinner, announced by advertisement, was a hoax. Edwards, the spy, saw to it that the government knew all the details of the conspiracy he had helped to foment. The conspirators were seized, Thistlewood only after a struggle in which he killed a Bow Street runner. They were tried in April: five were sentenced to transportation, five to death. On the scaffold Thistlewood declared in his broad Lincolnshire vowels: 'I desire all here to remember, that I die in the cause of liberty'.

John Stanhope, *Cato Street Conspiracy*, 1962.

**THOMAS WOOLER** (1786-1853) was a Yorkshire-born printer who had served his apprenticeship in Shoreditch and learned about politics in the small debating societies which met at the Mermaid, Hackney. In 1808 he became printer and editor of *The Reasoner*. In 1815 he founded *The Stage*, in which rather laboured satire and high-flying rhetoric anticipated the style of *The Black Dwarf*. This latter paper, published each Sunday morning in Sun Street, Finsbury, commanded for a time the largest radical audience after the *Political Register*. The post-war years were the heyday of radical journalism, a time when Lord Eldon could speak of 'wagons filled with seditious papers in order to be distributed through every village, to be scattered over the highways, to be introduced into cottages', when there was 'scarcely a village in the kingdom that had not its little shop in which nothing was sold but blasphemy and sedition'.

From its foundation in 1817 until its demise in 1824 *The Black Dwarf* was influential; during Cobbett's absence in America it led the field. Sherwin's *Register* and Wade's *Gorgon* were perhaps the *Dwarf*'s closest rivals. Wade's fortnightly *Black Book* was deadly in its documentation of sinecures, nepotism and corruption in church and state. The *Black Dwarf* excelled in vivid presentation of radical themes. Wooler used to set up his articles in type direct, without manuscript. His style was grandiloquent. He believed in organization upon the open and constitutionalist pattern. 'Let us look at and emulate the patient resolution of the Quakers. They have conquered *without arms* — without *violence* — without threats. They conquered by union.' He was also ready to go further, if constitutional means should fail. 'The *right* of the people to resist *oppression always exists*, and ... the *requisite power* to do this always resides in the *general will* of the people.'

In June 1817 Wooler was put on trial before Mr Justice Abbot and a special jury, for some passages in an April issue in which he had denounced ministers for 'infamous duplicity and dreadful treachery' (they had suspended the Habeas Corpus Act) and for sacrificing 'that constitution which France had never thought of assailing'. Wooler undertook his own defence and 'won the applause of a great part of the audience, which the sheriffs found it difficult to repress' (*Annual Register*). A verdict of 'guilty' was recorded. During his subsequent trial on a second charge, that of having derided the right of petitioning, it was revealed that three of the jurors had dissented from the original verdict. The second trial ended with a verdict of 'Not Guilty'. The Crown had hoped to muzzle *The Black Dwarf* before it gained too strong a hold. They would have been wiser to accept Wooler's contention that the finding of the first jury constituted an acquittal. They presented him with valuable advertisement for his journal and his cause. And they had exposed themselves to a further attack upon the way in which London special juries were named. After Wooler, the pamphlet-publisher Hone was tried on three counts and found 'Not Guilty'.

In 1819 Wooler took part in the election of Sir Charles Wolseley to be 'legislatory attorney' for Birmingham — and, like Wolseley, he was imprisoned for eighteen months, in Warwick gaol. Searching for other means of employment he had sought to become a barrister, but the Benchers of Lincoln's Inn refused to take him as a student. So he became a prisoner's advocate at the police courts, being employed in this capacity by the well-known Old Bailey lawyer, Samuel Harmer. After the Reform Act of 1832 he declared that he was finished with politics for 'these damned Whigs have taken all the sedition out of my hands'. He had contributed to their success. He has an important place in the long struggle for the freedom of the press.

W. D. Wickwar, *The Struggle for the Freedom of the Press*, 1928.

**RICHARD CARLILE** (1790-1843) was the son of a Devonshire shoe-maker, who became the leading personality in the fight for the freedom of the press in the early years of the nineteenth century. He had but a year or so of grammar school education at Ashburton in Devonshire and he was largely self-taught. He worked in turn as a chemist's shop-boy in Exeter and a journeyman tinsmith before settling in London in 1813 as a mechanic. He wrote of his youth: 'I was a regular, active and industrious man, working early and late ... and when out of the workshop was never so happy anywhere as at home with my wife and two children.' Often he missed meals and 'carried home some sixpenny publication to read at night'. So it was that he encountered the works of Tom Paine, at a time when he had lost his livelihood in the post-war depression and was trying to make a living as a newsvendor.

Paine's *Rights of Man* had been a textbook for extreme radicals of his time. Because he was logical and eloquent in a superficial way, he was an effective propagandist: how effective can be seen in the discipleship of men like Carlile. Writing of himself, as he was in 1817, when about to set up as publisher, Carlile described how he had read the *Age of Reason* in that year, 'found the validity of the Christian religion fairly investigated, and felt himself honestly and conscientiously impelled to support the negative side of the question'. In 1818, having published Sherwin's *Political Register* and written some irreverent parodies, Carlile announced the re-publication of the *Age of Reason* as Paine's *Theological Works*. It was expected that the government would indict; sales were brisk. A new periodical, *The Deist*, followed — and the government was forced to act. Two months after Peterloo (1819), Carlile's trial began. He failed to repeat the successes of Wooler and Hone, and was sentenced to three years' imprisonment and a £1,500 fine; and because he could not pay his fines he remained in Dorchester gaol for nearly six years, until ministers found that his case had become a notorious scandal. But Carlile was not silenced. With the aid of his wife, sister, shopboys and volunteers who came from all over the country to help him, he kept open the 'Temple of Reason' and secured the continued publication of the *Republican*. 'THE SHOP WILL NOT BE CLOSED AS A MATTER OF COURSE'.

The result of the government's persecution and Carlile's defiance was that he became the hero of the anti-clericals. In these years of debates about the rôle of church and dissent in

education, and of the *Extraordinary Black Book*, which revealed
the vast and ill-distributed wealth of the Church, secular movements took fire 'like whins on a common' (Thompson). There
were large and enthusiastic audiences for Carlile's meetings. In
1830 he founded the Rotunda and published its proceedings in his
*Prompter*. Weekly religious debates were sustained for a time by
the exciting diatribes of Jones, the veteran Jacobin, Taylor, the
evangelist of atheism who preached in full canonicals, and Zion
Ward, interpreter of the revelations of Joanna Southcott.

Carlile was imprisoned again in 1831 for refusing to pay church
rates. He maintained the fight to the end, and was not finally
released until 1835. By then he had become almost irrelevant to
the radical cause. Narrow, egotistical, cross-grained, Carlile went
on fighting the battles of the past. He could not adjust his ideas to
social changes. He loved to shock, as when he dated the *Republican* 'In the year 1822 of the Carpenter's wife's son', but he dealt
too much in generalities to be effective as a teacher. His importance had been that of personal example. He had provided a
dramatic illustration of the importance of free speech.

E. P. Thompson, *The Making of the English Working Class*, 1963.

HENRY HUNT (1773-1835) was the greatest demagogue of
the reform movement. He came of a prosperous farming family
of Upavon, Wiltshire. A man of exceptional physique, made to
attract attention, Hunt was a strong boxer, a good shot and a
dashing rider to hounds. He was naturally aggressive and boastful. He was fined and imprisoned for challenging a yeomanry
colonel in 1800, and, ten years later, for assaulting a gamekeeper.

He was at first a prominent loyalist in his county and raised a
troop of militia. In 1806, however, Cobbett printed *Hunt's
Address to the Independent Freeholders of Wiltshire* in the *Political Register*. He had joined the radical front. He contested Bristol
in 1806, Westminster in 1818 and Somerset in 1826 before becoming at last member for Preston in 1830 (one of the few constituencies which, having enjoyed a popular franchise, actually lost
voters by the Reform Act of 1832). The frustrations of the masses
and the lack of a mature political organization favoured the cult
of personality. His bell-like voice carried for great distances, an
important asset in those days for politicians and evangelists. He

brought to the cause of reform bravado which made him the scourge of ministers and the idol of the crowd. In 1802 he went to live with a Mrs Vince, a friend's wife, at Brighton, choosing that place, he said, because the Prince Regent and Mrs Fitzherbert were openly living there in sin! He subsequently secured a legal separation from his wife and lived faithfully with Mrs Vince. 'Beware of him', said Cobbett (but before he met him), 'he rides the country with a whore.' He was a handsome man and something of a dandy, proud of his size and 'the neatest and firmest of legs'. His famous white top hat was to become a symbol of the purity of his cause.

Hunt was principal speaker in the Spa Fields meetings of 1816. More spectacular and more serious was the Manchester meeting of 16 August 1819, when 60,000 people assembled in St. Peter's Fields to hear Hunt address them upon parliamentary reform. At the Manchester Radical Sunday School the monitors wore locket-portraits of 'Orator' Hunt around their necks. The meeting in St. Peter's Fields was to have been a triumphant rally of the radicals of Lancashire, a peaceful demonstration. Because of the clumsy and panicky handling of the Manchester yeomanry, the day ended in bloody disaster. Fifteen deaths and more than four hundred injured hardly constitute a 'massacre'. But the word rang through the country. Peterloo became a potent myth. Hunt had arrived, to the accompaniment of massed bands playing 'See the Conquering Hero Comes', in a barouche covered with blue and white flags and drawn along by the people; they, in Bamford's words, had sought to disarm criticism 'by a display of cleanliness, sobriety and decorum such as we had never before exhibited'. They had been ordered to bring 'no other weapon than that of an approving conscience'. Hunt probably knew better than most the risks involved in such a large gathering. To the magistrates the banners, the caps of liberty, the precise formations, had the look of an insurrection. Soon after the band had struck up 'God Save the King', the magistrates ordered his arrest. This was the cause of the yeomanry's gallop through the crowd, from whom they were 'rescued' by the hussars, striking with the flat of their sabres. Hunt was received in London more like a hero than a prisoner. Elaborate arrangements had been made for his reception. *The Times* estimated at 300,000 the crowds through which he passed. He was tried for an 'alleged conspiracy to alter the law by force and threats and for convening and attending an illegal, riotous and tumultuous meeting', found guilty with four others, and sentenced to two-and-a-half years' imprisonment (the longest sentence). 'The Champion of Liberty' became 'Saint Henry of Ilchester'.

Hunt emerged from Ilchester gaol a quieter man. He wrote memoirs there which were dedicated to radical reformers, but were largely concerned with himself: as a record of the movement they are almost worthless — and they do not commend the author. His egotistic, quarrelsome character did not mellow well. Lancashire was loyal to him but he made a poor member of parliament. No doubt he was one of Wellington's 'shocking bad hats'. It was more serious that he was incapable of political manoeuvre and compromise. He had lived too long in the exciting world of monster processions and petitions. Place said of him, 'Hunt says his mode of acting is to dash at good points and to care for no one; that he will mix with no committee, or any party; he will act by himself'. He was alone among radicals in refusing to agree to the terms of the Reform Bill. To the end he championed adult male suffrage: 'Universal suffrage — or nothing!' He also introduced the first parliamentary motion for female suffrage. He was rejected by the voters of Preston in 1833 and died two years later. He was buried in Mrs Vince's family vault.

Donald Read, *Peterloo, the Massacre and its Background*, 1958.
Joyce Marlow, *The Peterloo Massacre*, 1969.

**GEORGE LOVELESS** (1797-1874) was the leader of the group of Tolpuddle labourers who were sentenced to transportation for administering illegal oaths. Because of the publicity aroused by the case, the subsequent reprieve of the men, and the stimulus that their 'martyrdom' gave to radical movements, the Tolpuddle men have an honoured place in English social history.

Undoubtedly they were doing more than they realized when they met on 9 December 1833 for a ceremony of initiation into the 'Tolpuddle Friendly Society'. It was hoped that it would become part of a Dorset network of such societies which would eventually be incorporated into the Grand National Consolidated Trades Union — that ambitious organization whose collapse in 1834 was to be such a serious setback to the growth of trades unionism. An informer, present at the meeting, supplied details to the local magistrate. The six principals (one of whom, James Hammett, was not present at the meeting) were sent for trial at Dorchester Assizes. They were found guilty and, on 19 March 1834, sentenced to be transported 'to such places beyond the seas as His Majesty's Council, in their discretion shall see fit, for the term of seven years'. The indictment was based upon a strained interpretation of the Mutiny Act of 1797 which had been passed to cope with mutinous seamen in wartime. The government, prompted by an energetic magistrate, James Frampton, decided to use the trial as a means of checking what they regarded as a contagious spirit of village democracy. With this policy Williams, a newly appointed judge and a keen Whig, was fully in sympathy. The trial was therefore a political demonstration as much as an exercise in law.

Loveless, married, with three children, was the best educated of the group, having taught himself to read and write. Like his brother he was a Methodist. A local preacher of some renown, he had even managed to acquire a small theological library. To zealots like Frampton, to be a Methodist was to defy the proper ordering of village life under squire and parson. Loveless's record speaks for his determination and intelligence; he was a sober, earnest and purposeful man. Orator though he was, only exceptional circumstances made such a man into a militant radical. The 'Captain Swing' riots of 1830 had been a desperate movement of protest against intolerable conditions. Rising population, the effect of enclosures in grain producing districts and the introduction of new labour-saving machinery combined to bring a docile peasantry to mobbing and organized destruction. Nowhere in England were agricultural wages lower than in Dorset — or in Dorset than in the Tolpuddle district. When local farmers reduced them from nine to eight shillings, at the end of 1832, a deputation of villagers, with Loveless as spokesman, met the magistrates and farmers. They went back to work, apparently expecting some improvement. But wages were further reduced. Loveless may be believed when he said that it was 'impossible to live honestly on such scanty means'. By October 1833 he had made contact with Owen's Union. A meeting to hear officials from London was held in Tolpuddle. Since the repeal of the Combination Acts there was nothing illegal about such a proceeding, but the men needlessly exposed themselves by holding an initiation ceremony.

Below an imposing painting of Father Time, as a skeleton with a scythe in his hand, the initiates took an oath not to reveal the members or the activities of the society. It was the oath that betrayed them.

Loveless's colleagues went to Australia, he, in 1834, to the penal sub-colony of Van Diemen's land. At home the London Dorchester committee was founded to obtain redress. Thomas Wakley M.P. marshalled a campaign of petitions and pressed the new Home Secretary for a reprieve. Russell, unlike his predecessor Melbourne, was sympathetic. Eventually a free pardon was conceded (March 1836). Despite frustrating delays the men were traced. Loveless with his brother and their families, and James Brine, went to Greensted in Essex where an eighty acre farm had been bought for them by public subscription. Loveless was welcomed in Chartist circles. His pamphlet, the *Victims of Whiggery*, attacked the political establishment and exposed the cruelties of transportation and the conditions of the penal settlements. It was perhaps, however, to escape from politics and publicity that the Loveless family, with the other Tolpuddle men (except for Hammett) decided to emigrate to Canada (1844).

There Loveless farmed and prospered, and built a Methodist church. Before his death an Act of Parliament had set the British trades unions upon a sound legal footing (1871). In 1872, Joseph Arch, another Methodist, founded the National Agricultural Workers' Union. Loveless had the satisfaction of knowing that — to quote the words of his memorial in Siloam cemetery: 'The case of the Tolpuddle martyrs became a turning point in labour laws and practices in the United Kingdom.

Joyce Marlow, *The Tolpuddle Martyrs*, 1971.

**EDWARD JENNER** (1749-1823), physician, saved countless lives by his demonstration that immunity from smallpox could be obtained by vaccination with the virus of the milder cow-pox or vaccinia. The son of a Gloucestershire clergyman, apprenticed to a surgeon of Sodbury, he later studied medicine under John Hunter, who became his life-long friend and taught him that the study of medicine could be transformed by a methodical and broad scientific approach. Today, when specialization in depth and on the narrowest of fronts is leading advances in medical science, it is remarkable to think of Jenner pursuing at once the study of botany, zoology and geology. He began to practise at his native town of Berkeley in 1773 and became a Fellow of the Royal Society in 1788.

Inoculation with the virus of smallpox itself as a preventive had been pioneered by Lady Mary Wortley Montague early in the century and was not uncommon. But it was hazardous and suspect on religious as well as on clinical grounds. Jenner made a study of the incidence of cow-pox and examined the tradition that dairy-maids and others employed with cows did not take the smallpox. He experimented exhaustively with inoculations with cow-pox and then smallpox; the latter did not develop and his theory was proved. In a series of publications, culminating in 1800 with *A Complete Statement of Facts and Observations*, he stated the case for vaccination. He established an institute for the supply of cow-lymph and secured grants from Parliament in 1802 and 1806 amounting to £30,000 for the spread of the practice. Soon opposition died away and he became celebrated and admired. Seventy leading physicians signed a declaration affirming their confidence in the vaccine. In 1814 he was interviewed by the Tsar and the King of Prussia. He received many gifts from grateful people, but he made no attempt to make money from his discovery or to exploit fashionable interest. After a brief stay in London he returned to Gloucestershire and busied himself with the propagation of his treatment.

After the example set by the Scandinavian and several German states, vaccination was made compulsory in England in 1853 and the disease which had been so dreaded and dangerous became virtually extinct. The work of Louis Pasteur and others upon immunology in other diseases was directly inspired by Jenner. All who have bared their arms to the doctor's needle should bless the name of Jenner, whose statue in Gloucester Cathedral records a generous, warm-hearted and supremely useful life.

Dorothy Fisk, *Dr. Jenner of Berkeley*, 1959.

**THOMAS TELFORD** (1757-1834) was born at Glendinning in Eskdale. His father was an 'unblameable shepherd', in the phrase of his son's epitaph — and his upbringing in the little thatched cottage was simple. He received a sound education, however, at

*Thomas Telford*
(Artist: William Brockedon)

the parish school, left at fourteen and learned to be a mason. For some time he worked on the fast-growing New Town of Edinburgh; to this we may trace his admiration for the severe formality which characterized Scotland's late Georgian architecture. He also planned for himself the life of a poet; at least one of his poems, 'Eskdale', has a certain conventional charm — but he was to find another outlet for creative energy. In 1782 he took the high road to England and found work on Somerset House, then on Portsmouth Dockyard, where he was foreman mason. In 1786 he was appointed Surveyor of Public Works for Shropshire. The north of Shropshire, on the border of Worcestershire and Staffordshire, was being enriched at this time by industrial development; the very names Coalbrookdale and Coalport, with their associations with iron and china, suggest the source of this activity.

Telford was nothing if not versatile. He was the first to excavate Roman Uriconium (Wroxeter). At Buildwas, near the original iron bridge at Coalbrookdale, which had merely imitated in iron the conventional structure of a stone bridge, he built a second — lighter, flatter and with single span arch. He built and improved roads, dressing the roads with small fragments which made the surface impervious to water. He built churches: at Bridgnorth a grave, handsome design which takes full advantage of its site at the end of East Castle Street; two octagonal churches at Malinslee and Madeley. He supervised the restoration of Shrewsbury Castle for Sir William Pulteney and built a pleasant gazebo, red sandstone and again his favourite octagonal shape, on top of the mound.

Telford's Ellesmere canal was the first of some twenty projects on which he was employed. This one is notable for its two aqueducts. The greater one, Pont Cysylte, carries the canal 127 feet over the river Dee, in an iron trough fifteen feet wide, on iron arches mounted on eighteen piers of stone across a valley which, by means of a vast embankment, he narrowed to a thousand feet. The aqueduct, which took eight years to build, can be seen today, a remarkably impressive record of the confidence and energy of this time. Between 1803 and 1822 he was engaged upon the building of the Caledonian Canal which proved to be more formidable than expected; locks and cuttings had to be made through solid rock in some places. He was less disappointed, however, in his Swedish enterprise, the Gotha canal, for which he designed the locks and bridges between 1808 and 1810. For his work on this great waterway, joining the North Sea and the Baltic, he was rewarded by a Swedish knighthood.

In 1803 Telford had been put in charge of Highland works, the start of a connexion with his native country which transformed the wild and inaccessible north. In the course of his labours, in romantic country but often in very simple constructions, he built over a thousand bridges and about a thousand miles of road. His iron bridges are not all to the taste of those who look for the picturesque and like lichened stone and mossy humps. Telford is essentially a practical man of the iron age. But he did not lack a sense of style and he had a strong awareness of the need for works to be in harmony with their surroundings. Some of the bridges of Pontifex Maximus, as his friend Southey called him, are beautiful; notable examples are Craig Ellachie and Cartland Crags. Telford also worked on some forty harbours. No single man did more to improve the economic potential of the Highlands.

Meanwhile Telford was also responsible for the improvement of the Holyhead road, from Shropshire, through Wales to Anglesey. It culminated in what is perhaps his most famous work, the suspension bridge over the Menai Straits, with a span of 550 feet, utilizing Captain Brown's new principle, the flat link iron chain. It was opened, at Telford's request without special ceremony, in 1825. In the same year he was appointed engineer to the new project of St. Katherine's Dock in London. For five years more after the completion of this scheme in 1829, Telford was continually busy, on projects of many sorts, building up a large staff of pupils who were to carry on his work into a more scientific age. His pre-eminence is marked by the fact that he became President of the new Institution of Civil Engineers in 1820. He was a reserved man, who could be stern at times, and he never married, but he inspired great devotion. That admirers included Southey and Campbell, the poets, need not surprise us, for the heroic creativeness of his work is in tune with the romantic spirit of the time. He was indifferent about money and prestige. He was buried however, in Westminster Abbey, a fitting honour for one of the finest men of his time.

L. T. C. Rolt, *Thomas Telford*, 1958.

JOHN RENNIE (1761-1821), engineer, was born at Phantassie in Haddingtonshire. He was a typical product of the thorough education available to Scottish boys at this time. From his father's farmhouse he went to a parish school at Prestonkirk and thence to the burgh school at Dunbar. He also learned practical skills from a millwright on the Phantassie estate, Andrew Meikle, inventor of the threshing machine. From Edinburgh University he went to England to study the work of Brindley, Boulton, Watt and other pioneers. In 1783 he encountered Watt, another Scotsman and it was for him that he executed his first important commission, the Albion flour mill at Blackfriars. Remarkable for the use made of iron, as well as of steam power, this mill laid the base of Rennie's career. From the experience gained in its construction he was able to design other mills; amongst other projects were new machinery for the Mint, and saw mills for Archangel. In an age of expanding demand and a lack of trained engineers a man like Rennie could not be a specialist. Transport in general and canals in particular, however, provided the richest opportunities. In 1804 his Rochdale canal was opened; its digging along a hilly Pennine route had necessitated the construction of elaborate works to maintain the water level.

Miles of rich, brown farmland, now many feet below the level of the fenlands roads, attest to the success of Rennie's drainage work in South Lincolnshire. More imposing memorials are however to be found in the London bridges which he designed and built. Early essays in the analysis of the problems of span and tension and some designs for other bridges which were not carried out preceded the maturity of his best work. His first important bridge, at Kelso, had the elegant semi-elliptical arches and Doric ornamentation which later characterized Waterloo Bridge. The roadway was level, instead of the steep crown typical of most earlier bridges; this is to be found, too, in his first English bridge, over the Wytham at Boston. The Waterloo bridge was designed to harmonize with the river front of Somerset House, for Rennie was a man of his time in appreciating that utilitarian structures should be in harmonious relationship with near-by buildings. He was remarkably resourceful in the face of technical problems. His bridge, founded on coffer dams, 120 feet in span, had nine arches; the piers were ornamented with Doric pilasters. When he came to design a second Thames bridge, at Southwark, authorized by Parliament in 1814, he found the river very deep and the tides rapid at the point chosen for construction. To obtain the widest possible waterway he therefore built a bridge of only three cast iron segmental arches; the central one, of 240 feet span, sprang from robust stone piers and was the largest yet attempted in cast iron. When the old London Bridge was found to be unsafe, Rennie, asked to report on the situation, declared that an entirely new bridge was wanted. He completed a design just before his last illness. Appropriately his son, John Rennie, thirty years old when the first pile was driven in March 1824, carried out the work. At its opening in 1831 he received the knighthood which his father had earlier declined for himself, the first civil engineer to be honoured in this way.

Rennie encompassed an enormous amount of work. At the New London docks he made extensive use of steam engines for pumping and pile-driving. At the East India Docks, he had cast iron in the roofing of warehouses, railways and machinery for handling the heavy goods. He improved the navigation of the River Clyde, remodelled the harbours of Holyhead and the docks of Grimsby and Hull. It seems likely that the Bell Rock Lighthouse was his. He was certainly the main authority behind the building of the Plymouth breakwater which, when it was completed in 1848, had used 3,760,444 tons of stone. He was made a Fellow of the Royal Society in 1798 and on his death was buried near London Bridge at St. Paul's. Simple, unassuming, downright in character, he lived for his work. It remains to record the one noble project that wilted for want of support: a waterway for ships from Portsmouth to London. There survives but a forlorn piece of this conception in the weed-strewn Wey and Arun Canal.

C. T. G. Butcher, *John Rennie*, 1960.

**RICHARD TREVITHICK** (1771-1833), engineer and inventor, designed the first efficient railway locomotive. Faults of temperament, shortage of capital and a run of bad luck combined to cheat him of the fame and fortune which he surely deserved. When he died, in relative poverty and obscurity, the 'railway age' had begun.

The son of a mining engineer who was himself a noted expert in pumping machinery, Trevithick was a wayward boy and a problem to his parents and teachers. He showed signs of the impulsiveness that was to mar his career. But he also displayed an inventive capacity that was perhaps all the stronger for his lack of formal education. His physical strength became a legend among the hardy miners of Illogan and Camborne. On one occasion he lifted a cast iron pump weighing nearly a ton; on another he threw a ball over Camborne's church tower, standing near enough, it was said, to touch the base with his foot! Equally impressive were his repairs and improvements to mining machinery. In this practical school, where there was fierce competition between designers for valuable orders of pumping and other machines, Trevithick learned to think boldly. He invented an improved stationary steam engine with the high pressure that James Watt had been afraid to use because of his fear of explosions, but which was necessary if locomotion were to be achieved.

Trevithick was only thirteen when Murdock set his tiny model locomotive chuffing along a footpath by Redruth church. Murdock became discouraged about the feasibility of steam traction but Trevithick realized that his own more powerful engine, running on rails, had a promising future. Claims are hard to disentangle, but most authorities accept that Trevithick's tramway travelling engine, at Penydarron in South Wales, was the true pioneer of railway engines. Trevithick went there to construct a forge engine, then he designed (about 1801) this engine for transporting metal from the furnace to the forge. Owing to the weakness of the lines and the breaking of tram plates it was eventually relegated to the rôle of a stationary engine; but not before its use had been justified beyond doubt.

In 1808 Trevithick set up a circular railway in a field near the site of the future Euston station. Here, for a shilling, adventurous Londoners could travel behind Catch me who Can, a steam engine which regularly ran at twelve miles per hour. When a rail broke and the engine ploughed off into soft ground, Trevithick, who was already embarrassed by the failure of a scheme to construct a driftway under the Thames, abandoned his experiment. In 1812 we find him urging the merits of his steam engines for agricultural purposes. It seemed a wild idea at the time but his estimate of the use of steam for ploughing and threshing was both realistic and prophetic. In 1816 he went to Lima to work on the restoration of silver mines by using modern pumping machinery. Revolutionary disorders eventually destroyed Trevithick's machines and his brilliant prospects. Pressed into the army, he promptly invented a new gun! Between 1822 and 1826 he was engaged in mining operations in Costa Rica.

Trevithick was returning destitute to England when, by extraordinary chance, he met Robert Stephenson, in an inn at Cartagena. The younger man, whose father, George, was already establishing himself as a railway engineer, was destined to win fame and wealth in the 'railway age' that was to transform Britain's countryside, society and economy. Trevithick was to end in a pauper's grave at Dartford. His last years had been spent in typically bold schemes. Just before his death he designed a gilded cast-iron column, that was to be twice the height of the Great Pyramid, to celebrate the passing of the Great Reform Bill.

H. W. Dickinson and A. Titley, *Richard Trevithick*, 1934.

GEORGE STEPHENSON (1781-1848), the first of the railwaybuilders, was born in 1781 at Wylam, a colliery village in Northumberland. His father was employed as an engineer in charge of the steam engines used for pumping and winding at the pits. From the start the steam engine and the wooden tracks of the wagon-way were familiar features of his world. His family was poor and George was illiterate until the age of eighteen.

The story of his education is one of the finest sagas of 'selfhelp'. At night-school, after his day's work, he learned to read and write and to do arithmetic. At the age of twenty-one he was appointed engine man at the Willington colliery; in the same year he married. He worked furiously to keep his family and to educate his only son, Robert: cobbling shoes, mending watches, or stevedoring in the Newcastle docks. At length he was able to send Robert to school at Newcastle. Throughout their lives they were partners and Robert became a celebrated engineer before his father's death.

Stephenson had many interests — at about the same time as Davy he invented a miner's safety lamp — but he was concerned chiefly with the steam locomotive. The practical need for this was plain, since horsepower was inadequate and laborious; the technical problems also appealed to his inventive mind. Other attempts had been made, such as those of Cugnot (1770), Symington (1786) and Murdoch (1786) to make road locomotives, but without success because existing road surfaces would not bear their weight. But Trevithick in South Wales, and Blenkinsop at Leeds had more recently been successful with tram engines for colliery working.

*George Stephenson*
(Artist: Henry William Pickersgill)

Stephenson's first engine, the *Blucher*, was made for the proprietors of Killingworth colliery in 1814; it incorporated Trevithick's device, since neglected, for piping back the steam into the chimney of the engine, increasing in this way the draught and power of the engines. When Edward Pease, a Quaker coal-owner, secured the passage of a bill, in 1821, for the construction of a railway between Stockton and Darlington, Stephenson persuaded him to use steam locomotives and was appointed engineer of the project. Stephenson's greatness was not as a technical innovator; here he was one among several. But as a civil engineer, an organizer of technical resources, he was superlative. He conceived of the railway as a whole enterprise. Something in the way that he had risen, by overcoming one difficulty after another, gave him a rugged confidence in his own judgement; indeed few men's decisions have been so crucial for the future. He showed by the success of his Stockton and Darlington railway, 4ft. 8½ in. gauge (still the standard), that goods and passengers could be carried efficiently along the line.

The project for a tramroad between Liverpool and Manchester was mooted independently; it arose primarily from the need to break the canal's monopoly in communications between the fast-growing towns and was opposed by canal companies as well as by landowners. The Tyneside mechanic often got the better of the professional lawyers ranged against him. 'Suppose, now, that a cow were to stray upon the line and get in the way of the engine, would not that, think you, be a very awkward circumstance?' 'Yes', replied Stephenson, 'Very awkward — for the coo.' His work upon the construction of the 31-mile line which traversed the notorious Chat Moss showed that his confidence was not misplaced. A complex organization had to be created for the flow of materials and the handling of labour. When completed, the line had the first railway cutting in England, at Olive Mount, sixty-three bridges and the great Sankey viaduct, built mainly of brick. It was the first of those viaducts, usually graceful, even adding to the beauty of the valley they crossed, which were to become a feature of the landscape. Stephenson also won the competition for the best locomotive with the 'Rocket', capable of nearly thirty miles an hour although the directors only stipulated ten. In the same year, 1829, the Liverpool tunnel was opened. In the following year the line was opened. When Huskisson was knocked down and fatally injured, Stephenson himself drove the dying man to Manchester at full speed.

Stephenson built the Manchester and Leeds, the North Midland and the Grand Junction railways. He retired from active work in the forties but continued to advise and influence. He was consulted in Belgium and he surveyed in Spain. He took an interest in the education of working men and in pursuits less serious. He birds-nested in spring and grew melons in summer in his delightful garden at Tapton near Chesterfield. It is pleasant to record one of the more eccentric of his achievements. By encasing cucumbers in glass tubes he at last persuaded them to grow straight — a matter which had long occupied his attention.

L. T. C. Rolt, *George and Robert Stephenson*, 1960.
S. Smiles, *George and Robert Stephenson*, new ed. 1904.

**JOHN LOUDON McADAM** (1756-1836) was a road-builder whose name became a part of the English language. He was born at Ayr, went to New York at the age of fourteen, became a successful merchant, and returned to his native country in 1783 and bought an estate at Sauchrie in Ayrshire. As deputy lieutenant of Ayrshire and trustee of a turnpike trust he encountered problems of road-making. He spent thousands of pounds on his own experiments and travelled widely, inspecting roads.

In 1798 he moved to Falmouth as agent for re-victualling the navy. In 1815 he became surveyor to the British Turnpike Trust and, using his own system, set about rebuilding 180 miles of local roads. His method was relatively cheap since he believed that the hard-laid stone base, as used by Telford, was unnecessary. 'As no artificial road can be made so good as the natural soil in a *dry state*, it is necessary to preserve this state.' The earth had to be properly drained and kept dry by spreading on it a layer, about ten inches deep of small graded stone chips. After this had been flattened by traffic, two additional layers were put down. The result was 'a solid road, of clean, dry stone, or flint, so selected, prepared and laid, as to be impervious to water; and this cannot be effected unless the greatest care be taken that no earth, clay, chalks or other matter, that will hold water, be used with the broken stone; which must be so laid, as to unite by its own angles into a firm, compact and impenetrable body'.

He was impoverished by his single-minded efforts and in 1820 he petitioned Parliament for compensation. A special investigation was made and a report recommended his methods. Parliament voted a grant of £2,000, hardly over-generous in relation to the social value of his work. In 1827 he was made Surveyor-General of Metropolitan Roads. His methods were soon widely adopted and the basic principle was retained even when tar was added to make tarmac. It was his new roads that made possible the express coach services, the best in Europe, with an average speed of nine to ten miles an hour.

R. Devereux, *J. L. McAdam*, 1936.

**SAMUEL CROMPTON** (1753-1827), whose spinning 'mule' helped to transform the textile industry, was the son of a yeoman farmer who also had weaving interests. The old house, mullioned and gabled, where Crompton grew up, Hall i' th' Wood, near Bolton, is now a museum. Here Crompton worked at perfecting his cotton-spinning machine between 1774 and 1779.

He had begun his researches in order to remedy the defects of the jenny and there is no reason to suppose, as has been suggested, that he re-invented it. Crompton was a retiring man with no ambition to make a fortune and at first he only used the machine himself in his own workshop. But the fineness of his thread attracted jealous attention, spies bored holes in his walls and climbed up ladders, and to protect himself he had apparently to destroy the machine or take out a patent. Since part of his invention was simply an adaptation of Arkwright's water frame, he decided to present his machine to the public; he received the promise of a subscription but not all of it was paid by the manufacturers. Crompton was independent to the point of perversity. When a few years later he invented a carding machine, he at once smashed it, exclaiming: 'They shall not have this too!' He set up his own spinning mill, first at Oldham, then at Bolton, but he had no talent for management which, in those grimly competitive times, required ruthlessness and a certain rough cunning as well.

Crompton's career is very different from that of Arkwright who, with no greater inventive talents, made himself a millionaire. Crompton could not thrive; even his workmen were enticed away by rivals. But he would not come to terms and he refused when Robert Peel offered to take him into a partnership which would have been both convenient and profitable. In 1802 he received about £500 from a new subscription list, in 1812 a parliamentary grant of £5,000, which was mostly spent in paying his debts. Lean, ascetic in appearance, with notably large eyes, Crompton did not look like a pioneer of industry and he benefited little from his machine. When he visited textile factories in 1812 before presenting his petition to Parliament, he found that his mule was used in hundreds of factories, with a total of four or five million spindles. The once-popular jenny was vanishing and with it the cottage system. Weaving, too, was transformed, for the new fine thread made it possible for British manufacturers to produce delicate muslins which had formerly been the monopoly of the Indians. Samuel Crompton, for all this, died a poor man.

S. J. Chapman, *The Lancashire Cotton Industry*, 1904.

JOSEPH BRAMAH (1748-1814), inventor, was born at Stainborough, near Barnsley, where his father was tenant of a small farm. He began to work on the farm after leaving the village school, but at the age of sixteen he suffered an injury to his leg which left him very lame. He became apprenticed to the village carpenter. He then went to work in London with a cabinet maker and soon set up a small business. At the age of thirty he made his first invention after working on the cupboards within which water closets were then usually placed. His improved water closet (1778) was soon much in demand. He earned a greater fame, however, as a locksmith. His improved, unpickable lock was the product of years of experiment. In 1784 passers-by could see in his window in Piccadilly: 'The artist who can make an instrument that will pick or open this lock shall receive two hundred guineas the moment it is produced.' Sixty-seven years later an American mechanic succeeded in opening the lock after working at it for two days.

Invention bred invention. The complicated construction of his lock impelled Bramah to design new machine tools. The Science Museum in London displays Bramah's milling cutters, a machine for sawing slots in lock barrels and a spring-winding machine made on the lines of a screw-cutting lathe, which was a forerunner of Maudslay's superior lathe. Bramah was extraordinarily versatile. He made a hydraulic press (1795) and a beer-pump for drawing beer from the cask. His wood-planing machine was used for many years in Woolwich Arsenal. For the Bank of England he produced an ingenious machine for numbering banknotes. He was one of the first to propose the application of the screw propellor. It was when he was supervising the use of his hydraulic press in uprooting forest trees one December day that he caught cold, which developed fatally into pneumonia. The Yorkshire yeoman had earned the title of father of machine tools. It was not only his inventions that were important (he took out eighteen patents in all) but the effect of his work on other craftsmen. Without their work the mechanization of industry would have been retarded. They were of crucial importance.

S. Smiles, *Lives of the Great Engineers: Toolmakers*, 1904.

**HENRY MAUDSLAY** (1771-1831), inventor, was the son of William Maudslay, a joiner by trade who made textile machinery before joining the artillery as a wheelwright; he was wounded and discharged but found work at the Woolwich Arsenal. Henry was born there and his first job was making and filling cartridges. He moved to the blacksmith's shop and acquired local fame as a metal worker; when he was eighteen Joseph Bramah, the Barnsley inventor, sent for him. He was received suspiciously by the foreman because he had not served an apprenticeship. He proved his skill on the spot by renovating an old vice. At twenty-eight Maudslay was Bramah's head foreman. He had helped to make the first Bramah safety lock and he had married Bramah's housemaid, Sarah Tindel. But he was refused a rise in wages — he was paid 30s. a week — and so he left and set up his own workshop and smithy just off Oxford Street. He later moved to a larger workshop in Cavendish Square, where he eventually employed eighty men.

His first important improvement was the slide rest ('Maudslay's go-cart' and a boon to operatives who hitherto, when using a lathe, had to hold the cutting tool against the revolving metal, which made it hard to maintain level pressure and was also very tiring). His screw-cutting lathe was produced in about 1800. Leonardo da Vinci had first designed some such machine. The Frenchman Senot had produced a model in 1795. Maudslay's was enormously superior, combining slide-rest lead screws and change-gears in a screw-cutting lathe that could achieve remarkable accuracy. Hitherto, every screw thread had to be made by hand and each nut was different from another. It was left to his pupil

Whitworth to standardize screw threads. One feature of Maudslay's lathe is that it is made entirely from metal; it marks the abandonment of wood in the construction of metal working machines. Accuracy was the hall-mark of all his work. His bench micrometer, which served as the ultimate standard in his workshops, was a court of appeal, and he called it the Lord Chancellor.

Maudslay's biggest commission came from the Admiralty during the war. They wanted pulley blocks in large numbers: one battleship alone used 1,400 blocks. Marc Brunel designed a labour-saving machine for making them and Maudslay was commissioned to put his designs into effect. He completed the task in six years. There were 43 machines to carry out each operation from cutting the elm logs to completing the pulley blocks — machines for sawing, boring, mortising, shaping, rounding and milling, all worked by a 32 h.p. steam engine. The machines were successful and costs and time were cut; some of the machines were still in use until recently at Portsmouth dockyard.

Among the patents Maudslay took out were a calico printing machine, a differential gear hoist, and a machine for softening water by aeration. He had eventually to move his expanding business to a disused riding school in Lambeth. There the sign of Maudslay, Sons & Field was erected. In 1826 Thomas Allen described his 'extensive factory ... steam engines, tanks for shipping, and all works connected with various factories, are here executed in the best manner'. Clement, inventor of the metal-planing machine, Whitworth, who standardized screw threads and exhibited at the Great Exhibition a measuring machine capable of measuring to one millionth of an inch, and Nasmyth, inventor of the steam hammer, were the most famous of Maudslay's pupils. Nasmyth recalled his insistence upon the strictest accuracy: 'By a few masterly strokes he could produce plane surfaces so true that when their accuracy was tested by a standard plane surface of absolute truth, they were never found defective'.

Henry Maudslay, who liked to remind his employees of the virtues of economy and simplicity — 'Put to yourself the question, "What business has it to be there?", avoid complexities, and make everything as simple as possible' — was the perfect model for Samuel Smiles and his theme 'self help'.

J. B. Jeffreys, *The Story of the Engineers*, 1945.

JOHN DALTON (1766-1844), scientist, was the son of a West-morland handloom weaver. His mother, Deborah Greenup, was the abler and stronger of his Quaker parents. It was the Quaker master of a school at Pardshaw Hall, John Fletcher, who first set John on the road to learning from which he was never to deviate. Another Quaker gentleman, Elihu Robinson, noticed and encour-aged the boy's interest in science. Dalton set up a school in a barn at Englesfield, in 1778. The school failed after two years and for a time he supported himself by labouring work. In 1781, with his brother, and a sister for housekeeper, he started a school in Kendal. The Daltons were stern disciplinarians and John was too absorbed in his private studies to be a successful schoolmaster. A close friend at this time was John Gough, the blind scientist whom Wordsworth describes in 'The Excursion'. With Gough to teach him mathematics, Dalton immersed himself in the study of science.

In 1793 he became professor of mathematics at the New Col-lege, Manchester, and in that year appeared his *Meteorological Observations and Essays*, maintaining the electrical origin of aurora borealis. His subsequent papers, *The Constitution of Mixed Gases* and *The Expansion of Gases without Heat* (1801) established meteorology as a science — and his name as a scientist. He set out the rule that all gases expand equally with equal increment of temperature. In *The Absorption of Gases by Water* (1803) he first set out his explanation of the properties of gases; later he applied the same ideas, demonstrating that com-bination can be recognized as the union of discrete particles with definite weights characteristic of each element.

His interest in meteorology first led Dalton to think about the way in which matter is constituted. Analyses of air showed him that it was made up of the same proportion of oxygen and nitro-gen, with small quantities of water vapour and carbon dioxide. He knew that these gases are not in combination and have different densities. The heaviest of them should then sink to the bottom, the lightest rise to the top. That this is not the case he explained by the Lucretian idea of minute particles of different sizes in movement. To the old atomic conception he added the new view that matter was composed of a large number of elementary, homogeneous and distinct substances which are themselves composed of indestructible atoms; the atoms of any particular element are like each other but different from the atoms of other elements.

Dalton's complete theory was formally enunciated in 1808. His *New System of Chemical Philosophy* (1808-27, in successive numbers) has acquired classical status. He then went further to show that it should be possible to determine the relative number of atoms combining to form a compound, and the relative weights in which the constituent elements combined to form that compound. Inevitably Dalton made mistakes: it is more remarkable that he was as accurate as he was. He could have little idea, for example, of the number of atoms that form compounds. Davy at first rejected the atomic theory, but subsequently called it 'the greatest scientific advance of recent times'.

One contemporary described Dalton's appearance as 'repulsive': his voice was 'harsh and brawling; his gait stiff and awkward; his style of writing and conversation dry and almost crabbed'. He turned down an offer by Mr Strutt of Derby of a home and a laboratory, with £400 a year. He would not be tied and preferred to lodge in the house of some Quaker friends. He earned little and lived sparingly. When asked why he had never married he said 'I never had time.' Thursday afternoons saw him at bowls at the Dog and Partridge. Every year he walked in the Lakes: he was a lover of mountains and climbed Helvellyn more than thirty times. It is tempting to see him as another Dominie Sampson, but there was nothing of the failed or feeble about Dalton. He was always neatly dressed in his Quaker knee-breeches, dark grey stockings and broad-rimmed beaver hat and white neckcloth. Fellow scientists were struck by his likeness to Roubiliac's statue of Newton. It is noteworthy that he was colour-blind; his account of his own condition in 1794 was the first to identify the disorder, which was now known abroad as Daltonism.

Both Dalton's conceit and integrity were grounded in the simple virtues of a north-country yeoman. To a student who had missed a lecture and wanted him to testify that he had attended the complete course he solemnly delivered the entire lecture. But to any man who was so bold as to ask him for a scientific opinion he would answer: 'I have written a book on that subject. If thou wishest to inform thyself about the matter, thou canst buy my book for three shillings and sixpence.' When he died his remains were visited by 40,000 people: over a hundred carriages escorted him to his grave.

H. Roscoe, *John Dalton*, 1895.

WILLIAM MURDOCK (1754-1839), mechanic and inventor, introduced lighting by gas. During his work in Cornwall, as works manager for Boulton and Watt he conducted experiments with a view to using inflammable gas obtained from coal for lighting. He successfully lit his own house and later installed gas lighting in Boulton's Soho works. The peace of Amiens (1802) was celebrated with a brilliant display of new lighting, to 'the astonishment and admiration' of the people of Birmingham who went to see it.

Murdock's father was a Scottish millwright. William followed the same trade, but in 1777 he came south, looking for experience, and in particular for work on one of the new steam engines. When Boulton interviewed him he noticed him twiddling his hat: it was made of wood to his own design. Boulton took him on and sent him to oversee the firm's machines in the Cornish mines. Not the least of his duties was to watch for patent infringements. Murdock had to be tough as well as devoted. He seemed to live for his machines. He was once found asleep, heaving at his bed post, calling out, 'Now she goes, lads, now she goes!'

To steam engine construction Murdock contributed the 'sun and planet' motion and the 'bell-crank' engine. In 1810 he took out a patent for making stone pipes and the invention of 'iron cement' is also attributed to him. A story is told of him that well illustrates his resourceful character. On a visit to Manchester, one of the first cities to be lit by gas, he was invited to the house of a friend who lived outside the illuminated part of the city. Murdock walked with his friend past the gas works. He went in, took a pig's bladder from his pocket, filled it with gas, placed the stem of an old tobacco pipe into the neck of the bladder, and thus produced a flow of gas and a flare of light to guide them along the dark roads. As he grew older Murdock became modestly prosperous, but he went on working. On the lawn of his house at Handsworth stood a quaint garden ornament. It was 'the first piece of iron-toothed gearing ever cast'.

SIR HUMPHREY DAVY (1778-1829), chemist, inventor and savant, was born at Penzance, the son of a Norfolk wood-carver who had settled in Cornwall; his mother kept her family with a milliner's shop after the early death of her husband. Humphrey was educated at Penzance and Truro grammar schools and early showed a fanciful, ingenious cast of mind. At seventeen he was apprenticed to a surgeon and plunged into the study of moral philosophy. Soon, however, scientific matters claimed his attention.

Davy was lucky in being patronized first by Davies Gilbert, then by Dr. Beddoes who gave him a job at his 'Pneumatic Institution' at Bristol. Davy made here the acquaintance of Coleridge and Southey; he had something of a poet's temperament and he was also a lively and charming talker. In 1798 he published his findings, somewhat hasty ones, on Heat and Light. Then he embarked upon experiments in the inhaling of nitrous oxide which nearly killed him. In 1801 he took the post of Assistant-Lecturer in Chemistry at the 'Royal Institution', a society which had lately been founded for scientific experiment and, as befitted 'the age of improvement', for the diffusion of scientific knowledge for the benefit of society. Davy's lectures and his novel experiments enjoyed a *succés d'estime*. One of Gillray's caricatures represents Davy assisting in the treatment of a gentleman with 'laughing gas'.

Davy became Professor of Chemistry at the Institution; in 1803 he was elected Fellow of the Royal Society. He set no limits upon his studies and experiments, always looking for results, searching for the relationship of one subject to another and the application of theory to practical analysis or use. He is said to have dipped his fingers in an inkpot if he wished to erase a line and to have left his apparatus in a bewildering mess. Worse than his untidiness was his reluctance to pursue a single line of inquiry in depth. He was, however, a superb teacher, inspiring others to follow the lines that he suggested. With the versatility of genius he ranged from the application of chemistry to painting and farming to an attempt to unroll and decipher the papyri discovered at Herculaneum.

Davy's fame rests chiefly upon his great discovery that the alkalis and earths are compound substances formed by oxygen united with metallic bases. He not only discovered chlorine to be an element but discovered its practical uses too. (He was the first to use the word *element*, defined in the modern chemical sense.) He decomposed potash in 1807 and subsequently soda and the alkaline earths, baryta, strontia, lime and magnesia; he discovered the new elements: sodium, barium, strontium, calcium and magnesium. He did not discover iodine but was the first to show what good use could be made of it. By one invention he saved many hundreds of lives. After an investigation of fire-damp, his safety lamp, perfected in 1815, made possible deeper and safer coal working. He refused to be paid for this or to take out the patent which might have made him rich.

Science then knew no boundaries, even in wartime: in 1813 Napoleon granted Davy a special permit to go to the Continent. He took his young protégé Faraday with him, met the best scientists of Paris — Ampère, Berthollet and others — and experimented in one laboratory after another, in Florence, Rome and Naples. At Pompeii he researched into the composition of the colours of the paintings. In 1812 Davy had been knighted, and married a rich widow, Mrs Apreece. She was a haughty and unsympathetic woman who treated Faraday like an apprentice. Davy must indeed have been exasperating at times, egotistic and bumptious. When he became President of the Royal Society he showed a notable lack of tact. His health began to deteriorate about 1826; he went to Italy and died at Geneva. His mind, it seems, was active to near the end. His last important work was given to electromagnetic research.

Sir H. Hartley, *Humphrey Davy*, 1966.

**THOMAS BEDDOES** (1760-1808), physician and political radical, was among the most original and influential men of his day in the field of medical science. From a Shropshire boyhood and Bridgnorth grammar school, he went to Oxford. He was briefly in Edinburgh and Paris, where he met Lavoisier and other notable chemists, before returning to Oxford, as Reader in Chemistry. His liberalism and early sympathy with the ideals of the French Revolution were unwelcome there. So he went to Bristol to establish a hospital which, because he favoured the use of gas for respiratory complaints, he called the Pneumatic Institute. The chief of his chemical laboratory and his responsive disciple, was the young Humphrey Davy.

Beddoes was the central figure of a group of Bristol intellectuals. Coleridge and Southey were among those he befriended. Like that other wide-ranging intellectual, his contemporary Erasmus Darwin, he brought imagination and keen observation to a variety of interests. His novel, *Isaac Jenkins* (1793) made a strong and well-received case for temperance. His son, Thomas Lovell Beddoes (1803-49), poet and playwright, inherited his father's tendency to explore and question, but with it a depressive temperament, susceptible to the more morbid aspects of Gothic romance. Wandering about disconsolately, mainly in Germany, he worked for twenty years at his most famous poem, *Death's Jest Book*. He died by his own hand.

**SIR CHARLES BELL** (1774-1842), biologist, explored the anatomy and physiology of the central nervous system and discovered the distinct functions of the nerves. 'They will hereafter put me beside Harvey', he wrote, to a friend, of discoveries which were indeed the greatest contribution to physiology since the demonstration of the circulation of the blood.

Bell was the youngest of six children of William Bell, a Scottish episcopal clergyman. His mother — herself, too, the daughter of an episcopal clergyman — was a sensitive, artistic woman, who undertook much of the teaching of her children. One brother became a noted surgeon, another a professor of Scots law at Edinburgh. Charles loved drawing and he was one of many biologists who have been first drawn by their skill in art to the study of anatomy. While still a student at Edinburgh, he compiled a *System of Dissections*. In 1802, in connexion with his brother's lectures, he published a series of engravings of the brain and nervous system. In 1804 he came to London but found difficulty in establishing himself until the publication, in 1806, of his popular *Anatomy of Expression*, in which he set out to explain the mechanism of familiar ways of expression besides criticizing well-known works of art. West, the president of the Academy, promoted its publication, Queen Charlotte read it for two hours, the Nawab of Arcot ordered a copy bound in red morocco and satin. Bell taught artists and entered society — but he had yet to establish himself as a scientist. Between 1807 and 1830 he studied, dissected, lectured and wrote: gradually he developed his theories about nerves until in the latter year he published his collected papers under the title *The Nervous System of the Human Body*. It detracts in no way from his achievement that, in Paris, Majendie came independently, and later (1821) to Bell's first conclusions about the existence of the motor and sensory nerves.

Bell's principal work was on the double spinal roots from which most of the nerves arise. He showed that two nerves are necessary to a muscle, one to inform the brain of the sense of an action, the other to execute the action. The spinal nerves have filaments of both kinds, but their anterior roots from the spinal cord are always *motor*, their posterior roots *sensory*. The fifth cranial nerve is a motor as well as a sensory nerve; while it supplies the face with sensory branches, the motor nerve of the facial muscles is the *portia dura* of the seventh nerve. From his discovery of its true function the *portio dura* is often spoken of as 'Bell's nerve'. His inquiries into the functions of these nerves were prompted by observation of the results of accidents in men — but carried on by experiments on animals. The latter caused misgivings which suggest that he would be shocked by the way in which vivisection is now tolerated by educated people. Of some experiments he wrote: 'I cannot perfectly convince myself that I am authorized in nature or religion to do these cruelties.'

Bell was a sensitive man, a lover of the countryside and especially of fishing. In manner he tended to be grave and abstracted, though Cockburn said of him: 'If ever I knew a generally and practically happy man it was Sir Charles Bell.' He wrote a great deal, mostly about surgery; in 1832 appeared a paper on the organs of voice. With Brougham, to whose friendship he may have owed his knighthood, and Horner, he played a part in the foundation of London University. He was a tireless lecturer. In 1809 he went to Haslar hospital to help treat the wounded from Corunna and in 1815 to Brussels for the same purpose after Waterloo. He was conscientious in his practice at the Middlesex Hospital. He would examine a patient with the greatest care and in silence, before the assembled students, before retiring from the bed and offering his considered diagnosis, remedy and forecast of the likely outcome. As an operating and consulting surgeon he was not outstanding. Failing health and the preference, perhaps, for a more academic life may have prompted him to accept the chair of surgery at Edinburgh in 1836. He was staying at the time of his death at Hallow Park near Worcester and in Hallow Church there is to be seen a memorial to him, with an inscription by Lord Jeffrey.

G. Gordon-Taylor and E. W. Walls, *Sir Charles Bell, His Life and Times*, 1958.

**WILLIAM SMITH**, geologist (1769-1839), a self-educated surveyor, engineer and collector of fossils, first obtained an insight into the nature of strata while cutting canals. He discovered distinctive groups of fossils in different stratas. 132 years after the zoologist Martin Lister had proposed to the Royal Society a map showing the different kinds of British 'soiles', in 1815, Smith published the first coloured geological map. On a scale of five miles to an inch, his map shows twenty different rock formations for which he used the familiar local names, like London clay. His companion work, *Strata Identified by Organised Fossils* (1817), illustrated the organic remains characteristic of each rock unit. His general conclusion, that each formation is possessed of properties peculiar to itself [and] has the same organised fossils throughout its course' was the first clear statement of the principal of faunal sequence: the basis for world-wide correlation of fossiliferous strata into a coherent system. He showed that there are two different kinds of order in nature: one, in spatial arrangement of rock units; two, in succession of ancient forms of life.

Smith's pioneering map-making was followed up by George Greenough, who gave up his seat in parliament (1812) to devote himself to geology, formed a Geological Society and produced geological maps of England and Wales, and, later, of India. Whether Smith's influence is gauged by the scholars and scientists who thronged his soirées, by the fashion for fossil hunting that made the specimen bag, with pick and hammer, near-essential accoutrements for a Victorian gentleman's country holiday, or by the steady erosion, long before Darwin wrote, of belief in biblical accounts of the creation, it can be seen to be immense. Not for nothing has he been called 'the father of British geology'.

**CHARLES BABBAGE** (1792-1871), inventor, was the pioneer of the digital computer. He spent much of his life working on his Difference Engine, which was designed to calculate any table of numbers by the aid of differences, at a speed far exceeding that of any human mind: at an early trial it produced figures at the rate of forty-four a minute. In 1823, the Chancellor of the Exchequer, 'Prosperity' Robinson, gave him £1500 to complete the machine. But Babbage, an inventor to the core, underestimated the constructional complexity of his ideas. Ministers grew impatient. Wellington backed him with £3000 more, but Peel, refusing further help in 1842, expressed the instincts of the majority when he said to his friend Croker 'I should like a little previous consideration before I move in a thin House of country gentlemen a large vote for the creation of a wooden man to calculate tables from the formula $x^2 + x + 41$'.

By then, Babbage's engineer had walked out, taking most of the plans with him. This engine was never finished, but parts of it can still be seen in the Science Museum. Meanwhile, the inventor's mind had moved on to his Analytical Engine. This, which he worked up between 1842 and 1848, he saw as superseding the Difference Engine, through its range and complexity. It was based on the punched cards, designed for a loom by Joseph-Marie Jacquard in 1801, the hole corresponding to a lifted thread and the blank to a depressed one. Babbage used this concept numerically, in a way which those who developed the digital computer a century later recognised as anticipating the binary system.

Babbage's restless mind was full of ideas. He invented the heliograph and the ophthalmoscope. He suggested the use of a moving belt for short distance railways, of the sort now to be found on escalators and in the larger airports. He used his analytical skills; to point Rowland Hill towards the Penny Post, and for insurers to produce the first reliable actuarial life tables. He searched for the foolproof betting system. He could pick any lock, and decode most cyphers. But he became a bitter man. His Engines were never completed, and so were not displayed in the Great Exhibition. He was often passed over the positions he coveted. Although he had regularly collected the good and the great at his parties earlier on, only his family attended his funeral in Kensal Green Cemetery.

Maboth Moseley, *Irascible Genius*, 1964.

**SIR CHARLES LYELL** (1797-1875), geologist, was the author of the *Principles of Geology* which may be compared with

Darwin's *Origin of Species* as a contribution to the great earth-quake in nineteenth-century thinking about the universe, the creation and the nature of God. It dealt a mortal blow to the old 'catastrophic' interpretation and to the idea of universal and immutable laws of the universe, though these laws continued to be stoutly, sometimes (as by Gosse) eccentrically, defended.

Lyell was the eldest son of Charles Lyell, botanist and student of Dante, of Kinnordy in Forfarshire. The family lived in the south of England during his boyhood and the son's taste for natural history was encouraged by his father's interest and by the freedom of his life in the New Forest and Sussex. At Exeter College, Oxford, he was an indifferent classic but a keen student of entomology until Dr. Buckland's lectures attracted him to geology. The discovery of the difference between successive faunas was then so enlarging the subject that a correct understanding of its principles had become essential to the zoologist who wished to understand the relations between existing genera and species. Lyell's whole scientific work stemmed from the notion that the processes of the past must be judged by those currently in progress. 'We must preach up travelling as the first, second and third requisites for a modern geologist.' This dictum of Lyell's later life was based on his own experience of extensive travel: in 1817 he was in the Grampians, Mull and Staffa; in 1818 he inspected the Juras and the Alps.

He intended to study for the bar but weak eyesight thwarted him. He worked for the Geological Society, carried out intensive field studies and corresponded with foreign experts. In 1827 he was briefly on circuit, having taken up legal practice, but geology had already become his life. In the autumn of 1828 he was to be found walking and riding mule-back around Sicily, studying the evidence of recent mountain building. He realized that the relative ages of the later deposits could be established by the proportion of living to extinct molluscan species which they contained; hence came his division of tertiary strata into eocene, miocene and pliocene. This long-accepted classification, and his account of the way in which fossiliferous deposits could have been slowly raised above the sea appear in his *Principles*, published by Murray in successive volumes between 1830 and 1834.

From the start the book, constantly revised by Lyell, enjoyed wide circulation: the twelfth edition was issued in 1875. Some criticized Lyell for taking insufficient notice of Hutton's work: since Hutton, however, the science of paleontology had introduced a new field of evidence. Lyell's appeal to existing causes may suggest that his 'uniformitarian' doctrine is opposed to that of evolution — and he certainly opposed Lamarck's theory of transmutation of species until Darwin produced what seemed to him to be convincing evidence. Darwin himself paid tribute to his work, though Lyell's book *The Antiquity of Man* (1863) treated the theory of the origin of species with reserve.

Lyell was unusually open-minded, always ready to alter his position in the light of new evidence. Though contemporaries used to talk of his 'Lord Chancellor manner', his was a liberal and tolerant mind. Dean Stanley wrote of him: 'From early youth to extreme old age it was to him a solemn religious duty to be incessantly learning, constantly growing, fearlessly correcting his own mistakes. ... Science and religion for him not only were not divorced but were one and indivisible.' All his life he continued to travel and study. He was a sociable man of wide sympathies; in friendships, as in intellectual pursuits, he ranged beyond his own circle and subject. Charles Darwin was to speak affectionately of his 'morning house of call' when he lived at 16 Hart Street, London. Lyell was not a tall man but an unusually high, wide forehead would have given him a fine presence if his very short sight had not made him stoop and peer.

T. G. Bonney, *Charles Lyell and Modern Geology*, 1895.

**GEORGE WILLIAM MANBY** (1764-1854) was one of the first pioneers of rescue work at sea. He was born at Downham Market in Norfolk. Having joined the militia, he was appointed in 1803 to be barrack master at Yarmouth. He often heard of shipwrecks and, like other people, he at first regarded them as unavoidable. Dickens in *David Copperfield* paints an unforgettable picture of a storm shipwreck on this stretch of coast and in 1807 many witnessed just such a scene. The gun-brig *Snipe* was wrecked and sixty-seven persons perished within sixty yards of the beach. After the gale had subsided one hundred and forty-seven bodies were washed up on thirty miles of coast. It occurred to Manby that a line might be thrown to a threatened vessel from a gun. In 1783 he had fired a line over Downham Church from a mortar and he began a series of trials based on this experiment. It was difficult to attach a rope to the shot without its snapping, but at length strips of raw-hide closely plaited were used. In 1808 an opportunity came for him to test his invention. The brig *Elizabeth* was discerned about a hundred and fifty yards from the beach, helpless in a gale. The crew were lashed to the rigging with no means of rescue and great waves were breaking over them. The mortar was brought, a line thrown over the ship, a boat hauled off by it and seven men brought to land.

In 1810 a grant of £2,000 was made for Manby to research into sea-rescue. He was commissioned to report on the dangerous stretches of coast from Yarmouth to the Forth and as a result fifty-nine mortar stations were erected. Manby also attempted to devise shells filled with burning composition so that a crew could see the trajectory of a line being fired towards them. When quite old he made a journey into the northern seas in order to test a new kind of harpoon. He also attended to improvements in lifeboat methods. He became a Fellow of the Royal Society and received several foreign awards and decorations for his life-saving inventions.

**THOMAS GIRTIN** (1775-1802), painter in water-colour, a dark, handsome, big-boned lad, was born the son of a London ropemaker in the same year as Turner, with whom he grew up as his closest friend. Together they waited upon Dr. Thomas Monro, that remarkable young physician who cared not only for the King but for John Cozens in insanity, and who gathered to his home in Adelphi Terrace a company of young artists which included, at one time or another, Cotman, de Wint, John Varley and Linnell. To these he offered, on the one hand the mundane benefits of a square meal and half-a-crown an evening for their attendance, on the other his encouragement and criticism and the opportunity to see and copy from his portfolio of Gainsborough and Sandby, Hearne, Rooker and Cozens, the patriarchs of English water-colour art. Even before this acquaintance Girtin had exhibited at the Royal Academy (1794) and had taken, perhaps with Turner, a tour to the North in fulfilment of a commission to paint 'Monastic Remains and Ancient Castles' — the first of several such professional tours he made, each of which yielded immediate fruit, for he was one of the first of English painters to complete his pictures out-of-doors. He joined in forming perhaps the earliest sketching-club, of which Francia was a member (later Bonington's master), as well as Cotman, Callcott and others. By 1800 Girtin was in poor health; he was pressed by demands from illustrious patrons; he had in hand an oil panorama of London (108 feet × 18 feet) for Lord Essex; the incessant labour coupled with the long hours of exposure had aggravated a lung complaint. After the Peace of Amiens, he sought health in Paris, and there painted a series of exquisite street-scenes which bear the mark of Canaletto (with whose English work he was certainly acquainted). He died in 1802.

Bonington also died at 27; and their deaths were equal losses to English art. 'If Girtin had lived, I should have starved', said Turner; and while that is a generous exaggeration, it is argued that Girtin's style was so clearly defined at his death that a prolonged life would have turned him into a mannerist. Certainly he chose his style more quickly than Turner — a habit of low tones and muted colours, with a wonderful feeling for architectural and natural scale, the grandeur and the weight of ancient buildings, the breadth of lands which sweep away (all detail suppressed) into the infinity of sky — and he never had Turner's thirst for fresh experiment. But his drawings became less topographical and more atmospheric as he advanced, and some of his latest (e.g. *Subject from Ossian*) suggest that he might have followed the same way as Turner with a slower and more cautious step. Girtin is said to have been the first English artist to use water-colour habitually to *draw* with; this is only to say that he 'tinted' (laid water-colour over an inked outline) a good deal less than his predecessors; and there is no distinct division in the development of the technique. But it is certain that in his short life he led English water-colour from the nursery to maturity.

His character has suffered from being described by Edward Dayes, a considerable water-colourist, who had Girtin as apprentice, imprisoned him for not serving out his indentures, and seems to have nourished spite and (natural) jealousy against him. By other accounts, 'honest Tom Girtin' was a faithful friend, open-handed and kind, who preferred the company of the lower orders only because he disliked the affectation of the higher.

Jonathan Mayne, *Thomas Girtin*, 1949.

*Joseph Mallord William Turner*
(Artist: self)

**JOSEPH MALLORD WILLIAM TURNER** (1775-1851) would be named by many people as the greatest of English painters.

A visitor to the Royal Academy in the 1830s, if he went on one of the 'varnishing days' which preceded the annual exhibition, would have observed an elderly gentleman with a deep-weathered complexion and sharp, restless eyes under a tall, black hat; a black tail-coat, with the sleeves too long, surrounds his stubby body; his prominent nose is almost in contact with his canvas, so closely does he concentrate; and frequently he mutters to himself or makes an unintelligible joke. He has been here since breakfast and he will not leave before dark. He is in a state of constant activity, for he has learnt to rely on these three days in which to finish off his paintings which are to be exhibited. But he is not concerned only with himself: from time to time he will stump about the room, give oracular advice to a young Associate with a gruff 'Humph!' or 'What-r-doing?', and, if he spots a particularly delectable blob of colour on someone else's palette, he is quite likely to scoop it up and transfer it to his own.

The old man will die in the year of the Great Exhibition, leaving to the nation over two hundred oil-paintings, no fewer than nineteen thousand water-colours and drawings, and a fortune which (but for the artifices of lawyers) would have gone to the support of needy artists.

His father was a barber; his mother went mad. Turner himself was born in Covent Garden, and died in Cheyne Walk; and, despite an extraordinary amount of travelling, he remained a Londoner at heart. Ruskin, who, with *Modern Painters* (1843-60) constituted himself Turner's champion at a time when people were finding it harder and harder to understand the master's work, compares in a famous passage (Vol. V) the youth of Giorgione, passed in the golden city of Venice, with that of Turner, spent in the slums of London. Perhaps it was Turner's acquaintance with the broad river, which he loved to frequent, on which he and his father went fishing from a small boat (it is, so far as we know, the only hobby he had), beside which he died, that first awoke in him an almost proprietary sense of the glory of nature.

Another life-long loyalty was to the Royal Academy. He was admitted a student at the Academy Schools in 1789, at the age of 14; he first exhibited in the following year; and was elected A.R.A. only nine years later. He was R.A. in 1802, and Professor of Perspective there from 1808. For a man as solitary as Turner, who refused social ties and latterly lived secretly under an alias, the Academy was an essential anchor of stability and something like a home.

The secrecy in which he enveloped his activities has created special difficulties for his biographers; the earliest of whom (Walter Thornbury, 1861) preferred to give credit to a series of disreputable calumnies about Turner's private life than to believe what has emerged as the truth: that no modern artist has given such single-minded devotion to his work, and that his mysterious shifts were nothing else than an attempt to secure for himself conditions in which he could work with perfect concentration. Thus the story of his life — 'public' or 'private' — is the story of unremitting work. And, because he was capable of working on widely different compositions at the same time, attempts to classify his product, or to divide his life into stages of development, are bound to be imprecise. But certain generalizations can be made.

First, his oil-paintings form a small proportion of his total product. Because he was careless about technique and stored his paintings in alarming conditions of dirt and damp at his gallery in Queen Anne Street, many have lost their original brilliance. Yet their importance as a guide to his aspirations at all times of his maturity, and in particular in the last dazzling years, is indisputable. Water-colour, it is true, most naturally suited the impalpable nature of his imagery; so that, the more he sought to master the use of oils, the more he used them like water-colour. Yet it is the glory of oils that (if handled by a genius) they *can* be used like water-colour, and give an added depth and brilliance. Secondly, his procedure was to travel widely and light, making sketches (but no more) on the site. Scores of notebooks are filled with these precise notations of place and weather; but, perfect as many of them seem, none was intended to be a 'finished' picture. That came later, months or years later, when separate impressions were blended into a careful studio painting, in water-colour or in oils.

Many of his paintings passed to the engraver, or were engraved by Turner himself. The first to be so handled was the great *Shipwreck* of 1805 (Tate Gallery), an oil-painting which shows Turner's early mastery of the violence and depth of ocean. After that appeared by degrees the plates for the *Liber Studiorum* (a conscious imitation of Claude's *Liber Veritatis*), for *The Rivers of England, The Rivers of France*, the illustrations to Rogers's *Italy* and the Waverley Novels, and several other series. So popular were the engravings that copies found their way into the humblest homes. Here was the substance of his livelihood: it helps to explain why he was able to hoard his paintings and even buy them back into his own collection.

Next, it is said that Turner was unhappy in drawing the human figure. That is a just objection: in landscape he could group figures to advantage, but individually his figures are uninteresting and awkward. This can be explained in terms of his preoccupation with nature, or with the equally grand and mysterious impressions derived from the antiquity of buildings. His life shows that he was comparatively indifferent to human society. And Claude, who, along with Rembrandt, was his chief example, had equal difficulty in drawing the human figure.

This deficiency of Turner's work can also be explained in terms of his increasing impatience with mere detail. His artistic life can be seen as a progression from the scrupulous topographical drawing of his youth — when, in the company of Thomas Girtin, he toured the 'picturesque' buildings and scenery of England and Wales and attended that genial patron Dr. Monro — to the bewildering, explosive visions of his last phase. These last paintings, although splendid in their breadth, are compounded of numberless stipplings and flakes of colour. So that it is not the case that he dispensed with detail, but rather that he dispensed with the traditional *furniture* of paintings, with detail which did not contribute to the overall effect of elemental mystery. Here was his point of greatest distance from the pre-Raphaelites, who succeeded him in time; and it is not surprising to find that the human figure was part of the detail with which he desired to dispense.

In this progression there are certain milestones. The first oil-painting he exhibited was *Fishermen at Sea: off the Needles* (1796; on loan to the Tate Gallery). It is of special interest because in it Turner at once displays two themes which were to be characteristic: first, the Rembrandtian theme of local concentrations of light; secondly (and here Turner was attending to the normal facts of vision), the gathering of the interest of the picture into the central oval, leaving the edges undefined. *The Shipwreck* (1805: Tate Gallery) is an exaltation of the same themes.

His first visit to the Alps (in 1802, during the Peace of Amiens) aroused a hunger in him and revealed to him a realm in which he was to do some of his most original work. *The Falls of the Rhine at Schaffhausen* (1806: Boston) and *Snowstorm: Hannibal*

*Crossing the Alps* (1812: Tate) were the mature fruits of the 400 drawings which he brought back — though it is true that the second-named, which in its violence looks forward to his last period, was also derived from a thunderstorm he witnessed on the Yorkshire moors, when he was staying with his friends the Fawkeses at Farnley Hall.

But meanwhile he continued to work in imitation of — or rather in competition with — the Dutch sea-painters and Claude. It was Walter Fawkes who bought *The Dort* (1818), one of the most perfect of Turner's water-scenes in the Dutch style. And *Crossing the Brook* (1812: Tate) is a sublime recollection of Claude. But in the 1820s and 1830s Turner began to handle these traditions much more freely. His first visit to Venice (1819) gave him a new insight into the possibilities of water-scenery, a view which was to emerge most splendidly in *The Burning of the Houses of Lords and Commons* (1835: Cleveland), *Norham Castle* (1840s: Tate), and the great Venetian water-colours; while his treatment of classical subjects — as *The Bay of Baiae* (1823: Tate) and *Ulysses Deriding Polyphemus* (1829: Tate) — was similarly enriched by his first-hand experience of the Italian landscape.

Another household at which Turner was welcome was that of Lord Egremont at Petworth. He began to paint there in 1809; it was there, in the winter of 1830, at the height of his success, that he filled a sketchbook (now in the British Museum) with the most astonishing series of impressions, high-speed records in water-colour of the Christmas visitors, of the rooms and decorations of the house, and of the winter skies; and it was there, in 1836 or so, that he painted in oils his *Interior at Petworth*, one of the earliest paintings of that final phase during which (in Kenneth Clark's words) 'the idea that the world is made up of solid objects with lines round them ceased to trouble him'.

For that is the characteristic of his final period — form gives place to atmosphere. *The Slave Ship* (1840: Boston) is transitional: the items of the picture, down to the manacled leg in the foreground, are recognizable, but they are used, not so much to tell a story, as to create an overall sense of horror so stark that Ruskin, whose father gave him the picture, could not live with it. In *Snow Storm: Steam Boat off a Harbour's Mouth* (1842: Tate), *Yachts Approaching the Coast* (1840s: Tate) and *Rain, Steam and*

*Speed: the Great Western Railway* (1844: National Gallery) the form is minimal, yet not so that the meaning is lost. But they are paintings of pure weather, and they were done from personal observation. For, just as Turner had stood and sketched the night-sky made lurid by the burning Houses of Parliament, so now, at the age of nearly seventy, happening to be out in a small boat in a violent storm, he had himself tied to the mast, so that he could stay on deck for four hours and see into the heart of the storm. Shortly before his death, he was making studies of ice-bergs ... 'Life piled on life were all too little'. He died on 19 December 1851, and was buried in the crypt of St. Paul's, next to Sir Joshua Reynolds.

John Gage, *J. M. W. Turner, 'A Wonderful Range of Mind'*, 1987.

JOHN CONSTABLE (1776-1837), landscape painter, is perhaps the most popular of all English painters. For most people he is *the* artist of the English countryside. He was born at East Bergholt, a village lying on one lip of Dedham Vale on the border between Essex and Suffolk. His father was a wealthy miller, and John began work in Flatford Mill and was known as 'the handsome miller' before Sir George Beaumont, whose mother lived in Dedham, persuaded him to have a shot at an artistic career. After one false start in London, he entered the Royal Academy Schools in 1799, at the unusually late age of twenty-three.

He was quick to realize that, given his intimate knowledge of the English countryside, the result of an abiding love, he could do for it, and for English art, something which had never been done before, something very like what Wordsworth (whose poems he admired) was doing in poetry: to show it as it really was. Wordsworth was escaping from the eighteenth-century tradition which invested nature with formal qualities, mainly mythological and anthropomorphic, that acted as barriers to a simple appreciation. In landscape painting, the situation was somewhat more advanced. The thickest barriers had already been pierced by the Dutch seventeenth-century artists, and their work had been continued by Wilson and Gainsborough. But it was still widely felt that a painted landscape should have an element of unreality about it, and this view showed itself most obviously in the preference for brown tinting over green. Sir George Beaumont, for example, although in other ways very good to Constable (he had first aroused his interest in great art by showing him a work of Claude's), was one of the most vocal advocates of the 'brown' school, and felt that there was something vulgar about a green tree. Now it is Constable's *greenness*, the greenness of the greenest country on earth, which is his most original feature; to which he added a unique sense of (to use his own words) 'the dews — breezes — bloom and freshness, not one of which has yet been perfected on the canvas of any painter in the world'. He was the first to understand fully, for example, the *reflective* power of foliage, how it glitters even when dry, and how the advent of dew or rain enhances the reflection. The minute flecks of white by which he rendered this effect were disparaged in his day as 'Constable's snow'; but foreigners were more appreciative. C. R. Leslie, his first biographer, describes how one who had been at the Paris Salon of 1824, where *The Hay Wain* won a gold medal, wrote to Constable: 'I saw one draw another to your pictures with this expression, "Look at those landscapes by an Englishman — the ground appears to be covered with dew."' All this was the result of the closest observation; and he applied the same quasi-scientific approach to his study of clouds, which above all dictate the mood of his paintings. It is well known that Fuseli called to the Academy porter, 'Strowger, bring me my umbrella, I am going to see Mr Constable's pictures'.

Constable was never so obsessed with being original as to deny his debt to earlier masters of landscape, Claude, Gaspard Poussin, van Ruisdael, Wilson, and Gainsborough. One of his earliest exhibited paintings (1802: Victoria and Albert) is a view of Dedham Vale, with a marked compositional similarity to Claude's *Hagar and the Angel*, which Sir George Beaumont had allowed him to copy as a boy. And Sir George also owned Rubens's *Château de Steen*, one of the most 'modern' of early landscapes, and a picture which certainly influenced Constable.

The story of Constable's life can be briefly told. He first exhibited in the Academy in 1802. In 1816, at the age of forty, after a delay long protracted by her family, he married Maria Bicknell, whom he had known since childhood. She brought him not only profound happiness, but financial independence, so that he could now paint just what he liked. From now on we find him painting a large landscape for the Academy every year; it is a sign of the

*John Constable*
(Artist: Ramsay Richard Reinagle)

meticulous care he gave his 'finished' pictures that he might take a year over one of them. He was not elected R.A. until he was fifty-three, and this has been taken as a sure sign that he lacked the appreciation of his contemporaries. Certainly there were critics who did not spare him, as well as a wider suspicion of one who was a 'mere' landscape-artist; but in general he seems to have been held in repute, and within months of his death the National Gallery had begun a collection of his pictures. His main influence, however, was cast in France. His success at the Paris Salon of 1824 has already been mentioned. The young Delacroix saw *The Hay Wain* there, and is said to have hurried home and repainted his great *Massacre at Scio* in a fresher vein. Thereafter Constable influenced the French Romantic painters and, to a limited extent, the Impressionists. His influence does not obviously appear in England until the work of Wilson Steer.

As seems to be the rule with people who have moments of sublime experience, depression alternated with sublimity. The attacks of critics wounded him, and at the same time sharpened his tongue for retaliation. But he inspired, and kept, a few deep personal friendships. In 1828 Maria died of consumption. Constable was heart-broken: he wore mourning for the rest of his life. The intensely dramatic *Hadleigh Castle* (1829) is a token of his deep distress. The melancholy side of his nature now became uppe most, as he buried himself in his work. He died suddenly in 1837.

Constable's geographical range was small. He did not care for the wilder aspects of nature: the glaciated mountains and tormented seas which Turner loved, depressed him by their very idea. He never set foot abroad. Mostly he divided his time between Hampstead Heath and the Stour Valley (with visits to Brighton for Maria's health). He liked to make repeated studies of the same landscape, until he knew it intimately. To the end of his life, even in the last, darker years, he derived from nature moments of unaffected joy. 'Lovely', he wrote on one occasion, 'so much so that I could not paint for looking.' The sketches in which he registered this joy, hurried notes of wind-blown trees and rich fields with clouds flying, are amongst the most personal things in painting. His next step towards a 'finished' painting was to make what he called a 'study', usually indoors on a canvas as large as that he intended for the final version. In this 'study' he worked out the principles of the picture, the tonal disposition, the subject-matter, the distillation of a single pictorial idea from the wealth of material stored in his memory and sketches — and did so with much powerful, expressive handling that today it is these studies, which were never intended to be exhibited, which strike us as his finest work. Unfortunately he never escaped from the feeling that exhibited work must be 'finished' — or was it simply a desire to meet his critics half-way, that obliged him to make a further, 'final' painting, greatly elaborated, and thereby lose something of the immediacy of his original vision? A comparison of, for example, the *Study for the Hay Wain* (Victoria and Albert) with the work as exhibited (now in the Tate) will make the point clear.

There is no room to list his works. Some are familiar from countless reproductions. Certain of the sketches and studies can be seen in the Victoria and Albert Museum, and much of his more finished work in the Tate Gallery. After visiting them, it is difficult not to agree with the force of his own vindication: 'I never saw an ugly thing in my life.'

Leslie Parris, Ian Fleming-Williams and Conal Shields, *Constable, Paintings, Watercolours & Drawings*, 1976.

**RICHARD PARKES BONINGTON** (1801-28), painter, died, like Girtin, at the age of twenty-seven, and, with Girtin, is mourned as one whose brilliant promise was not fulfilled.

Owing to something disgraceful in the conduct of the father, who was a gaol-governor turned portrait-painter, the family was obliged to move from Nottingham to Calais when the boy was about sixteen. Here he had lessons from Louis Francia, who, after belonging to that brilliant group which Dr. Monro gathered round him in London at Adelphi Terrace, had returned to his native town. In 1820, he entered the Ecole des Beaux Arts in Paris, and began to work in the studio of Baron Gros, who had been an official artist of Napoleon's triumphs, and had chosen for him the pictures looted from Italy. Through Gros, Bonington was introduced to the Romantic movement and to Delacroix, and it was at the Salon of 1824 that the two young friends were affected by Constable's *Hay Wain*, which won a gold medal. Although Bonington shows the influence of both Delacroix and Constable, he won a gold medal at the same Salon on his own merits. And his reputation soon spread to London with pictures sent for exhibition there. Success was coming quickly to him; and it was well it did, for, after a journey to Italy, he contracted tuberculosis, and died in London in 1828.

His range is very wide, and is throughout informed by a marvellous lightness of touch. His brilliant draughtsmanship and crisp handling of paint extended as well to the human figure as to the architecture of building or of landscape. He is at his best in effects of wind and water, and his richly-coloured pictures glow with light. He and Constable had more influence on French painting than any other English artists.

Carlos Peacock, *Richard Parkes Bonington*, 1979.

**BENJAMIN WEST** (1738-1820), history and portrait painter, was born in Pennsylvania of a Quaker family, and only came to London in 1763 after making the trip to Italy which was practically the *sine qua non* of ambitious artists. Here he very soon (and perhaps surprisingly for an American in those days) gained the king's patronage — to which in part he must have owed his being chosen a founder-member of the Academy (1768) and his election as President on the death of Reynolds (a position he held with generosity and great decorum for nearly thirty years). The public — as well as those who should have known better — applauded, even revered, his history paintings, of which it is sadly true that they are 'only great by the acre' as Hazlitt said. Although the introduction of modern costume and the commemoration of modern events gave them an immediacy which previous history paintings had lacked, there is little to be found in them beyond conventional expressions, sombre colours, and competent paintwork — one longs for something either to praise or to damn. The works of his contemporary John Singleton Copley, who was also a popular history-painter of American birth — such works as *Charles I demanding the Surrender of the Five Members* or *The death of the Earl of Chatham* — have more verve in them and more truth. But of the two, West was the public figure: only it was not sufficiently seen that his strong suit was not the heroic murals of Windsor and of Greenwich, not even the mere canvas-displays like *The Death of General Wolfe*, but an unassuming and agreeable series of portraits.

Helmut von Erffa and Allen Stanley, *The Paintings of Benjamin West*, 1986.

**SIR THOMAS LAWRENCE** (1769-1830), portrait painter, was the grand-son of clergymen on both sides, but his father descended to keeping a public house in Bristol, where Lawrence was born. In 1772 the family took The Black Bear at Devizes, an inn frequented by fashionable travellers on the Bath Road — to whom the infant Lawrence exhibited his astonishing precocity at drawing likenesses. He was a public figure before he was ten; his talents were in demand at Oxford and at Bath, to which successively the family migrated; and by the time Lawrence began his brief stint at the Academy Schools in London at the age of eighteen, he had had an education which barely extended beyond the perilous arts of ingratiating himself with his patrons. But there is no minimizing the impression he made on London. This was something new, a virtuoso who was not only young but extremely good-looking. Sir Joshua was sage; the Court was charmed. Lawrence painted the Queen at Windsor — that familiar portrayal of the plain lady in white silk which, for a lad of twenty, is simply a masterpiece — and although the painting failed to please their Majesties, the royal favour was exerted, first in pressing Lawrence on the Academy as early as 1790, and then (1792) in appointing him to succeed Reynolds as Painter-in-Ordinary before he was even elected R.A. From here success was assured him, even if death had not deprived him of his rivals, Reynolds in 1792, Romney in 1802, Hoppner in 1810. The Prince Regent made an exception to his rule of enmity to his father's friends; honoured Lawrence with knighthood in 1815; and commissioned him to anticipate the camera by painting the portraits of the monarchs, statesmen and generals who had made the allied victory in the late war. Thus the Emperor of Russia and the Holy Roman Emperor, Blücher and Suvarov, Richelieu and Tschernitschev, and the rest of the heroes who at London in 1815, and at Aix in 1818, met to parcel out Europe, gave sittings in turn to Lawrence, and were gathered once and for all to the walls of the Waterloo Chamber at Windsor. From Aix, Lawrence went on to Vienna, to paint The Archduke Charles; and to Rome, to paint Cardinal Consalvi and what is perhaps (for its revelation of character) his *chef d'oeuvre*, the crafty-benign portrait of Pope Pius VII. On the night of his return to England in 1820, he was elected P.R.A. to succeed Benjamin West; in 1823 he advised on the purchase, from the estate of his late friend Angerstein, of the collection which made the nucleus of the National Gallery; and so he continued, in a position of unapproached authority, until his sudden death, leaving 1700 brushes in his studio and a very valuable collection of old-master drawings. Apart from his art, he was a fencer, a boxer and a billiards-player. He was curiously unable to keep himself financially solvent — which his taste for drawings only partly explains. He was a lonely man and probably unhappy. Despite or because of early affairs with the daughters of Mrs Siddons, he remained a bachelor — but a bachelor who was qualified to gladden the hearts of ladies of rank, and even used the opportunity of doing so: he was, in short, something of a philanderer.

In his painting the reading of character tends to be skin-deep only: expert in depicting courtliness and all the superficial graces of the Regency period, he seldom comes up to the qualities of wisdom, long-suffering or magnanimity (his *Warren Hastings* is an obvious exception). The deficiency can hardly have been one of education (as has been suggested), since it was least obvious in his earliest work: *William Lock of Newbury* (1790), *Captain Moore* (1792), *Viscount Barrington* (1792), are as profound as they are brilliant. But later, whether from overwork or from that degeneration which commonly afflicts the manhood of infant prodigies, the perception is slacker, and there is more truth than falsehood in Haydon's ungentle criticism that Lawrence 'flattered the vanities of the age, pampered its weakness and met its meretricious tastes. His men were all gentlemen with an air of fashion and the dandyism of high life — his women were delicate but not modest — beautiful but not natural, they appear to look that they may be looked at and to languish for the sake of sympathy.' However that may be, the best of his works are so striking as to have become part of the very language of portrait-painting; and *Elizabeth Farren* (which, with *Pinkie*, opened the door to romantic portraiture), *Princess Lieven*, *Lord Mount-stuart*, *William Lamb* and the various paintings of the Duke of Wellington and the Prince Regent, are as distinctive emblems of their age as Hilliard's *Young Man* or Van Dyck's *Charles I* of theirs.

Kenneth Garlick, *Sir Thomas Lawrence*, 1989.

SIR DAVID WILKIE (1785-1841), painter, was one of the long line of 'sons of the manse' who have won fame south of the

Border. His father was minister of the village of Cults, in Fife, and no doubt viewed with circumspection the hardening resolve of his third son to become an artist. But such was the boy's talent that eventually he was sent away to study art at the Trustees' Academy in Edinburgh. In 1804 he returned to Cults, and there painted his first important picture in the style which was to make him famous. It is a *genre* painting, a study of the neighbouring fair of Pitlessie, and, although wanting in colour-sense, it is a remarkably fresh and vigorous observation of village life. Its success led to portrait-commissions in the neighbourhood, but that did not satisfy him; in the summer of 1805 he took ship for London, and entered the Academy Schools.

He made the most of the opportunity, which in those days only London offered, to study the old masters. As might be expected from *Pitlessie Fair*, he was profoundly impressed by Teniers, the Flemish *genre* painter of the seventeenth century; and it was on the strength of *Pitlessie Fair*, which the buyer had lent to Wilkie to show to would-be patrons, that he obtained from Lord Mansfield the order for *The Village Politicians*. He proceeded with other *genre* paintings in the Dutch and Flemish manner, with undertones of Hogarth: one of the best is *The Blind Fiddler*, commissioned by Sir George Beaumont, whose sensible and generous patronage of young artists is a feature of these years. Such paintings made a rapid success for Wilkie. The tall and ungainly youth, with his thatch of sandy hair, his east-coast intonation, and his truly Scottish incapacity for seeing a joke, was yet so well received that he was elected A.R.A. in 1809, although eight days short of the minimum age, and R.A. two years later.

In 1810 his work was interrupted by the first serious onset of a type of neurasthenia which made him virtually incapable of working. Nevertheless in 1812 appeared *Village Festival* (for John Julius Angerstein, the connoisseur whose collection formed the basis of the National Gallery), and *Blindman's Buff*, a picture in which the energetic movement of a crowd of children is held in splendid balance. Soon after came *The Letter of Introduction*, where a dour bachelor, in dressing-gown and skull-cap, scrutinizes the references of a self-conscious young aspirant. Wilkie's reputation travelled abroad: in 1820 he finished, for the King of Bavaria, *The Reading of the Will* (Munich), perhaps the climax of his *genre* painting. The family has gathered round the lawyer in the parlour of the deceased, but what a family it is! — drawn in a crescent from the tender figure by the fire, patiently awaiting the best or the worst, to the florid lady of uncertain years, who has burst in on the proceedings, somewhat late, but claiming all for herself. It seems that he studied to express in a single picture the whole range of human emotion; and the picture is lovingly perfected to the last detail. About the same time he painted, for the Duke of Wellington, *Chelsea Pensioners Reading the Gazette of the Battle of Waterloo* (1822: Apsley House). When exhibited, it was phenomenally popular: people queued to see it.

In 1822, George IV paid the first royal visit to Scotland since the Union. Scott was master of ceremonies; Raeburn was knighted; Turner was there, filling his sketchbook as usual — and so was Wilkie. For him, the fruit of the expedition was two large commemorative paintings: a life-size full-length portrait of the kilted monarch, a little flattering, and the gorgeous *Entry of George IV into Holyrood House.* By the time these were finished, the interest of Sir Robert Peel, and the personal knowledge of the King derived from the one or two sittings which he gave for the Scottish pictures, secured for Wilkie the position of King's Limner for Scotland, which fell vacant on Raeburn's death in 1823.

But in 1824 Wilkie had a recurrence of his nervous illness, induced by overwork and family troubles. He travelled abroad for three years and, while he gradually recovered his health, he imbibed ideas which were to alter fundamentally the character of his work. Especially he was influenced by the paintings of Velasquez which he saw in Madrid. On his return his technique becomes much looser and broader. He seems to have thought that his earlier works were too laboured, and to have attempted a more rapid execution. His figures are now no longer simply part of the pattern, but fill the canvas. These are fine pictures — the huge *Sir David Baird Finding the Body of Tippoo Sahib* (Edinburgh Castle) is one of the finest — but they are not unique, and there were many who regretted his deserting his familiar vein. In 1836 he was knighted, and in 1840 set out for the Holy Land in search of fresh material. He died at sea off Malta on his way back. There was a nationwide outburst of regret, but the most eloquent tribute was Turner's *Peace: Burial of Wilkie at Sea* (1842: Tate).

Wilkie's habit of working a species of bitumen even into his highlights, so as to avoid the 'chalkiness' which he abhorred, and to give more depth to his shadows, has caused many of his paintings to darken and crack. It is therefore all the harder for us to account for the enormous respect in which he was held by contemporary artists. John Martin placed Wilkie alongside Leonardo and Raphael and other imperishable giants in his *Last Judgment* of 1853. Nevertheless Wilkie brought English *genre* painting to its highest pitch since Hogarth; he had many followers in the nineteenth century; and it is a part of the simplicity of his character that, unlike Hogarth, he was innocent of social satire. Sir Robert Peel, as he lay dying, asked that Wilkie's *John Knox Preaching* (1832: Tate) should be placed within his sight.

Lindsay Errington, *Tribute to Wilkie*, 1985.

**SAMUEL PALMER** (1805-81), landscape painter and etcher, was a visionary, like his friend and mentor William Blake; and the best of his visionary paintings were done before the accession of Victoria. Thereafter his life (for forty years) seems something of an anti-climax, in terms of experience as well as of expression — though he created some most lovely pictures, and though there was a 'sunset-touch', a few years at the end during which he recaptured much of his earlier vision.

He grew up on the southern edge of London, where the countryside invaded the town: the son of a bookseller. Both father and mother were Baptists; and although Palmer later joined the Church of England — as the church which most appealed to his romantic temperament by colour, liturgy, music, architecture — yet the strict religion of his early home profoundly influenced his life. His mother died when he was thirteen; but her place was taken by the remarkable Mary Ward, his nurse, devoted friend, and (to a degree) inspirer.

His father was that unusual thing: a father who *wanted* his son to be a painter, and was prepared to support him until he was successful. He also instilled in him a strong love of Nature. In his fourteenth year, the boy had three pictures accepted for exhibition at the Royal Academy, and two at the British Institution. His friendship with the landscape-painter John Linnell helped to form his taste by pointing him towards the Renaissance masters. To that he added a devotion to poetry, especially that of Milton, and especially Milton's own landscape, of dewy mornings, of shepherds sheltering from the heat of noon, and (above all) the magic of night, of woods and pastures sunk in darkness

'till the moon
Rising in clouded majesty, at length,
Apparent queen, unveil'd her peerless light,
And o'er the dark her silver mantle threw.'
(Paradise Lost IV.606-9)

It helped of course that Milton was a Christian, and his great poem a Christian document; for thus his high authority could be cited for Palmer's lifelong certainty that the purpose of art is religious. 'Genius', Palmer wrote, 'is the unreserved devotion of the whole soul to the divine, poetic arts, and through them to God; deeming all else, even to our daily bread, only valuable as it helps us to unveil the heavenly face of Beauty'.

Linnell introduced Palmer to older artists: to William Mulready, to John Varley, and (during 1824, at Fountain Court, in a meeting which was the most important of Palmer's life) to William Blake himself. To say that Palmer was captivated is hardly enough. Was not Blake the complete visionary, who as a boy had seen God looking in at the window, and the trees in Peckham thronged by starlike angels? Was he not a metaphysical poet? Was he not the illustrator of Milton, of Virgil, Dante, and of the Bible itself? Was he not also a transparently good man, indifferent to money or fame, whose life was simple and spent in the world of spirit?

Under Blake's influence, Palmer's leading motives were drawn together, as yarns are twisted to make a strong rope. Blake taught him to perceive 'the soul of beauty through the forms of matter'. From there it was a short step to holding that beauty was an aspect of God, art a sacrament, and the artist a kind of priest. Blake wrote: 'Prayer is the study of art; praise is the practice of art'. This idealism appealed to friends of Palmer also (he had a gift for making and keeping friends). A group of artists came together — including George Richmond and Edward Calvert, distinguished both then and later — who had fallen under Blake's spell, and by whom the primacy of the imagination, and its religious task, were unquestioned. Paradoxically in view of their youth and optimism, they called themselves the Ancients.

In 1826, for the sake of Palmer's health, his family moved out of London, to Shoreham in Kent. This opened the brightest period of Palmer's life, and the years in which he did much of the work which was unique to him (though it must be said that the *most* idiosyncratic — the haunting drawings done only in sepia mixed with gum — were created before the move to Shoreham). The place itself was still a rural paradise. The Ancients came down in force, for longer or shorter visits. They prayed together, worked at their painting, walked the hills at night like the exiles in the Forest of Arden, 'fleeting the time carelessly as they did in the golden world'. Palmer was happy — never so happy as during those few years at Shoreham; and he did a series of paintings which are among the best things of the nineteenth century: ideal landscapes of a world of innocence, rich fields and ancient woods lit by sun, moon, stars, bright clouds — all 'charged' (in the words of his contemporary, Hopkins) 'with the grandeur of God'.

It goes without saying that these pictures — and most of his later works — are quietist if not escapist. He loathed the creeping industrialisation of England — the 'uglification' of a supremely beautiful countryside. The coming of the railways appalled him: what would he have made of the motorcar with its crude intrusions into the privacy of the human soul?

Then, in the early 1830s — the idyll ended. Palmer was very hard up. His father and his brother had returned to town. The circle of the Ancients dispersed. Palmer's own vein of high inspiration seemed to be exhausted. Finally, in 1834, he too went back to London. He was only 29.

And three years later, the beloved Mary Ward died. With no-one to look after him, Palmer at last married Hannah, the daughter of John Linnell. They scraped together enough to allow them to spend two years in Italy. But they returned to poverty, and the confinement of London. Linnell proved to be a difficult father-in-law; and Hannah and Palmer were never really *ad unum* — except in the black days after the death of their elder son, a boy of great promise, in 1861, at the age of nineteen. (They had already lost their daughter at the age of three.)

Italy had turned Palmer's work in a new direction. He was excited by the landscape of the Campagna, its Virgilian echoes, and the treatment of it by Poussin and Claude. He made some marvellous paintings in Italy (there are two panoramas of Rome to be seen in Birmingham, and a third in Cambridge); but the note which was Palmer's alone has gone from his work. From now on, he is a watercolourist — and a colourist — of the very first rank, but not alone in that; and his pictures, though wonderfully poetic, are less obviously pictures of his dreams.

At last, an enlightened lawyer (who was Ruskin's solicitor) commissioned Palmer to do a series of etchings illustrating Milton's *L'Allegro* and *Il Penseroso*. It was four years since the boy's death; Palmer's religious faith was stronger again; he had moved back to the country, to Redhill; and he entered with delight into this work. Then he began also to etch illustrations to a translation he had made of Virgil's *Eclogues*. He lavished care on these series, so that they occupied him until his death. He was treading in the steps of Blake once more; and his landscapes now show touches of Claude. But also — in *The Lonely Tower*, *The Bellman*, in *Opening the Fold* — we are back in the unmistakably Palmerian world, of shepherds folding their sheep under starlit skies, of a village sunk in sleep or waking to the dappled clouds of morning. The magic has returned. The ordinary is transfigured, idealized.

Dressed often in an ankle-length coat and a beaver almost as high as himself, Palmer made an eccentric figure, and there is no doubt that he was an oddity. But his jolly companionship, his sense of the ridiculous, his sheer goodness, as well as admiration for his artistic powers, won and kept him many firm friends — of whom the most faithful of all, George Richmond, was beside him at his death.

One child survived, Arthur, and wrote his father's *Life*. Some of Palmer's best work is in the Ashmolean Museum, Oxford.

Lord David Cecil, *Visionary & Dreamer*, 1969.
Raymond Lister, *The Paintings of Samuel Palmer*, 1985.

**JOHN NASH** (1752-1835), architect, was with Sir John Soane the principal exponent of that phase of neo-classicism which is called the Regency style. Architects working in the Regency style combined a scrupulous eclecticism with a splendid bravado: like the pure 'Grecians' of the time, Wilkins and Smirke for example, they went back further than the Romanism of Sir William Chambers and the Adam brothers, to the fountainhead of the classical style, the Greek columns and entablatures — but then they proceeded to take liberties with them; and, not content with that, they went on to borrow, and often to mix with their neo-Grecian endeavours, the outstanding features of the Gothic style and of those styles which Sir William Chambers and others had made familiar, the Chinese, the Indian and the Egyptian. For this work Nash, with his abounding self-confidence, was peculiarly well-fitted; and fortune gave him the largest opportunities.

But he was in his mid-forties before he came to the public notice. He had studied architecture in his youth; then with the help of a small legacy, he had set up as a builder in London, but had gone bankrupt, and taken refuge in Wales and the West Country. Here he began to prosper, and in 1796 he returned to London to work in an informal architectural partnership with Humphrey Repton, the landscape-gardener. Two years later he married a Mary Anne Bradley, who seems to have been on intimate terms with the Prince of Wales, for from now on he was assured of royal favour, and was soon able to part company with Repton and to set up on his own account.

It was now that he began to design the small country houses — 'villas' — which improved roads were bringing within the range of city-workers; to embellish older houses with Gothic additions in the manner of Wyatt; and to exercise great ingenuity in planning country cottages which should be ornaments to the estates on which they were scattered (and of which the most coherent group is that of Blaise Hamlet, near Bristol).

Wyatt's sudden death in 1813 benefited Nash in two ways. He became (with Soane and Smirke) one of the three new Deputy Surveyors to the Board of Works. And, having already worked for the Prince at Carlton House, he was naturally chosen in Wyatt's stead to carry out the desired 'improvements' to the Brighton Pavilion. By 1818, the Pavilion had emerged in its present form; and the bizarre exterior, which has echoes of the Taj Mahal but partakes of a score of other influences too, is largely Nash's own.

By 1818, Nash was already far advanced with a more grandiose scheme. In 1811 the lease of 'Marylebone Park' reverted from the Duke of Portland to the Crown; and it was proposed that this land should be developed and linked to Whitehall by a great north-south route. In July 1811 the whole scheme was entrusted, by the influence of the Prince (now Regent), to Nash. It was a wise choice; for perhaps only Nash had the scale of vision (he was never one to become enmeshed in detail), the toughness and tenacity (for his plan involved widespread demolition of property), and the entrepreneurial capacity (he risked his own fortune on what was technically an official scheme) to complete the undertaking. The speed with which the work progressed is the best evidence of his capacity. Of course he was assisted by modern materials: stucco is used throughout, and many of the columns are of cast iron. And the design of the individual houses was left to fellow-architects. But Nash was the overall director and, if the finished work seems ill-considered and sometimes negligent, that was the price paid for his energy.

Of course, Nash's plan was never completed. He and the Prince intended that it should eclipse Napoleonic Paris. It never did that: the geometric regularity of large-scale town-planning has never appealed to the British genius. But even today, after redevelopment and blitzes, enough survives of what was completed to enable us to see the degree of originality and adventure. Nash intended that the route should run from Carlton House, on the north side of St. James's Park, to the new Regent's Park. But in 1825, the Prince (now King), tiring of Carlton House and its associations, ordered its destruction. In its place were built the great Carlton House Terraces. They formed the southern terminus of the route, which then proceeded northwards through Waterloo Place, Lower Regent Street and Piccadilly Circus (truly a circle in those days). Then came the first bend to the left, up the famous colonnaded quadrant of Regent Street (but Regent Street has been entirely remodelled in this century). Crossing Oxford Street at Oxford Circus, the route took a second leftward bend in Langham Place (where Nash's new church of All Souls closed the view up Regent Street), and proceeded along Portland Place (already built by the Adam brothers). Here Park Crescent and the terraces facing Park Square made — and make — a splendid entrance to the Park, which is itself bordered by Nash terraces. It is amusing to follow this route and see how much of Nash's work survives. Cumberland Terrace, flanking the Park on the east side, is perhaps the finest, for it was intended to face a 'villa' to be built in the Park for the Prince himself. But the spirit of Nash's London can still be caught by one who stands in Waterloo Place.

The third large item of royal patronage was the rebuilding of Buckingham House, which George IV wished to occupy as a palace in place of Carlton House. But, because of the high cost, Nash's commission was suspended on the king's death (1830) and his operations obscured by his successor. The Marble Arch, which he intended as an entrance, has found another resting-place. In 1835 Nash died in his Gothic castle on the Isle of Wight, and with him finally died the Regency.

Michael Mansbridge, *John Nash, A Complete Catalogue*, 1991.

SIR FRANCIS LEGGATT CHANTREY (1781-1841) would, in most people's estimation, share with Flaxman the honour of being England's greatest sculptor. Where Flaxman excelled in the grace of small monumental sculpture, Chantrey excelled primarily in the portrait-bust and the statue.

He was a Yorkshireman of farming stock who, having tried his hand at wood-carving and portrait-painting, found his true bent in modelling portraits, a kind of combination of the two, and an art which he largely taught himself. He made a reputation for himself in his native Sheffield, then came to London in his mid-twenties, where he received the generous encouragement of Nollekens, and married a wife, Mary Ann Wale. She brought him sufficient capital to buy a house in Belgrave Place, where he lived for the rest of his life.

In 1811 he had his first taste of success, when he exhibited in the Royal Academy the portrait-bust of the veteran radical politician Horne Tooke. This remarkably assured work made his name overnight. In the same year Thomas Johnes of Hafod, the Welsh scholar, wishing to commemorate his much-loved only daughter who had died as a child, invited Chantrey to undertake the commission. The huge family-group which resulted was placed in Wyatt's little church at Hafod, but destroyed in 1932 by one of the fires which were the curse of that romantic place (though fragments can be seen there to this day). The central figure of the dying girl harked back to Thomas Banks's beautiful *Penelope Boothby* at Ashbourne (1793), and, as in Banks's statue, there was no allegory. This was the first of Chantrey's breaks with the eighteenth-century tradition. 'I hate allegory', he said; 'it is a clumsy way of telling a story ... To produce real effect, we must copy man, we must represent his actions and display his emotions.' Hence the refreshing breath of realism in Chantrey's works; yet it is a realism which he managed to keep on the right side of sentimentality — though some would say he crossed the dividing-line in *The Sleeping Children* of 1817 (Lichfield Cathedral). That babes-in-the-wood memorial to two girls who had also died young, where one clutches a bunch of fading snowdrops, is a kind of double version of *Penelope Boothby*, with a certain loss of simplicity. But it caused a tremendous stir. 'Such was the press to see these children', writes Chantrey's biographer Holland, 'that there was no getting near them: mothers with tears in their eyes, lingered and went away, and returned; while Canova's now far-famed figures of Hebe and Terpischore stood almost unnoticed by their side.' Though neo-classicism in English sculpture was still far from dead — indeed Chantrey himself reverted to it in his monuments in relief — here was one nail in its coffin.

Another nail was Chantrey's increasing use of modern clothing, or at least of clothing which escaped from the classical tradition. He suited the clothes to the sitter: for example, his bust of *Sir Walter Scott* (1820: Abbotsford), the most popular of all his portrait-busts, is clothed in a tartan plaid secured by a tartan-brooch. Chantrey preferred the broad planes offered by simple clothing, to the replicated drapery in which the neo-classicists found their rhythm.

And how well he could model a portrait! The tale of his busts and statues is a very long one, and his sitters included many of the more remarkable of that remarkably rich period. Along with scores of their subjects, each of the four monarchs of the period sat to him while reigning. Bishops and judges, peers and politicians, artists and scientists, men of learning and men of wealth, followed suit. There seemed to be no character which he could not portray: whether it was the sagacity of age (*John Raphael Smith*, 1825: Victoria and Albert; and *Joseph Nollekens*, 1817: Woburn Abbey), the pathos of promise interrupted by death (*Francis Horner*, 1820: Westminster Abbey; and *Bishop Reginald Heber*, 1826: St. Paul's), the glow of youth (*Edward Johnstone*, 1819: Birmingham), or the loving serenity of a woman (*Mrs Jordan*, 1824: Earl of Munster Collection; and *Mrs Boulton*, 1834: Great Tew). But any description of his work is bound to deteriorate into a catalogue. There is a fine gathering of Court of Session judges, erected by public subscription, in the Parliament Hall at Edinburgh, easy to visit and appreciate.

And if one asks what, beside his insight into character, made him such a great sculptor, the answer is his rendering of flesh in marble, as lifelike as Nollekens's and more so.

> *Pygmalion niveum mira feliciter arte*
> *Sculpsit ebur ...*

and, like Pygmalion's ivory image, one of Chantrey's portraits will soon start into life.

It is a credit to William IV that he knighted both Westmacott and Chantrey in the year of his accession. Chantrey died in 1841, having destined his fortune, after his wife's death, to the purchase for the nation of works by British artists (the Chantrey Bequest).

S. Dunkerley, *Francis Chantrey, Sculptor,* 1995.

**THOMAS BRUCE, 7th EARL OF ELGIN** (1766-1841) was responsible for the importation into England of the most famous collection of classical sculpture in existence. The Elgin marbles are one of the most spectacular and priceless of all the treasures housed in the British Museum.

After his older brother died, having held the title for only a few months, he became Earl at the age of five. He was educated at Harrow and Westminster schools and then went to the University of St. Andrews. His first marriage was in 1799 to Mary Nisbet of Darleton, but it was dissolved by Act of Parliament in 1808. In 1810 he married Elizabeth Oswald, daughter of the Member of Parliament for Fife. He was himself a representative peer of Scotland for fifty years. He joined the army in 1785 and rose eventually to the rank of Major-General in 1814, but most of his time was spent on diplomatic missions. When war broke out with France he went as envoy to the Court of Brussels, but when the French armies overcame the Netherlands he was sent to Hesse and then to Prussia. He witnessed at close hand the unsuccessful Austrian and Prussian campaigns against the French. In 1799 he was sent as a special representative to the Turkish Court at Constantinople. This was the time of Napoleon's Egyptian expedition and

Lord Elgin remained at Constantinople until the French had been finally driven from the Ottoman Empire.

The Turkish Empire covered Greece, Asia Minor and the Middle East. Lord Elgin used his influence and his position to rescue many remains of Grecian art. He got permission from the Turkish authorities to have artists measure, sketch and record the details of classical sites and monuments for posterity; also 'to take away any pieces of stone with old inscriptions or figures thereon'. He made a large collection of moulds, statues, reliefs, vases, coins, and also measurements and plans of the greater Greek buildings. In 1802-12 a series of shiploads brought them back to England. He stored them privately. He asked the British Government to purchase the collection for the nation and after some years of negotiation the Committee of Supply of the House of Commons in 1816 voted that it should be purchased for £35,000, which was less than the collection had cost Elgin in transport and restoration. It was taken to the British Museum and placed in a temporary room erected to receive it. At the same time the Earl and his family were made hereditary trustees of the Museum. He has since been revered as one of the great Hellenists — or denounced by other Hellenophiles, such as Lord Byron, as a rapacious vandal. His behaviour was certainly haughty and high-handed, quite in keeping with the age of Wellington and Castlereagh. He could argue, however, that he had saved from certain neglect and probable destruction priceless works of art.

**SAMUEL WESLEY** (1766-1837) was the greatest English musician of his time. He was the son of the hymn writer Charles Wesley and the nephew of the founder of Methodism. Both Samuel and his brother Charles were child prodigies — indeed there were two other musical prodigies in the late eighteenth century who fulfilled their early promise to some extent: Stephen Storace and William Crotch, but none so great as Samuel Wesley. At the age of eight he completed an oratorio, *Ruth*, which gained him the description 'the Mozart'. He studied the organ, violin and harpsichord and he and his brother gave concerts in their London house for seven years in the rôles of boy composers and performers.

At the age of twenty-two, to the displeasure of his family, he became a Roman Catholic. In later life he returned to Anglicanism and denied having ever become a convert, saying that his interest in Catholicism had been limited to Gregorian music, but in fact a letter from Pope Pius VI exists which clearly indicates his conversion. This is an important aspect of his life; another, which may explain his curious denial, is that three years later, at the age of twenty-five, he fell into a deep excavation and damaged his brain, an injury which left him nervously ill and thereafter eccentric, illogical and confused.

Mrs Vincent Novello, the wife of the music publisher, wrote this to him: 'I knew him unfortunately too well. Pious Catholic, raving atheist; mad, reasonable; drunk and sober. The dread of all wives and regular families. A warm friend, a bitter foe; a satirical talker; a flatterer at times of those he cynically traduced at others; a blasphemer at times, a purling Methodist at others.' He was certainly well known in England as a conversationalist and a highly cultured, unconventional man, and as the greatest organist of his day. His main effort was devoted to spreading the works of J. S. Bach (whom he referred to as 'St. Sebastian') by playing them up and down the country; perhaps it was therefore a just reward that his own compositions were more famous in Germany than in England. These were mainly for the Roman mass and other services, the most famous being an eight-part motet *In exitu Israel*. Others were *Exultate Deo* and *Dixit Dominus*. Later he wrote music for the Anglican mass and a great many glees and songs, symphonies, concerti, solos and chamber music, but never anything for the stage. His was original and vital music.

Because of recurring insanity he never became the permanent organist at a great church and instead spent his life from 1824 as organist of Camden Chapel (St. Stephen's), Camden Town. That honour was left to his illegitimate son, Samuel Sebastian Wesley, who became a much appreciated and influential cathedral organist and composer of English church music.

**SIR HENRY ROWLEY BISHOP** (1786-1855) was the first musician to be dubbed a knight by the sovereign — by Queen Victoria in 1842. He was for many years the most prominent and prolific composer in England and his contemporary critic Leigh Hunt wrote 'It is seldom that Mr Bishop's music is not worth hearing.'

However, he has been more recently described by Percy Young as '... the tawdry Bishop who had reduced opera to the lowest form of light entertainment with a view to bringing English opera into line with continental standards' and Arthur Jacobs says he '"adapted" (i.e. did artistic violence to) Mozart's and other operas'. Indeed, today Bishop is remembered almost solely by 'Lo, here the gentle lark' and by a 'Sicilian air' which was the recurring theme song in his opera of 1823 *Clari, or the Maid of Milan* and which is none other than 'Home Sweet Home'! Thus a musical giant of the early nineteenth century, in terms of output rather than talent, is dwarfed by history. But was he completely unaware of the mediocrity of his own music?

All Bishop's training came from an Italian teacher, Francesco Bianchi, and this foreign influence remained with him all his life. His genuine gift was for the invention of melody and he was a prolific composer of stage pieces: more than a hundred cantatas, oratorios, glees and the infamous arrangements of operas by Arne, Rossini, Cherubini, Meyerbeer and Mozart into which he introduced his own themes. His popularization of music for a public who, with the advent of machinery, had the leisure and money to hear and see music performed was the beginning of the mass-culture music of Victoria's reign. Musical taste was dictated from below and Bishop's work, with few exceptions, was truly 'box office'.

He was a founder member, in 1813, and occasional conductor of the Philharmonic Society. In 1839 he took the degree of Bachelor of Music at Oxford, his exercise being performed at a festival conducted by him. He then became conductor at the Ancient Concerts, under the direction of the Duke of Wellington, which were devoted to the traditions of Purcell, Handel and the madrigalian composers, and he held this post for eight years. In 1841 he was elected Professor of Music at Edinburgh — in 1843 he was asked to resign, for he was rarely in Edinburgh and never gave any lectures! Nevertheless, he received a knighthood and in 1848 was awarded the Chair at Oxford. In 1853 he wrote an ode for the installation of the Earl of Derby as Chancellor of the University and received the degree of Doctor of Music, the ode standing as his exercise. Perhaps this was the most suitable title ever given him!

Bishop's moment of truth appears to have been a brief one.

One of his operas, *Aladdin* was a failure and in 1840 he wrote in a letter: 'I have been a slavish servant to the public; and too often, when I have turned each way their weathercock taste pointed, they have rounded on me and upbraided me for not remaining where I was!' This would seem to be the natural, yet ironic, revenge of the public upon this defacer of great composers, but in fact we see that Bishop's career was thereafter appreciated and regularly heralded with every kind of honour. Thus one must assume that public taste at all levels was very low indeed. It was an age of intense commercialism and great demand for 'entertainment' and English music did not flower again until late in the nineteenth century.

R. Northcott, *The Life of Sir Henry R. Bishop*, 1920.

**JOHN KEATS** (1795-1821) died four months after his twenty-fifth birthday. His last year was largely consumed by mental and physical suffering. He had not been a precocious boy; nor, until 1817, could be devote himself wholly to writing. Up till that time he had been a student, and latterly practitioner, of medicine. In a short space Keats became one of the world's great poets.

He still lives vividly today, in his letters and some of his poems. He seems to appeal directly to many who can only approach Wordsworth or Shelley as historians or critics. He is also a poet's poet. Tennyson rated Keats above all others of his century. Pre-Raphaelites and aesthetes, Morris, Swinburne, Wilde, saluted him as their master, pioneer of art for art's sake — a prejudiced view for, as another poet, Hopkins, said, dismissing his defects as due to his youth, he was 'made to be a thinker, a critic as much as a singer or artist of words'. A twentieth-century devotee of Keats was Wilfred Owen.

Some prime romantic conceptions appear in Keats. He was inspired by nature; he believed in 'the holiness of the heart's affections and the truth of imagination'. 'A fine writer', he once wrote, 'is the most genuine Being in the world.' But he was temperamentally averse to extremes: he accepted human limits. The elements of didacticism, or escapism that some find disturbing in other romantic poets are absent from Keats. This poet of tender sensibility was also a man of common sense; 'he had flint and iron in him', said Matthew Arnold, after reading Keats's letters.

*John Keats*
(Artist: Joseph Severn)

Keats's mind was a masculine one and he was an excellent
critic. As T. S. Eliot said, 'There is hardly one statement of Keats
about poetry which ... will not be found to be true. ...' He wins

friends, as he did in his lifetime, by his delight in things for their own sake, by his generous feelings for people and by his lack of conceit. As Arnold saw, 'his love of beauty was an intellectual and spiritual passion'. The poet, said Keats, must be a monk in imagination's monastery: he embraces its discipline so that he can more fully comprehend the joy and pain of actuality. Keats did not aspire to be a prophet or crusader. He was a craftsman — and no poet has ever applied himself more intensely to his craft. For him there was 'no fiercer hell than the failure in a great object'. He received two cruel and uncomprehending reviews of his first ambitious work *Endymion*. Yet he went on to what Gittings has called 'the greatest year of living growth of any English poet'.

Heredity rarely explains genius. Keats's forbears only suggest that John, like his brother George, might have prospered in commerce. Thomas Keats married his employer's daughter, Frances Jennings, and came to manage his livery stables at Moorfields, just outside the City. When he died, after a fall from his horse, John, the eldest of his four sons, was eight. His widow, pretty, and impetuous, married again; her mother, Mrs Jennings, took the children to live with her at Edmonton. Chancery suits wasted the money intended by Jennings for his wife and children. Frances soon left her second husband and returned to live with her mother and children. Fifteen months later, in March 1810, she died, probably of tuberculosis. John had nursed her tenderly: suffering and responsibility tried him young. At fourteen he was the male head of his family.

Since 1803 John had been at school under John Clarke at Enfield. (There had been talk of sending him to Harrow — where he would have been Byron's contemporary!) He was a lively, popular boy, open and generous but with a sort of 'terrier courage' when he was roused. He once attacked a teacher who boxed his brother Tom's ears; when he was older he trounced a butcher's boy whom he found maltreating a kitten. He read history and classical mythology, storing his mind with narratives and images which were soon to reappear transformed in verse. He began a prose translation of the *Aeneid* (which he completed after he left school) and discovered astronomy, music — and liberalism in the pages of Leigh Hunt's *Examiner*. He soaked himself in books with such delight that they became parts of his creative imagination. Spencer, Chapman and Drayton, later and most important, Shakespeare, were among the authors who became part of this transforming experience. It was when writing about *King Lear* that he wrote of that attitude to life which embodies 'negative capability' and which 'is capable of being in uncertainties, mysteries, doubts, and does without any irritable reaching out after fact and reason'.

The trust fund set up for the Keats children was badly managed. Keats could have gone to Oxford; instead he was articled to Thomas Hammond, an apothecary surgeon of Edmonton, and stayed with him for four years, studying the theory and practice of medicine. Fortunately Keats was near enough to Clarke to see him regularly, borrow books and talk about poetry. Of all poets Spencer, with his suggestive epithets and rich imagery, was the most attractive. Keats went through the *Faerie Queene* 'as a young horse would go through a spring meadow — ramping'. His first poem was 'Imitation of Spencer', written when he was eighteen. Sonnets and odes that followed in 1814 and 1815 all show the same natural fault of artificiality, the same predictable enthusiasm. Keats was straining to achieve a poetic manner, using a language that may have seemed fresher, less derivative to him than it does to us.

Before he moved to Southwark in October 1815, to complete his training at Guy's Hospital, he was a committed poet. As he worked at practical anatomy, assisting at operations, witnessing pain and death, his mind was often elsewhere. We are told that he always sat beside a window, and talked of nothing but poetry. He still fell naturally into stale idioms; he conceived an unfortunate admiration for the verse of Leigh Hunt. It was Hunt, however, who first published a poem, 'O Solitude', by Keats, in the *Examiner*, and his friendship encouraged Keats in fast and fluent writing. Another friend of this time was the painter Haydon, a total artist, passionate and reckless. Keats, who had qualified and been licensed to practice medicine in July 1816, made himself a home with his brothers in Cheapside and announced that he was going to be a poet. His first collection of poems was published in March 1817. One evening that winter Hunt and he were dining together and gave each other crowns of laurel and ivy to wear; visitors called, Hunt was embarrassed and removed his crown; Keats, unabashed, kept his on. He used to write under an engraving of Shakespeare's head; he read Shakespeare with a new determination to master his craft. The result was *Endymion* (April 1817-February 1818), in his own words 'four thousand lines of one bare circumstance', the love of Cynthia for the mortal Endymion. His concern in the poem is human experience raised to the imaginative 'sublime'. In the course of writing the poem he wrote to a friend: 'What the Imagination seizes as Beauty must be Truth — whether it existed before or not — for I have the same idea of all our Passions as of Love, they are all in their sublime, creative of essential Beauty ... However it may be, O for a life of sensations rather than of Thoughts!'

Hazlitt influenced Keats in his important conception of a poet as a purely creative being without individual character or identity, who passed, as Hazlitt said, 'through every variety of untried being'. The painter Joseph Severn noted his powers of observation: 'Even the features and gestures of passing tramps, the colour of one woman's hair, the smile on one child's face ...' The more mature Keats was, however, to recognize the poet's need for an ethical identity. He revered Wordsworth as the great poet of the age and liked to quote from 'Tintern Abbey' or 'Intimations of Immortality'. But he was opposed to 'poetry that has a palpable design upon us' for 'Poetry should be great and unobtrusive, a thing that enters one's soul.' What he admired in a poet was the capacity for sympathetic identification with some object dearer to him than himself. Nor was this theory unrelated to his life. He was by nature generous of time and sympathy towards friends and family. He was at home in the 'racketing' of literary London: there in 1818 he met Wordsworth, Lamb, Shelley and Joseph Severn. But his brother Tom, sickly with tuberculosis, had first claim on him and he went to look after him in Devonshire. In June his brother George left for America with his young wife — a great blow to Keats.

To escape from his sadness and to gain experience he set off on a tour with Charles Brown, walked 650 miles in the now conventional territory of romance, saw the Lakes, Scotland, climbed Ben Nevis and sailed out to Staffa. He returned awakened in sensibility but physically exhausted: Tom was now very ill and until his death at the end of November Keats scarcely left him. Living in the stuffy Hampstead sickroom, serving his brother with tender care, sleeping little, working on the first draft of 'Hyperion', Keats entered his maturity as man and poet. The experiences of twenty-three years had been vivid, exciting, often beautiful, sometimes cruel. One blow he should not have had to suffer was the scornful attack of Lockhart in the August issue of *Black-wood's* magazine. Keats, as the principal representative of the 'cockney school', was told to go back to the shop: 'It is a better and wiser thing to be a starved apothecary than a starved poet.' Croker's criticism in the *Quarterly Review* was even more damaging because more judicious, the work of a critic of sharp intelligence but no spark of poetic feeling. Keats made a defiant response. 'The genius of Poetry must work out its own salvation in a man: it cannot be matured by law and precept, but by sensation and watchfulness in itself.'

1819 was a miraculous year. For a time Keats was happy. He shared a house with Charles Brown; he met Fanny Brawne and experienced the passionate longings of first love. Two intense personal drives merged in one frenzied activity. He wanted to marry Fanny and to write poetry, not only because he loved it — but to live and provide for her. He had debts; George had lost money in America. In the early part of the year he wrote 'The Eve of St. Agnes'. With 'Hyperion' this poem shows that he has come of age: Milton and Spencer no longer dominate, the richness is all his own. 'Hyperion' is one of the few great pieces of epic poetry in the language; it can only be called a failure by the high standards that Keats set himself and sometimes attained. The shorter narrative of 'The Eve of St. Agnes' speaks of the emotion of young love — and contains the finest description of cold in our literature. It was written fast, but, as always, Keats revised carefully, looking for ways of replacing the general by the concrete and tactile. He was suffering from painful sore throats, but his mood was often elated. 'The faint conceptions I have of Poems to come brings the blood frequently into my forehead', he wrote to Woodhouse. In May 1819 he wrote the 'Ode to a Nightingale', and 'Ode on a Grecian Urn', the 'Ode to Melancholy' and the 'Ode to Indolence'. He was obsessed by the transitoriness of love and beauty. The attraction of the urn and the nightingale is that they are above the process of change and decay. In the summer he stayed with Brown on the Isle of Wight: he rewrote much of 'Hyperion', which became 'The Fall of Hyperion', and 'Lamia'. In the latter poems there is a harder brilliance, nearer to Byron's style. Like most of Keats's poems it centres on a conflict (his love of freedom against his love for Fanny?) between idealistic aspiration and realistic disenchantment. In September he wrote the 'Ode to Autumn', his most perfect expression of the elegiac mood: serene but overshadowed by sadness. We can only record these facts and marvel.

A reaction after his labours is not surprising. He and Fanny were tacitly engaged in the winter. His love-letters record his urgent but undirected desires. Then there was the onset of the tuberculosis that he had probably contracted from Tom, and pressing material worries: he had written what he must instinctively have known was great poetry, but he was living by money forwarded by his publishers. He decided to be a journalist 'on the liberal side of the question'. He wrote a satirical piece, 'Cap and Bells', about the marital troubles of the Regent. Was Keats, we may wonder, deliberately staying on the surface for fear of letting the intensity of inward experience overwhelm him? As he wrote to Fanny: 'I am very lax, unemployed, un-meridianed and objectless these last two months' (November). George returned in January to raise money from their trustee; some of it was Keats's, but he was too diffident to press his own claims. Soon afterwards he had a bad haemorrhage. He said to the faithful Brown as he coughed up blood: 'I know the colour of that blood; it is arterial blood; I cannot be deceived in that colour; that drop of blood is my death-warrant; I must die.' He was comforted in his slow decline by belated praise for his poems of the previous year. Leigh Hunt took him in till August; then he went to the Brawnes' house, where he had the harrowing experience of seeing Fanny daily, of seeing her drift away from him, and having to release her from the engagement. He was frantic at times with jealousy and despair, but brave and without self-pity. He dreaded having to leave England, but friends arranged for him to sail to Italy with Joseph Severn, who proved a sympathetic companion.

Dying slowly in the house by the Spanish steps in Rome (the house which is still preserved as a Keats museum), tended by Dr. James Clark, vomiting blood and kept alive only by the vitality of youth, fully aware from his medical knowledge of what was happening to him, Keats maintained his outward-looking spirit to the end, constantly concerned about Severn's work and the time he had to spend on his patient. He died on 23 February 1821. An autopsy revealed that the lungs were quite gone. 'Tell him', wrote

Leigh Hunt to Severn (thinking that Keats was still alive), 'tell that great poet and noble-hearted man, that we shall all bear his memory in the most precious part of our hearts, and that the world shall bow their heads to it as our loves do ... Tell him he was only before us on the road, as he was in everything else.'

W. J. Bate, *John Keats*, 1963.
Robert Gittings, *John Keats*, 1968.

**PERCY BYSSHE SHELLEY** (1792-1822), poet, was the son of a Sussex baronet, Sir Timothy Shelley, of Field Place, Horsham, and of Elizabeth Pilfold. Timothy's father, Bysshe, the first baronet, had married heiresses, Mary Michell and Elizabeth Perry, and had large estates. Timothy was briefly in Parliament. His wife was handsome in a rather stately way, a good letter-writer and a lover of the countryside. Field Place was a delightful old house for an imaginative child: 'very rambling, with long passages and odd corners, turnings and recesses, floors on different levels', set in a park, with fine trees and large gardens. Percy, a beautiful child, was the eldest of seven. His father 'read the Classics and other Books with him in the full hopes of making him a good and Gentlemanly Scholar'.

As a child Percy displayed a precocious inventiveness: he told his family and the servants fabulous stories about dragons and spirits. In his holidays he would divert himself, between shooting, riding and inspecting sheep, by writing poems. He had a good memory and ear: Gray's *Ode on a Favourite Cat* he reproduced entire after one reading. Two other traits hinted at a future less conventional than that of scholar-squire. He noticed the poverty of country people and planned to do something about it. One boyish scheme was to educate an orphan girl. He once made a stir at a dance by selecting for his partner a girl who was sitting out: she had been seduced and was being ignored — and that was enough for him. The miniature painted by the *émigré* duc de Montpensier, in 1802, depicts a sensitive but confident face. In the same year he was sent to his private school, Sion House Academy. He suffered the shocks that other boys from spacious, cherished homes, unacquainted with school, have endured at the hands of boarding school bullies. He retreated into solitude and books — preferably thrillers, strong stuff in that heyday of vampires and

*Percy Bysshe Shelley*
(Artist: Amelia Curran)

spectres. 'While yet a boy I sought for ghosts', he wrote in the first line of *Hymn to Intellectual Beauty*, and 'called on poisonous names'. He dreamed dreams that transcended mere schoolboy curiosity about the unknown. These lines from the dedication of

*The Revolt of Islam* describe an intense experience which may belong to the years of Sion. He was crying, one 'fresh May-dawn', outside the schoolroom with its 'harsh and grating strife of tyrants and of foes':

> So without shame I spake: 'I will be wise,
> And just, and free, and mild, if in me lies
> Such power.'

Eton in 1804 began a time of liberation, despite the temporary constraints of fagging, the 'Shelley-baiting' and later the 'fierce dominion' of Dr. Keate, who taught Shelley in the VI form. In July 1810 he translated half of 37 books of Pliny's *Natural History*! Keate noticed that he fell into metrical rhythms even in his Latin prose. He gave his housemaster a shock with an electrical machine. Astronomy also fascinated him. 'His jubilee was night. His spirit bounded on the shadow of darkness, and flew to the countless worlds beyond', wrote one contemporary. One friend, Halliday, recalls of Shelley 'the sparkling poetry of his mind', which 'shone out of his speaking eye, when he was dwelling on anything good or great'. As later at Oxford he threw a romantic haze over the countryside, transforming what he saw into a land of enchantment. What great walkers those romantics were — even Coleridge! Shelley was 'strong, light and active', Hogg wrote of him at eighteen, and well-suited 'to perform, as it were, a pedestrian steeplechase'.

Shelley went up to University College, Oxford. Imagine the clerical university, the factiousness of an inbred society, tutors who were aggravated by his civil rejections of their views, and the young scholar, idealist and egotist in a combination which would not have been so unusual if he had not also been so strong-willed: conflict was inevitable. Shelley read a lot: Plato, the Greek dramatists, historians, Shakespeare; he studied logic and science; above all, encouraged by his father, who urged him to compete for a poetry prize, he plied his pen. Of his interests at this time *A Poetical Essay on the Existing State of Things* — an early form of *Queen Mab* — may have been typical: the profits were intended for Peter Finnerty, who was in gaol for writing a 'libellous' letter against Lord Castlereagh. He also wrote *The Necessity of Atheism*, prepared with his friend Thomas Hogg and published by Philadelphia Phillips at Worthing. Written a stone's throw from the College chapel which symbolized the Anglican supremacy, this anonymous tract argued logically from the premise that 'The senses are the source of all knowledge to the mind'. It was sold at his printers and sent out to heads of colleges and bishops. Shelley and Hogg were expelled. Shelley had been a peacock in dress and pursuits. He went for country walks armed with a pair of duelling pistols. He played all the parts as though he had never expected to stay long. But he was 'good-natured and kind' — and he was only eighteen. And he, of all people, never knew an Oxford summer! A pleasant Oxford story may be his memorial, to go perhaps with the effigy by which the College made amends. Hogg tells of the young philosopher on Magdalen Bridge, grasping a baby from his mother's arms, inquiring 'in a piercing voice, and with a wistful look, "Will your baby tell us anything about pre-existence, madam?"'.

Timothy offered his son a voyage to the Greek islands on condition that he parted from Hogg. Shelley refused: he also rejected a generous offer by the Duke of Norfolk to accommodate him in due course with a parliamentary seat at Horsham. Only the good offices of an uncle secured him an allowance. Shelley stayed in London, wrote satires of the Prince Regent, even threw them into carriages attending a Carlton House banquet. He attended anatomical lectures at Bart's, and visited Cwm Elan in Radnorshire, the estate of Mr Thomas Grove, father of the girl whom Shelley had wanted to marry. He then married another, Harriet Westbrook. Sixteen years old, a school friend of his sisters at Clapham, brought up to strict principles, she had met Shelley, been disturbed by his atheism and fallen in love with him. On 28 August 1811 they married in Edinburgh. He inscribed the register: 'Percy Bysshe Shelley, farmer, Sussex'.

Shelley returned from a stormy visit to his father to rescue his wife from Hogg, who had taken too literally Shelley's views on the sharing of property, and in November 1811 settled in a cottage near Keswick. There he met Southey whose reaction was amused: 'Here is a man who acts upon me as my own ghost would do. He is just what I was in 1794.' Shelley was predictably disappointed. He dashed off to Dublin with a stirring *Address to the Irish People*. He suggested religious toleration for all at a Catholic emancipation rally, and was hissed out. The autumn of 1812 saw the Shelleys at Tremadoc helping William Madocks to reclaim marshland behind a sea-wall and build the town of Portmadoc. An attempt was made, one February night, to murder the poet. By whom, or why, has never transpired. Out of such experiences a more mature person and a greater poet was made. He intended to measure the quality of life by 'enthusiast feeling' in 'actual living', rather than by 'some grey veteran's of the world's cold school'. He remained true to this: the Shelley who was drowned in Italy was little different from the Shelley, self-deluding, quixotic, impulsive, who sent off copies of his *Letter to Ellenborough*, some by balloon and some in bottles down the Bristol Channel, and who, in 1813, brought out his private edition of *Queen Mab*. His friend Hookham had declined to publish this 'philosophical poem', which employs an un-Shakespearean fairy queen to utter lectures on politics and religion. Godwinist in anticipation of human growth toward justice and perfection by the operation of free minds, vehement in denunciation of kings, priests, statesmen, commerce and war, it is diffuse but not vague. This least indolent of romantics had acquired experience through wide reading — and his notes to the poem, on such matters as vegetarianism, indicate a bold intelligence.

Shelley's domestic life was one of constant motion. In June 1813 Harriet had a baby girl. He collected a *coterie* in London, centring upon J. F. Newton, a vegetarian, mystic and student of the zodiac. Amidst debts, borrowings, poems and hypochondria (he believed for a time that he had contracted elephantiasis), such relationships kept him stable. The strain on Harriet was immense. In March 1814 they were remarried, with proper formality, at St. George's, Hanover Square. In the summer of 1815 they separated: his mind suffered, 'like a little kingdom, the nature of an insurrection' for he had fallen in love with Mary Godwin, the daughter of William Godwin and Mary Wollstonecraft. Mary proposed that they live together — Mary as sister, Harriet as wife! Shelley felt that Harriet could not be a partner of his life: she could not feel poetry nor understand philosophy. She resented the false gods and demanding friends — Godwin above all.

In the summer of Waterloo Shelley lived at Bishopsgate, near Windsor: to this period belong *Summer Evening Churchyard* and (December) *Alastor or the Spirit of Solitude*. The latter's theme is that self-centred seclusion is punished by a daemon of ruin — but it may also be read as an elegy for the lost dreams of youth. In

May 1816 Shelley and Mary went to Geneva. There they met Byron, and Claire Clairemont. The poets' encounter was mutually inspiring: they boated together, recited and made poetry, and told stories. Mary's story, *Frankenstein*, was the most successful. Shelley returned in September with the third canto of Byron's *Childe Harold* for the printer, and Claire, carrying Byron's child, the future Allegra. In October 1816, Fanny Imlay, the daughter of Mary Wollstonecraft by her first marriage, committed suicide: neglected by Godwin, she had adored Shelley. Then Harriet was found drowned in the Serpentine (December 1816). Suicide is most probable, since she seems to have been rejected by her family. Well might Shelley now 'stare aghast'. Was he doomed to destroy those who loved him? At the end of the month he married Mary at St. Mildred's, Bread Street, for form's sake, on Godwin's insistence. But he was sick at heart. He offered a home to Claire and Allegra (born in January) and filed a suit in Chancery for custody of Harriet's children which was refused by Lord Eldon.

In December 1816 Leigh Hunt honoured Shelley, Keats, Reynolds and Byron, in his manifesto *Young Poets*, as the men who would re-animate English poetry. It was at Hunt's cottage in Hampstead that Shelley met Keats. Keats was lost in Shelley's 'daedal round with nature, and his Archimedean endeavours to move the globe with his own hands'. It was at Hampstead that Shelley rescued a woman having a fit: this was one of his 'most ordinary actions'. Among those whom he met were Hazlitt, Haydon, Severn and Horace Smith, a city man. They all left descriptions from which a composite picture may be formed. Fair, freckled, light-brown hair, delicate-looking, a gentle expression, a light voice (Haydon thought it 'feminine', Hazlitt 'shrill'), intensely blue eyes which seemed (Severn) 'to dwell more on the inward than the outward aspect of nature', slender, slightly drooping figure, unmistakably 'a *gentleman* ... one that is gentle, accomplished and brave' (Smith).

Albion House, Marlow, was to be his Dove Cottage: here he could husband his resources and observe nature. He lived sparingly; his diet was largely vegetarian; he walked a great deal and rowed on the Thames. Here he was seen 'with his hat wreathed with briony, or wild convolvulus; his hand filled with bunches of wildflowers plucked from the hedges as he passed ...'. The abstracted poet was also the warm-hearted squire: there were coins and blankets for the poor, visits to cottages, amateur medical advice: some of the country people liked the man whom their betters declared to be an atheist and seducer. At Marlow he wrote *Laon and Cynthia* (later published as *The Revolt of Islam*), with the revealing sub-title *The Revolution of the Golden City: A Vision of the Nineteenth Century*; its preface announced that the poem was written 'in the cause of a liberal and comprehensive morality'. Cynthia has been called the first 'new woman' in our poetry; she is as intelligent as she is passionate. But Hunt's judgement, 'The work cannot possibly become popular', was an understatement. Shelley wrote as if he had never met any real people, because he deliberately set out to be universal and abstract. In *Prometheus Unbound*, a greater poem in three Acts (a fourth was added, more lyrical but obscure and not obviously related), *Prometheus* embodies his Platonic idea that 'reasoned principles of moral conduct' are useless unless man can learn what is beautiful and virtuous.

Suffering from ill-health for which a damp house and his importunate father-in-law may be held to blame, Shelley was persuaded to go to Italy. He and Mary left in March 1818 after a hasty christening of their son and daughter and Allegra. Harriet's children had to be left behind, of course: when Charles Bysshe died of consumption in 1826 his old grandfather, who had brought him up fondly, simply described him on his memorial as 'grandson of Sir Timothy and Lady Elizabeth Shelley'. The Shelleys enjoyed a leisurely journey, taking in the sights while Shelley gathered inspiration for the glorious poetry of his last period. Some of the shorter poems, such as *Stanzas written in Dejection near Naples*, witness, however, to distress. His infant daughter Claire died in September 1818 at Venice, where Shelley stayed with Byron. In June 1819 his son William died at Rome. Then his servant Paolo attempted to blackmail him over the parentage of a mysterious infant. When 'my poor Neapolitan', as Shelley called the supposed mother, died in the summer of 1820, he wrote: 'It seems as if the destruction that is consuming me were as an atmosphere which wrapt and *infected* everything connected with me'.

He sought solace in intense writing. In 1819 he wrote most of *Prometheus* (at about the same time Beethoven was composing his *Choral Symphony*) and the *Cenci*, a Webster-like drama, regarded by St. John Ervine as proof that Shelley 'knew the tricks of the theatre trade by instinct'. *The Mask of Anarchy*, a manifesto directed to the working men of England, was composed in generous rage after he heard of Peterloo (August 1819). Some of his noblest lyrical poems also belong to this year, notably the *Ode to the West Wind*. In 1820 the Shelleys settled in Pisa with their baby son Percy, who had been born the previous November. Beside much else Shelley wrote the satirical drama of *Oedipus Tyrannus* or *Swellfoot the Tyrant* (King George IV).

The romantic Skythrop in Peacock's satirical novel, *Nightmare Abbey*, sold but seven copies of his treatise 'upon reforming the world' but he was undaunted. Shelley recognized and enjoyed his friend's caricature of himself: he, too, sold but seven copies of *Oedipus*. The *Epipsychidion*, 'an idealised history of my life and feelings', originated with his meeting with Emilia Viviani in a convent near Pisa. He had fallen briefly in love with her — and may have wanted her to elope. Very different is the *Adonais*, an elegy suggested by the death of Keats — more about Shelley than about Keats, and most about the condition of mankind.

> Life, like a dome of many-coloured glass,
> Stains the white radiance of Eternity,
> Until Death tramples it to fragments.

In this incomparable poem Shelley indeed obeyed Keats' injunction to him 'to be more of an artist'.

In prefaces to his works Shelley expounded political and moral views. As he told Peacock, he considered poetry 'very subordinate to moral and political science'. When, however, Peacock wrote his *Four Ages of Poetry*, arguing that poetry was a primitive thing, Shelley accepted the challenge. Philip Sidney, author of *Apologie for Poetrie*, was one of his idols. He wrote his great essay, the *Defence of Poetry*, in the vein of Sidney. Poetry, he affirms, 'lifts the veil from the hidden beauty of the world, and makes familiar objects be as if they were not familiar'. Shelley also draws upon his own experience: 'When composition begins, inspiration is already in the decline, and the most glorious poetry ... is probably a feeble shadow of the original conceptions of the poet.'

Shelley's last poem, aptly called *The Triumph of Life*, shows that he was at the height of his powers. In his insistence upon 'the contagion of the world's slow stain', Shelley seems to be giving up the idea that earthly happiness is possible: the word 'triumph' is surely intended ironically. The poem, which Eliot held to be his wisest and best, ends abruptly with the line: 'Then, what is life? I cried'. There is an urgency about the verse, as if Shelley has much to say in a hurry: he is looking on in a vision at a crowd of people hastening blindly along a dusty road. The poem was written in a lonely house on the Bay of Spezia. In June Shelley heard of the arrival of Leigh Hunt in Italy: he and his friend Williams set sail for Leghorn. The meeting with Hunt was a happy one: they planned a new journal.

On 8 July Shelley and Williams left Leghorn for Lerici; they sailed into the haze of a coming storm; the boat was swamped by a heavy sea — she appears to have been rammed by a *felucca*. Some Italian fishermen knew that they had money on board. The bodies were washed up near Viareggio. In Shelley's pocket was a volume of Keats's poems 'doubled back, as if the reader, in the act of reading, had hastily thrown it away'. On 15 August 1822, in the presence of the quarantine officers, Italian soldiers, Trelawney, Hunt and Byron, Shelley's corpse was burned, on a funeral pyre. The flame looked 'as tho' it contained the glassy essence of vitality'. Byron turned away from the Virgilian scene and swam out to his ship. The heart was sent to Mary; the ashes to the Protestant cemetery at Rome.

Edmund Blunden, *Shelley*, 1946.
N. I. White, *Shelley*, 2 vols., 1947.

**MARY WOLLSTONECRAFT SHELLEY** (1798-1851) wrote *Frankenstein*. In play and film its story has so caught and held the imagination of successive generations that the single fact might be held sufficient to justify her inclusion among the famous. Indeed she might otherwise chiefly be known as the poet's second wife: no mean qualification either since William Godwin's daughter came as near as any woman could to meeting Shelley's requirement for life partnership: 'one who can feel poetry and understand philosophy'. Aged sixteen she eloped with Shelley to form the notorious *ménage à trois*, with Claire Clairmont, through whom their fortunes became intertwined with those of Byron. After two suicides, those of Mary's half sister, Fanny, and Shelley's deserted wife, Harriet, in December 1816, her relationship was formalised by marriage. Already she had borne a son, William. There would follow Clara and Percy: the latter would inherit the Shelley baronetcy. From 1818 the Shelleys lived in Italy: Venice, Rome, Naples, finally Pisa. In June 1819 William died. In July 1822 Shelley was drowned. Thereafter Mary lived mainly in England, reconciled to her father, giving her time mainly to editing and publicising her husband's poems, educating her son, writing more novels. *The Last Man* (1826) is usually held to be the best of them: it describes the future destruction of the human race by a plague. Her *Journal* is a rich source for those seeking to track Shelley's life and enter his mind. She did not marry again.

*Frankenstein* had been published in 1818. Subtitled *The Modern Prometheus* it narrates the dire consequences that arise after a scientist has artificially created a human being. There is much of Godwin in the manner and matter of the book: chains of the mind, the power of truth, the virtues of republicanism. More generally it is of its age: Rousseau would recognise Frankenstein's creation, archetypal man in the state of nature, virtuous until corrupted by his treatment by other people. It is redolent of the darker side of Romanticism. Within the Gothic *genre*, it offered a sustained metaphor for the upheavals of the age. Shelley contributed much. The intense household, at once idealistic and self-absorbed, reading adventurously, revelling in speculation and story-telling, provided the perfect ambience. *Frankenstein* remains Mary's creation, its unique character her incontestable achievement.

Muriel Spark, *Mary Shelley*, 1987.

**GEORGE GORDON, LORD BYRON** (1788-1824) was born at 16 Holles Street, London, the son of Captain John Byron and his second wife, Catherine Gordon, formerly a Scottish heiress of better birth than education. By his previous marriage, to Lady Carmarthen, Captain Byron had one surviving child, Augusta. The son of 'Foul-weather Jack', the Admiral Byron of circumnavigation fame, he was a handsome, extravagant rake: by 1786 he had exhausted his wife's fortune and was compelled to live abroad; he died in poverty at Valenciennes. Mrs Byron retired with George to live in Aberdeen. They were poor, their

*George Gordon Byron, 6th Baron Byron*
(Artist: Richard Westall)

home was bleak, her temper was ungovernably violent; her lame son loved, feared and resented her. In 1798 his great-uncle died at Newstead Abbey, whither he had retired, with his mistress and a single servant, after killing one of the Chaworth family in a duel.

Byron, now sixth lord, and his mother found Newstead

dilapidated, and the estates encumbered by debts, so they had to live in a modest house in the neighbouring town of Southwell. In 1801 Byron was sent to Harrow, where he earned the nickname of 'the Old English Baron' and was admired for his personality and prowess at games: he boxed, swam in 'Duck Puddle' and played cricket against Eton. He remained, however, morbidly sensitive about the malformation of his right foot which made him limp. He enjoyed declaiming his own verse and speeches. Dr. Drury, the headmaster, grew tired of his escapades and lectured him: 'Because you are about to leave Harrow, it is no reason for you to make the house a scene of riot and confusion.' Byron later, however, remembered Drury with affection and respect and his son Henry Drury became a close friend. The attractions of Harrow were enhanced by the dullness of his life elsewhere. Southwell he wished 'to be swallowed up by an earthquake'; at fifteen he had fallen in love with Mary Chaworth, 'the morning star of Annesley', little older than himself; she preferred a local squire and Byron was deeply mortified: had he not heard her refer to him as 'the little lame boy'? At Trinity College, Cambridge (1805-8) his trusted school friend, Edward Long, helped to keep him in relatively sober ways, in what he called 'a villainous chaos of din and drunkeness, nothing but hazard and burgundy, hunting, mathematics and Newmarket, riot and racing'. Soon, however, his debts began to mount and he had to retire to his mother's house for a time. His first volume of poems, *House of Idleness* (1807), was properly 'cut up' by the *Edinburgh Review*. In January 1809 with *English Bards and Scotch Reviewers* he revenged himself upon the *Edinburgh Review* and showed a talent for satire in the Augustan manner. To celebrate his coming of age he took possession of Newstead, threw a bibulous party for his friends, who proclaimed him 'abbot' and drank his health out of a skull. He had a last violent scene with his mother and then (June 1809) left England for a grand tour.

For two years, with his devoted valet Fletcher, he travelled at random about the Mediterranean countries, going as far as Smyrna and Constantinople. The journeys were the making of the poet. In exotic and unfamiliar scenes he could shake off the introspective melancholy that so readily settled on him. On his return to England, for example, we find him writing: 'My whole life has been at variance with propriety, not to say decency ... my existence a dreary void.' His mother died just before he could reach Newstead to see her. At the same time his friend Charles Matthews was drowned: 'Some curse', he said, 'hangs over me and mine. My mother lies a corpse in this house; one of my best friends is drowned in a ditch.' The histrionic touches, even in grief, are typical. He brought home a poem from Greece which Robert Dallas, a remote relation and a warm admirer, submitted to John Murray. Murray wished apparently to call these Spenserian stanzes *Child of Harrow's Pilgrimage*. Perhaps fortunately, Byron's title, *Childe Harold's Pilgrimage*, prevailed. It appeared in March 1812, just after Byron's much-praised maiden speech in the House of Lords (an attack on the Frame-Breaking Bill and a sane, compassionate and well-documented statement of the workmen's case) and it was an instant success. Byron had written a racy traveller's journal in verse, a novelty in itself, and introduced the 'Byronic hero'. In the words of the *Edinburgh Re-view* 'There is … something piquant in the very novelty and singularity of that cast of misanthropy and universal scorn, which we have … noticed as among the more repulsive features of the composition'. The author could now be inspected by society.

He was about five foot eight, slender but well-knit. He could swim five miles and he was a good enough boxer to spar with 'Gentleman' Jackson. He had thick reddish hair, which was usually darkened and glossy with macassar oil and curled on his forehead; a straight line of nose and forehead; a full, sulky mouth with lips which 'fell singularly at the corners' and a heavy jaw. He could be easy with his friends; in large assemblies he tended to look supercilious. Aggressively masculine in his attitude to the other sex, whom he professed to treat as dolls, he was also feminine in his vanity, in his need to be noticed, and in his love of gossip. His lameness was hardly disfiguring, but it gave to his walk a smoothly gliding appearance. His be-ringed hands were delicately white. Appearance, rumour, legend, the lionizing tendencies of hostesses of the *beau monde*, the giddy atmosphere of 'the year of the waltz', Byron's own eager assuming of the part of literary lion, all contributed to a social sensation. Pope — whom Byron so much admired — could perhaps have done justice to the scene: Byron's own letters give a sufficiently vivid account of a time when, we are told, his name occurred so often at dinner parties and so excitedly that its repetition — Byr'n-Byr'n-Byr'n —

sank into a low continuous murmur. He became entangled with the unfortunate Lady Caroline Lamb. He grew more contemptuous of what passed for convention in Regency society. In January 1815, however, he married Annabella Milbanke, Lady Melbourne's niece, a girl of strong principles who loved Byron enough to want to rescue him. He behaved abominably and the marriage was a disaster. Moody and petulant, he was unmoved even by the birth of a daughter, Ada, in December, and they separated in January 1816. His wife seems to have become convinced that Byron had been enjoying an incestuous relationship with Augusta and that it was the end of this relationship that had made Byron so morose and cold in marriage. That Byron, obsessed by what he called 'the nightmare of my delinquencies' and convinced that he was ruled by destiny, was capable of such incest we may still doubt; Augusta was a passive, fond, receptive person. She surely meant no harm — and may have done none. The facts are mercifully obscure.

When the separation proceedings were complete Byron left England for the last time (April 1816), leaving behind frustrated bailiffs and a hum of scandalous gossip. The famous chestnut hair was already greying. He travelled across the Low Countries with his personal physician, Dr. Polidori, and settled beside Lake Geneva. There visitors included the Shelleys and Claire Clairmont, step-sister of Mary Godwin (Shelley's mistress and future wife). Shelley found Byron 'a slave to the vilest and most vulgar prejudices, and as mad as the winds.' After some time in his company, Claire returned to England to give birth to his daughter, Allegra. After touring the Bernese Alps he went to Milan, where he discarded Dr Polidori, and came to live in Venice (November 1816). Its decaying splendour suited him well. He wrote prolifically, mainly at night when his imagination was inflamed; he swam tirelessly, spent many hours over dressing — and drinking — and made love almost indiscriminately. He escaped from remorse and fatal *ennui* by escapades which he delighted to report. Margarita Cogni, 'wild as a witch and fierce as a demon', is among the memorable portraits in a famous letter to John Murray. He grew more debauched; health and temper suffered, as Shelley found when he visited him in 1818, the year in which he began *Don Juan*. The countess Guiccioli established him as her accepted lover in the Guiccioli palace in Ravenna. Her husband was apparently complaisant, and her brother Pietro Gamba drew Byron into the nationalist movement.

In the summer of 1821 Gamba's intrigues were unmasked by the Austrian authorities and they were banished from Ravenna. Byron followed them to Pisa and then to a villa near Leghorn. In April 1822 Allegra died at her convent; in June Shelley was drowned. Leigh Hunt had come out to plan a paper, *The Liberal*, with Shelley and Byron, but he had little in common with Byron and they soon quarrelled. Byron's craving for action was aroused by news that a Whig committee had been formed in London to aid the Greek rebels. He was invited by the committee to represent them in Greece. His sensible analysis and prompt actions show that he had the instinct of a man of action, though he had not been trained as either diplomat or soldier. The Greeks were divided and his main task was to sort out their claims. At the beginning of 1824 he was at Missolonghi, a poor little town among mosquito-ridden swamps. He came home soaked after a ride, caught a fever and died. To the end he was brave, active, and cheerful in adversity. His body was brought home to be buried in the family vault at Hucknall Torkard in Nottinghamshire. His spirit lived to inspire thousands who had never seen him.

Goethe called Byron 'the greatest genius of the century'. He possessed 'a high degree of that daemonic instinct and attraction which influences others independently of reason, effort or affection, which sometimes succeeds in guiding where the understanding fails'. Mazzini said: 'He gave a European rôle to English poetry. He led the genius of England on a pilgrimage through Europe.' Romanticism was to become identified with Byron but Byronism was a personal presentation of a movement that Byron scarcely understood; in him, it was more of a life-style than a coherent philosophy. From the English viewpoint he is out of the main stream of romantic poetry. Fellow-poets tended to regard him as an alien. Wordsworth found his style 'slovenly'; Coleridge dismissed *Don Juan* as Byron's 'last flash poem'. Keats wrote of him: 'He describes what he sees — I describe what I imagine.' Shelley alone among the great poets admired Byron. He saw that in *Don Juan* Byron put much of his real self. Natural, unaffected, racy, ebullient — like his letters that used to be read out loud at gatherings of his friends — the style of the poem is suited to his theme. Lyrical description, rough satire, long narrative periods and outbursts of personal feeling are all easily conveyed. His carelessness and use of slang are a virtue in this poem: they add to the effect of conversation. Mockery is the essence of the poem — for so Byron sought to reconcile the perpetual war of feelings and intelligence.

Writing what was both a romantic epic and a realistic satire, Byron spoke to his generation of reawakened liberals. His reputation in Europe is not therefore entirely based on misconceptions, nor on the fact that his verses translate easily. He appealed because he was an aristocratic rebel, a rejector of established systems, an aggressively self-assertive personality: a lustful *milord anglais* who went off to die for Greek freedom. Even in his prose there was a vital spirit. His influence upon English poetry has waned; much of his satire is as dead as its victims; critical appreciation has restored *Don Juan* and perhaps *Vision of Judgement* to their rightful place as satirical masterpieces, but few would put him on the same level as Wordsworth, Keats or Shelley. Insincerity, theatricality, lack of imaginative depth characterize his writing when he strays away from his own emotional experience.

Biography confirms many of the impressions of contemporaries. Whether 'Mad, bad, dangerous to know', as Caroline Lamb called him, or simply a near-helpless victim of heredity, upbringing and environment, Byron was incapable of behaving for long in a rational and decent manner. As rake and scribbler he performed with genius. The essence of it was the sheer energy with which he felt and suffered, energy which he could not direct for long to practical ends; and his unique gift of self-projection. To Byron may well be applied the depressing words of Paul Valéry: 'We love only ourselves.'

Ed. J. Murray, *Lord Byron's Correspondence*, 2 vols., 1922.
P. Quennell, *Byron: the Years of Fame*, 1935; *Byron in Italy*, 1941.
L. A. Marchand, *Byron, a Biography*, 3 vols., 1957.

**SIR WALTER SCOTT**, Baronet (1771-1832), poet and novelist, was the son of Walter Scott, Writer to the Signet, and of Anne Rutherford, daughter of Professor Rutherford of Edinburgh. On his father's side he was descended from one of the many branches

of the Buccleuch family. Edinburgh and the abrasive but cultured
life of its lawyers and academics, the Borders and the traditional
life of the laird, provided the background of his life and writing.
He was born in a wynd in the Old Town — such a one, perhaps,
as is described by Stevenson in his essay. When a baby he became
crippled in the right leg and he walked with a limp all his life.
With his friend John Irving he composed romances. Following
what he called the 'principle of romantic research' he read Dante
and fastened 'like a tiger, upon every collection of old songs
and romances which chance threw in my way'. He went for long
country walks 'for the pleasure of seeing romantic scenery'. The
spirit of story-telling possessed him as he stood on the field of
Bannockburn or tramped across the Pentland Hills. 'In crossing
Magus Moor, near St. Andrews, the spirit moved me to give a
picture of the assassination of the Archbishop of St. Andrews
to some fellow-travellers ... and one of them, though well
acquainted with the story, protested my narrative had frightened
away his night's sleep.'

Many childhood months were spent on his grandfather's farm
in Teviotdale. The delicate child grew up a tall man, strong, a
great walker and a tireless horseman. The de'il's in ye, Sherra',
Archibald Park would say; 'Ye'll never halt till they bring ye
hame with your feet foremost.' From Edinburgh High School, in
1783, he went to the University. At first he worked as writer under
his father, but soon decided to become an advocate. In 1792 he
was called to the Scottish Bar. As readers of Cockburn will know,
this was a brilliant period in Edinburgh's history. There were
giants on the bench and in the university. Young men disputed and
philosophized and pursued their own forensic or literary ambi-
tions; it was a prolific, slightly arrogant society. With the intellectual side of his professional community Scott was out of
sympathy. The prevailing mood was Presbyterian, if not free-
thinking, while his sympathies were Episcopalian and Jacobite.
As a political movement Jacobitism was dead, but Scott's romantic imagination fed upon the stories of those who had been out in
the Forty-Five. As he reacted against the rationalism of the urban
patriciate, so he dwelt more fondly on the ballads, songs and tales
of Old Scotland. He dwelt securely, however, in both worlds and
his attitude was ambiguous. The conflict of Jacobite and
Hanoverian is the theme of three of his greatest novels, *Waverley*,

*Sir Walter Scott, 1st Baronet*
(Artist: Sir Edwin Landseer)

*Rob Roy* and *Redgauntlet*, and inspires some of his finest writing. His treatment of this subject gains by his being able to see, feel and present both sides of the embittered question of loyalty. The Augustan, Johnsonian side of him was as strong as the sentimental. There was nothing sham or make-believe about his espousal of the dying Gaelic civilization. His was a true sympathy founded upon massive reading amongst chronicles and plays, deepened throughout his life by the observations of a countryman and by his acquaintance with ordinary folk.

Scott's view of history was a fanciful one: intuition, knowledge and imaginative sympathy operated in a creative harmony. He ever preferred the particular to the abstract. As he said in a letter of 1808, he had been 'an antiquary many years before (he) thought of being a poet'. The reading of Percy's *Reliques*, together with his own love of Scottish stories, led him to collect and improve upon old ballads. In *The Border Minstrelsy* (1802) he could be antiquarian, scholar, historian, critic and poet. He went on naturally to composing poems and then prose stories of his own. So close are Scott's writings to his own nature that they may justly be called a labour of love. He early practised his pen with translations from German authors. He acquired enough of this and other languages — French, Italian, Gaelic — to enrich his store of tales. His remarkable memory ensured that he would forget little of what he learned. The novelist grew out of the poet, the poet out of the 'sentiments, manners and habits' of the past.

Scott responded, as a stout Tory, to the challenge of the French war and became quartermaster of a volunteer regiment of Edinburgh dragoons. In 1797 he married Charlotte Carpenter, daughter of a French widow who had taken refuge in Britain, and settled in Castle Street. In 1799 his father died; in the same year Scott became sheriff-deputy of Selkirkshire. His extensive rambles along the Marches, his 'Liddesdale raids', bore fruit in the *Border Minstrelsy*, then (1805) in his first and best long poem, *The Lay of the Last Minstrel*.

The *Lay* was a mighty success. Scott reached the public which later lionized Byron. The *Lay* was followed by *Marmion* (1808) and *The Lady of the Lake* (1810). Later poems, *Rokeby*, *The Bridal of Trierman*, *The Lord of the Isles* and *Harold the Dauntless* were less well received. The epic is a heavy diet and readers were sated. Those who read them may still be stirred by passages of *Marmion* and the *Lay*, as by the light and noise of a thunderstorm. Scott was a born minstrel; he caught the elemental moods. Significantly, a great admirer was to be Thomas Hardy. He composed swiftly, much of it on horseback. The insight of, for instance, the speech of Rhoderick Dhu in *The Lady of the Lake* is rare. Too much of the verse has an air of false melodrama today: sham-Gothick. The stories are diffuse, the language conventional; above all Scott was inhibited by polite usage from using the dialect or depicting the habits of ordinary Scots. He was not so inhibited in his Scottish novels and it is this closeness to nature and to his own experience that makes them, especially the early ones, when his vision was fresh and his intellectual strength unimpaired, so far superior to the rest.

In 1805 he settled at Ashiestiel on the Tweed but he kept up his legal work; in 1806 he got the reversion of a clerkship to the Court of Session. To help an old schoolfriend, and to further his own literary career, he became a partner in James Ballantyne's printing business. He edited Dryden, wrote for the *Edinburgh Review*; then with more enthusiasm, for the Tory *Quarterly Review*, started by Murray in 1808. With capital, and pledges beyond his means, he backed Ballantyne's publishing ventures. Naïve in money matters, Scott was involved in speculation and capital liabilities greater than he realized. Meantime his affairs prospered. In 1812 the clerk died and he came by a larger salary. Money flowed in from his verse romances and he invested it in a dream: he bought the estate of Abbotsford on the Tweed and set about improving it. Readers of Lockhart will recall the place which house and estate occupied in Scott's affections. Abbotsford, with its walls of old suits of armour and its library of 20,000 volumes, reveals the complex personality of the man as well as anything that he wrote. He longed for a great estate: to be an improver and benefactor, to keep open house. He insisted upon having the house lit with gas: he loved a bright light, because it was gay and exciting, and ignored the immense cost of installation. At the same time he hankered after simple ways and his entertainment was homely as well as splendid.

His literary life, too, is full of contradictions. A first impression is one of stamina, *Old Mortality*, *The Black Dwarf*, *Rob Roy*, *The Heart of Midlothian*, *A Legend of Montrose*, *The Bride of Lammermoor* and *Ivanhoe* were all written between 1817 and 1820, when he was involved in much legal business, suffering crippling pain from gall-stones and rheumatism; also writing essays and reviews — and planning developments at Abbotsford. It is an example of artistic fertility, A. N. Wilson suggests, comparable to Michelangelo's ceiling in the Sistine Chapel, or Mozart's symphonies.

'They cannot say but what I had the crown', he wrote in his journal in 1827: he composed in different veins with extraordinary self-confidence. At the same time he persisted in an amateurish, anti-intellectual, casual tone: 'amusing myself with composition, which I felt a delightful occupation, I could also give pleasure to others' (Introduction to *The Chronicles of the Canongate*). This ambivalence surely came from a personality of many sides. The wordy antiquary of his ponderous introductions, the eighteenth-century gentleman, the sharp lawyer, the traditionalist are all to be found in his novels, sometimes in startling juxtaposition. In his worst books there is artificial writing and weary reading. In the best he is sufficiently detached as an artist, sufficiently involved as a man, to present living studies in depth — a Meg Merrilies, a Bailie Nicol Jarvie, or, both containing a good deal of himself, a Frank Osbaldistone, an Alan Fairford: all in a convincing frame. Indeed Scott presents the greatest diversity of realistic human characters outside Shakespeare.

Scott's edition of Swift came out in 1814. But this year was notable for a more seminal event. Hunting for fishing tackle in a drawer he came across the unfinished manuscript of a story he had written in 1805, but put away when he had shown it to a friend who was cool about it. Now he completed it. On 7 July *Waverley* was published, anonymously. Scott despised literary fame just as he disliked literary conversation: to 'talk book' was no substitute for life and the novel was not, in his eyes, a high form of composition. Few men have written so well, with such a modest opinion of what they were writing. Yet he found in *Waverley* and some of the romances that followed by 'the author of *Waverley*' (his identity was readily guessed at by his friends but not avowed by him until 1827) a richer vein than in his poems. *Guy Mannering*, *The Antiquary*, *Old Mortality*, *Rob Roy*, *The Heart of Midlothian*, *The Bride of Lammermoor* and *A Legend of Montrose* are drawn from the century between the Civil War and the Forty-Five; from a turbulent century as well known and described, albeit from the standpoint of the Scottish laird, as if he had lived amongst the Covenanters, Jacobites and the ordinary men he describes so well. 'The unexpected newness of the thing, the profusion of original characters, the Scotch language, Scotch scenery, Scotch men and women, the simplicity of the writing, and the graphic force of the descriptions — all struck us with a shock of delight'.

What Scott did was to put life into history by showing history as life. When he left Scotland, still more when he left recent history for the middle ages, the story-teller was still effective. But to the lover of Scott, *Ivanhoe*, *Quentin Durward*, *Peveril of the Peak*, to name the best known, perhaps, of the non-Scottish novels, may seem false coin. Scott, spurred on by his wretched publishers, was writing outside his province. When he returned, in 1824, in *Redgauntlet*, to Scotland and to his own life — for this book is written around his memory of his father and scenes of his boyhood — he wrote another novel of genius. It is full of the tense and tragic conflict of his best work. He is dealing with a practised hand with two worlds he knew well: lawyer and Jacobite laird in a balance of opposites. For good measure, in 'Wandering Willie's Tale', there is thrown in one of the finest short stories in the language.

He worked according to a strict regimen, writing much before breakfast, completing a novel sometimes in about three months. His writing tended to be planless, his plot developing as he went along. He found time, too, for the life of the laird, supervising the planting of trees and the clearing of rides; he was busy in Edinburgh affairs, a firm Tory, more trusting than discreet in his choice of friends and support of local factions. No man had trained so hard to beat the French, practising with his troop for hours at sabring turnips on sticks: 'Cut them down, the villains, cut them down!' When George IV made his memorable visit to Edinburgh in 1822 and put new life into Highland traditions by parading in Royal Stuart tartan, Scott, who had become a baronet in 1820, invited caricature by the fervour of his welcome. But George, for all his follies, was an admirer of Scott's novels. The unreformed constitution became objectionable to most Scots before 1832 because the burghs were notoriously at the disposal of the ministry, but Scott defended the *status quo* with ardour.

More damaging to him were errors of judgement in his private life. He was fleeced by the local farmers, who understood his ambition to make a large estate. When his publishers were ruined in the financial panic of 1825 and he became liable for debts of £130,000, he had few resources to meet his creditors. With heroic confidence he set himself to pay all by his writing, refusing all offers of help: 'This right hand shall pay it off.' *Woodstock*, the work on which he was engaged, fetched £8,000, the monumental *Life of Napoleon*, his greatest incursion into history, in nine volumes, £18,000. Within a few years his creditors had received a dividend of six shillings in the pound. But the art of his novels, and his health, failed under the strain. He earned vast sums, too much for the good of his art — for facility was his enemy — but always too little for his creditors. His delicate sense of honour ruined his last years. The man emerges a hero, but the wastage of a great art remains a tragedy of literature. There is more of the antiquarian, less of the natural story-teller, in *The Chronicles of the Canongate, The Fair Maid of Perth, Anne of Geierstein*. His wife died; then in 1831 the beloved grandson Johnnie Lockhart, for whom he had written a boy's history of Scotland, *Tales of a Grandfather*. From a voyage to the Mediterranean he came home a broken man to die at Abbotsford in September 1832.

The event was received as a public calamity. No author has left a stronger impress of integrity and goodness. In his fine essay on Scott, Hazlitt, a stern critic of his political views, wrote of the essence of his genius: 'Our author has conjured up the actual people he has to deal with ... in their habits as they lived; he has ransacked old chronicles, and poured the contents upon his page; he has squeezed out musty records; he has consulted way-faring pilgrims, bed-rid sybils. He has invoked the spirits of the air; he has conversed with the living and the dead, and let them tell their story in their own way; and by borrowing of others has enriched his own genius with everlasting variety, truth and freedom.' The virtues of the man are inseparable from those of the writing: simplicity, unpretentious humour, fortitude and a pleasing absence of guile. After death he received his due in one of the most readable of literary biographies. Let the sceptical reader who wishes to be introduced to the author of *Waverley* read Lockhart's account: 'Scott's Den', 'Scott at Breakfast', 'Scott's Raid into Liddesdale' — these are descriptive essays worthy of the master. They should, however, be treated only as a beginning, for Lockhart was often inaccurate and sometimes unfair. Buchan and Lang are also entertaining but they follow the master very closely. If he wants an appreciation of Scott's greatness as a novelist he should turn to Cockshut's critical appreciation: or to that of a fellow novelist, A. N. Wilson. Then he may read or re-read *Waverley* and its peers and discover for himself what the world has largely forgotten, that Sir Walter Scott is one of the select company of the world's great novelists.

J. G. Lockhart, *The Life of Sir Walter Scott*, 1848, Everyman ed., 1906.
A. O. J. Cockshut, *The Achievement of Walter Scott*, 1969.
A. N. Wilson, *The Laird of Abbotsford*, 1980.

JOHN GIBSON LOCKHART (1794-1854) was for twenty-seven years the successful editor of the *Quarterly Review*, the journal which competed for literary excellence, critical impact and political influence with the Whig *Edinburgh Review*. He is best known, however, as the biographer of Sir Walter Scott, his father-in-law. Besides numerous occasional pieces, some ballad poems and four novels he wrote lives of Burns and Napoleon. Clever, fluent, aggressive or sympathetic as occasion demanded, in none of that varied work did he excel. In the seven volumes of *The Memoirs of Sir Walter Scott* (1836-8) subject and biographer interacted to produce a masterpiece. The second half of the twentieth century has seen a flowering in the *genre* of literary biography: with new techniques, insights and resources come different critical standards. In the ample, traditional style, within its conventions, Lockhart can be placed on a level with Boswell: two Scotsmen — and two writers who so knew and revered their subjects that they lived, felt, thought and spoke for all time. No less than Boswell, he had the talent, and tact, to depict genius.

Lockhart was the second son of a Lanarkshire minister. His precocious scholarship set him, aged fifteen, on the high road that other clever Scotsmen have trodden: from Glasgow High School and University to Balliol College, Oxford. He won a First, went to Germany, and paid the obligatory visit to Goethe at Weimar. At the Scottish bar he was unsuccessful, so his thoughts turned to literature. With John Wilson he became the mainstay of *Blackwood's* magazine. His caustic wit was wellsuited to the thrust and parry of Edinburgh's intellectual journalism. In 1818 he first met Scott who recommended him to Ballantyne, the publisher, and suggested that he take over editing the *Edinburgh Annual Register* which Scott was keen to relinquish. In 1820 he married Scott's eldest daughter, Sophia.

In 1825 he went to London, to the *Quarterly Review*, and a wider fame. His *Life of Scott*, known to many in the abridged version of 1848, brought acclaim, though some thought that his account lacked reverence. He was faithful to his declared intent of 'making use, wherever possible, of his own letters and diaries'. It was his wish 'to let the character develop itself.' So the reader comes, not only to know the man, but to see the growth of the writer. Let one passage speak for the whole. There is a dinner party on a warm Edinburgh night in June 1814. The young men go to the library; it has a north window which looks obliquely upon Castle Street, and so on another lighted window where a hand can be seen writing, writing, pausing only to place another sheet upon the pile. Is it an attorney's clerk finishing some work? 'No, boys', the host exclaims: 'I well know what hand it is — 'tis Walter Scott's'. 'This', comments Lockhart, 'was the hand that, in the evenings of three summer weeks, wrote the two last volumes of *Waverley*.'

Sir Walter expected to found a dynasty of Scotts at Abbotsford. Yet of his four children, the elder son died soon after their father: both Lockhart's sons died also. By 1854 only Lockhart's daughter, and her daughter, remained of the family. His own health was broken, his spirit crushed. He travelled to Rome but returned to Abbotsford to die.

**FRANCIS JEFFREY, LORD JEFFREY** (1773-1850), lawyer and critic, was the son of George Jeffrey, depute clerk of the Court of Session, and of Henrietta Louden. He was educated at Edinburgh High School along with Brougham, Horner and Cockburn. He was at Glasgow University and, for a year, at Queen's College, Oxford, which he did not enjoy. He was admitted to the Scottish bar in 1794 but secured few briefs. He was a Whig and the Tories then held the establishment, legal as well as political, in a firm grip. Literature offered brighter prospects.

With the enterprising and generous Constable as publisher, together with Sidney Smith, the original projector, Brougham and Horner, fellow-luminaries of the Speculative Society, Jeffrey started the *Edinburgh Review*. 'Every Tory principle being absorbed in the horror of innovation', Whiggery appealed to intelligent men who were prepared to postpone professional advancement in return for the luxury of free expression of ideas. At first, however, the *Edinburgh* was not entirely partisan. Tories like Scott approved. After the notorious Cevallos article (number 26) which Jeffrey wrote with Brougham, it became more decidedly Whig in tone. In 1809 the *Quarterly Review* was started by Lockhart and Tory friends. The two papers had much in common: serious but biased analysis of political issues, and literary criticism in a classical and conservative manner. Dogmatic and ruthless in matters of taste, Jeffrey pounded romanticism in the person of Wordsworth. In political questions the papers adopted predictable lines, the one broadly reflecting Fox-Grey Whiggery with a strong admixture of the more radical Brougham, the other being Pittite and clerical, with a flavour of Southey-type paternalism.

As the Whigs came more into their own, Jeffrey's practice at the bar grew steadily, though he was never one of the great advocates. In 1820 he became Lord Rector of Glasgow University: a mark of recognition. He became Dean of the Faculty in 1829 and retired from the editorship of the *Edinburgh* in that year. 1830 saw a Whig government at Westminster and Jeffrey Lord Advocate, with a seat in Parliament successively for Malton and Edinburgh, and responsibility, in his official capacity, for the Reform Bill for Scotland. In 1834 he reached his summit as a judge in the Court of Session. At the time of the disruption he gave a momentous decision for the free church. He was lucky in his biographer: that doughty Whig and entertaining *raconteur*, Lord Cockburn, who became Solicitor-General in 1830, wrote eulogistically about his friend. We learn of his high moral character, his gaiety, industry and courage. His writing presents several of the more obnoxious features of Whiggery: the *Edinburgh* was notably arrogant and obtuse in its condemnations of the British performance in the Napoleonic wars. But Jeffrey must be judged by the standards of his day. Canning and Cobbett were his contemporaries, Brougham his colleague, Lockhart his rival: was he less fair in controversy than any of these?

All Jeffrey's best work was done for the *Edinburgh,* anonymously and hurriedly. He was aggressive but bore no malice. In 1806 he accepted a challenge from Tom Moore as a result of an article in the *Edinburgh*. Fortunately they were arrested in time to prevent their doing each other — or more likely themselves — any injury. They afterwards became great friends. Tories said of Jeffrey that he 'left a small library and a large, well-stocked cellar'. Cockburn more pleasantly recalls the hospitality of Craigbrook, where Jeffrey went to live in 1815. 'No unofficial house in Scotland has had a greater influence on literary or political opinion ... The Craigbrook Saturdays during the summer session! Escape from the court and the town, scenery, evergreens, bowls, talk, mirth, friendship and wine ...'

Henry Cockburn, *Life of Jeffrey*, 1852.

**THOMAS HOOD** (1799-1845), poet, was both popular and influential in his day. His fanciful humour reached many through the annuals he helped to popularise. In more serious vein he showed a sympathy for misfortune and misery which went deeper than mere desire to entertain. He was a man of fine sensibility who knew what it was to suffer.

He was born at Errol, the son of a bookseller. As a boy he was sent to London to work in a counting house. Tuberculosis soon threatened and he was sent back to Scotland, to live with relatives in Dundee. He wrote poems and articles but still thought of himself mainly as a draughtsman. He loved drawing and would adorn his writings with quaint illustrations. In 1818, he returned to London to be apprenticed as an engraver. In 1821 he became subeditor of *The London Magazine*. Some good poems date from the next few years. Marriage, in 1825, brought new incentive to earn: he lived comfortably before a publisher's failure, in 1834, forced the family to live abroad. In 1840 they were rescued by friends and returned home. For all their excellences poems like *Eugene Aram*, *The Plea of the Midsummer Fairies*, and collections of poems, many light and occasional, like *Hood's Own* and *Whimsicalities*, have not endured as might have been expected. When, however, for *Punch*, in 1843, he wrote *The Song of the Shirt*, he struck a deeper vein. The plight of the seamstresses was the more poignant because of the contrast with the unawareness of the fashionable lady: she dealt only with the employer: so polite to the lady, so ruthless to the seamstress. *The Song of the Shirt* was still being read when Millais' picture 'Stitch, Stitch, Stitch' appeared in 1876. Dress-makers were still being exploited. It does not detract from the power or effect of the poem. Hood was ailing when he wrote it. Dying, he was comforted to hear that Queen Victoria had determined to grant his widow a pension.

THOMAS DE QUINCEY (1785-1859) cuts an odd figure among the literary men of his time. He was known to magazine readers universally as the English Opium Eater. He lived a life so isolated and eccentric that it is hard to find the right place or description for him. He was a romantic, one of the first to appreciate the poetry of Wordsworth, and yet he was untouched by the excitements of the French Revolution. He was a deep-dyed conservative who detested the French and maintained his faith in England's aristocratic institutions. When he turned unsuccessfully to fiction, he adapted a Gothic style reflecting his own taste: he preferred the novel of sentiment and horror, as written by Mrs Radcliffe and 'Monk' Lewis, to the more robust work of Smollett and Fielding. He fled from reality and took refuge in mediaeval castles, ghosts, knights in armour, clanking chains and maidens in distress.

Eventually de Quincey came to explore the workings of the mind in a more personal way (if one excepts Boswell) than any writer before him. This captive romantic did his finest work in the field of subjective writing. *Confessions of an English Opium Eater, Suspiria de Profundis, Autobiographic Sketches* and *Reminiscences* (in which he gives a life and individuality to men like Lamb and Wordsworth that he was unable to give to his fictional characters) make up a distinctive contribution to literature. In one of his essays he distinguishes between the literature of knowledge and the literature of power. 'The function of the first is *to teach*; the function of the second is — *to move*: the first is a rudder; the second, an oar or a sail. The first speaks to the *mere* discursive understanding; the second speaks ultimately, it may happen, to the higher understanding or reason, but always *through* affections of pleasure and sympathy'. De Quincey's numerous writings, history, politics, theology, in the first category, have sunk into oblivion; in the second category he still has power to move us.

The family of de Quincey only assumed the 'de' after the death of Thomas's father in 1793. He was a middle-class merchant who had written a book on his English travels. One connexion of the family was a squire, last of a long line, whose decay de Quincey fondly describes. He admired his mother but: 'If I could presume to decry a fault it was that she turned the chilling aspects of her high-toned character too exclusively upon those whom, in any degree, she knew or supposed to be promoters of evil.' She was impatient of complications and subtleties. De Quincey was nothing if not complicated, and experienced often what he called 'the pressure on the heart from the *Incommunicable*'.

For three years he was tutored by his guardian, the Reverend Samuel Hall, then sent to Bath Grammar School; the family had moved to Bath from Manchester in 1796. In 1800 he travelled for a time with Lord Westport, an Etonian son of a friend of his mother. In November he went to Manchester Grammar School. In July 1802 he ran away: 'With my own headstrong folly for law and impulse, I set off on foot; carrying a small parcel with some articles of dress under my arm, a favourite English poet in one pocket, and an odd volume, containing about one-half of Canter's *Euripides* in the other.' With a small allowance from his mother he set off on the walking tour of Wales which he describes in the first part of the *Confessions*. In November he took the Holyhead Mail from Shrewsbury to London and spent there a winter which he recalled as a hideous dream of poverty and squalor. Mr Brunell, the seedy attorney of Greek Street where he lodged, and Anne, the sixteen-year-old prostitute who befriended him, stand out from the murk and mystery of his description with almost Dickensian power. Poor Anne of Oxford Street, whose surname he never discovered, who disappeared without trace! De Quincey ensures that she will not be forgotten.

Reconciled to his family, de Quincey went up to Worcester College, Oxford. It was in the autumn of the following year, 1804, that he first took opium to combat a severe attack of neuralgia. He was soothed and excited, though he did not become addicted at once. In May 1803 he had written to Wordsworth the letter of one who had discovered a new god. In the summer of 1807 he met Coleridge and arranged to make an anonymous present to him of £300. In November he went with Coleridge and his family to the Lake District, and there first met Wordsworth. The poet was kind, de Quincey ecstatic. In the following year he left Oxford — in the middle of an examination! — and later went to stay with the Wordsworths. He helped to see the poet's *Convention of Cintra* through the press. In October 1809 he came to Grasmere to live in Dove Cottage, which the Wordsworths had recently left. His friends' interest gave way to disapproval when, in 1817, he married Margaret Simpson, the daughter of a local farmer, a few months after she had given birth to his child. At this time he was drenching himself in opium. His drugged reveries and agonized awakenings must have been a trying experience for the girl. She made him a good wife — and he loved her, though he provided poorly for her. In 1830 she threatened to commit suicide; in 1835 their eldest son, William, died; in 1837 Margaret died. They were then living in Edinburgh, pursued by creditors.

De Quincey's acquaintance with the northern capital began in 1820 when he started to write for *Blackwood's Magazine*, after a short time as editor of the *Westmorland Gazette*. He quarrelled with Blackwood and went to London, where he wrote for the *London Magazine*. In September 1821 the *Confessions* began to appear: in the following year they were published in book form. In 1826, when the *London Magazine* had been sold, he started to write for *Blackwood's* again. In 1828 he returned to Edinburgh. At one time, after his wife's death, he was actually imprisoned for debt. Adam Black secured his release in return for articles for *Encyclopaedia Britannica*. In 1842 his soldier son, Horatio, died in China. After having successfully curbed his opium eating he relapsed in 1844; in general, however, he was able to subsist on small quantities of laudanum, as he explains in a passage of self-justification in the *Confessions*.

His eccentricities grew on him with age. He would drink up the contents of old medicine bottles in the hope that a composite mixture would have a good effect. He stored his tattered manuscripts in a tin bath and always carried a little brush with him so that he could dust them before giving them to the printer. He was careless about fire. On one occasion his hair was set on fire as he sat too close to a lamp; he brushed away the flames and went on reading. At the end, as he flitted from lodging to lodging, he was living almost entirely within himself: clothes and money mattered little. He remained perfectly polite, however, gentle, and a pleasing talker. Opium may have contributed to the imaginative depths of his best writing, but it certainly made him more dreamy and diffuse. He should not be blamed for the uneven quality of his writing. He was forced to write too much by the cruel economic laws of a writer's existence. What, then, is left? Some passages of his prose are among the most evocative in the language. At his best de Quincey can depict the twilight world between reality and nightmare, look into the darker aspects of London, treat with death (as in *Murder as One of the Fine Arts*), and convey in a unique way the symbolic meanings of what he sees.

E. Sackville-West, *A Flame in Sunlight*, 1936.
H. A. Eaton, *Thomas de Quincey*, 1936.

**THOMAS LOVE PEACOCK** (1785-1866), novelist, was born at Weymouth, the only child of a London glass merchant who died when he was three. His mother was a woman of intelligence whose favourite reading was Gibbon; his grandfather, Thomas Love, a retired, one-legged navy man, was also influential in his upbringing. He left school at thirteen and was thereafter self-educated. He became none the less an accomplished Grecian. Hellenism seasoned his writing but did not provide the main inspiration. His novels are largely conversation pieces in which story and scene play a subordinate part. Indeed, they can be called criticism in novel form. In the process of exposing the foibles and fallacies of others, Peacock reveals a great deal about himself: a Regency Aristophanes, a witty egotist, with a good deal of Rabelais thrown in — and a strong line in eighteenth-century Gibbonian rationalism.

Peacock did not depend solely on writing for a living. For a time (1808-9) he was a merchant, then under-secretary on a warship. From 1819 to its demise in 1856 he was an examiner in the East India Company. This occupation left him a good deal of time for writing. His friendship with Shelley, too, undoubtedly stimulated him: later he described, in *Fraser's Magazine*, his friendship with the poet between 1812 and 1822. Shelley, who provided him with the original of Skythrop in *Nightmare Abbey*, needed practical and patient friends in his intense and restless existence. It was Peacock's cool and original appraisal of poetry as a primitive thing, and of the present age of poetry as an age of brass, in *The Four Ages of Poetry* (1820) that provoked Shelley to write his *Defence of Poetry*. Peacock was not entirely serious in his part of philistine, though he had a great aversion to the poetry of Wordsworth. We need not regret that he wrote *The Four Ages* since it elicited such a lyrical response. Idealist and cynic — it was an improbable relationship, but not an unfruitful one.

Peacock produced his first poems in 1804 and wrote at intervals afterwards. His best lyrical poems are scattered through his novels, however. All but one of the novels were written between 1816 (*Headlong Hall*) and 1831 (*Crotchet Castle*). *Gryll Grange*, which some find the most enjoyable, is a *tour de force*, an old man's book, written in 1860. What will the reader find in these books, which are different from anything else in our literature? The contemporary debate is presented in terms of comic exaggeration which anticipates Dickens but draws upon the novels and plays of the past, the tradition of Fielding and Ben Jonson. The characters are often easily recognizable because of the simplification and prejudice which is perhaps Peacock's limitation as a critic, though part of his merit as a satirist. Mainchance Villa (in *Melincourt*) is the new residence of Peter Paypaul Paperstamp, with whom Mr Feathernest, Mr Vamp, Mr Killthedead and Mr Anyside Antijack discuss a letter from Mr Mystic, of Cimmerian Lodge. They are considering the best means to be adopted for finally and totally extinguishing the light of human understanding. Mr Forester (Shelley) and Mr Fax (Malthus) arrive: the latter is the champion of pure reason. Soon Paperstamp, whom the reader may already have identified as Wordsworth, and Feathernest (Southey) raise the cry, 'The Church is in danger'. Vamp (a Tory reviewer) applauds: 'It is an infallible tocsin, for rallying all the old women in the country', and Paperstamp observes that 'a little pious cant goes a great way towards turning the thoughts of men from the dangerous and jacobinical propensity of looking into moral and political causes for moral and political effects'. Thus Peacock canes the romantic poets, as elsewhere the political economists, high and dry Tories, or, in relatively gentle mood, in *Gryll Grange*, the high fanciful idealist, Mr Falconer, far-gone in hagiolatry, living in a tower, chaste but attended by seven beautiful sisters.

Two of Peacock's novels are different from the others: *Maid Marian* (1822) and *The Misfortunes of Elphin* (1829) are romantic stories, the first derived from Robin Hood, the second from Celtic legends. Peacock married a Welsh girl, Jane Gryffydh, and knew a little Welsh. There are pastoral scenes and verse in these books, besides satire. As a form of bardic light opera, the 'War

Song of Dinas Vawr' in *Elphin* is very fine. Irony prevails, however, and the romance is never offered straight. Moreover the characters are mostly shadows. For most people the novels of talk will give most pleasure. The reader may look in vain for depths in Peacock. He perceives very clearly the antagonistic forces in the world about him: 'The sentimental against the rational, the intuitive against the inductive, the ornamental against the useful, the intense against the tranquil, the romantic against the classical' (*Crotchet Castle*). When we think of Hazlitt or Coleridge, however, and the way in which their thought reached beyond this opposition, we see that the entertaining Peacock but skimmed the surface of his times. As his granddaughter recorded, 'He would not be worried'.

O. W. Campbell, *Thomas Love Peacock*, 1953.

WALTER SAVAGE LANDOR (1775-1864) was a gifted author; also a fine-looking, thin-skinned, irascible man, whose life was much taken up with quarrels: with his father, Rugby schoolmasters, Oxford dons, wife, Welsh tenants — indeed any person or authority in a position to offend him; also, however, a man whose long life was adorned by some notable friendships in his literary world.

Standing eccentrically alone, having the means to buy the estate of Lanthony with its ruined abbey, and to write without needing to, he was a compound of classic and romantic: an accomplished Latinist, his choice of classical subjects was conditioned by romantic influences. Neither his epic, *Gebir*, for example, nor his drama *Count Julian*, is classical in shape or spirit. Some of his early lyrics, plays and heroic poems were translations from his own Latin. His aim in poems was to achieve perfection of form and it was only in disenchanted middle age, as he despaired of winning readers, that he affected to regard poetry simply as an amusement. To the last, to quote George Sainsbury, 'he retained that strange occasional command of perfect phrase which was his special merit and privilege.'

It is, however, for his prose that Landor is now best remembered, and the best of it is to be found in *Imaginary Conversations*. Two volumes appeared in 1824, a third in 1828, and he went on adding to them almost to the end. Again the reader has to be selective, allowing for the crotchets and prejudices, the kind of impetuous harangue that Dickens portrayed — and it was instantly recognised — in *Bleak House*'s Mr Boythorne. He may find himself in the impressive train of admirers, from Southey and nearly all of the romantic generation, to Browning, Tennyson and Dickens and, most enthusiastic of all, Swinburne. Or he may be one of the many whom this most fastidious of writers expected to remain uncharmed. They may indeed miss in Landor, among so much that is pretty and charming, that which is to be found in the best critics: the comment that is truly enlightening, and the passion that can communicate at the deepest level of feeling. It is significant that Hazlitt, who was such a critic, found him wanting in those respects. But Landor, who looked always to have the last word, should be allowed it here: 'I shall dine late but the room will be well lighted and the guests few but select'. This was the man who had written to the Bishop of St. David's, ungraciously tardy in reply to Landor's offer to restore Llanthony church: 'God alone is great enough for me to ask anything of twice.'

Malcolm Elvin, *Landor*, 1958.

ALFRED MYNN (1807-61), cricketer, was a yeoman of Kent and among the greatest of early cricketers. Others could be chosen to represent the early days of the game, for instance, Beldham, one of the heroes of Hambledon so graphically described by John Nyren: 'Michael Angelo should have painted him ... great in every department, but his peculiar glory was the cut. His wrist seemed turned on spring of the finest steel. He took the ball, as Burke did the House of Commons, between wind and water; not a moment too soon or too late'. From the start cricket tempted men to such rapturous prose and flights of imagination. Alfred Mynn had no Nyren to celebrate his skills but he was the first to be generally acknowledged among cricket's champions. He was rather over six foot tall, and twenty stone in weight, but 'there was nothing clumsy about him. He was stately and dignified at all times'. Tall-hatted, he managed to deliver, round arm, at a disconcerting pace (the bowler's arm was not allowed to rise above his shoulder till 1835). There is some evidence that he could also bowl a leg-break. How he dominated the rough pitches of those days and impressed his personality on fellow players can be judged from these memorial lines, by W. J. Prowse: no other game could inspire such a requiem.

'With his tall and stately presence, with his nobly moulded form,
His broad hand was ever open, his brave heart was ever warm.
All were proud of him, all loved him. As the changing seasons pass,
As our champion lies a-sleeping underneath the Kentish grass'.

**JOHN JACKSON** (1769-1845), boxer, lifted the sport above its level of lethal, bare-fisted combats in makeshift rings, before seedy, raucous crowds, behind 'The Fancy', whose entry qualification was willingness to bet huge sums. Jack Broughton, heavyweight champion from 1734 to 1750, had introduced some rules under which — if they were enforced — it was forbidden to hit an opponent who was down or to grasp him below the waist. After him, Daniel Mendoza was held to be the first boxer to be scientific in his approach, with emphasis on footwork. Gloves would not be worn till later in the century, but in 1839 the London Prize Ring rules defined the size of the ring and extended the list of fouls to include butting and biting. But Jackson's influence extended beyond science and rules. The sport already had its fashionable spectators. Hazlitt's memorable essay conveys something of the thrill of a great fight as he goes post-haste to Newbury to see Tom Hickman the Gas Man fight Jem Belcher the Game Chicken. Through 'Gentleman' Jackson it came to be more of a sport for the amateurs for whom the 'Queensbury Rules' would eventually obtain. Patronised by 'The First Gentleman', the Prince of Wales, he ran a boxing academy in London. Byron was one of his pupils and rewarded Jackson with a line in *Don Juan*. Jackson was renowned for feats of strength: he could lift ten hundred-weight and a quarter. With his teaching, and some notable victories came wealth and position as a respectable member of society.

# FURTHER READING

In this necessarily short list are some books which will provide a background to the particular studies and supplement to books already listed.

J. Steven Watson, *The Reign of George III, 1760-1815*, 1960.

R. Christie, *Stress and Stability in Late Eighteenth Century Britain*, 1984.

J. D. C. Clark, *English Society, 1688-1832*, 1985.

Eric J. Evans, *Britain before the Reform Act, 1815-32*, 1989.

Asa Briggs, *The Age of Improvement*, 1959.

Linda Colley, *Britons, Forging the Nation, 1707-1837*, 1992.

T. W. Moody and W. E. Vaughan, *The New History of Ireland, vol. IV*, 1986.

P. Morgan, *A New History of Wales: the Eighteenth Century Renaissance*, 1982.

T. C. Smout, *A History of the Scottish People, 1650-1839*, 1970.

Clive Emsley, *British Society and the French Wars, 1793-1815*, 1979.

Frank O'Gorman, *Voters, Patrons and Parties: the Unreformed Electorate of Hanoverian England, 1734-1832*, 1989.

T. Dickinson, *Liberty and Property: Political Ideology in Eighteenth Century Britain*, 1977.

J. Cannon, *Aristocratic Century: the Peerage of Eighteenth Century England*, 1984.

D. Landes, *Unbound Prometheus, Technical Change and Industrial Development*, 1969.

P. Mathias, *The First Industrial Nation, 2nd edn.*, 1983.

J. D. Chambers and G. E. Mingay, *The Agricultural Revolution, 1750-1880*, 1966.

P. Horn, *The Rural World, 1780-1850*, 1980.

H. C. B. Rogers, *The British Army of the Eighteenth Century*, 1977.

P. J. Marshall, *Bengal: the British Bridgehead. East India, 1740-1828*, 1988.

N. A. M. Rodger, *The Wooden World: An Anatomy of the Georgian Navy*, 1986.

Michael Lewis, *The Navy in Transition, 1814-64. A Social*

*History*, 1965.

E. R. Norman, *Church and Society in England, 1770-1970*, 1976.

Roy Porter, *English Society in the Eighteenth Century*, 1982.

John Chandos, *Boys Together, English Public Schools, 1800-64*. 1984.

F. K. Prochaska, *Women and Philanthropy in Nineteenth Century England*, 1980.

David Owen, *English Philanthropy, 1660-1960*, 1965.

Jane Ridley, *Fox Hunting*, 1990.

K. V. Thomas, *Man and the Natural World, 1500-1800*, 1983.

J. Burke, *English Art, 1714-1800*, 1976.

Kenneth Clark, *The Gothic Revival, revised*, 1962.

Maurice Bowra, *The Romantic Imagination*, 1950.

I. Watt, *The Rise of the Novel*, 1957.

# INDEX